P9-DVN-942

ALSO BY CHRISTOPHER ANDERSEN

JAGGER UNAUTHORIZED

MADONNA UNAUTHORIZED

CITIZEN JANE

THE BEST OF EVERYTHING
(WITH JOHN MARION)

YOUNG KATE

THE SERPENT'S TOOTH

THE BOOK OF PEOPLE

FATHER

SUSAN HAYWARD

THE NAME GAME

Christopher Andersen

SIMON & SCHUSTER

NEW YORK
LONDON
TORONTO
SYDNEY
TOKYO
SINGAPORE

Michael

UNAUTHORIZED

Jackson

Simon & Schuster
Rockefeller Center
1230 Avenue of the Americas
New York, NY 10020

Designed by Barbara M. Bachman

Manufactured in the United States of America

1 3 5 7 9 10 8 6 4 2

Library of Congress Cataloging-in-Publication data is available.

ISBN 0-671-89239-8

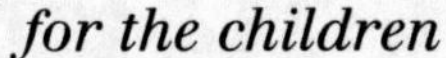

for the children

AUTHOR'S NOTE

In early 1991, while I was still hard at work on my biography of Madonna, a fellow journalist called in the middle of the night with an amazing story. Two former employees at Michael Jackson's Neverland Ranch claimed to have seen Michael fondling a little boy. Not just any boy, but one of the biggest child stars in the world. My initial reaction of shock and disbelief led me to begin an investigation of my own into the life of the world's most famous human being.

More than two years after that initial phone call, another boy accused Michael of sexually molesting him—explosive charges that led to both civil and criminal investigations. After *People* magazine and CNN reported in the fall of 1993 that I was writing *Michael Jackson: Unauthorized,* one of the principal investigators in the civil case admitted to me that I had been placed under surveillance. As both sides scrambled for information that would either prove or disprove the charges against Michael, I had inadvertently become part of the story.

A daunting amount of research is required for any comprehensive biography, and this was certainly true in the case of *Michael Jackson: Unauthorized.* Even more time was spent in pursuit of sources: friends, family, neighbors, teachers, coworkers, employees, and business associates. Some of the sources asked not to be identified in this book. I respected their wishes.

On several occasions I telephoned and wrote Michael Jackson in an attempt to arrange an interview, but he declined. A number of people close to Michael expressed a willingness to speak on the record until they were instructed not to, either by Michael himself or by members of the Jackson family. Fortunately, there were hundreds who were willing to talk candidly with or without Michael's official approval.

Through it all, Michael continued to astonish me at almost every turn. He remains what he has always been: the most celebrated, controversial, and consistently puzzling cultural figure of his time.

Christopher Andersen

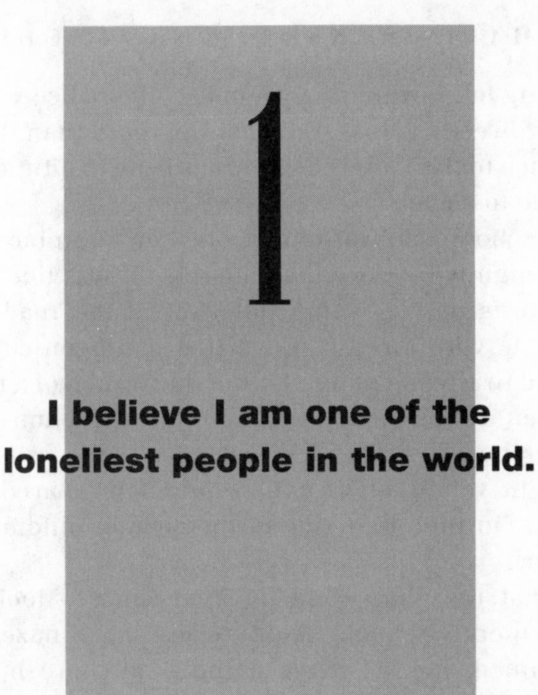

1

I believe I am one of the loneliest people in the world.

On August 21, 1993, sirens screaming, lights flashing, the fourteen cars and vans that made up the police motorcade snaked along Highway 154 toward Los Olivos, shattering the Saturday afternoon calm of the Santa Ynez Valley. The long drive up the California coast from Los Angeles to Santa Barbara had taken the motorcade past some of the world's most spectacular scenery. Yet as they turned eastward through the San Marcos Pass, even the jaded L.A. cops were impressed with the world they entered: an oak-dappled Shangri-la of undulating hills and sprawling ranchlands nestled at the foot of the mist-shrouded San Rafael Mountains.

Two and a half hours after leaving Los Angeles, the motorcade reached Los Olivos, a pristine hamlet best known in the region for its quaint, tourist-oriented art galleries and its Victorian gingerbread Grand Hotel. It was here that the entire convoy swung north onto Figueroa Mountain Road, churning up dust and sending skittish livestock scurrying up the brown, corduroy-textured hillsides.

For the next five miles the police saw horses, cattle, a barn or two—but no people until they reached their destination: the mock Tudor gatehouse that guarded the entrance to Michael Jackson's Neverland ranch.

Before turning left toward the gatehouse, the police were stunned at what they saw directly across the road. Not more than thirty feet away was the entrance to the Family School, a private institution for children from ages three to eleven.

The Family School logo was emblazoned on a rainbow-colored sign, and the waist-high wire fence that encircled it was tied with pink ribbons. In the foreground—within full view of the road—was a playground complete with a red rowboat that had been converted into a sandbox, an old tire swing hanging from the branch of a massive weeping willow, even a rope ladder leading up to a treehouse. Toward the rear of the clapboard, single-story school building was another play area with bright yellow playground equipment geared to somewhat older children. On the other side of the school building there was a basketball court.

Knowing what they had come to Neverland to look for, the police officers merely shook their heads in amazement. "Jesus Christ," exclaimed one. "There's nothing out here but a bunch of kids."

The Family School had been in operation for sixteen years before Michael Jackson decided in 1988 to buy the 2,700-acre Sycamore ranch directly across the road. Jackson's business advisers had wondered why their client was so intent on buying so much property in such a remote location and strongly advised against it.

Curiously, Michael's only other neighbor on Figueroa Mountain Road was yet another school, tony Midland Prep. With a student body of eighty-two, Midland offered its students horseback riding and mountain hiking expeditions as well as a rigorous academic courseload. Even in this distant, sparsely populated canyon, Michael Jackson was secure in the knowledge that Neverland would always be surrounded by children.

The dozen police vehicles, sirens still screaming, pulled up to the Neverland gatehouse. A stunned security guard emerged from his post and, visibly shaken, confronted the officer in the lead patrol car. "We have a warrant to search the buildings and grounds," the police captain told the guard, "for evidence in relationship to a complaint involving a child."

Neverland's own security cameras, meanwhile, were capturing the confrontation on video. Inside the house, some of Jackson's household staff of fifty-six (not including forty groundskeepers) watched the drama unfold on closed-circuit television.

"I can't let you in without authorization," the guard at the front gate protested.

"Stand aside," the captain said, "or you'll be arrested for obstruction of justice."

The guard rushed back to his electronic controls in the guardhouse, and within seconds the massive iron gates swung open. The motorcade drove through, and the first sign the police saw as they approached the crest of a hill was CHILDREN AT PLAY.

The motorcade sped up the winding, half-mile-long drive—past the man-made lake with its arched stone bridge, waterfall, and swan boat; past the two hundred animals in the private zoo; past the Ferris wheel, the bumper car tent, the lollipop red miniature train, and the carousel that played "Like a Virgin"; past the candy-striped popcorn stands and the mock Indian village complete with teepees; past the water fort designed personally by Jackson and his once best friend Macaulay Culkin; past the pool, the basketball courts, the playground, the trampoline, and the two-story video arcade; past the gazebo where he gave away Elizabeth Taylor in marriage. There were countless statues of children, and wherever the officers looked, there seemed to be a swing hanging from a tree limb. More accustomed to patrolling the mean streets of downtown Los Angeles, they stared in gapemouthed wonder. "Do you believe this?" one asked his partner. "My kids would go *crazy* here."

The motorcade pulled up the drive to the front of Neverland's main house, a hip-roofed Scandinavian chalet, and the forty uniformed officers poured out of their vehicles and onto the flower-bordered slate walkway. The front door swung open, and a Jackson aide was presented with a search warrant. Incredulous, he scanned the precisely worded, single-spaced document. Under the heading *Items to Be Seized:*

1. Any photographs, slides, negatives, or video recordings of male juveniles, dressed, nude, and/or in sexually explicit poses.
2. Any undeveloped film.
3. Diaries, telephone books, address books, correspondence, or other writings tending to identify juveniles who have been victims of sexual abuse.
4. To photograph the interior and exterior of the locations for identifying purposes and to corroborate witness statements and descriptions.
5. Items of identification including but not limited to . . .

The officers stepped inside the house and gazed up at a two-story-tall painting by David Nordahl that loomed over the foyer. The surreal portrait depicted a beatific Michael in a swirling firmament of cherub-faced children. As they made their way through the mansion, the police would encounter five other paintings showing Jackson surrounded by adoring youngsters.

With the help of locksmith Duane Bole of the Bee Safe Lock & Key Company in nearby Santa Maria, the officers gained entry to the main house's thirty-five rooms, as well as to the stables, guest house, and several outbuildings. Before he unlocked a single door, Bole was required by the police to sign a confidentiality statement promising not to discuss the raid on Neverland or what he witnessed there. "I was just there to do a job," he later said. "Michael Jackson has done a lot of good in the world. I hope the police don't find what they're looking for."

For the next five hours police combed every square inch of Neverland. They looked through every closet, cabinet, and cupboard, under beds, behind curtains, and inside lampshades. They pulled out desk drawers and checked for items—a photograph, perhaps—that might be taped underneath. They scoured refrigerators, pantries, and medicine cabinets. They looked inside toilet tanks.

Brett Barnes stood to the side, wide-eyed with confusion and fear, as the uniformed men and women swarmed over Neverland. One of the chosen few boys Michael referred to as his "special friends," Australian-born Brett, eleven, was staying at Neverland while Michael was off on the second leg of his *Dangerous* tour. Normally Brett would spend all day, every day, in Michael's company and even share Michael's bed. Despite the fact that his mother and sister were with him, Brett was trembling.

That evening the unwelcome visitors to Neverland left, carting cardboard boxes brimming with photographs, notebooks, and videotapes. Employees at the ranch, surprised by the swiftness of the raid, if not by the nature of the investigation itself, peered cautiously from upstairs windows or pretended to be going about their business. "Mostly we stayed as far away as possible," said one, "so we wouldn't get involved."

At the same time one group of police officers rifled through Jackson's personal effects at Neverland, another was searching Jackson's two-bedroom condominium on Galaxy Way in Century City. The heavily guarded, bunkerlike condo complex is regarded as one of Los Angeles' most exclusive addresses. But the inside of Michael's condo looked more like a day care center or the showroom of a toy manufacturer. The walls were plastered with Disney posters, the floors strewn with computer games, puzzles, children's books, and expensive gadgets of every conceivable kind. After four hours the police walked away with more than twenty boxes of videotapes, photographs, picture albums, and files.

Halfway around the world, Michael Jackson had just checked into his suite at Bangkok's luxurious Oriental Hotel when his criminal attorney, Howard Weitzman, called with news of the police raid. Jackson had known for weeks that the bomb he had tried so frantically to defuse was about to explode. To prepare for this inevitability, he had even arranged for Anthony Pellicano, the ubiquitous, sharkskin-suited "private investigator to the stars," to accompany him to Thailand. Pellicano had spearheaded behind-the-scenes efforts to forestall a scandal, and at this perilous juncture Michael wanted him close at hand.

Still, nothing had prepared anyone in the Jackson camp for the uncharacteristically swift and decisive police action. Clearly they had not anticipated that law enforcement would swoop down on Neverland and the Century City condo as soon as Jackson left the country.

"How could this happen?" Michael demanded to know. "How can they do this to me?"

"They had a search warrant," he was told. "It's legal."

Michael became unraveled. "But why? Why are they doing this to me?" He was sobbing loudly now. The strange, whispery falsetto that Weitzman usually strained to hear was gone now. "I love children," Michael pleaded. "Everybody knows that. *I love children!*"

Michael threw down the phone and began stamping his feet, overturning tables, and throwing chairs. "Why is this happening?" he yelled, pounding his fists against a wall. "I never hurt anyone!" With that he sent a vase of flowers and framed photographs flying off a dresser with one sweep of his arm.

Promising Michael that he would handle everything, Pellicano boarded the next plane back to Los Angeles. Meantime Michael refused to eat or speak for the next twenty-four hours. Periodically he would break down, sobbing uncontrollably.

Of even more concern to those around Michael was his growing dependence on pills. Since severely burning his scalp while filming a Pepsi commercial in 1983, he had undergone a number of surgical procedures and had become hooked on painkillers in the process. Now, under the added stress of the charges being leveled against him, he was adding sedatives to the mix.

Jackson did manage to pull himself together enough to telephone Brett at Neverland and reassure the boy that it would all blow over. "Don't worry," he told his special friend. "It's all a big mistake. Everything will be all right."

Despite the dramatic and highly public manner in which they were carried out, the public would remain unaware of the police raids for the next forty-eight hours. Around 1:00 A.M. on Monday, August 23, freelance television journalist Don Ray was jarred awake by an anonymous caller. "A search warrant has gone down," said the voice on the other end of the phone. "In fact, *two* search warrants have gone down."

"Where?" asked Ray, still half asleep.

There was a long pause. *"Neverland,"* said the voice.

Ray paused a moment. "Neverland?"

"Yes."

Ray was still at a loss. "You mean Peter Pan's been busted?"

"No, no," replied the frustrated caller. "Does 'moonwalk' mean anything to you?"

"What, MTV? Hmm . . . You mean *Michael Jackson?*"

With that the caller said that both Neverland and Jackson's Century City condo had been searched. He would not tell Ray what the police were looking for, but he did say that they had used a local locksmith to gain access to a certain room for which even Jackson's household staff did not have keys.

Later Monday morning Ray pulled out the Yellow Pages for Santa Barbara County and, starting with the A's, went down the list of local locksmiths. His second call was to Bee Safe Lock & Key.

Lockmith Duane Bole admitted to Ray that he had accompanied police to Neverland the previous Saturday, but beyond that he was sworn to secrecy. Still, it was enough to persuade Los Angeles' NBC affiliate, KNBC, to run with the story that police had searched Jackson's homes.

"It was then," Ray would later recall, "that Anthony Pellicano did the unthinkable." Before KNBC could air its story, Jackson's "security consultant" went before television cameras to proclaim that there was no truth to the charges that Michael had abused a young boy. Instead, insisted Pellicano, it was just another extortion attempt—one of twenty-five to thirty attempts made against Jackson each year.

"A demand for twenty million dollars was made and presented, and it was flatly refused," Pellicano told the astonished reporters. "We had no intention to do anything with it, we wanted to see how far they went. They made threats that they wanted to go to the district attorney's office, and I said, 'Go.' I said, 'Why are you waiting?' When we would not pay, a phone call was made to Child and Family Services, which started this whole investigation."

Ray could scarcely believe what he was hearing. Until Jackson's own spokesman volunteered this information, no one knew the nature of the investigation. "We had Mr. Pellicano," said Ray, "to thank for first mentioning child molestation."

KNBC broke the story on the evening news that Monday, triggering a global media avalanche. PETER PAN OR PERVERT? screamed one *New York Post* headline. ROCK STAR IN MIDST OF CHILD MOLESTATION CASE blared the normally sedate *Times* of London.

Michael responded by issuing a statement through his criminal lawyer, Howard Weitzman. Before it was released, the statement was read to Michael over the phone. While claiming that Jackson was "horrified" by the "horrendous" allegations, the carefully crafted press release struck a self-assured note. The appearance of hysteria, Weitzman counseled, was to be avoided at all costs. "My representatives have continuously kept me aware of what has and is taking place in California," Michael's statement read. "I am confident the [police] department will conduct a fair and thorough investigation and that its results will demonstrate there was no wrongdoing on my part.

"I intend to continue my world tour and look forward to seeing all of you in each of the scheduled cities. I am grateful for the overwhelming support of my fans throughout the world."

Michael was pleased with the statement but insisted that one line be added at the end: "I love you all."

The next day Michael canceled his second show in Bangkok only three hours before he was to go on stage. "Because of the extreme heat and humidity," explained tour doctor Stuart Finkelstein, "Michael Jackson has acute dehydration and has been taking fluids intravenously."

Jackson's stated reasons for canceling the show were met with skepticism. Press and public alike observed that the weather in Bangkok was unseasonably temperate. Besides, both the temperature and humidity inside the stadium were carefully controlled. "Even superstars get sick," Jackson's public relations representative, Lee Solters, told reporters from Michael's hotel suite. "There was a lot of heat and humidity at the first performance. He expended an unbelievable amount of energy."

In truth Michael was on the brink of total emotional collapse, thanks in part to a steady diet of Percodan and Valium. In a state of deep depression, he was now alternately sobbing and vomiting.

Katherine Jackson had been trying to reach her son for hours, to no avail. Despite the fact that Michael worshiped his mother, even she found it impossible to break through the impenetrable wall of surrogates and sycophants that Michael had erected around himself.

Finally, one day after the story broke, the phone rang at the Jackson family's Tudor-style mansion in Encino, California. It was Michael. Katherine told her son that she believed in his innocence and was certain that he would be vindicated. But Michael was inconsolable. "If I come back home and I'm arrested," he cried, "I'll kill myself."

In Bangkok, Bill Bray, the grizzled chief of Jackson security and a father figure to Michael since the Jackson Five days, took this threat seriously and ordered a twenty-four-hour suicide watch to protect Michael from himself. Two guards were stationed in the hallway outside his sixth-floor suite, two inside, and another two on the balcony. Even when he walked from one room into another, Michael was shadowed by a bodyguard. For his own safety he was not to be left alone for a moment.

The scandal of the decade was only two days old when, on August 25, Michael made another telephone call to the woman he now considered to be his closest friend in all the world, Elizabeth Taylor. "I'm being crucified," he said, sobbing. "My life is ruined. The world sees me as this monstrous freak who abuses little boys. But it's a terrible lie, Elizabeth. You know I'd never do such an awful thing."

"I believe you, Michael," Taylor said, now crying herself. "For God's sake, don't do anything desperate. Hold on. I'll be there soon and we'll fight this thing together."

The next morning hotel maid Toi Saengswant let herself into Jackson's suite to clean the bathrooms when she heard strange, muffled sounds coming from a bedroom. She tiptoed down the hall and slowly pushed open the bedroom door. There, in the darkness, lay the most famous human being in the world—curled up in the fetal position, sucking his thumb and whimpering like a frightened child.

Yet for Michael Jackson—the man who was never a child and the child who never grew up—the worst was yet to come.

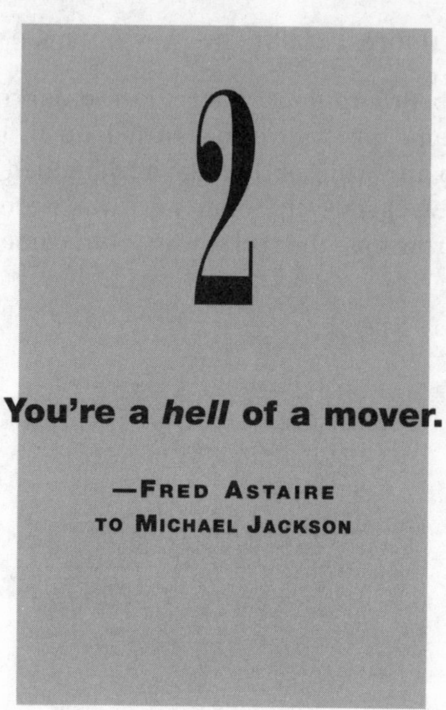

2

You're a *hell* of a mover.

—FRED ASTAIRE
TO MICHAEL JACKSON

On May 16, 1983—a full decade before the police raid on Neverland—Michael Jackson dazzled millions of television viewers with his show-stopping performance of "Billie Jean" on the NBC special *Motown 25: Yesterday, Today, and Forever.* Wearing a sequined black jacket, a black fedora that he flung into the wings seconds into the routine, his trademark white socks and single white glove, Michael erupted into a dizzying series of spins, pops, and glides. All were eclipsed by a gravity-defying step called the moonwalk.

With Michael as its glittering centerpiece, *Motown 25: Yesterday, Today, and Forever* rated as the most watched variety program in television history. The morning after it aired, Michael was eating breakfast with his longtime vocal coach, Seth Riggs, when the phone rang. On the other end was Fred Astaire. "Man," Astaire said, "you really put them on their asses last night."

There was a long silence while Michael, who had shaken hands with the legendary hoofer but never spoken with him at any length, considered whether or not this was a crank call. "Thank you," he replied cautiously.

"You're an angry dancer," Astaire went on. "I'm the same way. I used to do the same thing with my cane. I watched the special last night.

I taped it and I watched it again this morning. You're a *hell* of a mover."

Michael, in a daze, thanked Astaire once again in his barely audible falsetto whisper. Then he hung up, raced to his marble bathroom with the gold swan-necked faucet, and vomited. He was not accustomed to praise.

"You're doing it wrong," Joe Jackson thundered, shoving two of his older sons out of the way and planting himself next to seven-year-old Michael. The year was 1965 and the place Gary, Indiana. "You gotta do it like *this.*" The bearlike paterfamilias of the Jackson clan snapped his fingers, twirled clockwise, and dropped to his knee. The sight of their steelworker father lumbering through a dance routine as if he were one of the Temptations might have been abjectly ridiculous, but the Jackson boys knew from painful, welt-raising experience to keep their mouths shut and pay close attention.

All but tiny Mike, as he was always called by his brothers and sisters. Unable to suppress a giggle, he watched in horror as Joe pulled off his rawhide belt and, brandishing it like a bullwhip, lunged toward him. Easily faster than his father, Michael was usually able to elude his pursuer—sometimes pausing long enough, as his sister La Toya would later recall, to fling a shoe at Joe before scurrying out the door to safety.

But not this time. Just snaring the boy by his shirt collar, Joe lifted Michael off the floor. Michael stared defiantly into his father's green, reptilian eyes. "Thought you'd get away again, eh, boy?" he said, grinning. Michael braced for the sting of the belt, but instead his father merely lowered him to the floor and ordered him to stand still. The others held their collective breath as Joe went into his bedroom and returned with a .38 revolver. Michael stood, frozen, as his father aimed the pistol at him and slowly squeezed the trigger.

The pistol wasn't loaded, but everyone jumped just the same. After all, this was the same gun-obsessed family man—Joe kept firearms stashed under his bed, in closets, and in night table drawers—who once accidentally shot and wounded his own brother in the head during a hunting trip. Michael bolted for the kitchen door, the sound of his tormentor's demonic laughter fading behind him. "I am the Jo-Jo," he could hear his father call out after him. "Never forget that, boy. *I am the Jo-Jo!*"

Just as he would shape the dreams and fears of his children, Joseph

Walter Jackson was the product of a stern, devoutly Christian upbringing in rural Fountain Hill, Arkansas. The eldest of five children, Joseph was born in 1929 to high school teacher Samuel Jackson and his wife, Chrystalee. The fact that the beautiful Chrystalee King was sixteen and one of Samuel's students when he got her pregnant did not alter his perception of himself as a righteous, God-fearing man—although he did fear that the Ku Klux Klan might lynch him for what he had done to a pupil.

A strict disciplinarian and a cold, emotionally distant man, Samuel ruled his family like a demigod. Fearing that they would fall under Satan's influence if any of his brood so much as played a game of jumprope or stickball with the neighborhood children, Samuel decreed that no Jackson would socialize with outsiders. As the oldest, Joe was assigned the task of enforcing this draconian rule, dragging his younger brother and two surviving sisters (a third, Verna, died of polio at age seven) home to the Jackson family fortress whenever they ventured outside after school.

Michael Jackson was Samuel's grandson. He could, in fact, trace his roots in America back to the early 1800s. His great-great-grandmother Mattie Daniel was the offspring of a slave and the crippled daughter of a plantation owner.

Another distant ancestor was a Choctaw Indian named July Gale. July, who was called "Jack" during his days as an army scout, fathered a boy by a young slave named Gina. They called their son Nero. Despite the fact that his father was a free man, Nero was born into slavery because his mother was a slave. He became known as Nero, Jack's son—in time, Nero Jackson.

When Nero tried to escape, his cruel owner pinched his nose with red hot tongs, leaving the first Jackson to bear scars on his nostrils for the rest of his life. After the Civil War, Nero, who had learned native medicine from his Choctaw father, went into practice for himself. He amassed a small fortune as an Indian healer but spent much of it on alcohol and women. He died in 1934 at the age of ninety-six, leaving his son Samuel—Michael's grandfather—three hundred acres, but no money to pay back taxes. Samuel lost the property and pursued a teaching career.

Joe was fifteen when Samuel and Chrystalee Jackson divorced. It was decided that Chrystalee would take Joe's sisters and brother with her to East Chicago, Indiana. Joe was to accompany his father to Oakland, California, where Samuel remarried within months. Unhappy with that arrangement, Joe packed up and moved in with his mother and her new husband in East Chicago.

Over the next dozen years Samuel and Chrystalee would divorce their new spouses, reconcile and remarry one another, divorce again, and marry other partners again. This marital merry-go-round was made even more complicated by the free-spirited Chrystalee's extensive extramarital activities. Left to care for his siblings during their mother's long absences, Joe grew increasingly resentful.

Joe discovered an outlet for his pent-up feelings of rage and frustration: amateur boxing. He became so proficient at knocking out his opponents that, at seventeen, he dropped out of high school to compete in the Golden Gloves championships. Joe had an ear for music as well. When he wasn't flattening opponents with a lightning right hook, he played blues guitar with a local band.

Shortly after his eighteenth birthday Joe married a local girl, and the newlyweds moved in with her parents. They soon discovered that fidelity was not the groom's strong suit, however, and after ten months of bitter squabbling the union ended in divorce.

Watching this drama from the sidelines was Katherine Scruse, a diminutive, well-spoken young woman whom Joe had met at the birthday party of a mutual friend and whose light complexion reflected her mixed ancestry. A year younger than Joe, Kate had been born to a family of tenant cotton farmers in rural Russell County, Alabama, where her great-grandfather Kendall Brown had been a slave and a standout in the Baptist choir. It is to Brown, whose father was white, that she traces her family's musical roots. "People told me that my great-grandfather had such a wonderful voice," she later remarked, "so powerful and so strong." Kendall Brown would eventually change his name to Screws, after the family that owned him. His great-granddaughter had, in fact, been baptized Kattie B. Screws after an aunt but as a teenager legally changed her name to the less suggestive Katherine Esther Scruse.

Katherine was not yet two years old when she contracted infantile paralysis—a public health scourge that, twenty-three years before the advent of polio vaccine, was a leading killer of American children and young adults. At the height of the Great Depression, Kate's parents moved north to Indiana in hopes of finding employment to pay for their daughter's mounting medical bills. While her father, Prince Screws, worked as a Pullman porter, her mother, Martha, took care of Katherine and Katherine's younger sister, Hattie.

Unlike Joe's little sister Verna, Katherine survived polio—but not without paying a price. Struggling through childhood on crutches, she endured the merciless teasing of her classmates with a quiet dignity.

But the relentless taunts left lasting emotional scars, turning a sunny-faced little girl into an excruciatingly shy, introverted adolescent. "Children can be incredibly cruel," Katherine said. "But I think it made me a stronger person."

By the time she was a junior in high school, Katherine was able to toss aside her crutches, although the disease left her with a permanent limp. When she met Joe Jackson, Joe saw past Katherine's disability, perhaps because of his sister Verna's own tragic battle with polio; he recognized the tenacity behind the pretty face and shy smile. She, in turn, had had a crush on Joe even before he married his first wife.

Joe and Katherine were married on November 5, 1949, in a civil ceremony and three months later moved to nearby Gary, Indiana, where they began their married life in a tiny, one-story white clapboard tract house located on a corner lot just behind the Roosevelt High School baseball diamond. Their home was modest—two cramped bedrooms, a kitchen with a gas stove, a single bathroom. But these were by no means the ghetto conditions that would later be invented by Motown Records as part of the Jackson legend. The neighborhood, consisting of well-kept single-story dwellings divided by wood picket fences, would be more accurately described as working class.

Seven months after their wedding, Katherine and Joe Jackson became parents for the first time with the birth of Maureen Reilette, nicknamed Rebbie (pronounced Reebie) on May 29, 1950. Since Joe did not believe in birth control, others followed in rapid succession: Sigmund Esco, who would be called Jackie, arrived the following May 4, his mother's twenty-first birthday. Toriano Adaryll (Tito) was born on October 15, 1953, followed by Jermaine La Juane on December 11, 1954, and La Toya Yvonne on May 29, 1956.

Nine months later, on March 12, 1957, the Jacksons faced their first tragic loss with the death of Brandon. One of a set of twins born prematurely, Brandon was less than a day old when he succumbed to respiratory failure. The other twin, Marlon David, survived. They were dealt another blow when three-year-old Jermaine was hospitalized with a life-threatening case of nephritis, a kidney disorder. Jermaine pulled through, but hefty medical bills cut into the family's meager savings.

Then, on August 29, 1958, Michael arrived, followed on October 29,

1961, by Steven Randall (Randy) and, on May 16, 1966, by Janet Dameta.

Joe and Katherine reserved one of the bedrooms for themselves, but their sons were forced to sleep stacked one atop the other, literally. Michael shared a middle bunk with Marlon, wedged between eldest brother, Jackie, on the bottom and Tito on top. Little Randy slept on a sofa in the living room, with his sisters on a pull-out sofa bed a few feet away.

To feed and clothe his sizable brood, Joe worked days as a crane operator at American Foundries and the four-to-midnight swing shift at Inland Steel. Katherine was a part-time cashier's clerk at what was then Sears Roebuck, but it was not enough. The older children pitched in, mowing lawns, shoveling snow.

Michael was scarcely out of diapers when his father stumbled on a new and personally satisfying way to earn some extra money. Dusting off his old guitar, he teamed up with his brother Luther and four friends to form a rhythm and blues band called the Falcons. Performing hits by the then popular likes of Little Richard and Chuck Berry, the Falcons played local clubs and parties for $20 a night. The Jacksons' living room doubled as a rehearsal studio for Joe and his fellow musicians, and although banished to their room during these practice sessions, the three oldest boys—Jackie, Tito, and Jermaine—would sneak an occasional glance at their father ripping through "Good Golly Miss Molly" and "Tutti-Frutti." Michael would claim not to remember the Falcons. He later said his earliest memories are of his mother cradling him in her arms and serenading him with "Danny Boy" and "You Are My Sunshine."

As far back as anyone could remember, Michael loved music, and he loved to dance. Other family members used to laugh at the sight of eighteen-month-old Mike in the kitchen, gyrating to the rhythm of the washing machine.

Just as his father had shielded his children from outside influences, Joe forbade his children to play with or even talk to neighborhood youngsters. Ostensibly it was to keep the boys from being inducted into the roving gangs of juvenile delinquents that had begun to terrorize Gary in the 1950s and early 1960s.

Joe's solution was to "banish the outside world from our home," said La Toya, "until our world *became* our home." This enforced isolation also enabled Joe to exert total control over his family. Beginning with

Jackie, who by all accounts was his favorite victim, Joe routinely and savagely punished his children for minor infractions, real and imagined. Beatings were administered with razor straps, belts, wire coat hangers, rulers, switches, and fists. Bloody noses were not uncommon, and more than once one of the boys was knocked senseless.

Not even the girls were spared. When he was four, Michael went into the bathroom to discover six-year-old La Toya sprawled on the cold tile floor, sobbing and bloody. Joe had beaten her because she had received a bad report card. Michael merely stepped over her body and, without saying a word for fear of incurring his father's wrath, stood on tiptoe to reach the faucet and wash his hands for dinner.

Joe just smiled whenever one of his boys raised his fist in a rare gesture of self-defense. It provided an excuse to, in the words of one brother, "*really* beat the hell out of us." Almost disappointed that they wouldn't fight back more often, Joe resorted to buying the boys boxing gloves and pitting them against one another while he watched from the sidelines, urging them to knock each other cold. When they didn't, he chided them for being "sissies." Jermaine reacted by developing a stammer in second grade that persisted into his teens. That, predictably, made him the object of even more ridicule by his father—not to mention unfeeling peers.

The senior Jackson's reign of terror was psychological as well as physical. He would don a Halloween mask, then leap out from the shadows at his horrified children, often reducing them to tears. Michael and Marlon clung to each other in their bunk, terrified at the prospect of their father bursting out from a closet or suddenly appearing at their window, brandishing a kitchen knife. The louder his children's hysterical screams, the longer Joe rolled on the floor, laughing uncontrollably.

Even more hurtful was the emotional abuse he heaped on all his children. When he wasn't thrashing them with a belt, he reveled in chastising them verbally. Michael would later tell friends that he and his siblings were made to feel "worthless, that we couldn't do anything right."

As gentle, understanding, and affectionate as her husband was unremittingly cruel, Katherine—who along with Joe insisted that abuse never took place—tried to compensate for Joe's inability to express any love for his children. She lavished praise on her daughters and sons. But Katherine, who was also battered by Joe, did little to shield them from their abusive father. Vowing that her children would never grow up in a broken home as she had, she did whatever she had to do to please her husband. And if that meant never contradicting him or contravening his orders, so be it. The children would always refer to their father as "Joe" and Kate as "Mother"; they reserved the more endearing "Mama" and "Papa" for their maternal grandparents.

What held Katherine together was her unflagging religious faith. A strong moralist, she walked out of the Lutheran Church she had been attending when the minister confessed that he'd had an extramarital affair with one of his flock. She fled to the rock-ribbed Baptist faith of her Alabama forebears—until she learned that the preacher there was also carrying on with a female choir member.

It was around this time, shortly after the assassination of President John F. Kennedy in 1963, that Kate opened her front door to a young black man wearing a starched white shirt and carrying a Bible. Within weeks Katherine was standing by the side of the pool at Roosevelt High, waiting to be baptized as a Jehovah's Witness.

Although known as the Jehovah's Witnesses since 1931, the movement actually dated back to the late 1860s, when a devout Pittsburgh haberdasher named Charles Taze Russell gave up his business to spread the Holy Word. Jehovah's Witnesses are best known for their practice of "publishing," or door-to-door proselytizing. Members are expected to spend between ten and fifteen hours a week dispensing religious pamphlets and Bibles.

Their message is a stern one. Jehovah's Witnesses steadfastly believe that the world will soon be consumed in a cataclysmic clash between the powers of good and evil. According to this extreme branch of Protestant fundamentalism, the only survivors will be "the Remnant"—144,000 Jehovah's Witnesses hand-picked by Jesus to rule paradise on earth for one thousand years. Toward that end, Jehovah's Witnesses are urged to consort only with other Jehovah's Witnesses and, except when trying to enlist converts, avoid all contact with the outside world.

Jehovah's Witnesses must also abide by a strict code of behavior: no smoking, no swearing, no gambling, no drinking to excess, no fishing or hunting for sport. Dancing is tolerated, as long as it does not involve actual physical contact. The faith also condemns abortion, homosexuality, and premarital sex—all grounds for being summarily drummed out of the faith. Anyone who has been "disfellowshiped" in this manner is completely ostracized from all other Witnesses, including their own family members.

Moreover, Witnesses are not permitted to hold elective office, serve in the military, or pledge allegiance to any flag. They do not celebrate birthdays, anniversaries, or Christmas. Katherine abided by all the rules and restrictions of her newfound religion. Her parents did what they could to brighten their grandchildren's holiday season with parties and gifts—an indulgence Katherine tolerated grudgingly. But from the age of five Michael never celebrated Christmas like other youngsters. It was a deeply felt loss, and one of the reasons he would ultimately come to believe that his childhood had been stolen from him.

As much as the Witnesses' hellfire-and-brimstone message appealed to Kate, she did not force Joe or the children to join her church formally. Michael would distribute thousands of *Watchtower* pamphlets well into his adulthood, but he was not actually baptized into the faith until 1981. For his part, Joe accompanied his wife to the Kingdom Hall a few times, then stopped going out of boredom. Not that he objected to his wife's unflinching devotion to her religious beliefs. Anything that reinforced the family's insularity made it that much easier for him to remain in complete control.

When Joe was not home, Katherine loosened the reins a bit. The children would sometimes be allowed to play with the next-door neighbors—but only if they got home before their father returned from work. Since there was no money for music lessons, she even let them take Joe's cherished guitar down from the closet to strum when their father was at the plant. After a time it was clear to her that Jackie and Jermaine had inherited her singing ability and Tito his father's talent for playing intricate riffs on the guitar.

One day, inevitably, Tito was strumming a tune when *thwang*—a string broke. Horrified, the brothers slipped the guitar back into the closet and prayed that somehow they would be spared Joe's wrath. When he discovered what had happened, Katherine rushed to their defense. "The boys are good, Joseph," she insisted. "I mean, they are *really* good."

Joe was too blind with rage to hear. "He tore me up," Tito remembered. Through his sobs the boy told his father that he really could play. "Okay," Joe said, smirking, "let me see what you can do."

And he did, with Jermaine and Jackie singing along. Joe was stunned. The next day he returned home from work with a mysterious package and handed it to Tito. Inside was a red electric guitar. "Now," he said, glowering down at the boy, "practice!"

Having given up on his own dreams of stardom, Joe taught his sons everything he knew about playing rhythm and blues. Then, with the same harsh, unrelenting discipline that he displayed as a father, he force-marched them through three to four hours of daily rehearsal. "When the other kids would be out on the street playing games," Joe said later, "my boys were in the house working—trying to learn how to be something in life."

Meanwhile Michael soaked it all up from the sidelines. Family members remember being impressed by the three-year-old's "sweet" singing voice. By the time he was four, Joe's original notion of calling the group the Jackson Four would have to be changed to accommodate an additional member. Mike not only imitated his older brothers' moves to perfection, he surpassed them.

Initially relegated to playing the bongos, Michael would replace Jermaine as lead singer within a year. For his part, Michael was oblivious of the pain that caused Jermaine. While their father's brutality had rendered the other children soft-spoken and sensitive to the feelings of the others, Michael was totally self-assured from the outset. He told his brothers where to stand, how to move, how to sing, and, eventually, even what costumes to wear. La Toya recalled her mother sewing different outfits for the boys to wear on stage and then holding the costumes up for Michael's approval.

Neighborhood children who once taunted the Jackson boys for staying indoors to practice now lined up on the curb outside 2300 Jackson Street to hear them play. Michael was in the first grade when he made his solo debut, belting out a stirring rendition of "Climb Every Mountain" before the entire Garnett School student body. To his amazement he not only received a standing ovation, but reduced half the teaching staff to tears.

Not long after, Joe decided it was time for the boys to perform for the first time in public. With Jermaine singing lead this time, they performed their version of the Temptations' classic "My Girl" at a talent contest held in the Roosevelt High School gym. They followed up with "Barefootin'," thrilling the audience with Michael's oft rehearsed "spur of the moment" shoeless routine.

The Jackson brothers won the contest easily, and the awards soon began to fill the tiny house on Jackson Street. But the family continued to struggle financially. Joe still worked two jobs, and when he was not around to oversee the boys' rehearsals, Katherine monitored their performance. As soon as he returned home, she gave Joe a detailed and often scathing critique. Even though these reports usually resulted in more beatings for his sons, Michael and his brothers never blamed their mother. Indeed, as the only source of any parental love inside the home, she would remain above reproach. It was Joe who increasingly became the focus of their anger . . . and of Michael's hatred.

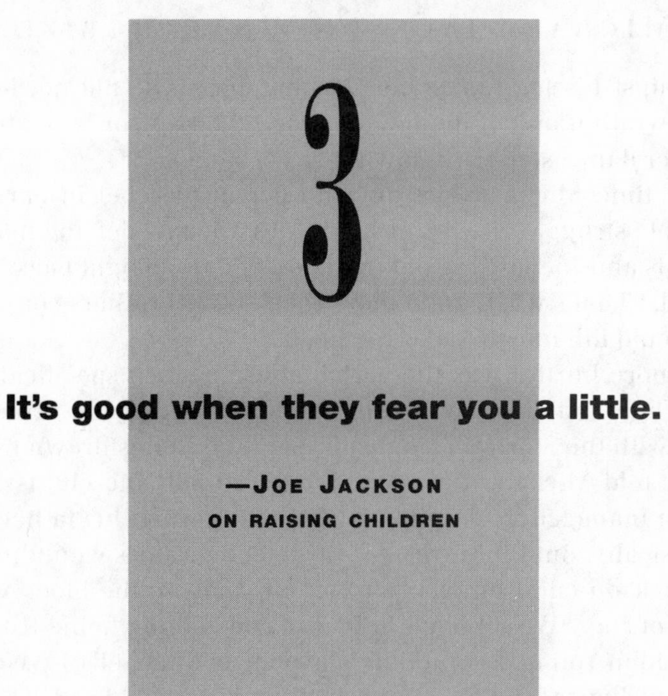

3
It's good when they fear you a little.
—Joe Jackson
on raising children

The Jackson brothers, now billing themselves as the Ripples and Waves Plus Michael, played their first nonamateur, pass-the-hat solo gig in the summer of 1964, promoting a sale at a local Big Top discount store. People crowded into the aisles to hear the Ripples and Waves Plus Michael do their own renditions of hits by the Temptations and James Brown. By now they were joined on the organ by Randy Rancifer and on the drums by Johnny Jackson (supposedly no relation, although Motown's image-molding publicity department would later describe him in the press releases as the boys' "favorite cousin"; whether or not he was technically a relative, Johnny Jackson was close enough to the family for Joe to be his legal guardian).

"The audiences ate it up," Jackie recalled of those early days. "Michael just blew them away. He was the main attraction, the star. We all saw that even then."

And no one more clearly than Joe, who focused his attention—and his wrath—on the family's spotlight-grabbing prodigy. Every day after school the boys lined up in the living room and, under their father's unforgiving gaze, rehearsed until they collapsed from exhaustion. Convinced now that his boys had serious commercial potential, Joe was more unmerciful in his demands than ever. Slapping a whip menacingly against his leg like some Gestapo guard, he did not hesitate to vent his wrath if one of the boys wandered off key or failed to execute the proper dance step with flawless precision.

By the time Michael was nine he began to rebel in earnest. The predictable struggle of wills ensued, with Michael defying his father at rehearsals and Joe lashing out in anger. "I'd try to fight back," Michael later said. "That's why I got it more than all my brothers combined. My father would kill me, just tear me up."

Even more hurtful was the verbal abuse heaped specifically on Michael. While audiences were already marveling at the three-foot-tall dynamo with the Shirley Temple dimples and James Brown moves, Joe routinely told Michael that he was ugly, stupid, and clumsy. Michael still often managed to scramble out of reach when his father attacked him physically. But there was no way to deflect Joe's wounding words.

The Jackson children weren't the only kids on the block who were terrified of Joe. "We all lived in fear of Joe coming home from work," recalled John Young, a sometime playmate of Michael's. "We'd be playing in their house, and one of the Jackson kids would yell. 'Here's Dad' —and we were all so afraid of him we'd run out the back window."

Once, Joe surprised them, found Michael and Young hiding under a bed, and dragged them out. He pulled out a pocket knife and held it to Young's throat. "I was about six, and my little heart nearly leaped out of my chest!" Then Joe snarled, "If I catch you playing in here again, I'll slit your neck open."

According to Young, Joe did this "several times" to neighbor children as well as to his own—"just to scare us, and it sure did! He didn't want his children playing around. He just wanted them to play music."

Whatever the ultimate psychic cost to Michael and his brothers and sisters, Joe's approach yielded the desired results. When Michael was seven the Ripples and Waves had vanquished a dozen other amateur groups to become citywide champions. And once they had conquered Gary, Joe set his sights on nearby Chicago. Before long the group had entered and won several talent contests there, and Joe—prompted by his ambitious and increasingly impatient wife—decided it was time for his sons to make the leap from amateurs to professionals.

On weekends Joe packed up the family's Volkswagen bus and drove the kids to Chicago, where they were booked into burlesque joints and bars with names like the Guys and Gals Club, Joe Cool's, Bill Street, and the High Chaparral. Life on the nightclub circuit proved anything but glamorous for the boys. They usually shared the bill with drunken, decidedly unamusing comics and over-the-hill strippers who flung their undergarments from the stage. Panties were particularly prized by audience members, who sniffed them and howled appreciatively.

"Some of the things I would see from the stage!" Michael recalled. "This woman, one of the stripteasers named Mary Rose, would take her drawers off and throw 'em out at the people. Aw, man! Ugh! That to me was awful!"

Joe not only condoned these sleazy antics, he forced Michael to join in. During his own spirited version of the Joe Tex song "Skinny Legs and All," Michael would jump down off the stage, run into the audience, scurry under tables, and look up the dresses of women customers. "When I ran through the audience, people would throw all this money on the floor," Michael said later, "tons of dollars, tens, twenties, lots of change. I remember my pockets being so full of money that I couldn't keep my pants up."

Notwithstanding the fact that it was certainly inappropriate and possibly illegal for minors to perform in bars and strip joints, Joe had no apparent qualms about exposing his children to such sordid goings-on. These out-of-town excursions also provided an opportunity for some extracurricular activity of his own. After their last show of the night, Joe would lock the boys in their motel room and head out on the town.

For the devoutly religious Katherine, the Jehovah's Witness who flinched if anyone so much as whispered God's name in vain, there could have been no excuse for such behavior. But steeped in piety, she simply looked the other way. As long as no one shared the lurid details with her—and, given her lofty moral perch, no one was about to—she feigned ignorance.

"Katherine knew all about the bar fights, the strippers, how Michael went up under women's skirts, everything," a longtime friend said. "But the only way out of Gary was through Michael." In one way, however, Kate was even more aggressive than her husband in pushing the act. "She was worried that if the Jackson Five, as they were now called, didn't make it big soon, it would be too late," the same friend recalled. "One day she turned to me and said, 'Michael is cute now, but he won't stay that way forever. Then what do we do? They've got to get a record contract *now.*' "

Joe knew even then that the Jackson Five's high-energy style was perfectly tailored for Detroit's hugely successful Motown label. He mailed a demo tape to the record company's founder, Berry Gordy, Jr., but it was returned without comment three months later. Still, he later said, "I knew the kids had something."

In 1967 the Jackson Five opened for Motown's own Gladys Knight and the Pips at Chicago's Regal Theater. Michael and his brothers so impressed Gladys during rehearsals that she arranged for several Motown executives to catch their performance that night. They did not share her enthusiasm, so for now the Jackson Five would have to settle for being up-and-coming stars on what was then referred to as the chitlin' circuit, the informal network of theaters across the country that showcased black talent. On weekends Michael and his brothers refined their act before large inner-city audiences in Kansas City, Philadelphia, St. Louis, Cleveland, Washington, D.C., Boston, and Phoenix. The schedule was grueling, but nothing could match the show business education Michael and his brothers were getting on the road. By Christmas of 1967, they were opening for performers like the O'Jays, Jackie Wilson, Gladys Knight and the Pips, Sam and Dave, the Isley Brothers, the Temptations—even James Brown. And while Jackie, Jermaine, Tito, and Marlon engaged in backstage horseplay between sets, Michael stood in the wings, a self-described "sponge" soaking up all he could from the biggest names in soul.

Only nine, Michael was already such a polished performer that other acts began sniggering about the "midget" those Jacksons were supposedly palming off as a child. Joe and Michael's brothers laughed whenever they heard remarks like that, but Michael, who often felt lost in this world of adults, cried. "I never could stand it," he later said, "when people made fun of me."

The group's next major challenge would be another amateur night—or rather *the* amateur night, at Harlem's famed Apollo Theater. A mecca for black talent since the 1930s, the Apollo was perhaps best known for its raucous Wednesday night talent contests. "The Apollo crowds are the toughest in the world," said singing star Luther Vandross, who would suffer the humiliation of three losses before finally walking away with the coveted first prize. "It takes guts, but if you can win them over, you *know* you've got the stuff to make it in the business."

On a steamy August night in 1967, the Jackson Five not only won handily, but received a rare standing ovation. Joe was ecstatic, but Katherine was more insistent than ever that the boys land a recording contract. Motown was ignoring them, but aspiring Gary songwriter-producer Gordon Keith was eager to sign them up for his local Steeltown label. The first time he watched the Jackson Five rehearse in their living room, Keith was aware of Michael's star potential. "Before they even started singing," he recalled, "Michael walked up to this cord that was stretched between Tito's guitar and amp. It was about waist high, and he jumped right over it. It seemed superhuman."

The Jackson Five's first single was released on the Steeltown label in the spring of 1968. Given the controversy that would surround Michael's adult life, the song's title—"Big Boy"—now seems almost tragically ironic. "Big Boy" debuted on Gary's WWCA radio and soon became a modest hit.

Buoyed by the success of "Big Boy," the Jackson Five returned to the Apollo—this time as a paid act. Before they went on, Michael watched in amazement as a striking young femme fatale slithered seductively across the stage, finally rousing the audience to its feet by whipping off her sequined top and cascading blond wig to reveal that she was actually a he. "I looked out at the theater audience, and they were *going* for it," Michael later recalled, "applauding wildly and cheering. Crazy stuff." More than just another random memory of his early days in show business, it was the first time Michael witnessed the way gender bending could be employed to excite and sway an audience.

A scout for the popular television series hosted by urbane Englishman David Frost happened to be in the Apollo audience that night and reported back to Frost's talent coordinators. A week later a producer for the show called Joe in Gary. Would the Jackson Five, the producer wondered, consider making their network debut on Frost's talk show?

For the next few days the family prepared feverishly for their first exposure on national television. Before they could make the journey to Manhattan, however, they had a prior commitment to fulfill—opening for Bobby Taylor and the Vancouvers, a minor Motown act, at Chicago's Regal Theater.

Although Diana Ross would later claim credit for discovering Michael, it was Bobby Taylor who—with the help of Gladys Knight—got on the phone and convinced Motown executive Ralph Seltzer to give the Jackson Five an audition. Joe was now faced with the choice of appearing on *The David Frost Show* or taking this one shot at a contract with Motown. Joe left for Detroit.

. . .

The great-grandson of a Georgia slave owner and a slave, Berry Gordy, Jr., had worked on a Ford assembly line until he wrote an R&B hit for Jackie Wilson, "Reet Petite," in 1957. Two years later Gordy borrowed $800 from relatives to start Tamla Records, which quickly became Motown (Tamla remained as the name of one of Motown's subsidiary labels).

Beginning with hits by Smokey Robinson and the Miracles, Marvin Gaye, Mary Wells, and the Marvelettes, the distinctive, up-tempo Motown sound proved equally appealing to white audiences. Gordy employed experts on fashion, dance, and etiquette to ensure that his artists would look and act as silken as they sounded. Over the next few years such Motown acts as the Supremes, the Temptations, Stevie Wonder, the Four Tops, and Martha Reeves and the Vandellas all but dominated the pop music charts—and made Gordy one of the most powerful men in the music industry.

In Detroit, on July 23, 1968, ten Motown executives scribbled furiously on yellow legal pads as the Jackson Five tore through one number after another.

When it was over, a cameraman retrieved the black-and-white film that had been taken of the audition. Motown executive Ralph Seltzer informed Joe that he would be getting back to him with an answer after Gordy had had a chance to screen the footage. Seltzer then shook Joe's hand and, without ever hinting at his reaction to the audition, politely thanked them for coming.

Utterly demoralized, Joe and his sons piled their equipment into the minibus and headed home—unaware that within hours of their departure Gordy had viewed the audition footage and ordered Seltzer to draw up the contracts. "Michael was a born star, a natural," Gordy recalled. Moreover, Motown was in a state of transition. Gordy was in the process of moving the company headquarters to Los Angeles, and Motown needed an infusion of fresh talent. Michael and his brothers were the ideal donors.

After an anxiety-filled weekend, the call finally came. Seltzer told Joe that his boss wanted to sign up the Jackson Five immediately. On July 26 Joe and his sons were summoned to Hitsville USA, Motown's headquarters on West Grand Boulevard in Detroit. This time the previously poker-faced Seltzer was ebullient. He handed Joe Motown's boilerplate contract, and without bothering to read it, Joe signed on the dotted line on behalf of his sons.

Ultimately this contract, which assigned to Motown all rights to the

Jackson Five name, would wind up at the center of a bitter legal dispute between the group and Gordy. Under its terms, for example, the Jacksons were to collect a royalty of about 3 percent on the wholesale price of every record—or a dime per album. Michael's share was just one-fifth of that amount: two cents.

None of that mattered at the time. Gordy himself took Michael and his brothers aside and confidently predicted that their first three recordings would shoot to number one. Over the next several months, while Motown lawyers worked on extricating them from their forgotten contract with Steeltown Records (Gordy would grudgingly agree to buy out that contract for a nominal sum), the boys attended school during the week and spent weekends recording at Motown studios in Detroit.

In September Gary's mayor, Richard Hatcher, invited his old supporters the Jackson Five to perform at a "Soul Weekend" campaign fundraiser. Motown's publicity machine would concoct the story that this was where Motown diva Diana Ross first "discovered" Michael Jackson. In truth she first encountered the Jackson Five at Gordy's Detroit mansion when they entertained at a celebrity-studded Christmas party there. Ross told the stunned Jackson clan that she had been asked by her mentor, Mr. Gordy, to take the newest Motown group under her creative wing. Then she knelt down and, beaming, affectionately pinched Michael's cheek.

Ross ("Diane" or "D" to intimates) would prove to be far more than just a professional mentor for Michael. As the music industry's slinky, feline cynosure of style and elegance, the lead singer of the Supremes was not only Motown's biggest star, but would soon become the biggest-selling female vocalist in history. In time Jackson's devotion to Ross—and his desire to emulate her—would verge on obsession.

The group's top priority for the moment, however, was to record something Mr. Gordy (all the Jacksons, including Michael's parents, called him Mr. Gordy) deemed worthy of release. Tensions mounted as the mogul rejected one effort after another.

At home in Gary, the family faced a crisis of a different sort. While Michael knew of his father's Vesuvian temper, he was too young to realize that Joe had been sexually abusing his sisters for years. While La Toya lay shivering next to Rebbie in bed, Joe would, according to La Toya, climb in with them.

La Toya would recall that as a teenager Rebbie begged her mother to get professional help for Joe. But Kate turned a deaf ear to her daughter's pleas. Only once, according to La Toya, did Katherine try to stop her husband from attacking their oldest daughter. "Joe," she cried, "can't you just leave her alone tonight?"

By the time her brothers landed the Motown contract, La Toya would claim Joe had already begun molesting her. "My father was like an animal," she recalled. "I was ten and eleven at the time. He'd say dirty things and touch my body inside my clothes. And I had to touch him in certain places."

It would remain unclear whether Janet Jackson was spared her elder sister's fate. La Toya later recalled that Rebbie approached her when they were both adults and asked, "Did he do it to Janet?" La Toya did not have the answer. In a display of solidarity, Rebbie and her parents would later deny that there had been sexual abuse in the family.

Katherine had reasons of her own to be fearful of Joe. The boys' new contract had done nothing to blunt Joe's anger. If anything, the added stress of having to produce a record acceptable to Berry Gordy heightened tensions in the Jackson household, and Kate was a frequent target. "He was always yelling and screaming at her," Michael later said of his father. "And he would beat her, too. I saw it so many times."

While Joe was out of town with her brothers, Rebbie asked for and got Katherine's permission to wed her childhood sweetheart and fellow Jehovah's Witness Nathanial Brown. The couple would live in Kentucky, where Brown had landed steady employment as a driving instructor.

Joe reacted to news of the engagement by flying into a purple-veined rage. He recognized that Rebbie, who had studied music as a child, had considerable potential. Among all the Jackson siblings, in fact, Rebbie's singing voice would come to most closely resemble Michael's as an adult. Ultimately Joe had plans to exploit the talents of all his offspring.

At age eighteen Rebbie eloped with Brown to Kentucky, becoming the first Jackson child to free herself from Joe's iron grasp. Rebbie's escape came none too soon. Michael later remarked that despite the family's phenomenal achievements, Joe would grow even more violent over the years. But for the moment, as he stood on the brink of one of the most remarkable careers in show business history, Michael thought only of Berry Gordy's words. "I'm going to make you," Gordy had said, putting his hand on the ten-year-old boy's shoulder, "the biggest thing in the world."

4

Diana Ross has told me that people in show business can get hurt. I don't see how, to tell the truth. Maybe one day I will, but I kinda doubt it.

—Michael Jackson at age twelve

After eight nail-gnawing months working twelve-hour days at Motown's Detroit studios, the Jackson Five had still not been able to write a single song that met Berry Gordy's exacting standards. Gordy was worried. He instructed the Jacksons to pack up and move to Los Angeles, where he could take a direct hand in shaping their sound. Joe and the boys moved, but being no less cautious than his sons' new mentor, Joe left Katherine behind in Gary with La Toya, Randy, and Janet—in the event that things might not work out as planned.

Michael, his father, and his brothers arrived in Los Angeles on August 9, 1969, and as far as they were concerned, they had landed in paradise—"like having the world transformed," Michael later said, "into a wonderful dream." But while the Jacksons gazed in wonder at the sunset and the swaying palms their first night in Los Angeles, a family of a different sort—Charles Manson's drug-crazed, Satan-obsessed "family"—was just a few miles away in a Bel Air mansion, slaughtering Sharon Tate and six others in one of American history's most heinous killing sprees.

These two simultaneous events—the Jacksons' arrival in Los Angeles to pursue their career in earnest and the grisly Manson family murders—were strangely interrelated. A palpable wave of fear swept over the city as homeowners bought attack dogs and hired armed security guards to protect them from LSD- and amphetamine-fueled intruders. To many, the savage, senseless killings were a fitting if brutal symbol of the sex, drugs, and rock and roll era. And in the Jackson Five (and particularly in Michael), America would come to see a new symbol, a fresh-scrubbed, clean-cut, nonthreatening antidote to the poisonous influences of the 1960s.

On August 10, 1969, Joe and his sons were whisked off to Diana Ross's sprawling house in the Hollywood Hills. She then showed them a copy of the invitation that had gone out to several hundred movers and shakers in the entertainment industry over her signature:

> *Please join me in welcoming a brilliant musical group, the Jackson Five, on Monday, August 11, 6:30 to 9:30 at the Daisy, North Rodeo Drive, Beverly Hills. The Jackson Five, featuring sensational eight-year-old Michael Jackson, will perform live at the party. Please come and listen to this fabulous new Motown group.*

Eight-year-old Michael Jackson? Embarrassed, he pointed out that he was actually ten; in fact, he was just a few weeks shy of his eleventh birthday. Michael was politely informed that making him seem younger would only enhance his image and the group's chances for success. For consistency's sake, *all* of the Jacksons had suddenly become two years younger. And while they were on the subject of image building, the boys were told that it would be best if they said that Ross had discovered them. The boys were to forget Gladys Knight and Bobby Taylor and all those who had gone before.

The group's unveiling at the Daisy, then one of Beverly Hills' trendiest discos, was a throwback to an earlier time when established cabaret stars introduced exciting new acts at the Copacabana or the Coconut Grove. The audience was heavily salted with Motown employees and their wives, but it was not necessary. The crowd went wild and broke into cheers when Gordy told them that the Jackson Five would be making their television debut on ABC's *Hollywood Palace* in the fall. The next morning's *L.A. Herald* and *Times* both published glowing accounts of the group's debut, saving their most lavish praise for Michael.

Their careers officially launched, the Jacksons buckled down to the business of recording a record that Gordy was willing to sell. Toward this end, Gordy and several other Motown producer-songwriters—West Coast creative director Deke Richards, Freddie Perren, and Fonce

Mizell—pooled their talents to come up with a winning formula. They called themselves the Corporation.

Richards, the Corporation's de facto ringleader, had just written a song for Gladys Knight and the Pips called "I Want to Be Free." Knight, robbed of credit for discovering the Jackson Five, would be robbed again—this time of a hit song. It was retooled for the Jacksons, and for the next six weeks, Richards worked day and night with the boys, trying to get the song—now retitled "I Want You Back"—honed to perfection. After twenty grueling takes, Richards was happy with the results. But not Gordy, who ordered them back into the studio. After half a dozen more tries, Gordy was finally satisfied.

Then came the business of marketing the group. Motown lived up to its motto—"the Sound of Young America"—not only by churning out hit records, but by grooming a stable of performers who looked and performed as smoothly as their sound—on stage and off. The responsibility of packaging urban African American talent so that it was acceptable to the largely white record-buying middle class had fallen in the 1960s to Motown's legendary Artist Development Division. But now that "Motown U" had officially been disbanded, Gordy assigned the in-house training of Michael and his brothers to his twenty-four-year-old assistant Suzanne de Passe. She brought in experts to teach the boys proper table manners (though Michael seemed intent on eating with his hands), and drilled them for hours on how to handle potentially embarrassing questions from the press.

It was hard work, and Michael was painfully aware of the childhood he was missing. He would later concede that he often looked longingly out the window of the Motown studios at kids playing in a nearby park, wondering what it would be like "not to have all the pressure."

Once de Passe had completed her handiwork, Gordy decided that the lead singer of his hottest new group needed some additional training in the finer points of being a star. That October Michael was separated from Joe and his brothers and set to stay with Diana Ross at her ranch house in the Hollywood Hills. Although Joe grudgingly agreed to Gordy's scheme, Katherine harbored grave doubts about what impact such a living arrangement might have on her impressionable son. Ever the devout Jehovah's Witness, she did not want her son sleeping every night in a household where there was smoking and drinking and God knew what.

Ross had more in common with the Jackson brood than Katherine knew. Brought up in a family of six crammed into a Detroit housing project, Ross had joined up with Cass Technical High School pals Mary Wilson and Florence Ballard (later replaced by Cindy Birdsong) to form a group called the Primettes—a female counterpart to the all-male Primes, who later emerged at the Temptations. When they first auditioned for Gordy in 1960, he told them to come back after graduation. They did, scoring their first hit ("Where Did Our Love Go?") in 1964.

Ross, who was in the midst of a torrid affair with the married Gordy, soon began to eclipse her fellow Supremes, and in 1968 the group was rechristened Diana Ross and the Supremes. When Michael arrived on her doorstep in the autumn of 1969, Ross was preparing to break away from the group and strike out on her own. Within a year the group's touching farewell song, "Someday We'll Be Together," would top the charts.

For now, however, Ross was totally absorbed in planning her solo career—leaving little time for her young charge. By all accounts she did little more than pat Michael on the head and reassure him repeatedly that he was destined for greatness.

Despite Ross's preoccupation with her own career, Michael's brief stay at her house made a lasting impression. Unknown to her, Michael made a game of spying on Motown's most regal star. When she rehearsed in front of a full-length mirror for hours, he crouched behind a sofa and studied her every slinky move and queenly gesture.

Ross's tempestuous affair with Gordy was also witnessed firsthand by Michael. Gordy and Ross argued ferociously and often. In short, Michael's surrogate parents were behaving in much the same way as his real mother and father, serving to reinforce the confusion in his young mind between adult heterosexual love and uncontrollable anger, between sex and violence.

Linking Diana Ross and the adorable Michael in the public mind served a dual purpose for Motown. It introduced a hot young group with across-the-board appeal to America, and it launched Ross as an independent entity. As part of that ruse, Michael was instructed to play Galatea to Ross's Pygmalion. And as is often the case with stars—particularly young ones—he came to believe his own publicity.

Over the years Michael would strongly imply that he and Ross became more than mere platonic friends. As a teenager he would tell interviewers that he had "shacked up" with Ross for "over a year," and that "Diana Ross was my mother, my lover, and my sister all combined in one amazing person."

With such hyperbolic flights of fantasy still well into the future, it was

Diana Ross who, as guest host of ABC's *Hollywood Palace*, introduced the nation to the Jackson Five on October 18, 1969.

That night marked the first time America heard "I Want You Back." The infectious tune and Michael's heartfelt delivery ("Oooh, baby, give me one more chance. . . . Won't you please let me back in your heart?") were enough to win over even this decidedly middle-of-the-road audience.

The single "I Want You Back" hit the record stores the following week and began its inexorable climb to the top of the charts. Nearly four months later the group's debut record knocked "Raindrops Keep Fallin' on My Head," the Burt Bacharach–Hal David theme from *Butch Cassidy and the Sundance Kid*, out of the number one spot.

That December—in time for Christmas—Motown released the boys' debut album, *Diana Ross Presents the Jackson 5* (after much in-house debate it was decided that the numeral *5* was more distinctive—more salable—than the word). On December 14 the Jackson Five went on *The Ed Sullivan Show* singing "Can You Remember?" and "I Want You Back." Sullivan had scored major coups broadcasting the first national television appearances of Elvis Presley and the Beatles. And judging by the excitement these five young men from Gary had created, he was certain he had once again uncovered the next pop phenomenon.

Over the next five months the Jackson Five would fulfill Gordy's prophecy as their first three singles soared to the top of *Billboard*'s "Hot 100." The follow-up to "I Want You Back" was pure bubblegum. Written by Deke Richards, Freddie Perren, and Fonce Mizell, it was called "ABC" and exemplified the bouncy, brassy schoolyard sound that was to be the group's winning formula in those early years. This time the lyrics—"A-B-C . . . as easy at 1-2-3"—were well within the grasp of a lead singer not yet out of the sixth grade.

"ABC" was released in February of 1970 and in just six weeks rocketed to the top, bumping the Beatles classic "Let It Be" out of the number one position. "ABC" would go on to sell 2.5 million copies and win a Grammy as the year's best pop song.

That May the Beatles were once again trounced by the Jacksons when "The Love You Save" (a not-too-subtle variation on the Supremes' "Stop in the Name of Love") replaced "The Long and Winding Road" in the top spot. Chockablock with Ross-inspired "ooohs" and the kind of soulful begging for which young Michael was already becoming famous, the record shared the reassuringly amateur sound of its predecessors.

To sustain their success over the long haul, the Jackson Five would have to prove they were capable of producing more than just tame teenybopper fare. Thus far Deke Richards and the Corporation had been responsible for all the group's material. Now Gordy took matters into his own hands and teamed up with Willie Hutch to create "I'll Be There."

With its wistful lyrics and soothing melody, "I'll Be There" would in retrospect seem like a sure thing. Once finished, even Gordy pronounced it "the perfect song." Still, the consensus inside Motown was that this what not what the group's fans wanted to hear; "I'll Be There," it was agreed, would flop miserably.

Even if this dire prediction did prove to be true, it seemed unlikely to derail the Jackson juggernaut. By this time Joe was confident enough to summon the rest of the family to California, and the Jackson clan moved into a nondescript, 3,000-square-foot house leased for them by Motown on Hollywood's Queen Road. The boys spent all their time at home rehearsing, and although Katherine enforced a strict ten P.M. bedtime, occasionally Joe would roust them out of their bunks for late night practice sessions "just to keep them on their toes."

Within days of their arrival on Queen Road, neighbors were complaining bitterly about the noise. Forced to vacate the premises, the Jacksons were relocated to another home leased for them by Gordy. A split-level, stucco-walled monstrosity, their new house clung to a Hollywood hillside. The interior was straight out of *The Brady Bunch*—open staircase, shag carpeting, cheap paneling, motel-modern decor.

Katherine was left with the formidable task of creating a homey atmosphere amid these transient surroundings; her sons had their hands full coping with their newfound fame. Like the lads from Liverpool, the kids from Gary were causing pandemonium wherever they went.

When the Jackson Five arrived in Philadelphia for their first concert appearance under the Motown banner on May 2, 1970, thousands of screaming teenagers mobbed the airport. No less harrowing was the atmosphere at the Philadelphia Convention Center, where a phalanx of dour-faced policemen held back a wave of hysterical adolescents who threatened to overrun the stage.

The scene would be repeated again and again that summer as the Jacksons played several concert dates to promote their second album, *ABC*. At each, the group had to be protected from crazed fans by a wall of security guards, then spirited off in a motorcade with sirens wailing.

So traumatic was the experience that young Michael often burst into tears as soon as the group reached the safety of their hotel.

That August, a month after the Jackson Five caused a near riot at the Los Angeles Forum, the group's first ballad hit record stores across the country. Contrary to expectations, "I'll Be There" zoomed to number one. Gordy had been proven right—and then some. The Jackson Five's first *four* releases had gone to the top of the charts—a first for any group. By the time the dust had settled, the Jackson Five could also boast that they had sold more singles than any other act in 1970.

The year 1971 began auspiciously with the release of their new single, "Mama's Pearl." A throwback to their traditional bubblegum sound, "Mama's Pearl" marked the first time they failed to reach the top spot—peaking at number two. But Gordy could hardly claim to be disappointed. At a time when some Motown stalwarts were losing their luster, he had tapped into a rich vein of platinum.

On January 31, 1971, less than eighteen months after they had left for Los Angeles, the Jackson Five made a triumphant return to Gary. As their limousine moved through the crowded streets of their old neighborhood, the house at 2300 Jackson Street—renamed Jackson Five Boulevard for the day—came into view. With its snow-covered front yard and tumbledown picket fence, the property looked amazingly small. On a tree in a front yard, someone had nailed a huge sign that dwarfed the house even further. It read:

WELCOME HOME, JACKSON 5
KEEPERS OF THE DREAM

5

For so many years I was called a thirty-five-year-old midget. Nobody believed I was a little kid.

"Rattler!" Before Michael realized what was happening, someone shoved him roughly into the pool—just out of reach of the poisonous snake that slithered menacingly nearby. As the rattler made its exit into the bushes, Michael, who had several pet snakes of his own, was crestfallen. "Darn it!" he yelled at his rescuer. "I didn't even get to hear his rattle shake or nuthin'."

The Jacksons' neighbors had come to accept the occasional visit of a rattlesnake or two—along with opossums, skunks, tarantulas, and other forms of wildlife that, despite the intrusion of civilization, continued to proliferate in the parched hills above Los Angeles. Shaken by Michael's close call at poolside, Katherine ordered Joe to find the family a new, more civilized place to live.

In March of 1971 Joe plunked down $250,000 on a stucco-walled split-level on Hayvenhurst Boulevard in the upscale San Fernando suburb of Encino. The property boasted an orange grove, an Olympic-size pool with a Jacuzzi and water-spouting Greek statuary, an archery range, a badminton court, a basketball court, a playhouse, and separate guest quarters.

The twenty-two-room mansion—which the Jacksons called Hayvenhurst—would undergo many renovations over the next decade, including the addition of a state-of-the art recording studio (with an adjacent snack-filled lounge the kids called the "Candy Store") and a screening room with thirty-two seats upholstered in plush red velvet. For the first time in their lives, the brothers had room for pets, and the Jacksons' personal zoo expanded rapidly. In addition to the resident German shepherds Lobo and Heavy, there was a wolf named Black Girl, Jeffrey the Mynah, Tweety Chicken, Peter Rabbit, and two boa constrictors—one belonging to Jermaine, the other to Michael. "I just got my boa," an ecstatic twelve-year-old Michael told a reporter. "It's even bigger than Jermaine's. But I don't have my mice anymore. They started multiplying and it got outrageous. They got loose in the house, too. Millions of them."

Michael's pet rodents had another unpleasant habit: when things got too crowded, they began devouring each other. "They'll do that," he said. "Yuck! So I put 'em outside. But it gets real cold in California at night, and they all froze to death. Funny, huh?"

Even though there were six bedrooms in the house, the children doubled and tripled up just as they had back in Gary: Jackie with "cousin" Ronnie, who still played backup for the group; Tito with "cousin" Johnny; Marlon with Jermaine; Janet with La Toya, and Michael with little brother Randy.

At first they were required to do chores around the house, just as they always had. "We don't have no maids, y'know," Michael boasted to reporters. But by the time Michael was thirteen, the whim of every Jackson would be catered to by a battalion of servants—including maids, gardeners, cooks, and chauffeurs.

All the amenities aside, it was not so much the opulence of their new surroundings that distinguished this from previous homes as the sheer isolation. High walls, imposing iron gates, and a small army of uniformed guards monitoring surveillance cameras now stood between the Jacksons and the outside world. Their new Encino abode was nearly forty minutes away from Los Angeles by car. Here, away from any corrupting outside influences, Joe could maintain complete control over his moneymaking brood.

Michael and his brothers worked overtime to pay for the upkeep on their gilded cage. That March Motown released one of the Jackson Five's most enduring hits, a Clifton Davis ballad called "Never Can Say Goodbye." Davis, an actor and singer, would be best known playing a handsome young preacher in the popular 1980s television series *Amen.*

The week that "Never Can Say Goodbye" plateaued at number two on the *Billboard* chart, Michael made a guest appearance doing his impression of Frank Sinatra on Diana Ross's first solo television special, *Diana.* Wearing a jaunty fedora, Sinatra's trademark raincoat slung over his shoulder, Michael belted out his satirical version of "It Was a Very Good Year"—without the faintest clue, he would later admit, as to why it was funny. "So long as they laugh when they're supposed to," he said with a shrug, "it doesn't matter if I get it or not."

Indeed, even among the squeaky-clean Jackson kids, Michael appeared to be the most resolutely accommodating. He would go out of his way to sign autographs or pose with fans for pictures, and thanks to his mother's civilizing influence, he was unfailingly polite in the presence of adults. La Toya, however, regarded Michael as nothing more than "a typical pesky brother. "He was so full of fun and outgoing," his sister said years later, "it's hard to believe that Michael and the adult Michael were the same person."

The Jackson children's carefully circumscribed world left little room for outside friendships. Nor did they have the opportunity to forge relationships with other children at school. Michael was briefly enrolled in the sixth grade at Los Angeles' Gardner Street Elementary School and spent a scant ten days attending Beverly Hills' Emerson Junior High before someone phoned the school and threatened to kill him. Katherine was so shaken by the anonymous death threat that she yanked both Michael and Marlon out of Emerson and placed them at Buckley, an exclusive private school in nearby Sherman Oaks.

Still, Michael spent little time in class; he owed virtually his entire education from age twelve on to Mrs. Rose Fine, a motherly tutor who accompanied the Jackson Five on concert tours, recording sessions, television tapings, wherever their work might take them.

The most outgoing and rambunctious of the Jackson kids, Michael also possessed a surprising mean streak when it came to his brothers and sisters. Continuing well into adulthood, he would constantly tease and belittle his siblings, sometimes reducing them to tears. He dubbed the somewhat chunky Janet "Dunk," short for "donkey." He called the round-cheeked La Toya "Moonface" but saved the most humiliating nickname for the acne-stricken Jermaine: "Rocky Road."

As they had done several times before, the Jackson Five went into the studio that May and recorded a song intended for another artist. Deke Richards had wanted Motown's newest acquisition, Sammy Davis, Jr., to record "Maybe Tomorrow." Legend or no, Davis was passed over in favor of Michael. Although not a huge hit—the ballad squeaked into the Top Ten—"Maybe Tomorrow" helped the group sustain momentum as it headed off that July of 1971 on its most ambitious concert tour yet—more than forty-five cities in less than two months.

Michael was at his most inventive on tour. To combat boredom on the road, Michael and his brothers played poker (Marlon's card-playing prowess earned him the moniker "Las Vegas") and Monopoly, had furious pillow fights, held races down hotel corridors, and threw water balloons off balconies.

While the Jackson Five juggernaut rolled across the land, Gordy and Motown were cashing in big on Jackson merchandise. Every conceivable item was emblazoned with the boys' wholesome young faces and the Jackson Five logo: lunchboxes, toys, posters, buttons, stickers, calendars, watches, T-shirts, jackets, sleeping bags, towels, and bedding.

For the boys, the ultimate pop culture kudo—their own Saturday morning cartoon show—came just as their fifty-city tour drew to a close in Honolulu that September. Michael and his brothers were the stars of *The Jackson 5 Show,* but they had nothing to do with it; they merely provided the musical portion in the form of excerpts from their hit records. They were paid only scale—about $350 each per episode—but for Michael, a devout fan of Roadrunner cartoons, it was an enormous thrill. "Funny, too," he once said, "because I hardly ever got to see it. We were always on the road, working. . . ."

Jacksonmania was in full swing throughout the balance of 1971 and well into the following year. A week after they made their debut as cartoons, ABC aired *Goin' Back to Indiana,* the Jackson Five's first prime-time special, on September 19, 1971.

An even bigger milestone was reached in October, when Motown released Michael's first solo effort, "Got to Be There." At Diana Ross's urging, Berry Gordy had decided it was time to take full advantage of Michael's star potential. Joe Jackson went along with Gordy's plan, with the proviso that the Jackson Five—with Michael as lead singer—would remain Motown's top priority. Little more than an overwrought variation on the previous year's megahit "I'll Be There," "Got to Be There" catapulted to the top of the charts by mid-December.

Michael had always been the center of attention, but with "Got to Be There" dominating the airwaves and a solo album of the same name flying off the shelves, he now all but eclipsed his brothers. With the possible exception of Jermaine, who would never forget the day he had been abruptly dumped as lead singer and replaced by Michael, the other Jacksons did not, in fact, resent Michael's growing celebrity. They had long been resigned to his preeminent position in the group. They were also now old enough to take advantage of some of the perks of rock stardom. While Tito and Jermaine were content tooling around Encino in their mother's jet black Audi, twenty-one-year-old Jackie overlooked his father's objections and bought a car of his own—a sporty Datsun 240-Z.

When Jackie crashed into another car and went careening through the windshield, he knew his father's reaction would be violent. "You fool!" Joe screamed, punching his eldest son and knocking him to the floor. Predictably, Joe seemed less concerned with Jackie's welfare than the impact his death or injury might have had on the group. "What would we do then, be the Jackson Four?" he shouted. "You think the fans would still love you with an ugly, scarred-up old face?"

Jackie had always taken more than his full share of abuse from Joe. All of the Jackson boys were still slapped, shoved, punched, and otherwise humiliated by Joe with regularity and often in full view of outsiders. But Jackie, as always, seemed to be the lightning rod for his father's unchecked anger.

The clash over his mishap in the 240-Z was the last straw for Jackie, who moved out of Hayvenhurst and into his own apartment. Professionally he was still very much under his father's thumb. "Even after he moved out," said La Toya, "he was afraid of Joseph. We all are to this day."

There were other compensations, however. By 1972 Jackie, described by his brothers as the "lover boy" of the group, was already cutting a broad swath through the groupie population. He was merely emulating his father; ever since Jackie could remember, whenever they were on the road Joe had made a point of bringing his young pickups back to the hotel so they could "kiss my boys good night."

Jackie's modus operandi seldom varied. At concerts he would pick one girl out of the audience, have her brought backstage, and then rendezvous with her at his hotel room.

Barely sixteen, Jermaine began his sexual career by sleeping with the groupies who had already been bedded by Jackie (as, on occasion, did his father, Joe). Eventually Jermaine would be regarded as the most promiscuous of the young Jacksons, sometimes picking two or three girls at a concert, then staggering their arrivals at his hotel room.

"Jermaine practically had a revolving door installed at the foot of his bed," said one roadie.

His hyperactive brothers had no qualms about performing sex acts in Michael's presence, even though he was only thirteen. The sleeping arrangements on the road were the same as they had always been. Michael and Marlon slept together while Jermaine had an adjoining bed to himself. Often Michael would be awakened by the sounds of moaning and thrashing about as Jermaine tried out a wide variety of sexual positions with his latest one-night stand.

By flaunting their sexual adventures in Michael's face, Jackie and Jermaine may have sought to educate their preadolescent brother as well as impress him with their manly prowess. But his exposure to raw, anonymous sex at such as early age served only to deepen Michael's sense of confusion about the relationship between men and women.

Despite Katherine's civilizing influence, it now appeared to Michael as if his brothers were turning out just like their father. The young women Jackie and Jermaine brought back to their rooms were, in Michael's eyes, coerced into performing what appeared to be unspeakably degrading acts. When they left, they often did so in tears.

Michael's premature sexual education might not have stopped there. Johnny Jackson, the "cousin" who lived with the Jackson family from 1967 to 1976, has claimed that Michael was sexually abused by a relative. Steeltown Records' owner Gordon Keith claims that Johnny Jackson has told him of stumbling upon the relative, a male employee, and twelve-year-old Michael. All three were nude and appeared to be sexually aroused.

Michael has never acknowledged having been sexually molested as a child. Whatever the truth, as with any physically and emotionally abused child, the deep wounds would not manifest themselves fully until adulthood.

Michael reacted to his brothers' sexual escapades by burying himself in his faith. He pored over the Bible, memorizing scripture and debating the finer points of the Book of Revelations with La Toya. Ironically, La Toya was forbidden by her Jehovah's Witness faith from listening to most of her brothers' early hit records. Relatively harmless lines like "shake it, shake it, baby" from "ABC" were deemed too suggestive. But as long as the records sold, Katherine was able to overlook this glaring contradiction of her religious beliefs.

Michael, who viewed his brothers' extracurricular activities as nothing less than a betrayal of the fans' trust and his own faith, took an active part in sabotaging their romantic forays whenever possible. If he noticed either Jackie or Jermaine pursuing a fan, or if he encountered an unfamiliar young woman heading toward their room, he stopped to warn them. Sometimes he even became confrontational, accosting female fans in lobbies and hotel corridors and demanding to know point-blank if they had "had sex" (or were planning to have sex) with one of his brothers. By all accounts, Michael's heartfelt entreaties had no effect; in each case the fan was willing to do whatever it took to sleep with a Jackson.

Quiet, stolid Tito, the Jackson child who bore the closest physical resemblance to Joe, was the exception. In late 1971, Tito and his high school sweetheart DeeDee Martes became engaged—secretly, since Joe had been cautioned by Motown that any marriage among the group's members could seriously undermine their status as teenage sex symbols.

Eventually Joe and Katherine grudgingly acquiesced to the marriage—but only after DeeDee had signed a prenuptial contract drawn up by the family's lawyers. The contract, which was intended for all prospective Jackson wives, essentially cut them off without a penny in the event the marriage broke up—a stipulation that would be of some considerable significance, since every Jackson son who married would, in fact, ultimately divorce.

Michael, who accepted without question the Jehovah's Witness tenet that sex is a marital "tribulation" that must be endured for the sole purpose of procreation, gave his parents and Motown executives no cause for concern. He was focused solely on his career—so much so that, while his brothers now seemed to be just going through the motions on stage and in the recording studio, Michael consciously worked on carving out a niche for himself as a solo act.

Before and after concerts, Michael no longer engaged in horseplay with his brothers. Instead he stayed to himself in his room, drawing caricatures on the sketch pad he always carried with him or catching up on his Bible studies.

In the spring of 1972 his remake of the 1958 Bobby Day ditty "Rockin' Robin" had been an enormous if somewhat incongruous hit for Michael, fluttering to number two on the charts. An animal was also the subject of Michael's next big single, although that could not have been deduced from the song. Nowhere in the lyrics to "Ben" was there any indication that the tune was, in fact, a paean to a rat.

Understandably there were misgivings when Michael was first approached to record the theme from the film of the same name. *Ben,* an offbeat, tongue-in-cheek horror story about a misfit boy whose best friend is a rodent, seemed to contradict Michael's squeaky-clean image. But given Michael's special fondness for the creatures, the movie and the song appealed to him.

The moviegoing public agreed. *Ben* was a box office hit, and the song went on to be nominated for an Academy Award. More important for Michael, "Ben" was his first solo record to reach number one.

With the biggest-selling record in the country to his credit, fourteen-year-old Michael began to chafe under the constraints of the Motown system. He now insisted on more control in the studio, and when producers three times his age refused to give it to him, he complained directly to Berry Gordy. A compromise was usually reached, but Michael, who would always trust his instincts, was seldom satisfied. "I could have done so much more with what I was given," he later said, "if they'd let me."

Joe viewed Michael's newfound independent streak with a mixture of glee and apprehension. On his own, Michael had already become a major profit center for Motown. That meant "twice the money," as Joe was fond of saying, as long as Michael's solo career did not jeopardize the Jackson Five—Joe's number one priority.

Joe also worried that headstrong Michael, the only one of his children who even dared to talk back, might try to wriggle free from his control. Thus far he had successfully managed to bully all his offspring into submission. Through a combination of beatings, intimidation, and ego-battering, Joe had effectively undermined their self-worth to the point where they felt utterly dependent on him. "You're all *nuthin',*" was his constant refrain. Michael, no less than his brothers, had felt he had no choice but to believe it. Until now.

One afternoon after returning home from yet another exhausting session in the recording studio, Michael went to the backyard cages where the mice were kept and plucked one out by the tail. He then brought the wriggling rodent to another cage, this one housing his eight-foot-long, ten-inch-thick boa constrictor. He grinned as he watched the snake ingesting the mouse whole. Sometimes Michael bestowed a name on the boa's hapless dinner. Today, that name was Joe.

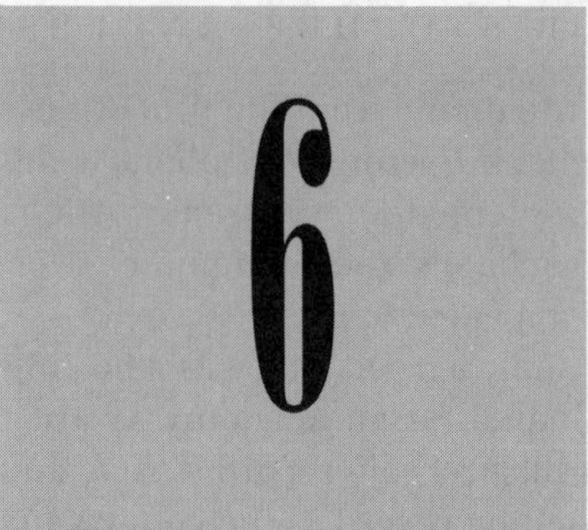

Everybody can't be as lucky as the Jacksons.

—Joe Jackson

The smell of smoke might have aroused Michael out of his deep sleep, if the pain—a sharp, searing shock that seemed to shoot up his leg to his brain—had not jolted him awake. He screamed and threw back the covers to see his father crouching at the foot of his bed, holding a match to his son's bare foot and laughing hysterically.

None of the Jackson children could ever be certain when their father would play one of his cruel practical jokes or when he might, without warning, strike out in an inexplicable fit of rage. Oddly, their success seemed to make him more volatile than ever. His personal arsenal of firearms had grown over the years, and more and more frequently Joe would pull out a pistol from a drawer, point it at one of his children, and pull the trigger. Fortunately the guns were never loaded.

It was only logical that when Joe began working into the night at his office in Hollywood and spending less and less time at home, Michael and the others were grateful. Katherine had her suspicions, but as long as she was not publicly humiliated by her husband's infidelities, she was willing to look the other way if it meant there would be some measure of tranquillity at home.

. . .

The Jackson Five (actually the Jackson Six, now that little brother Randy had joined the group) launched its first European tour in November of 1972. Their first performance promised to be their most exciting to date: a royal command performance at Albert Hall before Queen Elizabeth.

No one was prepared for the mayhem that ensued when the plane touched down at London's Heathrow Airport. Airport security guards tried but failed to hold back nearly ten thousand screaming young fans who engulfed the boys as they tried to make their way to waiting limousines. The mob ripped their shirts, yanked handfuls of hair out of their heads, and even stole their shoes. The most horrifying moment came when fans yanked at both ends of a scarf that was wrapped around Michael's neck. He was nearly strangled before a fast-thinking chauffeur shoved the girls out of the way and literally tossed Michael headfirst into the car.

Similar episodes occurred when the Jackson Five moved on to Paris, Munich, Frankfurt, and Brussels. In Amsterdam rampaging mobs smashed store windows and overturned cars.

Mass hysteria aside, the Jackson Five's recording career had begun a downward spiral the previous spring with the release of the lackluster "Little Bitty Pretty One" and continued that fall with "Lookin' Through the Windows."

Worse was to come. When it was released in February of 1973, the single "Hallelujah Day" was a disappointment; *Skywriter* arrived in record stores the following month and was an even bigger bomb.

In the middle of all this turmoil, Katherine dropped a bombshell. Shortly after the Jackson Five returned to the United States to tape their second television special, she had been informed by a so-called friend that Joe was being seen around town with Cheryle Terrell, a twenty-six-year-old Jackson Five fan who had a crush on Jackie. As had often been the case, Joe, then forty-six, moved in on the young woman—only this time a serious relationship had developed.

As long as he restricted himself to tawdry one-night stands, Katherine was willing to overlook her husband's philandering. But this particular affair had already lasted several months, and her pride would not allow her to accept the fact that her husband had a mistress. Katherine filed for divorce in Los Angeles Superior Court on March 9, 1973.

At Motown headquarters Gordy and his minions were acutely aware of the nasty legal battle that was about to take place—and how it could shatter the family's carefully crafted squeaky-clean image. "This was the all-American family," said one executive. "Now Katherine threatened to expose their perfect family life as the complete sham that it was. The whole company panicked."

Only a few inside Motown were privy to the divorce action, and they relentlessly pestered Katherine to drop it. The Jacksons were America's most beloved family, they told her, and by divorcing Joe she would explode the myth and destroy her children's careers.

Despite their pending divorce, Kate and Joe were the very picture of marital harmony that summer when they joined their sons on the group's first tour of Japan. Michael was an instant crowd-pleaser in Tokyo. The Japanese audiences behaved themselves, but those in Australia, the next stop on the tour, were more demonstrative. At a concert in Perth, Michael had to be whisked away by security guards when fans rushed the stage.

For all the hysteria on the road, the group's recording career remained stagnant. For the first time Joe now considered the possibility of leaving Motown and taking the Jackson Five to a label "where we'll be appreciated."

That August producer Hal Davis came up with "Get It Together"—a slick, less saccharine-sounding number that at least managed to make it as high as number twenty-eight on the *Billboard* chart. That mollified Joe. Still, there was no telling how long this reconciliation might last. To protect his interests, Gordy quietly moved to make the Jackson Five name and logo his own. The U.S. Patent Office granted that request in August of 1973, giving Motown sole dominion over the group's name.

Ultimately, the fact that the Jackson Five did not own the rights to their own name would come as a substantial shock to the Jacksons themselves. But for now it appeared that the group and Motown had stepped back from the brink of divorce at the eleventh hour.

So too had Joe and Katherine, who once again put the family's image above her own pride. While they were still in Australia, DeeDee Jackson gave birth in August to the first Jackson grandchild—Toriano Adaryll II (nicknamed Taj). Joe refused to let Tito fly home for the arrival of his first child.

Meanwhile Michael was about to acquire a new sister-in-law—all in the interest of keeping Motown and the Jackson Five together. Joe was now more convinced than ever that the Jackson Five was suffering from Gordy's inattention. What they needed was a personal tie to the company's founder—the sort of intimate connection that had worked such wonders for Diana Ross's career.

Joe did not have to look far. Although Gordy's nineteen-year-old daughter, Hazel, had long been enamored of Jermaine—the two had been dating on and off for several years—both families had played down their romance. Next to Michael, the soulful-looking Jermaine was the most popular Jackson—and generally regarded as the sexiest. In the face of harsh commercial reality, Joe now sought to cement an alliance with Gordy by marrying Jermaine to Hazel. That September six hundred silver-embossed invitations went out for what *Ebony* breathlessly billed as "what might be called 'the wedding of the century.' "

On December 15, 1973, Michael showed up in the Rodeo Room of the Beverly Hills Hotel to serve with his other brothers as an usher at Jermaine's lavish wedding (Jermaine chose Marlon to be his best man). *Ebony* had predicted the cost of the affair could exceed $60,000. Actually it topped $250,000.

At one point just days before the ceremony, yet another family crisis threatened to torpedo the whole glittering affair. Katherine received a tip from another friend that Cheryle Terrell was pregnant with Joe's child. As a result, a family member recalled, "Katherine just packed her bags and took off. She couldn't stand Joe's infidelity any longer."

Katherine reappeared in time for Jermaine's wedding. Whatever her personal pain, as always she was not about to risk a scandal that would ruin her son's wedding and tarnish the family image.

The group waited for Jermaine to return from his month-long European honeymoon before launching a ten-day tour of the West African republic of Senegal. It was the group's first trip to Africa, and Michael was excited by the long line of natives resplendent in tribal costumes performing a special dance in their honor when they arrived at Dakar International Airport. "Their drums and sounds filled the air with rhythm," Michael recalled. "I was going crazy. I was screaming, 'All right! They got the rhythm. . . . This is it. This is where I come from. The origin.' "

But Michael was also shocked by the living conditions of the Senegalese. The group had to make do without electricity, running water, or even modern plumbing. And while Michael took the opportunity to praise Africans as "the most talented race on earth," he made no secret of his desire to return to the princely comforts of his California home.

Once back in the United States, Michael and his brothers made their first real attempt to cash in on the emerging disco craze with the release of "Dancing Machine." The single, with its distinctive cutting-edge blend of contemporary dance music and R&B, was a benchmark of sorts for the group, and especially for Michael.

There had been a palpable fear that the Jackson Five would lose their core audience if they strayed too far from their tried-and-true recipe for bubblegum soul. "Dancing Machine" proved a necessary departure for the Jackson Five—a bold ploy to attract a new, more musically sophisticated audience without alienating their young fans. In truth their fans were growing up right along with them. The single went double platinum, rocketing to number two on the pop charts. "If they had stuck with what they were doing," said Dick Clark, "they probably would have fizzled out within a year. In this business, stagnation is death. Michael knows that better than anyone."

"Dancing Machine" also marked the first opportunity for the record-buying public to hear the new, more mature-sounding Michael. There had been much speculation about what puberty might do to Michael's voice, and rumors abounded about just what drastic actions Motown might take to preserve it. One scenario had large doses of hormones being administered to Michael; another even suggested that he might be surgically altered in the manner of Italy's seventeenth-century castrati.

Even to other family members, Michael professed not to care. Privately, in the words of a cousin, "Mike was going through hell. Once I remember his voice cracked, and you could just see this look of panic cross his face." Joe coped with this situation scientifically. Ballads were added to Michael's repertoire so that he would have the opportunity to "break in" his new voice.

As for the trademark bubblegum soul hits that were a pro forma part of any Jackson Five show, the group had a simple solution. They merely dropped the songs a half key or a full key so Michael would not have to risk a hernia straining for that high C. Gradually, tentatively, he was making the inevitable switch from boy soprano to tenor.

Michael claimed that during those awkward teenage years, "the biggest personal struggle I had to face was right there in the mirror." First he underwent a growth spurt between the ages of fourteen and fifteen, nearly shooting up to his full height of five feet ten inches. Suddenly he had to contend with the look of disappointment on the faces of people who came primed to see that adorable, chipmunk-cheeked little boy who sang "ABC" and "Ben." "They'd walk right past me," he recalled.

"I would say, 'I'm Michael,' and they would look doubtful. I was not the person they expected or even wanted to see."

Then there was the nickname bestowed upon Michael by Joe. "Hey, *Bignose,*" his father said with cruel delight. "Where did you get that from, eh, Bignose?" The brothers, retaliating for all the sniping they had endured from Michael over the years, took up the chant. "There's *Bignose!*" Michael proved less resilient than his siblings. Humiliated, he usually ran from the taunts, his eyes welling with tears.

Michael was also devastated when, at fifteen, he fell victim to a severe case of acne that left his face covered with pimples—divine retribution, his mother suggested, for the days when he had teased Jermaine with the nickname Rocky Road.

Michael's complexion problems left him nothing short of traumatized. He sought treatment from Beverly Hills' top skin specialists. Nothing seemed to work. And for over two years—until he finally outgrew the problem at seventeen—Michael became a virtual recluse, holed up in his room, always casting his eyes downward, never looking anyone directly in the face. For the first time he refused to pose for pictures and shied away from fans. "I can't stand it, La Toya," he confided to his sister, "I really can't."

To complicate matters, Michael also became obsessed with his weight. Each morning he would disrobe and weigh himself, then examine his body in the mirror for any signs of weight gain. If he could pinch even a fraction of an inch of flesh anywhere on his body, he would fast until he was satisfied that the "problem" was resolved.

To combat both his acne and his imagined obesity, Michael decided to forgo the oily French fries and potato chips he loved for the vegetarian diet that he supposed had cleared up brother Jermaine's complexion. Still, he suffered emotionally. His self-esteem was inexorably intertwined with his physical appearance, and his adolescent tribulations left deep psychological scars. "He never recovered," La Toya observed. "Once the most sociable and effervescent of my brothers, he was now painfully shy, something I don't think he'll ever overcome." Michael concurred. "It messed up my whole personality," he confessed.

If Michael was "disgusted" by what he saw in the mirror, as he claimed to be, the fans did not share his revulsion. On the road the adoring crowds were more frenzied than ever. And at their Encino home, fans gathered every day outside the gates, hoping for a glimpse of Michael. "My fans are my dates," he became fond of saying. "They're at our gate every day, and I'll go out and sign autographs." Would he ever venture outside the gate to actually meet these people? "No," he replied matter-of-factly. "Never."

One afternoon when Janet was home alone, an entire family somehow managed to make it past security and into the house. They seemed nice enough, so Janet treated them to a tour. Not long after, Michael was sitting in the den when a woman climbed over the gate, walked into the house, and plopped down on the couch beside him. "God sent me," she explained.

Not all intruders were so benign. Another woman materialized inside the house and, screaming that she had been put on the planet to bear Michael's children, pursued him until she was dragged off by security.

None of this apparently impressed Michael as much as the fan who asked him if he actually performed the same bodily functions as mere mortals. "In front of everybody, she asked me, 'Do you go to the bathroom?' " Michael said. "I was so embarrassed, I didn't know what to say."

The only place Michael ever felt truly confident was before an audience, where he could hide behind layers of stage makeup and his flashy moves. At no time was that more obvious than in April of 1974 when the Jackson kids—*all* the Jackson kids—made their Las Vegas debut.

For Joe's generation, Las Vegas had symbolic importance. The Strip had been a mecca for black entertainers since the days when Sammy Davis, Jr., played the Sands Hotel but was not allowed to stay there. But there were also hard economic reasons for headlining at one of the big hotels. If the Jackson Five was to survive in any form, it would have to complete the transition begun with "Dancing Machine." Joe reasoned that if they could prove themselves before an audience of white middle-class adults, then they would not be so totally dependent on the vagaries of record sales. They could always make millions playing before a sea of leisure-suited salesmen and their beehive-coifed wives. Elvis had discovered this; so had Ann-Margret, Cher, and even Diana Ross.

The Jacksons were booked into the newest and biggest hotel on the Strip, the MGM Grand. And as always, Michael was the riveting centerpiece of the show. "When we started out, I used to be little, cute, and charming," he told the crowd after the group's first explosive number. "Now I'm big, cute, and charming." Rail thin and over six feet tall in his platform shoes, he moved with the grace, self-assurance, and energy of an electrified Fred Astaire.

Still, the Jacksons felt there was much to learn from the master. On a night off, they flew up to Lake Tahoe to catch Elvis Presley's act at the Sahara Hotel and Casino. When they ventured backstage after the performance, Presley was obviously having difficulty winding down. He paced nervously back and forth, his white satin jumpsuit soaked with sweat.

Michael eyed the hulking, bloated, and obviously drugged Elvis warily. But Presley was delighted to see the Jacksons. "You guys are incredible," he said, pausing to shake their hands before he resumed his pacing. His pupils were pinpricks. "You started so young, it's really somethin'." Michael and the others were flattered when Presley rattled off the names of his favorite J-5 hits and complimented them on the smooth, high-tech sound of "Dancing Machine." He also stressed, sincerely if somewhat awkwardly, that rock and roll owed its existence to black performers and that the Jacksons were part of that musical tradition.

Michael and the others were flattered but also mortified by the obvious toll drugs were taking on Presley's health. As they turned to leave, Presley grabbed Michael's hand and squeezed it hard. "You kids be good," he drawled. Within two years, he would be dead.

7

One thing I'm not is stupid.

Michael trusted his brother implicitly. So when he called to say he was sending over two friends to get his autograph, Michael opened the door and welcomed the two attractive young women into his hotel room. It soon became clear that they had come for more than an autograph. Now that Michael was fifteen, it had been decided that he had remained celibate too long. The two prostitutes had been hired to put an end to his virginity once and for all. "They kept telling the press that Michael was this red-blooded American male," said a friend, "but it bothered Joe and the brothers that Michael didn't seem interested in girls at all." From a business standpoint alone, Joe recognized that Michael was growing into a handsome young man with bankable sex appeal. It did not bode well if he seemed uninterested in the opposite sex.

While one of the hookers began to disrobe, the other tried to unbutton Michael's shirt. He brushed her aside and headed for the door, only to find that it was locked from the outside. "Hey," he shouted. "Open the door. Somebody?" Although muffled, he could hear familiar laughter coming from the other side of the door. "Come on, guys. *Guys?*"

The experience of being locked in a room at the age of fifteen with two hookers was traumatizing for Michael and a pivotal event in his sexual development. At a time when most males are taking their first tentative steps into the sexual arena, Michael had already witnessed firsthand his father's infidelity and his older brothers' promiscuity. Now he was again being forced by his own family to confront sex in its rawest form.

Despite their most energetic efforts, the two hookers not only failed to arouse Michael, they reduced him to tears. They were even more confused when, as they put their clothes back on, he pulled a Bible from the bedstand drawer and began reciting scripture.

From that point on, Michael would use the Bible as his shield against any romantic involvement with a woman. Theresa Gonsalves, who years later would claim to be the inspiration for Michael's controversial number one hit "Billie Jean," learned that firsthand when she met Michael that year in Las Vegas.

Gonsalves had actually boasted to her schoolgirl friends in Boston that she would meet Michael by the time she was sixteen, and set out to fulfill that dream by peppering Michael with letters. She told Michael that she would fly to Las Vegas to meet him on her sixteenth birthday and even took a part-time job to pay for the trip.

The Jacksons were so impressed with Gonsalves's gutsy resolve that Katherine invited her to stay with the family when she finally arrived in Las Vegas as promised on the eve of her sixteenth birthday. Unfortunately, when she met Michael he was in a petulant snit, rudely issuing orders to his bodyguard, Bill Bray, and behaving, in Gonsalves's words, "like a spoiled brat." Bray, who over the next two decades would become one of Michael's closest confidants, didn't mind. "I'm Michael's chaperon and punching bag," he liked to quip.

Gonsalves found "very little to like about him at first. I was really disappointed when I met Michael. I thought: Here is this kid at sixteen bossing people around and doing whatever he wants." But over the next week Michael and Gonsalves, always surrounded by the other Jacksons, grew increasingly fond of one another. Her last night in Las Vegas, Michael asked her to stay behind with him in his dressing room while the rest of the family went out to dinner. Oh, boy, she thought, my chance to be alone with him.

Her hopes were dashed when he pulled out his Bible and began preaching on the evils of premarital sex. "The whole time he talked about his religion," she recalled. "I went home to Boston and started studying with the Jehovah's Witnesses." According to Gonsalves, Michael seemed preoccupied not only with the issue of sexual purity, but also with the existence of Satan—particularly demonic possession.

. . . .

Gloating in his victory over Gordy in the ongoing power struggle about the direction of his sons' careers, Joe signed up his sons to portray a family of slaves in a feature film called *Isoman Cross and Sons.* Not surprisingly, Gordy objected on the grounds that such grim subject matter might compromise the group's upbeat image.

Without Gordy's backing, the movie would never get off the ground, and a seething Joe responded by taking the family back to Las Vegas in August of 1974. It was while they were wowing yet another audience at the MGM Grand that, back at Centinela Valley Community Hospital in Inglewood, California, Cheryle Terrell gave birth to Joe Jackson's daughter Jo Vonnie (later changed to Joh Vonnie) Jackson.

Amazingly, after one of the shows, Joe called a meeting of his sons and proudly told them that they had a new half sister. Michael recalled that he was "so proud, like we should be happy for him. It made me sick."

It was only a matter of months before Michael, disgusted by his father's behavior and hoping that Katherine would be forced to divorce him, told his mother everything. She was devastated but did not want to give Joe the satisfaction of knowing that he had wounded her deeply. "On the surface, it looked as if everything were business as usual," said a friend. "But every once in a while she'd talk about that 'whore and her bastard child.' "

Joe was so brazen about Cheryle Terrell and their daughter that he bought them a three-bedroom house just minutes away from Hayvenhurst. By all accounts Joe treated his illegitimate daughter more like a favored grandchild, lavishing her with presents and affection. Soon he was spending more time with his new family than with his brood by Katherine.

Utterly humiliated, Katherine would ultimately manifest her anger in an unexpected way. One afternoon, after listening in on a particularly intimate phone call between Joe and Cheryle, Katherine followed Joe to her house and attacked Terrell in the driveway, slapping her across the face and shoving her to the ground.

For the first time, Katherine had given some vent to her true feelings. Michael reacted by once again begging her to divorce Joe. This time she packed her bags and left to live with her mother. A week later she succumbed to Joe's tearful pleadings over the phone and returned home. "What can I do, Michael?" she asked her disappointed son. "He loves me."

All this marital turmoil did nothing to dissuade the Jackson sons from taking wives at an early age. During a return engagement at the MGM Grand that autumn, Jackie quietly married Enid Spann, the twenty-year-old daughter of a successful black businessman and his Korean-born wife.

The state of the Jackson Five's marriage to Motown, meanwhile, was no less problematic. Michael's next solo album, *Forever Michael,* was released in January of 1975 and promptly sank into oblivion. Convinced that his son's career was being allowed to languish, Joe declared that Michael would never again record a solo record for Motown.

While his father ranted, Michael took matters into his own hands. Without consulting Joe or anyone else in the family, he arranged a private meeting with Gordy for May 14 at Motown headquarters. There was no doubt that, had he known, Joe would have forbidden such a summit.

"I know people don't think of me as tough or strong-willed," Michael later said. "But that day I was a lion." Michael laid all his cards on the table, complaining that he and his brothers resented the fact that they were given no freedom to write, produce, or own the publishing rights—these rights being particularly lucrative—to the songs they recorded.

Gordy was impressed, and so was Michael. At sixteen, he had proven to himself that he had the mettle to deal one-on-one with one of the most powerful men in show business. As the meeting ended, he still devoutly hoped that Gordy would accede to the group's wishes. "We all felt our roots were there," he said, "and we all wished we could stay."

Neither Joe nor Michael's brothers were amused. However noble his intentions, Michael had moved unilaterally to negotiate a peace with the man they now considered an enemy. As soon as he heard of Michael's meeting with Gordy, Joe called the brothers together for a meeting of their own. Only Jermaine was missing; Joe no longer felt Berry Gordy's son-in-law could be trusted with Jackson Five secrets. That night the four remaining brothers took a vote on whether to leave Motown. The vote was unanimous. It was agreed that Joe would secretly begin soliciting offers from other labels.

Within weeks Joe and Ron Alexenburg, president of CBS Records' Epic label, had worked out a deal that included a $750,000 up-front signing bonus and a royalty of 27 percent—*ten times* the group's royalty rate at Motown.

Money was certainly a major factor in their decision to sign with Epic. But it was not the only factor. Epic was fast establishing a reputation as a cutting-edge label, with a roster of stars that ranged from country legends Tammy Wynette and Charlie Rich to hard-rockers Ted Nugent and Jeff Beck to Patti LaBelle.

What most intrigued Michael about a deal with Epic would be the chance to work with producers Kenny Gamble and Leon Huff, chief exponents of what had become known as the "Philly sound." Even more significant, Epic, which also had its doubts about the Jacksons' unproven songwriting abilities, would allow them to submit two or three numbers for possible inclusion in each new album.

Whatever Joe's failings as a husband and father, Michael would later concede that his father's foresight kept them from becoming just another "nostalgia act." Had Joe not acted decisively, the Jackson Five would almost certainly have become another group of well-paid, creatively stymied has-beens.

All of the brothers were thrilled with the deal their father presented to them. All but Jermaine. Gordy had convinced his son-in-law that he was all but destined to take over as president of Motown. Jermaine had to decide whether he wanted to jeopardize that for an uncertain future at Epic.

Even as they performed a live show on the stage of Long Island's Westbury Music Fair, the wrangling went on—Jermaine arguing that the family should remain loyal to Motown, his brothers demanding that he join them in their mutiny. Then, between their first and second shows at Westbury, Jermaine received a phone call backstage from his father-in-law. News of the Jacksons' imminent defection had hit the newspapers, and now it was time for Jermaine to make his choice. With only minutes to go before returning to the stage, he walked out on his stunned brothers.

Moments later Michael returned to the stage. For the first time since they'd begun performing, Jermaine was not standing on Michael's left with his bass. "It was painful," Michael recalled. "I felt totally naked on stage for the first time in my life." Still, he ripped through the Jackson Five's repertoire with a passion and ferocity to compensate for the loss of his brother.

If Jermaine's absence had been noticed, the audience gave no sign of it: when it was all over, the crowd leapt to its feet and gave Michael three standing ovations.

8

People hurt each other over and over again. I spend a lot of time being sad. I'm just sad a lot.

The lunchtime press conference, held atop New York's RCA Building in the art deco aerie known as the Rainbow Grill, had the serious air of a United Nations conclave. Led by a somber Joe Jackson, the rest of the clan—without Jermaine—filed onto the dais and took their seats.

Only days before, the family had been shocked to learn for the first time that Motown owned the rights to the Jackson Five name and logo; Gordy had shrewdly (and quietly) registered the name with the U.S. Patent Office two years earlier. If they were going to leave Motown, they were informed curtly, they would have to come up with a new name.

No matter. Michael had suggested they merely call themselves the Jacksons, and the others nodded in agreement.

The June 30, 1975, press conference began with Joe proudly announcing that the Jackson family was leaving Motown for CBS's Epic label—despite the fact that the group's Motown contract did not expire until March of the following year. His stated reason for making the switch: "Motown sells a lot of singles. Epic sells a lot of albums. We look forward to selling a lot of albums."

Michael, wearing a black velvet jacket and plaid vest, was asked what benefit he thought might derive from the switch. "I'm sure," he said in a barely audible squeak, "the promotion will be stronger."

As for Jermaine, Joe insisted that his prodigal son would return. "Under his conditions," he allowed, "it'll take a while." Randy, who owed his newfound full membership in the group to Jermaine's departure, shifted uneasily on his seat.

Predictably, Motown filed a $5 million breach of contract suit (later increased to $20 million) against the Jacksons, and Joe immediately countersued—the first skirmish in the protracted legal war over the fate of Motown's last great group.

Charging malice on Joe's part, Motown issued a statement saying that Gordy "took these children from Indiana and made them the marvelous group they are today." Joe fired back: "It's *me* who discovered the Jackson Five. I rehearsed them every day." Meanwhile, Motown had released yet another Jackson Five album, *Moving Violation.* More money was devoted to promotion and distribution, but it proved too little, too late. *Moving Violation* generated not a single hit for the group.

Despite the fact that Motown had hundreds of unreleased Jackson Five songs in its inventory, Gordy insisted that the group return to the studio in the fall of 1975. "No!" thundered Joe when he received Gordy's summons. "That S.O.B. ain't gonna push us around no more, period."

The others agreed—all except Michael. He and Jermaine had had a special bond, and no one felt Jermaine's absence more keenly than Michael. But he also insisted that the Jackson brothers had a moral and legal obligation to fulfill the terms of their contract. "I know we have to at least honor our commitment to Berry or we're gonna lose the whole lawsuit," Michael said. "It's not right." Ultimately Michael was proved correct. After years of legal wrangling, the courts decided against the Jacksons, awarding Motown $600,000 in damages.

Despite his preeminence—or, more accurately, because of it—his brothers were loath to listen to Michael's opinions. "The others knew that he was the star," a family friend said. "They knew he could pull the plug on the whole thing any time he wanted. But *he* didn't know that at the time. Joe knew how to keep Michael in his place, and the brothers just went along with the program."

They ignored him again when Joe signed the Jacksons to star in their own CBS replacement series starting in June of 1976. Michael was already acutely aware of the negative impact television could have on a recording career. When it came to seeing rock stars struggling awkwardly through comedy sketches, familiarity definitely bred contempt.

"We shouldn't do it," Michael argued with his father and brothers. "Look at Tony Orlando. Look at Cher. It's gonna really hurt our sales." Once again, he was overruled. Despite little Janet's natural flair for comedy—her Mae West impersonation caught the eye of producer Norman Lear, who cast Janet in the hit CBS series *Good Times*—*The Jacksons* proved a major embarrassment to Michael. "We had to dress in ridiculous outfits and perform stupid comedy routines to canned laughter," he wrote in his autobiography. "It was all so fake.... It's crazy."

Still, after four shows *The Jacksons* was picked up for the 1977 season. But Michael, as it turned out, would not have to suffer much longer. That spring the show was canceled after it placed dead last in the Nielsen ratings.

At about the same time their first album on the Epic label, *The Jacksons,* hit record stores across the country. One cut from the LP, "Enjoy Yourself," was released as a single and within three weeks was perched within the top ten.

To push the album, the Jacksons hit the concert circuit in the spring of 1977. Once again Michael kept to himself. While his brothers partied, he agreed to a one-on-one interview over a home-cooked meal at the apartment of New York *Daily News* reporter Bob Weiner. Michael guzzled water and waved away an offer of red wine. "I don't drink or take any drugs," he declared, "and I don't want to experiment. If a person wants to get away from things, there are a million things to do outside of getting high."

While Weiner prepared the agreed-upon meal in the tiny kitchen of his apartment, Michael "made himself right at home," his host recalled. Without hesitation Michael plowed into the books, photographs, record albums, and knickknacks that cluttered the apartment. Suddenly he let out a horrified gasp, and his host ran out from the kitchen. Michael was staring at a calendar that featured a photograph of Jackie Onassis sunbathing in the nude at her villa on Aristotle Onassis's private island of Scorpios.

"Oh," Michael murmured, stricken at the sight of a topless Jackie. "Why did she pose for these pictures?"

"Since it's not every day that I encounter an eighteen-year-old millionaire with innocence intact," Weiner said, "I broke it to him gently that the photographs were taken without Mrs. Onassis's knowledge. He breathed easier."

Throughout the curious meal—which Michael ate entirely with his hands—he seemed distant, distracted, and, when it came to Jermaine's defection and gossip that the other Jacksons resented Michael's growing fame, defensive. "We're still a family," he insisted. "That's the most important thing."

After dinner Michael gravitated back to the trivia stockpile in Weiner's living room and, out of hundreds of records, chose the sound track from the big budget bomb *Bugsy Malone* to put on the turntable. "I love kids," Michael said wistfully, "and I loved this film because it has only kids in it. Do you like kids? I could photograph them all day."

The next evening, after the Jacksons shattered box office records at the Nassau Coliseum, Michael went out on one of his rare dates with a member of the opposite sex. After seeing *The Wiz* for the fourth time, he escorted the musical's tiny, Merman-voiced teenage star, Stephanie Mills, to the chic Park Avenue nightclub Regine's for dinner. Throughout dinner she flirted with him, brushing his hand with hers, bumping his knees under the table, even, for one fleeting moment, laying her head on his shoulder. With each touch Michael became rigid. And as his discomfort became more and more obvious, their unlikely chaperon for the evening, Andy Warhol, did what he always did best in such prickly social situations. Nothing.

Michael nibbled forlornly on a cookie while the rest of his party dined on pâté de foie gras, truffles, and filet mignon. Eventually the naive Michael asked the obviously gay Warhol why he had never married. "Don't you want children?" Michael asked.

Warhol pondered the question for a moment. "I want children," he finally replied, "but not my own." Michael's response, said another patron at an adjacent table, was to "smile that sweet, angelic smile of his."

If he was unsure of his place in the real world—especially in relation to the opposite sex—Michael had no doubts about his abilities when it came to writing songs. He considered it nothing less than a major breakthrough when Epic had allowed the brothers to contribute two of their songs to their new album, "Blues Away" and "Style of Life." Inspired by Jackie Wilson's touching "Lonely Teardrops," Michael wrote "Blues Away" to "overcome a deep depression . . . a way of laughing on the outside to stop the churning inside."

At this time Michael was certainly experiencing a considerable amount of "churning inside." Within the past year his father had practically moved in with his mistress and illegitimate daughter, his brother Jermaine had broken away from the family, his brother Jackie had filed for divorce (he and Enid later reconciled), and Marlon had announced that he had been secretly married to an eighteen-year-old fan, Carol Parker, for four months.

With the other four original members of the Jackson Five now married, attention focused on Michael's romantic interests, if any. The family was sensitive to rumors that he was either gay or asexual, and took pains to discuss Michael's prowess whenever possible in print. "Back in the early days," Marlon was quoted as saying, "Michael was something to keep up with where the girls were concerned. Believe me, Michael ain't a virgin. No way." Tito chimed in that Michael was "after all the girls," and even Jermaine went out of his way to call his brother "a real Romeo. Only he's shy about it."

At nineteen Michael was, in fact, a virgin. He confided to a friend that despite the thousands of women who had literally thrown themselves at him, he had never so much as kissed a girl.

Michael's sexual confusion was understandable. His entire life had been a lesson in abuse, dishonesty, betrayal, and self-deception. His stridently puritanical mother had taught him that sex outside marriage was a sin yet looked the other way when their father abused his sons and then took them to sleazy strip clubs to perform.

Joe's flagrant infidelities also sent a conflicting message—one reinforced by Jackie's and Jermaine's sexual antics on the road. And then there was the matter of Michael's traumatizing night locked up with two prostitutes.

Michael's tentative first steps toward a relationship with a member of the opposite sex occurred at a Sunset Strip nightclub called On the Rox. He was chatting with actor Ryan O'Neal when someone grabbed his hand and he turned to see Tatum O'Neal, Ryan's thirteen-year-old daughter, beaming. "It was serious stuff to me," he recalled of the moment. *"She touched me."*

They had much in common. Like Michael, Tatum had been exposed to the rough side of life at an early age. And, as with two other "important" women in Michael's later life—Brooke Shields and Elizabeth Taylor—O'Neal's childhood had, like Michael's, been sacrificed on the altar of stardom.

Michael's first real "date" occurred when Tatum invited him to a party at Hugh Hefner's Playboy mansion in Beverly Hills. Several of the guests peeled off after dinner to make love upstairs, and Tatum headed for the hot tub in the grotto. When Michael declined her invitation to frolic nude in the tub, a member of Hefner's staff brought them bathing suits.

They dated over the next two years, but Michael would not even kiss Tatum, much less get involved in a serious romance. Yet he would later insinuate that theirs had been a full-fledged affair. "I guess you'd have to say she was my first love—after Diana."

Michael was nothing if not fiercely loyal to his mentor, Diana Ross, and that loyalty was about to pay off yet again. Michael had already seen *The Wiz,* Broadway's Tony-winning all-black musical based on *The Wizard of Oz,* seven times when Motown announced that it was making the movie version with Diana in the lead role.

The original *Wizard of Oz* had been filmed on an MGM back lot in 1939, with Judy Garland playing the role of Dorothy. In *The Wiz,* Dorothy was no longer a spunky Kansas schoolgirl, but a more mature Harlem schoolteacher. And the yellow brick road wound through an urban Oz of slums and subways to an Emerald City of concrete and steel: the World Trade Center.

If Ross, at thirty-four, was a bit old to be playing Dorothy, no one had any doubt that lanky Michael would make the perfect Scarecrow, the role originally played by Ray Bolger. Michael had already turned down a starring role in the basketball movie *One on One,* which turned out to be a sleeper hit of 1979. ("I was waiting for a musical," he explained.) Now, at the urging of both Ross and Berry Gordy—who once again seized the opportunity to upstage Joe Jackson—Michael auditioned for and landed the part.

Predictably, Joe and his other sons saw this as an attempt by Gordy to drive a wedge between Michael and the family. There was also apprehension about any independent project that might set Michael apart from his brothers in the public mind. "The last thing Joe wanted," said one Motown executive, "was to see Michael make it as a movie star. That would have spelled the end of the group."

One week before he was to leave for New York to begin filming,

Michael decided to spend the Fourth of July holiday at Jermaine's house near the beach. He was wading into the surf alone when, inexplicably, he found himself gasping for breath. Trying not to panic, he staggered back to the house and collapsed. A half-hour later at the hospital, Michael awoke to the news that a blood vessel had burst in his lung, and that he suffered from a mild case of pleurisy. It would be advisable, said the doctor, for him to curtail his schedule. Michael managed a weak laugh.

On July 10, Michael and La Toya arrived in New York, where they set up house in a mirror-walled, thirty-seventh-floor apartment on New York's exclusive Sutton Place. It was the first time either of them had been away from Joe and Kate for any extended period of time. And La Toya's job, as set forth by their mother, was to make sure that absent-minded Michael was properly fed and clothed before he headed out to the set each morning at 5:30 A.M.

Universal Pictures announced the launching of *The Wiz*—at $20 million the costliest movie musical ever—at a lavish New York press conference in September of 1977. While reporters waited for Ross to make her grand entrance from the wings, the Afro-crowned Michael strolled in nonchalantly and waved hellow. "His unaffected charm shattered the pervasive aura of practiced glamour like a thunderclap," one reporter remembered, "and it shamed the pretentions of the painted lady sweeping in just behind him."

Virtually eclipsed by the movie's stars and its Oscar-winning director, Sidney Lumet, the show's musical director stood quietly to one side. His name was Quincy Jones, and he was destined to become one of the strongest influences in Michael's career.

When filming began, one of the things that appealed most to Michael about the role of the Scarecrow was the heavy makeup required. With his face still marred by acne, he actually looked forward to spending five hours a day, six days a week, sitting on the makeup chair, having putty trowled onto his cheeks.

He enjoyed hiding behind this Halloween mask so much, in fact, that he began wearing it home. One of his favorite pastimes was to stare out the window of his chauffeured limousine at children in other cars and wait for a reaction. "Whoa, they get frightened!" he said. "They don't know who or what it is! It's a trip! It's a secret . . . that's it. I like that it's—a secret."

Once back at the apartment, he often kept his makeup on, dancing for hours in front of the mirrors in full Scarecrow costume. "I forget everything else but the Scarecrow's world," he said. "It's a feeling of peace. It's just like . . . magic."

Michael might have seemed typecast as the Scarecrow, a good-natured but dim-witted character who is searching for a brain. As he neared adulthood, it was becoming increasingly clear to Michael that his formal education was sadly lacking. And never more so than, while filming a scene, he unintentionally broke up the crew during rehearsals by pronouncing Socrates "Soh-crates" (as in packing crates"). From the wings, Quincy Jones whispered the correct pronunciation—much to Michael's relief.

Anyone who spent time with Michael soon realized that his inability to pronounce the names of ancient Greek philosophers was not his only failing. No one, for example, had ever bothered to teach him how to eat with utensils. Rock journalist Timothy White recalled what it was like to dine with Michael and two record company executives at an elegant French restaurant in Manhattan. "When his Caesar salad is placed before him, he looks down at the plate, then at his silverware, and begins eating each dripping leaf with his spidery fingers, oily dressing accumulating on the tablecloth."

Michael, tucking his napkin into the collar of his T-shirt, then whispered to the waiter, "What's *qweech?*" When the quiche lorraine arrived, Michael "stabs his fingers into the steaming wedge, gathers up a gooey hunk, and begins gobbling it off his palm. 'It's like ham and eggs!' "

When he wasn't "licking his gooey knuckles," Michael also displayed an alarming ignorance of current events during this particularly revealing meal. He admitted that he had no idea what Watergate was all about. "It was terrible, wasn't it?" he said. "I guess it was. Have you met Nixon? Is he happy? I saw him on TV last year, and he looked so unhappy!"

When someone at the table alluded to then president Jimmy Carter's White House predecessor, an incredulous Michael gasped, "Excuse me? Vice President Ford was a *president?* Really? Boy, I gotta keep up on these things!"

Michael worked grueling eleven-hour days on the set of *The Wiz*, but that did not prevent him from sampling New York's frenetic nightlife. Indeed, he proved a tireless disco and party hopper, dancing into the late night hours and yet somehow managing to straggle into the studio on time the next morning.

Michael, a young superstar on his own for the first time in the Big Apple, was treating Manhattan like his own personal Oz. Unabashedly star-struck, he reveled in hobnobbing with the city's resident glitterati. The epicenter of this world was a surreal disco called Studio 54, where Mick and Bianca Jagger and their vampiric crowd came alive after midnight.

Truman Capote, who went several nights a week, called it "the nightclub of the future. It's very democratic. Boys with boys, girls with girls, girls with boys, blacks and whites, capitalists and Marxists, Chinese, and everything else—all in one big mix!"

Studio 54 also celebrated drugs with impunity. Several times each night a cocaine-snorting neon man-in-the-moon would swing down from the ceiling, its eye flashing red to the approving roar of the crowd. High in the tiered balcony, scions of the Kennedy, Rockefeller, and Vanderbilt families were among those snorting cocaine and amyl nitrite, oblivious of couples—gay and straight—that at any given time could be found having sex in the shadows.

Liza Minnelli accompanied Michael and La Toya on several of their nocturnal romps and made sure they were ushered by owner Steve Rubell to the sanctum sanctorum of Studio 54—the basement, a very private, carefully guarded catacomb where free drugs were dispensed like candy and the famous indulged in a wide range of sexual games.

Impossibly naive about cocaine and its effects, Michael and La Toya marveled at the inexhaustible energy and relentless good cheer of these disco denizens. Whenever someone stopped to offer him cocaine from the glass vial that hung around his neck, Michael would politely decline. "It's hard to believe," La Toya later said, "but we didn't know what cocaine was, what it looked like, or how you used it."

Michael did, however, appear to derive some voyeuristic pleasure from watching patrons turn on in other ways. Truman Capote remembered watching Michael stare intently as a man and woman engaged in a sexual act in the shadows. "We were all so used to that sort of thing," Capote said, "and I sort of expected him to be absolutely shocked. But he seemed to be studying them like they were mating panda bears in the zoo."

Many of Studio 54's regular customers were gay or bisexual, and most assumed that, given his high voice and effeminate mannerisms, Michael was gay. "Of course we thought he was gay—or at least bi," said one of the shirtless Studio 54 bartenders who was recruited personally by Rubell from one of New York's gay bars. He remembered a well-known designer "making an obvious pass at Michael. But Michael turned him down cold. If he did like men, that news wasn't for public consumption."

Michael was, in fact, already the subject of one of the wildest rumors in show business—that he was about to have a sex change operation so he could marry actor-singer Clifton Davis. Jackson was in the record section of a Sears department store when a girl rushed up to him screaming, "It isn't true! It isn't true!"

"What isn't true?" Michael asked.

"You're not a girl!" blurted the fan. Another fan, when she heard the news, reportedly committed suicide by jumping from the window of a high rise.

At the time when gossip about the two men was reaching a fever pitch, Michael and Davis had bumped into each other backstage after watching Diana Ross's act at Caesar's Palace in Las Vegas. After some awkward moments, Davis turned to Michael and cracked, "Hey, you're not a girl after all, are you?"

The sex change rumor had prompted Michael to launch a counter-offensive. "First of all," he told one reporter, "nothing is gay about me. Let me make this perfectly clear to everybody. Just because my voice is naturally high doesn't mean that I'm a homosexual."

But reminded by record company executives that it would not be politic to alienate a sizable segment of the record-buying population, Michael began to sound more diplomatic whenever a member of the press brought up the subject. "I'm sure we must have plenty of fans who are gay," he conceded. "That doesn't bother me in the slightest, but I'm not gay. You can print that." However, there was the occasional lapse: "It's disgusting to me," he once blurted out to a startled reporter, "that people think I'm gay."

Kate may have already had her doubts about Michael's sexual orientation, but she was not about to admit them, even to herself. "Michael is not homosexual, period," she stated, citing his strict adherence to the Jehovah's Witness faith. "It makes me crazy when I hear people say that. He knows his Bible, and he know it's against God."

As a practical matter, Michael knew that any public perception of him as a gay man could destroy his career overnight. Certainly the millions of teenage girls who accounted for the vast majority of the Jacksons' record sales would no longer fantasize about a young man who had no interest in the opposite sex. "I've met some very beautiful women during my travels," Michael tried to explain in a press statement, "but unfortunately many of them had personalities that were not to my liking. It's difficult to find beauty and kindness in one girl. But I'm sure that as time goes by I will run into the right young lady who will capture my heart."

She did not appear when he was shooting *The Wiz*, which proved to be a relatively painless experience for Michael. An exception: a rooftop scene in which Dorothy faints and the Scarecrow comes to her rescue. "I had to pick Diana up," recalled Michael, who weighed 115 pounds at the time. "But she was too heavy. I kept puffing away on the dialogue while I tried over and over again to lift her, until I finally made it."

No sooner was filming on *The Wiz* completed than CBS released the Jacksons' second album on the Epic label, *Going Places*. It went nowhere fast, failing to produce a single hit. And Michael was now convinced that the Jacksons' creative marriage with songwriter-producers Gamble and Huff was not working out.

Once again it was time to take action. Michael and his father marched to Black Rock, CBS's imposing midtown Manhattan headquarters, to confront Epic president Ron Alexenburg. Over an elegant lunch in CBS's paneled executive dining room, Michael came right to the point. "Epic has done its best," he said, "and it's not good enough. We want to be funkier, experiment with new sounds."

If the Jacksons were to remain with CBS/Epic, Joe continued, they would have to be allowed to write and produce their own songs. Otherwise, Joe and Michael informed Alexenburg, the Jacksons were ready to walk.

It was a daring gamble. Walter Yetnikoff, who would later emerge as Michael's champion at CBS, had already made the decision to buy out the Jacksons' contract for $100,000. It took impassioned pleas from Alexenburg and Epic's West Coast artist and repertoire executive Bobby Colomby to give them one more chance to make an album—this time on their terms.

Michael and Joe knew nothing of Yetnikoff's decision to release them from their contract; if they had, they most certainly would not have initiated the showdown at Black Rock. When Alexenburg later called to say that Epic was granting their request for what amounted to total creative control of their next album, they rejoiced. Nothing could have been better for Michael's flagging self-esteem. Even without his Scarecrow getup, he had faced down two of the most powerful men in the record industry—Berry Gordy and Epic's Alexenburg—and won. He was nineteen years old.

The Jacksons went to work on their their new album for Epic, and Michael asked Quincy Jones if he could recommend a producer. "Sure," Jones replied. "Me."

Hitting theaters across the country in November 1978, *The Wiz* proved to be a critical and commercial catastrophe. "A piece of fantasy," sniped one writer, "about as airy as an elephant dancing in quicksand." Nevertheless, Michael's ungainly Scarecrow was singled out for praise by several critics. And the movie also managed to produce a hit single: Michael's bouncy "Ease on Down the Road" duet with Ross.

Sidney Lumet, who with Ross took most of the blame for the film's failure, was unstinting in his praise for Michael. When *Soul* magazine's Randy Taraborrelli pointed out that the revered director was comparing him favorably to James Dean, Michael merely shrugged. "So," he asked quizzically, "who's James Dean?"

For the record, Michael claimed to be wholly unconcerned with *The Wiz*'s abysmal performance. Privately he fretted that the public's strong aversion to *The Wiz*—it had not merely failed, it had *bombed*—might end his acting career before it began. He was ready, however, to take a strong hand in the writing and production of his own album material. That was made abundantly clear with the release in late November, 1978, of *Destiny*, their latest effort for Epic. Propelled by "Shake Your Body (Down to the Ground)," the hit disco single written by Michael and Randy, *Destiny* went platinum, the brothers' biggest-selling album to date.

Once again Jacksonmania swept the globe. While his speaking voice had evolved into a breathless cross between those of Marilyn Monroe and Minnie Mouse, Michael sang with a newfound authority that clearly thrilled audiences. The adult Michael was proving even more irresistible to the squealing multitudes than his former cute self.

Intent on taking full advantage of *Destiny*'s impact, Joe brought in industry veterans Freddy DeMann (who later managed a promising young singer named Madonna) and Ron Weisner to co-manage the group. At their urging Michael embarked with his brothers on a punishing world tour.

As lucrative as the tour proved to be—grossing an estimated $750,000 for each of the brothers—Michael was less than thrilled with the fact that he shared equally with his brothers while doing the lion's share of the work. To compensate, he promised himself that the next time he stepped into a studio it would be to record his first solo album for Epic. "I hear an ideal record in my mind," he mused at one point, "maybe with Quincy Jones. We'll see."

Meanwhile it was evident to all around him that Michael was moody and withdrawn on the tour—partly because of the physical strain and partly because he yearned to strike out on his own. "He'd spend hours locked up in his hotel room," said one member of the tour. "Everybody knew you just left him alone."

"Something is really missing when I'm not on stage," Michael later said by way of explanation. "It may sound crazy, but I'm a stage addict. When I'm not on stage I have fits and I get crazy. I start crying and I act . . . I guess you might say weird and freaked out. I start dancing around the house. It's like part of me is missing and I have this wild craving for it."

Michael already seemed resigned to having a life only in the spotlight. "On stage is the only time I really open up. I say to myself, 'This is it, this is home, this is where I'm supposed to be, where God meant me to be. I feel so free, so unlimited on stage. I feel like I can do anything. It feels so good when the lights hit you and you feel the audience. I can almost taste that feeling now. I eat it up. Performing is better than anything else I can think of."

But once the cheering stopped, Michael withdrew into a private world. "When I'm not onstage," he said, sighing, "I sort of close down."

Still, he seemed to have a morbid fascination with the dark side of life. "I can't wait to see India," he would say. "I know what the rich are like. When I go to other countries, people say 'You wanna see the ugly part of it?' That's what I want to see! I want to see what it's really like to *starve.* I don't want to hear it, or read it. I want to see it. . . . When I actually looked into the queen's eyes, it was the greatest thing! And it's the same thing with starvation!"

Michael had also begun to exhibit a peculiar interest in the physically deformed, particularly those who had been forced to live out their lives as sideshow freaks. He was absorbed by the tragic yet inspiring life story of John Merrick, the so-called Elephant Man.

Suffering from neurofibromatosis, a rare neurological disease that left him severely deformed, Merrick was a sensitive, articulate man who spent most of his life as a sideshow attraction before becoming the darling of Victorian society. His touching plight spawned a hit Broadway play and an Oscar-nominated film directed by David Lynch. Michael sobbed his way through fifteen screenings of *The Elephant Man.*

"That story reminds me of me a lot," he said. "It makes me cry because I see myself."

The rest of the world was a long way from regarding Michael as a freak in 1979, but that was how he was beginning to see himself. "Off stage," said a friend, "Michael was very uncomfortable in his own skin. He didn't know who he was—or what he was."

Ongoing reports of well-meaning young women trying to rid Michael of his virginity once and for all added to the pressure. According to one tabloid story, at a party in the Los Angeles home of rocker Rod Stewart, Tatum O'Neal and a starlet tried to lure Michael to bed. Michael took Tatum's hand and was marching toward the bedroom when he turned and fled in terror. Later, Tatum reportedly shed her clothes in an attempt to seduce Michael; again he literally ran away. The starlet later denied the story and filed a lawsuit against the publishers.

Michael's contact with people outside the family now took place almost exclusively over the telephone, with one exception: children, in whose nonthreatening company he felt totally at ease. "Kids—love 'em," he said with a grin. Every week he spent some time either meeting seriously ill children or speaking with them over the phone. "They're the reason I do what I do."

Terry George was a star-struck twelve-year-old living in Yorkshire, England, when he first met Michael in February 1979. Armed with a tape recorder that his parents gave him for Christmas, George pursued his hobby of interviewing celebrities, photographing them, and collecting their autographs. "Nothing was ever published," he recalled. "I did it just for just for fun, just for the excitement of meeting famous people." Eventually the engaging Yorkshire youth had charmed Omar Sharif and Paul McCartney, among others, into talking with him.

When the Jacksons' Destiny tour took them to the nearby city of Leeds, young George went to the Dragonara Hotel and eavesdropped in the lobby. "I overheard the maids talking about how Michael had taken the entire top floor," he said, "so I took the lift straight up and knocked on the door."

"Yes?" said a small voice from the other side of the door.

"Are you Michael?" George asked.

"Yes."

George explained why he was there. When he told Michael he was only twelve, the door opened and Michael ushered him into the room. "I'm waiting for a phone call," Michael told him. "There is a boy on a life-support machine I talk to every day. They tell me it's the only thing that's keeping him going." Within moments, George recalled, the phone rang and Michael chatted amiably with the dying boy. "I was very impressed," George said. "He talked to this boy to keep him alive."

George's interview with Michael lasted thirty minutes, and he asked Michael, among other things, if he had a girlfriend. "He sort of scowled," George recalled, "and then said, 'No! I'm happy.' "

Another odd moment came when Michael told George that he was writing a song called "Always." "I want to cry on the record," he said. "I mean really *cry,* and I want people to cry when they hear me."

Michael, obviously impressed with the young fan, invited him to return the next day. "Here I was a scruffy little kid," George said. "For a pop star to be friendly to me, it was *breathtaking."* Before he left the next day, the two exchanged phone numbers and addresses.

A few days later Michael called the boy's home from London. George's mother answered. "Hi, it's Michael. . . . Is Terry there?" After Michael returned home to California, the calls continued. "He'd call me, or as soon as my parents went out to play bingo around ten at night, I'd call him," George said. "We'd talk for hours. We used to sing songs to each other, and he told me how much he wanted to work with Paul McCartney's group Wings and how much he loved Paul's work."

Their conversations would occasionally turn serious. "He seemed fascinated with the subject of child abuse," George said. "He asked all about how I was raised, if I'd been abused. He told me he had another friend at school—a very young friend, and that they talked about these things." Michael also confided in George about his family. "He didn't seem fond of the men in his family at all. I was surprised that he never talked about his brothers, and that he was obviously much closer to his sisters, La Toya and Janet.

"Michael was also fascinated about religion. He was always talking about it, quoting scripture. Michael kept promising to send me a Jehovah's Witness Bible. He asked me several times if I believed in God—obviously it was very important to him." As for the opposite sex: "Michael *never* mentioned women. I got the feeling that he wasn't of any particular sexual orientation."

It was right after one of their religious discussions in April 1979 that Michael suddenly switched gears. "Do you masturbate?" the twenty-year-old man asked his twelve-year-old friend.

"I sort of giggled and said, 'Yes.' I was embarrassed," George said, "and I didn't really understand what he was talking about."

George said he "kept trying to get him off the subject," but Michael persisted.

"Have you ever done it with cream?" Michael then asked.

"I was so confused," George remembered, "He meant hand cream, but I thought he meant, you know, *milk.*"

"Would you believe I'm doing it now?" Michael asked.

"I replied, 'Are you?' " George said. "I really didn't know *what* to say. I was shocked, panic-stricken. I wanted to hang up, but he *was* Michael Jackson, and I didn't want him to stop being my friend."

According to George, Jackson went on describing this sexual activity in detail for four or five minutes. "Most people don't even think Michael Jackson goes to the toilet, much less that he masturbates," George said. "Today you'd call our conversation phone sex, I suppose. But I don't believe it was a dirty old man thing. I think for Michael talking like that on the phone was a way of expressing affection."

Nor did George feel that he was the only person Michael talked with over the phone in this suggestive manner. "I have no way of knowing for sure," he said, "but it didn't take him long to get around to talking about sex. And he didn't seem awkward at all when he brought it up. Obviously, he really enjoyed talking to a twelve-year-old boy like that."

As their talks grew more frequent, Michael urged George to fly to California. "He told me I could stay with him at his place," George said. "I told him I couldn't afford the plane fare."

At first George's parents were proud of their son's friendship with one of the world's most famous men. Rather than erupt in anger when Michael called at 5 A.M., George's father bragged to friends that he had spoken with the superstar.

All that ended, however, when the family's phone bill for one month topped $600. "You've been talking to that Michael Jackson again, haven't you?" was the refrain around the George household for weeks, until they finally took the drastic action of cutting off Terry's access to the phone.

During his lunch breaks at school, George then began calling the Jackson family compound in Encino collect. La Toya or Janet would accept the calls, but Michael now seemed to be too busy to speak with George. Nor did he respond to George's letters.

Four years later George tried to rekindle their friendship when Michael arrived back in London for a recording session with McCartney. Michael looked startled when the husky seventeen-year-old reintroduced himself, "but he was very friendly. We talked for about ten minutes and made an appointment to get together the next day."

The meeting did not take place. And after several postponements, George confronted Michael as he got into his limousine outside the recording studio. "Michael got in the car and turned his back to me," George recalled. "I tapped on the window and called his name, but he wouldn't turn around. I asked why he was doing this, and he said, 'You've changed. . . .' "

George stood alone as the limo sped off. "I was nearly in tears," he recalled. "Michael lied to me. I felt used by someone who wanted my friendship because I was just a boy. Now I was a young man he just didn't want to know."

Later George saw Michael with "another young boy. I'd been replaced, and then it occurred to me: I was just one of many."

Following the Destiny tour, an exhausted, dejected Michael vowed to concentrate on his solo career. Joe, however, demanded that Michael continue to promote the *Destiny* album by giving interviews to the music press. Michael agreed, but only if the questions were channeled through Janet. That way, he reasoned, he was technically not answering reporters' questions as he had been directed to by Joe.

In this convoluted fashion, *Melody Maker* magazine's Steve Demorest interviewed Michael—directing his questions to Janet, who then relayed them to Michael as he sat next to her on the living room couch. He was not reluctant to discuss his overriding interest in children—although he declared he would never father one himself.

"One of my favorite pastimes is being with children—talking to them, playing with them in the grass," he told Demorest. "They say things that just astound you. They go through a brilliant, genius stage. But then, when they get to a certain age," he said with a sigh, "they lose it."

Michael spun around, tripped over his own feet, and slammed face first into the wooden floor. The accident, which occurred on stage at the height of the Destiny tour, provided him with what he had been wanting for years—a new nose.

Deeply self-conscious after years of taunting by his father and brothers—they still called him "Bignose" in front of strangers, bringing him close to tears every time—Michael yearned for a button nose like the one that belonged to his friend and mentor, Diana Ross.

Now that his nose was broken, he had his excuse. "I sometimes wonder," said a colleague, "if that was really an 'accident' at all."

Michael's nose was straightened and reshaped by a Beverly Hills surgeon for the first time in May 1979. Now when he looked in the mirror, he liked what he saw: a nose that no longer spread across his face like his father's. Over the next decade he would undergo a series of surgeries to eradicate every remaining trace of his father's brutish visage. "That's how much," said a family member, "he hates Joseph."

And as he would do after all future surgeries, Michael took home a little memento from his stay at the hospital: a small glass vial containing a purplish slice of his own nose cartilage.

At Hayvenhurst Michael seemed to retreat more and more into his childlike world. He visited Disneyland frequently, sneaking in through a back entrance and wearing a disguise to avoid recognition. At home he spent hours in his darkened room, watching television, venturing out to feed his pet boa constrictor or sing Jackson Five songs with his mynah bird, Ricky. After years of being told by Joe that he was ugly, Michael taught Ricky to say, "You're cute! You're cute!" whenever his owner walked in the room.

It was in early 1979 when Theresa Gonsalves first noticed that Michael "just wasn't growing up." The fan befriended by Michael in Las Vegas four years earlier had visited him on the set of *The Wiz* in New York and in California after the Destiny tour.

For four years Michael had avoided taking his driver's test because he claimed to be too shy to appear at the California Motor Vehicle Department and stand in line with the rest of the motorists. It took prodding from Katherine, who pointed out that he could not be dependent on chauffeurs forever, to persuade Michael finally to take his driver's test in 1979 at the age of twenty-one.

Behind the wheel of his Rolls-Royce for the first time, Michael, always tailed by his security chief and confidant Bill Bray, knocked over garbage cans and ricocheted off curbs. But when Gonsalves accompanied him for a drive around Los Angeles, she was less disturbed by his lack of driving skills than by his stunted emotional growth.

Michael slammed on the brakes when he spotted a small boy playing on the sidewalk. "Terry," he said, "I want you to steal that little kid's toy. Go ahead, take it and we'll drive away!"

"He seemed real serious at first," Gonsalves said. "Of course he wasn't, but that was the kind of thing he would do. He was still acting like a little boy."

By this time Michael already had seven nieces and nephews. He could scarcely have been described as a doting uncle. Despite their close proximity, he would go for months without seeing his brothers' children. He was nevertheless an avid collector of their artifacts: booties, locks of hair, crib blankets, first outfits, drawings, report cards, school projects. In a separate bureau drawer he preserved a dirty diaper from each child, apparently with its crusted contents still intact.

The odor emanating from Michael's diaper drawer was masked by the general squalor of his room. Of the three maids employed at Hayvenhurst, one was given the sole responsibility of tidying up Michael's room without disturbing the books, papers, games, toys, photographs, and half-eaten snacks that seemed to blanket every visible surface.

To further complicate matters, when he began recording his new solo album, *Off the Wall,* Michael made the conscious decision neither to bathe regularly nor to change his clothes—including his socks and underwear. His working-day uniform of torn jeans, frayed T-shirts, and tennis shoes with holes in them soon began emitting a pungent fragrance all their own.

The resulting stench in the studio became so unbearable for the other musicians—not to mention his own family—that La Toya, now the closest of Michael's siblings, was enlisted to get him to clean up his act. Although he still refused to wear new shoes, he began wearing freshly laundered jeans and showering a couple of times a week. (After the stupendous success of *Off the Wall,* Michael became so superstitious about this studied sloppiness that he went through a similar phase while working on each of his subsequent albums.)

When they were putting together *Off the Wall,* Quincy Jones coined a new, equally unflattering nickname for Michael: "Smelly"—although he was quick to explain that it had nothing to do with Jackson's pungent aroma. Presumably "smelly" was the equivalent of "cool" or "funky." Jackson was "so polite and proper," Jones said, "I can't even get him to say the word *funky.* Honest to God. . . . He'll say, 'That's smelly, man. Smelly jelly.' "

Michael was searching for a caring father figure, and he found it in Quincy Jones. Already a behind-the-scenes legend by the time he and Michael got to know each other on the set of *The Wiz,* "Q" had made a name for himself as a jazz musician and composer-arranger-producer for Tommy Dorsey, Count Basie, and Duke Ellington, among others. Beginning with Sidney Lumet's *The Pawnbroker,* he became the first black accepted into the exclusive fraternity of Hollywood composers, scoring dozens of major features from *In the Heat of the Night* to *In Cold Blood.*

Publicly Michael did what he could to quell mounting speculation that he was dissatisfied with the group and wanted to break out on his own. "My brothers and I get along fine," he told *Ebony.* "There's no ego problem with us. . . . It's just not the time to make any drastic change. I'll do more films and my own albums, but right now the group comes first. Anyway, I don't do very many things until a certain force tells me to do them. The force tells me when, and then I make my move."

Meanwhile Jones and "Smelly" were mapping out a strategy to make his new album—tentatively titled *Girlfriend,* after the Paul McCartney song written expressly for Michael—sound as different from the Jacksons as possible. Both headstrong perfectionists, Michael and Jones hit it off instantly. Trying to make the most of costly studio time, "Q" was accustomed to coaxing the best performance possible out of temperamental, often undisciplined stars. In contrast, Michael had prepared so thoroughly in advance that Jones often had a difficult time keeping up.

Such dedication exacted a price. One day Katherine was in the kitchen at Hayvenhurst when Michael stumbled into the room, gasping for breath. She sat him down and tried to reassure him that he was only hyperventilating. But Michael's breathing became more and more labored, and for a frightening moment it looked as if he were about to lose consciousness.

Katherine quickly summoned security chief Bray. "What's wrong, Joker?" asked Bray, who had called Michael "Joker" since childhood.

"I'm dying," Michael cried. "Please, get me to the hospital. Now! Please!"

Within minutes a team of emergency room physicians at Inglewood's Centinela Hospital were hovering over Michael. Their unanimous diagnosis: he had suffered a classic panic attack. The distraught patient was given oxygen and, after he had calmed down, was released with a mild prescription sedative. Katherine convinced her son to take the medication, but he became frightened as the pill began to take effect. This triggered yet another anxiety attack, and once again the troops mobilized to whisk him back to the emergency room. Several hours later, Michael, now convinced that the sedation would not kill him, returned home to rest.

When it was released in August 1979, *Off the Wall* caused an immediate sensation. Even the album cover sparked controversy. It showed Michael leaning up against a graffiti-covered wall, clad in a snazzy tuxedo and—at Michael's insistence—white socks. Even more startling was Michael's newly refined nose, which, it was widely noticed, now made the resemblance between him and his mentor Diana Ross undeniable.

Inside the glossy jacket was an innovative mix of swirling, rhythm-driven dance numbers, frothy love songs, and soul-searing ballads. To produce his signature sound, Michael, who neither read music nor played an instrument, claimed that songs arrived full-blown in his head. "I wake up from dreams and go, 'Wow, put this down on paper,' " he explained. "The whole thing is strange. You hear the words, everything is right there in your face. And you say to yourself, I'm sorry, I just didn't write this. It's there already."

Once he had played the song over and over in his head, he then sang it into a tape recorder, using his uncanny ability to impersonate instruments so that Jones and the other members of his studio team would understand the precise orchestration he had in mind: "I hear French horns first: *wa-wa-wa-wa.* Then the bass line: *ta-dum, ta-dum dum dum, ta-dum . . .*"

More than faintly reminiscent of the Jacksons' "Shake Your Body (Down to the Ground)," "Don't Stop 'Til You Get Enough" was actually the first song written solely by Michael. For this cut, Michael experimented with a ten-second spoken—or rather mumbled—introduction over a thumping bass line, all designed to build suspense before launching into the melody itself: "You know, I was wonderin' . . . you know, the force, it's got a lot of power, make me feel like a . . . make me feel like . . ." The tension was released with Michael's squeal and a cyclonic amalgam of soaring strings and thumping bass.

The provocative nature of the song's title did not elude Michael. Although he had yet to experience an intimate relationship with a woman, he had witnessed his brothers in the act frequently enough to know what meaning could be read into the phrase.

The title track ("Life ain't so bad at all, if you live it off the wall. . . .") also featured Michael's new piercing falsetto, but for the gentler "Rock with You" (written by Jones's close friend and former Heatwave member, Rod Temperton) his sound was considerably more subdued, more calculatedly sensual.

Surprisingly, when asked to name some of his favorite songwriters, Michael listed such veterans as Henry Mancini, Johnny Mercer, and Burt Bacharach alongside McCartney, Elton John, and Stevie Wonder. "There are a lot of kids, black and white," he said, "who won't even pick up a book, but they'll memorize lyrics to an Elton John song or a Stevie Wonder record. Messages in those lyrics can change a person's life."

As soon as Quincy Jones had played "She's Out of My Life" for Michael, "something clicked," Jones said. Days before he went into the studio, Michael had told his twelve-year-old English phone pal, Terry George, that he wanted to release a record in which he actually wept. "When he sang 'She's Out of My Life,' " Jones recalled, "he would cry. Every time we did it, I'd look up at the end and Michael would be crying. I said, 'We'll come back in two weeks and do it again, and maybe it won't tear you up so much.' Came back and he started to get teary. So we left it in."

Four cuts from the album—"Don't Stop 'Til You Get Enough," "Rock with You," "Off the Wall," and "She's Out of My Life"—would make it into the top ten, the first time ever for a solo artist. "Don't Stop 'Til You Get Enough" and "Rock with You" made it all the way to number one.

Released in August 1979, *Off the Wall* became a music industry event—in large part because, at a time when the industry was in an unprecedented slump, Michael's album sold a startling seven million copies.

But rather than savor the album's success, Michael, virtually friendless and imprisoned by his fame at the family compound in Encino, seemed to wallow in his isolation. "I may want to just go walking or sit in a tree, but everything we do is on TV or in the newspapers," he complained. "So you stay in your room all day. When you're a performer, people want everything. They pull your hair out, break down barricades. . . . It can be very scary."

Increasingly he turned to disguises—wigs, hats, fake beards, sunglasses—to venture outside the walls of Hayvenhurst. On his frequent trips to Disneyland—sometimes as many as three or four trips a week to the Magic Kingdom—Michael would sometimes stop at a souvenir shop and buy a pair of Groucho Marx glasses with the fake nose and mustache attached. This seldom worked, however, so he usually remained in the shadows, escorted by Disney employees through secret tunnels and passageways to the rides and attractions of his choice.

He also donned disguises when he went door to door with La Toya, spreading the word of God as a Jehovah's Witness. While he had little trouble fooling adults who answered the door, most children could be counted on to blow his cover with "Hey! What's Michael Jackson doing here?" He also encountered the usual problems faced by his fellow Witnesses. Irate homeowners yelled at him to leave them alone, doors were slammed in his face, and on at least one occasion an attack dog pursued him, ripping his pants leg as he dove for the limousine waiting out of sight around the corner.

Michael's most effective disguise was also his most bizarre. When he was determined not to be recognized, he donned the chador of a Muslim woman—with his white socks and tennis shoes poking out below the hem.

Michael was determined to mingle with the common folk—even if that meant taking risks. Wearing scruffy clothes, a tattered overcoat, a hat, and sometimes fake facial hair or a wig, he ventured into the seedier areas of downtown L.A. He told his father that he just wanted to hobnob with some of the city's more unfortunate citizens—the street hustlers, prostitutes, and drunks who hung out on the streets at all hours of the night.

In February 1980 Katherine, La Toya, Janet, and Michael gathered around the television set at Hayvenhurst to watch the Grammy Awards. It had been a bleak season for the music business as a whole, and Michael had been expected to reap the lion's share of Grammy nominations. Instead he had garnered only two. And when he won a single Grammy—for best male R&B performer—he burst into tears. Given the fact that such legends as Little Richard and the Rolling Stones had never won any Grammys, it seemed a bit of an overreaction.

While his mother and sisters tried to console him, Michael wept uncontrollably for several minutes. "How can they do this? This is so wrong!" he sobbed. Then he stopped abruptly and wiped the tears from his eyes with one hand. Shaking a clenched fist at the screen, he promised that his next album would be the biggest in history. "I'll show them," he swore. "Just you watch. . . ."

Two weeks later at three A.M., someone called Hayvenhurst with devastating news. Speeding along rain-slicked Cahuenga Boulevard behind the wheel of his girlfriend's Mercedes, eighteen-year-old Randy Jackson had spun out of control and slammed into a pole. Pried from the wreckage with the jaws of life, Randy was rushed to St. Joseph's Medical Center in Burbank.

When Michael, Katherine, Joe, and Janet arrived at the hospital, they were told Randy's legs were crushed and his pelvis cracked. They would almost certainly have to amputate one or both legs, the emergency room physician told them—if Randy managed to survive the night.

Miraculously, after months of physical therapy and equally intensive prayer by Katherine and her fellow Witnesses, Randy made a full recovery—so much so that seven months after his near fatal accident, he would be fit enough to participate with his mother and sister Janet in an alleged assault on a woman they believed was Joe's girlfriend.

Gina Sprague, then nineteen, began working as a secretary at Joe's Sunset Boulevard office in late 1979. Although she denied having an affair with him, Sprague's relationship with the boss was at the very least intensely personal. According to La Toya, Sprague publicly flaunted their relationship, going so far as to order expensive items from a Neiman-Marcus catalog and charge them to Joe's credit card while Janet and La Toya sat a few feet away in the waiting room.

More upsetting were Sprague's frequent calls to Joe at Hayvenhurst. More often than not it was Katherine who answered the phone. Finally, on October 15, 1980, Katherine angrily told Sprague to stop calling Hayvenhurst and to clear out of Joe Jackson's office—"or we're going to come and get you."

When Katherine phoned the office the next day, Sprague was still there. With Randy and fourteen-year-old Janet in tow, Katherine drove to the office and confronted Sprague. Sprague would later tell her account of the confrontation to law enforcement officials.

"Bitch!" Katherine screamed. "I told you we were gonna get you!" While she yanked Sprague's hair, Janet twisted her right wrist. Sprague was screaming for help when Randy pulled her out of her chair, slammed her to the floor, and then—along with Katherine and Janet—dragged her out of the office and into a hallway.

By then, Sprague said, Katherine was completely out of control, shrieking, "Bitch, you better leave my husband alone!" as she punched Sprague repeatedly in the face.

"Get out of here while you can," Sprague said, trying to protect herself. She was aware of how much damage such an incident could do to the family's vaunted reputation. "Get out before someone recognizes you." Katherine responded by taking a "blunt object" out of her purse and beating her with it while Randy held Sprague up against a wall.

At that moment, Jim Krieg, a guard employed by the Jacksons, appeared on the scene. "Leave, mister," Janet snarled. "This is a family affair." Then, as Randy tried to drag Sprague into a stairwell, Katherine ripped a gold necklace off the secretary's bruised neck. "Bitch," she said, "this belongs to *me*—not you!" With that they sped off, leaving Sprague, bloodied and bruised, slumped on the floor.

Within minutes an ambulance arrived and rushed Sprague to the hospital, where she was treated for a concussion as well as multiple lacerations and contusions. Initially the official line was that Sprague had been in an auto accident. But, according to Sprague, when Joe tried to buy her silence she became enraged.

Despite the attack, Sprague reportedly continued her friendship with Joe for several months. Nearly a year after the incident, however, she filed a lawsuit against him, Katherine, Randy, and Janet, demanding $21 million in damages. The defendants denied the attack ever took place, but three eyewitnesses backed Sprague's story. Privately Katherine allegedly admitted to friends and employees that she had beaten up "the bitch." The suit was eventually settled out of court for an undisclosed sum estimated to be in the neighborhood of $85,000.

"When Miss Katherine gets upset," Sprague said, "she fights." Yet Michael was shocked that his mother could behave in such an unladylike manner. He dealt with the assault on Gina Sprague simply by refusing to acknowledge to himself or to others that such an ugly incident had ever actually occurred. Even though he had been cordial with Sprague prior to the attack, he had no interest in her well-being and even professed not to know who she was. "Unless you are a child of Katherine's," Sprague said, "you are *nothing* to Michael."

While his mother was venting her rage over Joe's infidelities, Michael was striking up new friendships with a trio of screen legends on the New England set of *On Golden Pond*. Michael had met Jane Fonda a few months earlier in Los Angeles, and she was charmed by his diffident naiveté. "In some ways," Fonda mused, "Michael reminds me of the walking wounded—an extremely fragile person." Besides, it was refreshing to find someone who was totally unaware of her previous incarnations as Barbarella and Hanoi Jane.

She invited Michael to stay at her private lakeside cabin, and Michael later recalled being "all alone on the water" with Fonda, and "we'd just talk, talk, talk about . . . you name it: politics, philosophers, racism, Vietnam, acting, all kinds of things. It was magic."

Soon Fonda introduced him to her crusty father, Henry, whose reaction was predictable. "Dad didn't get Michael at first," Fonda said. "But he wasn't any easier to know than Michael, really." The two men sat on a dock, and Henry baited fishhooks for him; it was the first time Michael had ever held a pole. "My father and Michael had a lot in common," Fonda said. "They were both intensely private, incredibly sensitive men who really came alive when they were on camera or on stage. Dad thought Michael was weird, but he also ended up liking him —a lot."

Meeting the Fondas was considerably less daunting than coming face-to-face with Katharine Hepburn. When Jane introduced Michael to her, Hepburn "didn't know who he was or quite what to make of him," Fonda recalled. "She just shook his hand and walked away. But that's Kate."

Michael was very upset. Hepburn had snubbed him, and as unaccustomed as he was to rejection, he felt genuinely hurt. "Why doesn't she like me?" he wanted to know. "What did I say that made her mad at me?" For starters, Michael's unnerving falsetto whisper and strangely fey appearance plainly annoyed Hepburn.

But gradually Hepburn came around. Michael arrived on the set to watch the filming, armed with a tape recorder, and at the end of every take Hepburn would talk to him. "They sat on a rock, and he listened to her stories," Fonda recalled. "At the core of every anecdote she told was a lesson—the most wonderful, valuable, deep lessons for a young talent. She told him never to settle in, never to lose his hunger, his edge." After that, Hepburn and Michael became fast if decidedly unlikely friends, chatting over the telephone.

In 1981 Hepburn took her nine-year-old grandniece to see Michael at Madison Square Garden. Not surprisingly, it was Hepburn's first rock concert. And although the music was not particularly to her liking, she admitted that she was dazzled by the spectacle "like all the other kids in the audience. . . . He obviously," she said of her strange new friend, "knows exactly what he's doing."

What Hepburn was not prepared for, however, was the sheer pandemonium triggered by Michael's appearance on stage. "The crowd went completely wild," photographer David McGough recalled. "It was a total mob scene. I go to big concerts like that all the time, but I have to admit I was scared. It was fascinating to watch Katharine Hepburn's reaction. She sat still and stayed calm, but you could see the concern on her face. I could just see the headlines the next day: KATHARINE HEPBURN KILLED AT MICHAEL JACKSON CONCERT."

Michael had pragmatic reasons for fretting over the public relations ramifications of his mother's confrontation with Gina Sprague. At about the same time that Katherine, Janet, and Randy were accused of assaulting Joe's secretary, the Jacksons' *Triumph* album was released.

Perhaps to satisfy his brothers that he had not forsaken the group for his solo projects, Michael had put extra effort into *Triumph.* In the ground-breaking video for one cut from the album, "Can You Feel It?," the brothers strode across the earth like benevolent (if garishly attired) gods, showering light, color, peace, love, and pixie dust on the grateful multitudes below.

To re-create some of that magic when they took to the road to promote the album, Michael and his brothers hired celebrated magician Doug Henning to do the special effects. Aiming for the pop concert equivalent of Steven Spielberg's science-fiction film *Close Encounters of the Third Kind,* the show featured pyrotechnics, intricate lighting effects, and Michael vanishing in a puff of smoke at the climax of "Don't Stop 'Til You Get Enough."

For another "special effect," Michael had sought out the professional services of plastic surgeon Steven Hoefflin. Ostensibly to correct breathing difficulties caused by the first rhinoplasty, he had a second operation. His nose—narrowed, straightened even further by surgery—already looked too small for his face. Everyone was so preoccupied with the upcoming tour, however, that, according to one startled staffer, "no one seemed to notice. Not even Katherine."

Michael had only grudgingly agreed to tour with his brothers—it would be his last, he vowed to anyone who would listen—and when they were not on stage together, he distanced himself from them as much as possible. In the company of Bill Bray, he spent his off hours prowling city streets in disguise—sometimes browsing through toy shops and antiques stores, other times hobnobbing with derelicts and street kids.

Michael eschewed marijuana, cocaine, and hard drugs, but he may not have included prescription drugs in the same category. At least one acquaintance, June Scott, claimed that backstage at a concert in Ohio, she saw him take red devils (amphetamines). "Michael used to have to take red devils just to keep himself going. Then, of course, he'd have to take downers. When you look at all the pressure he's always been under, can you blame him?"

Whatever the causes, Michael's behavior had become increasingly unpredictable. During a visit to Atlanta, Michael donned scruffy clothes, sunglasses, and a slouchy hat. And with one of his bodyguards in tow, he cruised the city streets in his limousine.

After driving around aimlessly for over two hours, Michael, who had grown increasingly irritable, inexplicably ordered the car to stop. Then he bolted out of the limo and into an antiques shop, where the store owner, British-born John Nolan, was just closing up. Brushing past Nolan, Michael dashed to the back of the store and into a mirrored cabinet, closing the door behind him.

He came out of his hiding place a few moments later and commanded Nolan to take him on a tour of the downstairs showroom. "He looked so weird," Nolan remembered. "It was like talking to a child." When Nolan told him he was going to call the police instead, Michael blocked his path and, menacingly, reached into his pocket.

Nolan, who did not recognize Michael, assumed he was reaching for a knife. "I thought, Oh, God, this is death, one of us is going to die." At that point the terrified store owner punched Michael in the face, knocking him to the floor. Then, as Michael struggled to get up, Nolan grabbed him in a headlock and ran to the front of the store. There he crashed Michael's head through the door. Glass rained down on both men. Miraculously neither was seriously cut.

As Michael crouched on the floor in a daze, Nolan phoned the police. It was then that Michael's bodyguard barged into the shop. Nolan told him the Atlanta police were on the way. "I don't know why I don't take your head off," the bodyguard said. The police arrived, and while they were dragging Michael away, he reportedly turned to Nolan and screamed, "Englishman, I'm gonna kill you!"

At the time, a serial killer had murdered ten black children in Atlanta, and the city was in a state of near panic. Two hours after the brawl, an unnamed city hall official called Nolan and warned him that he might touch off a race riot if he insisted on pressing charges against the man who had invaded his shop. Nolan, still unaware of the intruder's identity, had no idea what the official was talking about—until he was driven by a downtown record store where Michael's face was plastered in the window.

Nolan, told that Michael had agreed to contribute $5 million to a fund for the families of the murdered children, dropped the matter. While acknowledging that an incident took place, Atlanta's deputy police chief William Taylor would later claim that Michael was never arrested, that no money had changed hands, and that Nolan had agreed not to press criminal trespass charges against Michael if Michael didn't press assault charges against him.

But the arresting officer in the case, Jeff Green, insisted that Michael had been arrested. He was quoted as saying that Michael's arrest record had been destroyed as part of a cover-up. "I don't know what happened to the records," Green said. "All I know is that they don't exist and they should. Something was worked out to let Jackson off the hook."

The Jackson family had nothing to say about the episode. Oddly, the family did report a different incident involving Michael that supposedly occurred at about the same time. Michael was innocently browsing through a convenience store when a white racist accused him of stealing a candy bar. The man allegedly screamed "Nigger!" at Michael and beat him repeatedly until the heroic Bill Bray came to the rescue. The family claimed to have filed a lawsuit, then dropped it when they decided the racist posed a threat to Michael's safety.

Not that Michael wasn't a target for obsessive fans; he was. He was so accustomed to receiving unsolicited photographs and offers of sex from adoring young women that by 1981 all such correspondence was destroyed almost as soon as it was opened.

No one proved more implacable than a certain teenager who inundated Michael with hundreds of letters in 1981. And although she was not the first woman openly to fantasize that Michael was the father of her baby, her letters had a psychotic ring to them that frightened Michael.

Because it was feared that she would show up at Hayvenhurst, guards were given her photo and warned that if they spotted her, they were to phone the police immediately. Her psychological stalking of Michael reached its climax when a gift box arrived containing a photograph of the woman and her child, a letter, and a gun. In the letter Michael's would-be lover said that she had an identical gun, and that she would use it to kill herself and her baby at noon the following Sunday. She insisted that Michael pick up the gun and, at precisely the same time, take his own life.

The incident disturbed Michael, but not enough to take any decisive action. Curiously flattered by the woman's obsessive persistence, he actually framed her picture and put the gun away among his other souvenirs. Thankfully the woman did not follow through with her part of the threat. The letters stopped by early 1982, after she was diagnosed with schizophrenia and committed to a mental hospital.

Both the *Triumph* album and the tour outperformed all expectations. In their attempt to outdazzle other top R&B groups of the time—particularly Earth, Wind, and Fire—the Jacksons had succeeded spectacularly. The tour netted $5 million—money Michael could easily have forgone but that was essential if the other Jacksons were to maintain their princely lifestyles.

Still, nothing the adult Michael had done with his brothers approached the impact of *Off the Wall,* and talk turned again to what now seemed to be his inevitable departure from the group. When asked if he planned to leave and focus solely on his own career, Michael said coyly, "Uhm. Yes and no. I can't really say. Uhm. It's hard to say right now. It's just something that has to happen on its own."

Michael's long-term strategy hinged on his hiring new management. Finding a replacement for his father did not take long. Along with Diana Ross, Neil Diamond, Bob Dylan, and George Harrison, Michael had been a client of top music industry lawyer David Braun since joining Epic. When Braun left his thriving practice to become president of PolyGram Records in October 1980, he turned Michael over to one of his eager young associates, a thirty-year-old onetime tax lawyer named John Branca.

Branca was shrewd, ambitious, and determined to help Michael realize his dream of becoming the world's richest performer. The chemistry between Michael and the coolly confident Branca was instantaneous; Michael trusted this savvy young attorney to accomplish what his father could not—so much so that when Braun returned to the law firm six months later, expecting to reclaim Michael as his client, Jackson stuck with Branca.

Branca's chief ally at Epic was none other than CBS Records' flamboyant and controversial president, Walter Yetnikoff. In sharp contrast with the youthful, suave Branca, Brooklyn-bred Yetnikoff was crude and bellicose. Once a diffident corporate lawyer, Yetnikoff had transformed himself into the most powerful man in the record industry, principally by bullying those around him. He was, in a word, simply too loud to ignore. "Nobody," Yetnikoff was fond of saying, out-*geschreis* me!"

Only two years earlier Yetnikoff was so convinced that the Jacksons—Michael included—were over the hill that he had to be talked out of cutting them loose from CBS. But now, while dealing with a stable of talent that included Barbra Streisand, Bob Dylan, Cyndi Lauper, and Meat Loaf, Yetnikoff always managed to find time for Michael. He was already convinced that with the right nurturing and promotion, Michael could become the biggest CBS star of all.

Rounding out the trinity that would become Jackson's private "Mafia" was CBS Records' promotion maven Frank Dileo. At five feet two inches and over 250 pounds (one wag dubbed him the "human cannonball"), Dileo cut a curious figure among the Brooks Brothers–clad executive on the thirty-fifth floor of Black Rock. Indeed, puffing on a Churchillian stogie and flashing a marble-size pinky ring, he looked more like a bookie than a world-class record executive. And for a time, that is precisely what he was. Specializing in college basketball, in 1977 and again in 1978 Dileo was convicted and fined for misdemeanor bookmaking.

During his five years as Epic's promotion director, Dileo played a significant role in making such around-the-bend performers as Meat Loaf, Cyndi Lauper, and Boy George household names. Known as "Tookie" to his friends, he was a firm believer in farming out records to well-connected independent promoters—a segment of the industry that flourished despite persistent charges of payola (in the form of cash and drugs), kickbacks, and intimidation. "Organized crime?" sniffed Dileo. "That's bullshit. There hasn't been organized crime since Capone died."

Dileo was destined to play a much larger part in Michael Jackson's career, but for now all Epic executives—not to mention millions of fans around the world—anxiously awaited Michael's follow-up to *Off the Wall*. Before he could get to that, however, Michael first had to fulfill a promise to a new friend. The friend was a little over three feet tall, had an index finger that glowed, and preferred to be known by his initials: E.T.

When he first saw Steven Spielberg's *E.T., the Extra-Terrestrial*, Michael "melted through the whole thing. The second time, I cried like crazy." Spielberg, meanwhile, could think of no one better suited to narrate the storybook *E.T.* album for MCA. "Michael is one of the last living innocents who is in complete control of his life," he told journalist Gerri Hirshey. "I've never seen *anybody* like Michael. He's an emotional star child."

Spielberg hired Quincy Jones to produce the LP, and together they approached Michael. "If E.T. hadn't come to Elliott," Spielberg told Michael, "he would have come to your house." Michael agreed to record the album but first he wanted to meet the star, and a photo session was arranged.

"It was so wonderful," Michael said with a straight face. "He grabbed me, he put his arms around me. He was so real that I was talking with him. I kissed him before I left."

During the *E.T.* recording sessions, Michael was overcome with emotion. "I felt like I was there, like behind a tree or something, watching everything that happened." When it got to the part where E.T. lay dying, Michael choked back very real tears. Spielberg and Jones decided to leave it in.

Spielberg now joined the chorus of powerful voices urging Michael to seek out film properties. The most vocal of these was Jane Fonda. One afternoon, while the two of them were riding in Michael's new white Rolls-Royce, she agonized over what film she might produce for him to star in. Suddenly the answer was staring her in the face. "I know what you've got to do," she said. *"Peter Pan."*

Michael began to cry. "Why did you say that?" he asked.

"Because," she replied, *"you're* Peter Pan."

"You know," said Michael, regaining his composure, "all over the walls of my room are pictures of Peter Pan. I totally identify with Peter Pan, the lost boy of Never-Never Land."

Francis Ford Coppola was working on plans to film a big-budget version of *Peter Pan,* and Fonda phoned him to campaign for Michael in the part. "Oh," she gushed, "I can see him leading lost children into a world of fantasy and magic." (Later, Spielberg planned his own Peter Pan movie with Michael in the title role. It evolved into the 1991 blockbuster, *Hook,* with Robin Williams in the role intended originally for Jackson.)

Meanwhile Michael had his hands full tackling other challenges. While still recording *The E.T. Storybook,* he flew to London to work with Paul McCartney at Abbey Road studios on "Say Say Say," which would go on to become the top-selling single of 1983. In return, McCartney had agreed to travel to Los Angeles to record one of Michael's songs—"The Girl Is Mine"— for his upcoming album.

It was during his stay at McCartney's palatial estate outside London that the former Beatle boasted to Michael that he owned the copyrights to scores of songs, ranging from standards like "Stormy Weather" to 1950s hit parade fare ("Autumn Leaves") to rock and roll classics like "Peggy Sue" and "Every Day." As schooled as he was in the music business, Michael was dumbfounded at the notion that the copyright owner actually got paid every time a song was performed live or played on TV or the radio. He was even more flabbergasted when he learned that McCartney's catalog of golden oldies earned him more than $38 million annually. This went a long way toward explaining why, in 1982, McCartney was considered to be the wealthiest man in show business.

The whole business of acquiring song copyrights came as nothing less than a revelation to Michael. Eventually McCartney would rue the day he ever breathed a word of it to his young friend.

As he flew back from London, Michael had more pressing problems on his mind. His "mother-lover-sister," Diana Ross, who by now had left Motown, was in the midst of recording her second RCA album, *Silk Electric,* and needed a surefire hit. Michael was "zooming along on the Concorde" when a song popped into his head. "I said, 'Hey, that's perfect for Diana!' " he recalled. "I didn't have a tape recorder or anything, so I had to suffer for like three hours. Soon as I got home I whipped that baby on tape."

"That baby" was "Muscles," an erotic paean to masculine pulchritude that raised eyebrows and set even Ross to wondering about Michael's motivation. Michael insisted that the song was about his pet snake, but the lyrics—"I want muscles / All over your body"—suggested that the author had something else in mind. No matter. Ross, thanks to her onetime protégé, was able to chalk up yet another hit.

Henry Fonda was so ill when he won his first Oscar, for *On Golden Pond,* that he could not attend the awards ceremony. Instead Jane accepted the statuette for her father, then hand-delivered it to him at his home in Bel Air. The Fonda clan—Jane, brother Peter, and Henry's fifth wife, Shirlee—were surprised that he had managed to hang on long enough to savor this last triumph.

Amazingly, Henry Fonda would survive another five months. By the time he died on August 12, 1982, the family almost felt a sense of relief. That night Michael rode over to Henry's Bel Air estate in his new black Rolls. There he sat with Jane, Peter, and Shirlee as they traded memories, laughed, cried—and carefully monitored TV news reports of the screen legend's passing.

Although never articulated, there were obvious reasons for the instant chemistry between Jane Fonda and Michael. Both had grown up in households dominated by powerful, often callous, always emotionally distant men. Fonda harbored some of the same deep resentment toward Henry that Michael felt toward Joe, and in that sense they shared the same psychic scars.

A week after Henry Fonda's death, Michael turned his attention to the turmoil in his own family as Katherine Jackson filed for divorce a second time on the usual grounds of irreconcilable differences. She asked for custody of Janet, the youngest of her nine offspring and at sixteen the only one who was still a minor.

The court papers also listed the couple's assets: Hayvenhurst; their condominium in the San Fernando Valley; a business known as Joe Jackson Productions; furniture and furnishings and other personal properties; various bank accounts; a 1974 GMC motor home; a 1971 white Rolls-Royce; a 1971 blue Rolls-Royce; a 1971 blue-gray Mercedes-Benz; a 1978 brown SEL Mercedes-Benz; a 1981 Toyota truck; a 1980 white Cadillac limousine; two boats (day cruisers); a trailer; and a Keogh retirement plan.

Years after she had made her first halfhearted attempt to divorce Joe, Katherine realized she still knew precious little about the state of the family's finances. She feared, however, that unless the court ordered Joe to stop spending, they might both end up with nothing. In her petition to the court, Katherine recalled that a year earlier Joe had told her they were "running short of money." When she asked him for specifics, he snapped back, "Stay out of the business!"

"From time to time thereafter," her petition continued, "he would talk about losing money. I would ask him if he would like me to help in his business office, and he would reply once again that I should stay out of the business. [Joe] has always had control of all of the money and would give me the monies that I needed from time to time."

Katherine suspected that Joe was siphoning off funds to support his mistress and their child. "I am informed and believe," she stated in her petition, "that within the last year, he has spent in excess of $50,000 on a young woman and has purchased for her parcels of real property from our community funds."

Katherine did not have to look far for proof that Joe was in dire financial straits, stemming largely from the dismal showing of his own small record label and several questionable investments. Joe had actually had to raise capital by selling Michael half of Hayvenhurst for $500,000.

Michael wasted no time virtually razing the existing house and replacing it with a mock Tudor mansion. The whole project would take nearly two years and transform the rather bland California ranch house into a sort of rococo fairyland, with tiered fountains, stained-glass windows, glittering chandeliers, circular staircases, marble floors, peacock-print upholstery, and ubiquitous bronze figurines ("Everything seems to be splashed with gold," observed one visitor).

One cavernous, oak-paneled room, incongruously dubbed the "den," featured an old-fashioned soda fountain where the Jackson children would make wide-eyed visitors strawberry milkshakes and banana splits. Above the elaborately carved, turn-of-the-century mahogany bar was a huge, leaded stained-glass window depicting a medieval knight in armor staring up at a black castle on a hill.

Outside, a brick footpath led past flower beds overflowing with azaleas, pink roses, and pansies to a pond where four black swans glided silently across the water. They were only a small part of the growing Hayvenhurst menagerie, which—in addition to the now famous Muscles—included llamas Lola and Louis, a goat named Mr. Tibbs, Jabar the giraffe, two deer (Prince and Princess), and male peacocks named Winter and Spring.

There was also a scaled-down replica of Disneyland's Main Street USA on the grounds, complete with turn-of-the-century storefronts and even Michael's own lifelike "audioanimatronic" Abraham Lincoln robot that amazed visitors to the Magic Kingdom. In the evenings, twinkling bulbs—the "Tivoli lights," Michael proudly, if uncomprehendingly, called them—outlined the mansion's graceful silhouette. When it was finally completed, the reconstruction of Hayvenhurst cost Michael in excess of $3 million.

Behind Hayvenhurst's fairy-tale facade, however, the marriage of Michael's parents was quietly unraveling. Katherine had been so discreet in filing court papers that the divorce action went virtually unnoticed in the press, much to the relief of Epic Records. For his part, Michael was delighted that his mother had summoned the courage to leave Joe —until it became clear that he had no intention of moving out. Joe's strategy worked. After months of giving depositions and filling out forms, Katherine would once again throw up her hands.

Michael harbored enough resentment toward Joe for both of them. But for now he had to put aside those bitter feelings and concentrate on the task before him. That August of 1982 Michael and Quincy Jones started work on a new album at L.A.'s Westlake Studios. Michael would dedicate it to his beleaguered mother. The working title was initially *Starlight*, but before long Michael and "Q" had come up with a new name for the album: *Thriller*.

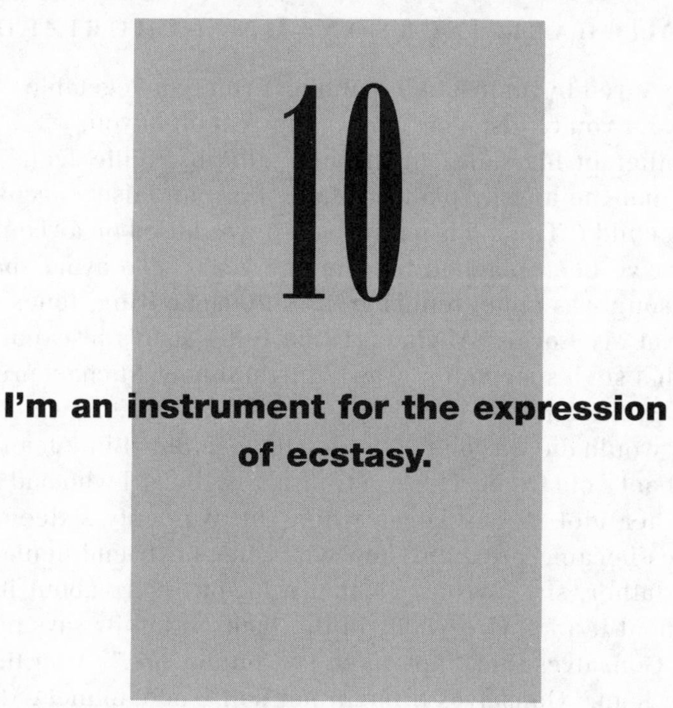

10
I'm an instrument for the expression of ecstasy.

"He's in full control," Steven Spielberg once observed of his enigmatic friend Michael. "Sometimes he appears to other people to be wavering on the fringes of twilight, but there is great conscious forethought behind everything he does. He's very smart about his career and the choices he makes. He is definitely a man of two personalities."

As they began to work on their next album, Quincy Jones could not have agreed more with Spielberg's assessment. "Michael's a truth machine," he said. "He's got a balance between the wisdom of a sixty-year-old and the enthusiasm of a child." Michael brought both his personalities to bear on the making of *Thriller.* While Jones culled three hundred songs, Michael was busy crafting his own—four of which would eventually wind up in the album.

Intensely personal and intentionally revealing, each of the new compositions offered a glimpse into Michael's secret world. Michael had actually written "Wanna Be Startin' Somethin' " years earlier during the *Off the Wall* sessions. A foursquare indictment of rumor and innuendo ("talkin', squealin', spyin' "), the song depicts Michael being skewered by gossips.

A few of the zanier lines dealt with Michael's own status as a celebrity being devoured by an insatiable public: "You're a vegetable / Still they hate you. . . . You're just a buffet. . . . They eat off of you."

Of another of his songs in the new album, "Billie Jean," Michael claimed that the angrily plaintive tale of a man falsely accused of fathering a child ("The kid is not my son") was based on a "composite of people we've been plagued by over the years." To avoid speculation that the song was about tennis great Billie Jean King, Jones fought to call it "Not My Lover." Michael, citing Billie Jean's bisexual lifestyle, argued that such speculation was highly unlikely. Michael prevailed.

Certainly the fan who had proposed a suicide pact in which she and her baby would die was one of those who inspired "Billie Jean." So, too, was Michael's old friend Theresa Gonsalves, the girl who had flown out to meet her idol in Las Vegas when she was only sixteen. In 1981 Gonsalves became pregnant, and when her boyfriend denied that he was the father, she "wrote Michael a lot of letters about it, and we talked about it a lot. Everybody in the Jackson family says he wrote it for me," Gonsalves said, "not *about* me, but for me." (After the release of "Billie Jean," Gonsalves brought her son, Todd, to meet Michael. "I said, 'Todd, this is the man who sings "Billie Jean," and you're Billie Jean's kid.' ")

In fact, the main inspiration for Billie Jean was an exotically beautiful, nineteen-year-old "Laker girl," a cheerleader for the Los Angeles Lakers basketball team. At one point the young woman had called Jackie Jackson's wife, Enid, from the hospital, claiming she had just aborted a baby and that Jackie was the father. Jackie denied the allegation but continued their steamy affair. On one occasion the Laker girl brazenly showed up at Jackie's home and was greeted at the front door by Enid, who, the girl said, proceeded to tie her to a chair and threaten her. Later Enid caught her husband and his girlfriend together on the backseat of the family Land Rover and, according to the Laker girl, roughed her up.

The affair, which finally led Enid to divorce Jackie, lasted fully eight years—ending only when his girlfriend launched her own recording career. Enid had been Michael's favorite sister-in-law. And although he admired the Laker girl's undeniably formidable talents as a dancer, choreographer, and pop singer, Michael would never forgive her for breaking up his big brother's marriage. "Billie Jean" provided the means for Michael to vent his bitterness toward Jackie's Laker girl lover: Paula Abdul.

By implying that Michael might actually put himself in a position to be sued for paternity, "Billie Jean" served another purpose. "You know, everybody thinks you're gay," Michael's vocal coach, Seth Riggs, blurted out one day.

"I know." Michael giggled. "The other day a big, tall, blond, nice-looking fellow come up to me and said, 'Gee, Michael, I think you're wonderful. I sure would like to go to bed with you.' I looked at him and said, 'When's the last time you read the Bible? You know, you really should read it because there is some real information in there about homosexuality.' The guy says, 'I guess if I'd been a girl, it would have been different.' And I said, 'No, there are some very direct words on that in the Bible, too.' "

A sexual undercurrent ran through "Billie Jean," and the lyrics ("Mama always told me to be careful what you do / Don't run around breaking young girls' hearts") reassured Michael's public that he had the appetites of any heterosexual male. "Michael was very upset that people thought he was gay. He'd cry about it," a friend said. "For the first time, people were saying, 'Wow, this girl says Michael got her pregnant. He's straight after all!' " Not unaware that the song would restore the faith of at least some of his female fans, Michael played up the real-life angle in interviews. " 'Billie Jean' is a result of a paternity suit," he later told a reporter. "I won't comment on whether or not the song is autobiographical, but it's real."

Quincy Jones knew that the album still needed an explosive, teeth-rattling track and for weeks badgered Michael to come up with one. The result was "Beat It," a macho foray into the realm of gritty hard rock. Featuring Eddie Van Halen's blistering guitar solo, the song's hard-driving, macho sound belied its nonviolent message aimed squarely at teens: that it's best to walk away from a fight. While recording "Beat It," the speakers overloaded and, according to Jones, "actually burst into flame"—something he had never witnessed before.

In sharp contrast, the McCartney-Jackson duet "The Girl Is Mine"—a verbal tug-of-war between two ardent suitors—was a blatantly syrupy confection. When McCartney blanched at a line that referred to the "dog-gone girl," Michael argued that he "wasn't going for depth—he was going for rhythm, he was going for feel. And he was right."

Michael took the same approach to "Human Nature," a ballad written by Steve Porcaro and John Bettis of the rock group Toto. This finely crafted song cast Michael as a solitary young man on a nocturnal stroll, declaring, "If they say Why? Why? / Tell them that it's human nature. . . . I like lovin' this way." Given the dubious nature of Michael's sexual orientation, that last phrase raised eyebrows among heterosexuals and delighted the gay community.

For the fluffy "Pretty Young Thing," written by Quincy Jones and James Ingram, Michael enlisted the help of his sisters La Toya and Janet to sing backup. Their voices were then run through an electronic blender that made them sound curiously like harmonizing chipmunks.

Such froth would be necessary, both Jones and Jackson reasoned, to offset the impact of the album's title cut. Designed as a link between the album's dark and light themes, "Thriller" gave Michael a chance to indulge his own taste for the macabre. Replete with such cliché horror movie sound effects as clanking chains, creaking doors, and wolfman howls, the Rod Temperton song wound up with a delightfully camp rap by none other than the reigning king of the B horror flick, Vincent Price.

The pressure to put all these parts together on record in time for the Christmas record-buying season was intense. Epic gave Michael and Jones just three months to record *Thriller*, insisting that it be finished by October 1, 1982, "do or die." To further complicate matters, Michael and Jones were not yet finished with *The E.T. Storybook*, and Jones was also juggling an album for disco diva Donna Summer.

This time the headstrong "Q" was more inclined to step back and let Michael take control in the studio. Sometimes Jones did not even bother to show up. Michael welcomed the responsibility, but the deadline pressure took its toll. And whenever he felt overwhelmed, Michael sought solace in the company of children. "When I'm upset about a recording session," he said, "I'll dash off on my bike and ride to the schoolyard, just to be around them. When I come back to the studio, I'm ready to move mountains. Kids do that to me. It's like magic."

Other times he would simply pull out one of the children's books or publications he always kept close at hand. "If I'm down, I'll take a book with children's pictures and look at it and it will just lift me up," he said. Again he stressed that simply "being around children is like magic."

Michael rushed through the process of mixing the tracks—adjusting the balance of vocals and instruments—to meet his deadline. When he and Jones finally sat down to listen to the album from start to finish, Michael was "devastated. *Thriller* sounded so crappy to me that tears came to my eyes." Indeed, Michael held his head in his hands and wept through each song. When the last cut was played, he bolted from the room and drove to the nearest playground for comfort.

Even the "magic" of children could not buoy Michael's spirits; he told Jones to call Walter Yetnikoff at CBS Records and tell him that *Thriller* would not be delivered on schedule. The entire album would have to remixed—a delicate, laborious process not unlike that of editing a film.

There were the customary tantrums and threats of lawsuits. But when the master to Michael's remixed *Thriller* was finally handed in a month later, everyone was, well, thrilled.

Not thrilled enough for Michael, however. While listening to the finished album for the first time, Michael's co-manager Ron Weisner and Quincy Jones cautioned Michael not to get his hopes up too high. Despite *Thriller*'s obvious hit potential, they pointed out that the record market was in such a slump, there was no way it could approach *Off the Wall*'s phenomenal run of eight million copies. Their prediction: a respectable sale of two million.

Michael blasted both men for their lack of confidence in *Thriller*, and the next day called Walter Yetnikoff to cancel the project. *Thriller* could be the biggest-selling album in history, Michael said, "but only if everybody gets behind it one hundred percent."

Yetnikoff's normal response to such demonstrations of artistic temperament was to throw a tantrum of his own. But he was impressed by Michael's determination. The CBS Records chief promised that *Thriller* would receive his full attention. The album was put on a crash schedule and shipped to stores on November 21, 1982.

Reviewers were ecstatic, praising "Jackson's joyously irrepressible performance" and proclaiming *Thriller* as "the latest statement by one of the great singers in popular music today." Vince Aletti of *The Village Voice* joined in the chorus, calling *Thriller* "as stunning and satisfying a piece of show biz escapism as anyone has turned out in years." But Aletti also sensed something more profound in its swirling undercurrent of paranoia. "In *Thriller*," he wrote, "Michael has begun to part the shimmering curtain of his innocence (it's magic, it's unreal) to glimpse darker, deeper things. Once that curtain is ripped down, the view could be astonishing."

Thriller would spend thirty-seven weeks perched at number one, spin off seven top ten singles, and overtake the sound track of *Saturday Night Fever* to become the biggest-selling album of all time—just as Michael had predicted. Eventually, forty-two million copies of *Thriller* would be sold worldwide. And when "Billie Jean" (the second single from the album to be released after "The Girl Is Mine") reached its peak, Michael became the first artist simultaneously to have the number one hits on the pop single, pop album, R&B album, and R&B single charts.

Michael would credit Frank Dileo, Epic's chubby, cigar-chomping promotion wiz, with masterminding *Thriller*'s assault on the airwaves. With "Billie Jean" still sitting at the top of the charts, Dileo urged CBS to release "Beat It"—a move CBS executives were convinced would dilute the impact of both songs. Dileo argued that each record would simply build on the other, creating an unstoppable momentum for the entire album. He was right. "Beat It" also made it to number one.

Dileo was valuable to Michael for more than just his marketing savvy. A fifteen-year veteran of the record industry himself, Michael was well aware that independent record promoters could determine whether a song got saturation airplay or was consigned to oblivion. More than any other Epic executive, Dileo maintained strong contacts with some of the key figures in this shady world. "He gets the job done," Michael observed of his new friend.

MTV also played a major part in *Thriller*'s phenomenal success. Ignoring the song's story line altogether, the "Billie Jean" video cast Michael as a dapper, elusive mystery man being pursued by relentless paparazzi. He vanishes and reappears at will; the sidewalk squares light up whenever his dancing feet actually touch pavement. The stark, avant-garde nature of the video introduced the world to a new, more sophisticated Michael—and marked his first step toward becoming the dominant figure in the world of music video.

Directed by Bob Giraldi, the award-winning maker of television commercials (and former husband of model Cheryl Tiegs), and choreographed by Broadway veteran Michael *(Dreamgirls)* Peters, "Beat It" stuck to the song's pacifist message. Cast as an urban youth fed up with the violence of his peers, Michael was the only thing that stood between two chain-wielding rival gangs out for blood. Shot in south-central Los Angeles with real-life gang members as extras, "Beat It" aimed for a certain verisimilitude. But while it may have worked a generation earlier, this *West Side Story* approach to street warfare now seemed hopelessly outdated. The image of macho gang members led by a snarling Michael through a series of balletic twirls and kicks seemed laughable.

Still, on the basis of Michael's name and the blockbuster success of the album, "Beat It" should have been automatically placed on the MTV schedule. It wasn't. Catering to a white suburban audience, MTV often rejected out of hand videos from major black artists. The "Billie Jean" video seemed innocuous enough to be accepted by MTV; unlike many black stars, Michael had an appeal that had traditionally obliterated racial boundaries. But "Beat It," with its menacing theme of black urban violence and gang warfare, was a different animal. The bombastic Walter Yetnikoff got on the phone to MTV chief Bob Pittman and, after what Yetnikoff referred to as a lot of "screaming and hollering"—plus the threat of withdrawing *all* CBS record videos—"Beat It" became an MTV staple.

His implausible tough-guy stance in "Beat It" might have caused a few chuckles, but no one was laughing at the superhuman ease with which Michael executed the video's grueling dance routines. His irrefutable technical skill was never more in evidence than on May 16, 1983, when an audience of over fifty million tuned in to *Motown 25: Yesterday, Today, and Forever* and were dazzled by Michael's gravity-defying powers.

Initially he refused his old friend Suzanne de Passe's invitation to appear on the NBC special honoring Motown's twenty-fifth anniversary. Accustomed to doing take after take during the making of his videos, he was reluctant to appear at a live taping where he was not in complete control. Moreover, his brothers had already accepted the invitation. Michael had worked hard to forge a solo career for himself; a reunion of the Jackson Five before a network audience, he felt, could only set him back.

Michael called up John Branca and co-managers Weisner and DeMann and told them how he felt. "Why should I do it?" he asked rhetorically. "I've worked this long to get away from the Jackson Five, and now *Thriller*'s going to put me on top. They may need me, but I sure don't need them."

Branca remained noncommittal, but Weisner and DeMann went out of their way to concur with Michael. Obviously Motown was just trying to capitalize on his huge success. And after the way Berry Gordy had treated the Jacksons at the end? "There is no way you can do this thing," DeMann told Michael. "Impossible. No way. We'll tell them to forget it."

The only voices in his camp actively calling for Michael to do the Motown television reunion belonged to Joe and Jermaine, and for obvious reasons. Over the eight years since Jermaine had made the decision to remain with Motown, he had recorded seven albums and eleven singles. Only one, 1980's "Let's Get Serious," had been a major hit. While Michael's *Thriller* dominated the airwaves, Jermaine left Motown to sign with Arista Records in early 1983. Although he was unabashedly bitter about Michael's success and openly blasted him in the press for "trying to be white," what Jermaine now wanted more than anything was a Jackson Five reunion.

At the very least, Michael's participation with his brothers would recapture past glories and give them the added exposure they desperately needed for their upcoming album without Michael. At most, it could mean the rebirth of the Jackson Five, with Michael returning to his role as lead singer and Jermaine rejoining the fold. But the mere fact that both his father and Jermaine backed the *Motown 25* appearance made Michael even more adamant in his opposition.

He did not budge an inch until Berry Gordy ambushed him at a recording studio and begged him to reconsider. When Michael demanded that he not only be given a solo spot, but that he use that spot to sing "Billie Jean," Gordy was dumbfounded. The show was a celebration of Motown, not Epic. The Supremes, Mary Wells, Stevie Wonder, Marvin Gaye, the Temptations, the Four Tops, Gladys Knight and the Pips, Smokey Robinson—all would be singing their Motown hits, whether or not they were still with the label. Couldn't Michael sing one of his Jackson Five hits?

"Nope," Michael replied with a shrug. "I sing "Billie Jean" or nothing. Take it or leave it." Gordy relented.

The result was one of the most talked about live performances in television history. After a tearful on-stage reunion with his brothers—including the prodigal Jermaine—Michael exploded into a lip-synched rendition of "Billie Jean."

For the first time, millions watched as Jackson appeared to defy the laws of physics with his moonwalk. Unknown to the public, Michael had secretly paid sixteen-year-old *Soul Train* dancer Geron Candidate (who went by the stage name Casper) $1,000 to teach him the step, which had actually been introduced by urban break dancers in the late 1970s. Technically this step, during which Michael appeared to be gliding in two opposite directions simultaneously, was not the moonwalk at all. It was known among street dancers as the backslide; the moonwalk was the backslide done in one complete circle.

No matter. It was Michael's moonwalk that brought the *Motown 25*'s audience of show business insiders to its feet, waving and cheering. The next day everyone was talking not only about his spectacular performance, but also about the mysterious sequined white glove he wore on his left hand. Like the moonwalk, Michael's lone glove had been around for years; he began sporting it in the late 1970s as a sort of homage to minstrel shows, and he even wore one on the cover of his *Off the Wall* tour album in 1980. No one, however, seemed to notice. Until now.

A few days after Fred Astaire had called to laud Michael for his *Motown 25* performance, he invited him to his Beverly Hills home and Michael taught Astaire, then eighty-four, to moonwalk. Gene Kelly dropped by Hayvenhurst to pay his regards. He praised Michael's "native histrionic intelligence and his great wit. He knows when to stop and then flash out like a bolt of lightning. There are a lot of dancers who can go ninety miles an hour, but Michael is too clever for just that."

As far as Michael was concerned, to be regarded as a peer by such show business giants was the ultimate accolade. "Can you believe it?" he later said. "Fred Astaire and Gene Kelly told me *I* was a great dancer! If I never get another award or another compliment, that will be enough."

It was enough for Gordy that *Motown 25* turned out to be the highest-rated variety show in television history. The show served as a kind of booster rocket for *Thriller,* propelling it even farther into hyperspace. By June of 1983 it was clear that *Thriller* would not only far surpass *Off the Wall,* but that it had the potential of ending up in the *Guinness Book of World Records* (as it eventually would).

Michael celebrated by ordering his attorney, John Branca, to fire Weisner and DeMann. The principal reasons for their dismissal: both men had agreed with him when he'd said he did not want to do the *Motown 25* special. "Look what could have happened," he complained, "if I'd followed their advice!"

Both men had no inkling of Michael's displeasure. In what would become his standard practice, Michael had smiled and chatted with them amiably only hours before their dismissal. In this case a tersely worded letter from Branca arrived on their desks, informing them their services were no longer needed. (DeMann bounced back quickly; within months he had signed a fast-rising new talent by the name of Madonna.)

Next on the chopping block was Joe. Michael was angrier than ever over the way his father continued to mistreat Katherine—over the years of philandering, the emotional neglect, the countless unrepentant acts of cruelty. Nor could he forget the humiliating abuse he had endured at the hands of his father as a child. "It was," said a former business associate, "payback time."

Once again Michael instructed Branca, who remained his closest adviser, to wield the ax. And determined to be well out of harm's way, Michael specified the precise time at which the messenger was to arrive at Hayvenhurst and present Joe with his pink slip.

Joe did not take being fired by his own son quietly. "What in the hell is *this?*" he raged, storming down the hall toward Michael's room. He would not find him there, nor anywhere else on the premises, for that matter. Soon anger turned to tears. Within days the brothers would also cast him aside, declining to renew their management contract with him. More than any single person, Joe was responsible for the success of all the Jacksons. No one could deny that in spite of everything, he had devoted his entire life to nurturing their careers.

So where was Michael? Joe asked.

"Why, Disneyland," someone answered. "Michael went to Disneyland."

Joe's public reaction to his abrupt dismissal was to behave as if it meant nothing. "I was there when it started," he said with a shrug, "and I'll be there when it ends." Meanwhile he led reporters to believe that the firing of DeMann and Weisner was his idea. Referring to the white "leeches" he claimed were living off his son, Joe said, "There was a time when I felt I needed white help in dealing with the corporate structure at CBS. . . ."

His blatantly racist remarks caused a furor within the entertainment industry. Michael responded by issuing a press release in which he feigned astonishment: "I don't know what would make him say something like that. To hear him talk like that turns my stomach. I don't know where he gets that from. I happen to be color blind. . . . Racism is not my motto. One day, I strongly expect every color to live as one family."

Both Joe and Katherine were apparently quite specific in their prejudices. According to La Toya, her father often complained about "those damned Jews," while her mother frequently talked of "Hitler's one mistake—he didn't kill all those Jews. He left too many damn Jews on this earth, and they multiplied."

While Joe seethed over being turned out by his own sons, Michael and his sisters cowered in their rooms at Hayvenhurst. All breathed a collective sigh of relief whenever he stormed out of the house, climbed into his Rolls, and left to spend the weekend with one of his mistresses.

Joe made up for these brief periods of peace whenever he was in residence. Nearly every day, one of the sons dropped by, often with his wife, and their visits frequently served as a catalyst for violence. No sooner had they arrived at the door one afternoon than Jackie and his wife, Enid, began squabbling about Jackie's ongoing affair with Paula Abdul. Joe, an obvious believer in extramarital activity, yelled at Enid to shut up, reducing her to tears. Jackie came to his wife's defense.

"Jackie and Joe began punching each other," Enid remembered. "Joe rushed from the room and came back waving a gun. He put it to Jackie's head and told him, 'Don't ever raise a fist to me again or I'll kill you!' "

A few days later Enid arrived at Hayvenhurst, and when she realized Jackie was not there, she said jokingly to Joe, "When he gets here, I'm gonna kill him."

At that point Joe pounced on Enid, dragging her into his bedroom and onto his bed. "He was lying there on top of me with his hands on my throat," Enid said, "when Katherine walked in. . . . I don't know whether Katherine saved me from a beating, a rape—or even death."

Like father, like son, Jackie often struck Enid in full view of witnesses and once, after punching her, ground the heel of his Gucci loafer into her open hand as she lay writhing on the kitchen floor in pain.

"It's a nice place Michael comes from," his friend Steven Spielberg observed. "I wish we could all spend some time in his world." Had he known the full truth, Spielberg almost certainly would have reconsidered. Michael's was a world of his own making: a world of illusion, isolation, emotional stagnation, and, inevitably, profound sadness.

It was also a world born of necessity. As long as his father's psychological reign of terror continued downstairs at Hayvenhurst, Michael felt he had no choice but to fashion a palatable environment for himself upstairs.

Although he was now twenty-five, leaving the nest entirely was not an option. "If I moved out now, I'd die of loneliness," he said. "Most people who move out go to discos every night. They party every night. They invite friends over, and I don't do any of those things. I would really die of loneliness."

So Michael retreated into a fantasy world of his own behind the brick-and-stucco walls of Hayvenhurst. Located just down the hall from La Toya's impeccably furnished suite was Michael's one-thousand-square-foot bedroom-playroom, complete with emerald green carpeting, fireplace, silk wallpaper, wooden shutters, private bath (with outdoor hot tub), a desk, a bureau—and no bed. Michael preferred to sleep curled up on the floor, staring up at the Peter Pan posters that seemed to hang everywhere.

No wonder. *Newsweek* had now officially dubbed Michael "the Peter Pan of pop," and although the planned feature film remake seemed to be going nowhere (Spielberg was having difficulty securing the necessary rights from the J. M. Barrie estate), Michael reveled in the comparison. He still dreamed about flying nearly every night—dreams that Freudians would quickly interpret as having a sexual connotation but that Michael chalked up to his childlike quest for "magic."

Michael was convinced that he could, in fact, follow in the flight path of his fairy-tale alter ego. "We *can* fly, you know," he said. We just don't know how to think the right thoughts and levitate ourselves off the ground."

Not that Michael didn't try. According to a young friend who visited him at Hayvenhurst, they would close their eyes, hold hands, and stand in the middle of his room and concentrate on floating to the ceiling. "I'd get bored after a half hour or so and play a game or something," recalled one boy years later, "but Michael just kept standing there with his eyes closed, wishing he could fly. Once he asked Tinkerbell to sprinkle him with pixie dust. No, I'm sure he wasn't kidding."

Michael was the first to admit that with the exception of children, he simply could not relate to others normally, period. "I hate to admit it," he told a visitor, "but I feel strange around everyday people. See, my whole life has been on stage. And the impression I get of people is applause, standing ovations, and running after you. In a crowd I'm afraid. On stage I feel safe. If I could, I would sleep on stage. I'm serious."

Since he had no concept of how to deal with real people, he decided to populate his environment with plastic ones. In his room were six mannequins—one Asian, one black, one Hispanic, a redhead, and two blonds. Michael dressed them in costumes from the 1920s and 1930s—fringed flapper dresses, ankle-length evening gowns, feather boas, and an assortment of hats. He also named each, and had spirited (if rather one-sided) conversations with them. To keep these store dummies company, more than fifty dolls—some dressed, some not—were scattered amid the papers, posters, and toys that littered his room.

"I guess I want to bring them to life," he said of his mannequin roommates. "You know what I think it is? Yeah, I think I'll say it. I think I'm accompanying myself with friends I never had. I probably have two friends. And I just got them. And they see you so differently. A next-door neighbor instead of a star. That's what it is. I surround myself with people I want to be my friends. And I can do that with mannequins. I talk to them."

Then there was the miniature Disneyland he was constructing alongside the house, where other animated creatures and characters would soon join his lifelike Lincoln robot. "These will be like real people," he boasted to yet another visitor. "Except they won't grab at you, or ask you for favors. This will be my own little part of Disneyland. I feel comfortable with these figures. They are my personal friends."

Just how terrified Michael was of the outside world became clear when family friend Dave Nussbaum asked him to have a bite of lunch. "I can't go out there—they'll get me for sure," Michael replied. Nussbaum asked him what he meant. "My fans are waiting outside the house," Michael said. "They're around the corner, and they want to get their hands on me. I know they don't want to hurt me, but they will without knowing it." According to Nussbaum, the "terror in his eyes was genuine" as Michael repeated the litany: "I just can't go out there."

Michael's unabashed withdrawal from reality did not faze anyone in his family. Katherine was happy as long as he was home; she and the other Jacksons catered willingly to his eccentricities. But others were concerned, foremost among them Diana Ross. "He spends a lot of time, too much time, by himself," she said. She rented a yacht and coaxed him into joining her and her daughters for a weekend cruise off Long Island, but he spent much of the time alone in his cabin. "Michael has a lot of people around him, but he's very afraid," Ross said. "I don't know why. I think it came from the early days."

Even when he ventured out socially, Michael found it virtually impossible to connect with adults. When Dick Clark, who had known him since he was ten, asked Michael to his spectacular Malibu estate for a small gathering, the reclusive superstar screwed up his courage and accepted the invitation.

One memorable aspect of the decor at Clark's house was the downstairs replica of a fully tiled subway station restroom, complete with urinal and a stall with graffiti-covered walls. Once inside the stall's swinging door, guests were invited to add to the graffiti. Hence the walls were covered with the signatures of every rock legend from Little Richard and Aretha Franklin to Elton John.

At one point during the proceedings, the host realized no one had seen Jackson for over an hour. He was, as it turned out, alone in the downstairs bathroom, scrawling all over the stall with a Magic Marker. "I didn't have the heart to spoil his fun," Clark recalled, "so I just went back upstairs to talk with all the boring grown-ups."

The first person allowed complete entree into Michael's fantasy world was Emmanuel Lewis, the three-foot-four-inch-tall star of the hit television series *Webster*. Michael had spotted "Manny" when he was doing commercials, months before the precocious twelve-year-old achieved prime-time stardom. Smitten, he called up Lewis's mother, talent agent Margaret Lewis, and asked if Lewis would like to spend time with him at Hayvenhurst.

On any given weekend the two could be seen at Hayvenhurst, darting in and out of bushes as they played hide-and-seek, wrestling on the grass, pretending to be Peter Pan's lost boys or cops and robbers, zipping around the courtyard in Michael's electric car. They also spent hours playing with Jackson's menagerie, speaking to Lois the llama in a baby-talk "language" invented by Michael.

Most of their time together, however, was spent in Michael's darkened, cluttered room, watching videos from Michael's large collection of horror movies or acting scenes from Disney classics. There were sleepovers—something Michael claimed he'd never had as a child—and the roughhousing and pillow fights that went with them.

During one overnight visit, Michael let Lewis in on a secret. He walked to the opposite side of the room and pressed on the wall, and—to Lewis's amazement—it opened up to reveal a secret corridor lined with children's books. The passageway led directly from Michael's bedroom out of the house.

Michael displayed the kind of physical affection toward Lewis that was never expressed among members of his own family. They often cuddled and hugged—moments actually captured on one home video taken by Michael's official "videographer," Steve Howell. In the video Michael was shown teaching his little friend a routine from "Beat It," full of hip swivels and pelvic thrusts. The video also showed the two giggling and whispering as they acted out their fantasy games. For his birthday Michael gave his diminutive buddy a $5,000 diamond-and-gold friendship bracelet.

The sight of Michael hauling around the forty-pound Lewis like a three-year-old was disconcerting. La Toya was concerned, but she soon learned that her brother's friendship with Emmanuel was a verboten topic. "If any of us suggested to Michael that he'd have a better time with somebody his own age," she said, "his eyes filled with tears. He obviously didn't like to talk about it."

Even Lewis's mother seemed willing to overlook twenty-five-year-old Michael's growing obsession with her twelve-year-old son—until, in 1985, they registered at a Beverly Hill hotel as father and son. When she learned of that, Margaret Lewis immediately severed their relationship.

"Michael was hanging around boys even before *Thriller* was released," recalled veteran photographer Vinnie Zuffante, who had spent over fifteen years covering Jackson. "He would go out wearing a disguise, usually a face mask. I would see him driving his black Rolls around Encino, headed for the pinball arcade."

Indeed, Emmanuel Lewis was not Michael's only playmate. As early as late 1982 there was usually a young boy in tow whenever Michael ventured forth in public. *Thriller* had been out two weeks when Michael took one of his young friends to a Queen concert at the L.A. Forum. The friend, who with his ten-year-old little brother often "hung out" with Michael at Hayvenhurst, rode along in Jackson's limo, then went backstage to meet Queen's flamboyant lead singer, Freddie Mercury. Jackson and Mercury had been friends ever since Michael urged Queen to release "Another One Bites the Dust" as a single. It went on to become a monster hit, and Mercury had been after Michael to record with him ever since. Mercury, who was gay, would die of AIDS in 1991.

Emmanuel Lewis and the friend who accompanied him to the Queen concert would be the first of a long parade of young boys recruited by Michael for the express purpose of recapturing his childhood—or, more accurately, creating the childhood he never knew. Yet in the autumn of 1983 Michael continued to lead a relatively cloistered existence. Twice a week he went door to door as part of his Jehovah's Witness field service. Four times a week he attended meetings at the local Kingdom Hall. On Sundays he fasted. He also locked himself in his room and danced to the point of exhaustion. No mirrors. "They make you pose," he explained.

If he shared his life with anyone, it was La Toya. The independent-minded Janet—who by 1983 had followed her brother's lead and undergone two rhinoplasties—also remained at Hayvenhurst; her room was across the hall from La Toya's. But she was already hot in pursuit of stardom as an actress. Starting in 1977 with the part of an abused child in the hit CBS sitcom *Good Times,* she went on to recurring roles in the long-running series *Diff'rent Strokes* and *Fame.* After long days on the set she usually locked herself in her room, afraid to get caught in the crossfire between Joe and Michael.

La Toya, meanwhile, had chosen to follow her brothers into music, and Michael did what he could to help her, co-writing and producing her single "Night Time Lover." "They were very close," said Michael's longtime publicist, Norman Winter. "They had an intense personal bond. I always felt that, at the time, Michael was as close to La Toya as he could be to anyone. It was not like your usual brother-sister relationship. They were more like giggly girlfriends, if you want to know the truth."

There evolved between Michael and La Toya a secret code of knowing winks and furtive glances. The even dressed alike, consulting on what to wear before going out in public. "They'd come down dressed in identical purple outfits, or wearing the same stretch pants and shocking pink angora sweaters," said one frequent visitor to the house. "Nobody said a thing."

An incorrigible gossip and self-confessed busybody, Michael tried to involve La Toya in his snooping expeditions. One of his favorite pastimes was what he called "rambling": essentially invading others' privacy by rifling through their things when they weren't around.

No sooner would an agent, lawyer, or business associate step out of the office than Michael would begin rifling through desk drawers, looking over private papers, peering into closed cabinets. At other people's homes he snooped through refrigerators, closets, medicine chests. As soon as his host reappeared, Michael would be gazing nonchalantly out a window, leafing through a book, or, if he could manage it, in his original spot. No one suspected a thing.

Michael told La Toya, who witnessed many such episodes, that rambling was his way of getting behind the facade most people presented to the world. "If you really want to know somebody," he told her, "look in the very bottom of their bedroom drawers."

When the family journeyed to Alabama for the funeral of Michael's maternal grandfather, Michael declined to attend the actual services. Instead he stayed behind at his grandparents' house, where he and Bill Bray searched for mementos and bundles of cash that Michael's grandfather had reputedly stashed away over the decades. During this treasure hunt, Michael proceeded to loot the premises of jewelry, knickknacks, and other souvenirs he could find.

It was while rambling through his father's bedroom suite at Hayvenhurst that Michael made one of his more shocking discoveries. Reaching beneath the bed, he felt a metal object and slowly pulled out a loaded Uzi machine gun.

Ten months after its release, *Thriller* was still the number one album in the country and selling at the astounding rate of two hundred thousand copies a week. Convinced that another blockbuster video would help maintain momentum to propel the album well into 1984, Michael began work on the video for *Thriller.*

Jackson's video library of horror films included John Landis's tongue-in-cheek *An American Werewolf in London,* one of the films that Michael watched repeatedly with his young friends. Michael wanted the fourteen-minute-long *Thriller* video to be a mini-horror film, and, working with Landis, came up with a concept that married *I Was a Teen-age Werewolf*—somewhat familiar territory for Landis—with the egregious gore of *Night of the Living Dead.*

In the video's opening scene, set in the 1950s, the beautiful, twenty-three-year-old Ola Ray is out on a date with Michael, her wholesome-looking boyfriend, when—thanks to the special-effects genius of Rick Baker—he is transformed into a werewolf. As he gets ready to pounce, the audience suddenly realizes this is a movie within a movie; Michael and Ola are alive and well in 1983, watching all this transpire on the big screen.

Ola, too frightened to watch the rest of the film, leaves the theater with a taunting, playful Michael in hot pursuit. When they pass a cemetery, an assortment of oozing corpses rise from their graves and join Michael in a macabre dance. Before long these zombies in varying states of decay chase our damsel in distress to her home and—in a scene straight from *Night of the Living Dead,* begin crashing through the walls. In the end, she is awakened by Michael. Why, it's all been a horrible dream, of course. But as Michael turns toward the camera we see what poor Ola can't: his malevolent grin and demonic yellow eyes.

When La Toya saw the video for the first time, she instantly recognized the beast Michael had transformed himself into. He had patterned the terrifying creature on their father, Joe.

Fred Astaire had told Michael he was "an angry dancer," and he was right. Michael's dancing could be electric, pantherlike, explosive, sensual—but seldom joyful. "I never smile," he once said, "when I dance." Michael channeled into his work all the pent-up anxiety and rage over what his parents had done to him. Every soul-wrenching performance was an unspoken indictment of Joe.

The *Thriller* video would cost twenty times the usual amount, or about $600,000—nearly all of it covered by John Branca's deft handling of presold distribution deals. Even more daring, Branca and Jackson borrowed an idea from Hollywood and commissioned a promotional documentary on the making of the video to be called—what else?—*The Making of* Thriller.

"To me he's like a Zen monk," said Jerry Kramer, director of *The Making of* Thriller. "He is so focused on a singular goal, his work, his art. He's constantly trying to take it to a higher level."

As usual, Michael impressed all around him during the two-week shoot with what dancers called his "superhuman drive." At one point choreographer Michael Peters was rehearsing twenty dancers in groups of five. By the time they were finished with their routine, all the dancers were sweating, panting, and gulping Gatorade. Michael, wearing a heavy leather jacket, worked out with each group, and never reached the point where he was breathing hard, much less near collapsing from exhaustion. At the end of the day Kramer asked Michael where he was going. "Home to practice," he replied.

His costar, Ola Ray, was not required to dance in the video, but she was under a strain nonetheless. Aware of Michael's strict religious beliefs, she had concealed from him the fact that she had posed nude for a *Playboy* centerfold in 1980. "He never mentioned it," she recalled. "He wasn't aware, so it didn't cause any problems."

Actually Michael was more concerned that Ray might wonder why he did not try to seduce her. Model and former child star Brooke Shields, whom he had met before only briefly and scarcely knew, provided a convenient excuse. Michael told Ray repeatedly that he and Shields were deeply in love. "He talked about her a lot," Ray remembered, "saying that he spoke to her on the phone most days and really thought a lot about her."

Michael went further to dispel any doubts Ray might have had about his sexuality. "One day a gay guy and his friend came onto the set. Michael said, 'Look at him, he's got his *boyfriend* with him.' He thought the whole thing was really funny." Ray's final verdict: "He's so pure it's scary. He's a space person."

In fact, Michael was now hanging out with Marlon Brando's long-haired, husky son Miko. "They seemed to be best friends," Ray observed. "They were together all the time."

Michael was actually more interested in the senior Brando and what he represented on screen. After screening *The Godfather* dozens of times, Michael—whose fascination with organized crime matched his interest in the macabre—now found it impossible to distinguish between Marlon Brando and Don Corleone. The night Quincy Jones introduced his old friend Marlon to Michael, Jackson was so dumbstruck that all he could do was awkwardly compliment the three-hundred-pound onetime matinee idol on his appearance.

"You should see me," said Brando, dripping with sarcasm, "in the shower." Brando then proceeded to tell a rapid-fire series of dirty jokes, all sprinkled liberally with profanity. Michael merely stood in the center of the room, cupping his hands over his ears.

After Michael hired Miko as his personal assistant and bodyguard, however, his relationship with the senior Brando warmed considerably. Over the next several years Michael would seek Marlon Brando's counsel on a number of career matters. In turn he telephoned to offer moral support when Brando's son Christian shot and killed the lover of Brando's pregnant daughter Cheyenne (Christian was sentenced to ten years in prison for the slaying, and Cheyenne tried to commit suicide).

Weeks before *Thriller*'s scheduled premiere on MTV, the elders at Michael's Kingdom Hall got wind of the video's occult theme. Michael was hauled before a panel and warned that if he did not destroy the video and renounce his own fascination with satanism, he would be "disfellowshiped"—banished from the faith. For Jehovah's Witnesses, that was tantamount to being banished from heaven for all eternity. Michael was crushed.

It was not the first time Michael's fame had raised hackles among the faithful. Despite the fact that he and his family contributed not only time, but tens of thousands of dollars to the church, many resented Michael's fame. Over the years there was muffled criticism of his music, his suggestive dancing, his flashy sex symbol image, his heavy use of makeup even when he was not on stage, and—most disturbingly—recurrent rumors to the effect that he was gay. For Jehovah's Witnesses it was the one unpardonable sin.

Michael had resisted all previous attempts by the elders to influence his art or the direction of his career. But now that they were threatening to kick him out, he was terrified. Whimpering, he called John

Branca and ordered him to burn the master tape. Branca thought otherwise. Without *Thriller* there could be no *The Making of* Thriller. Too much was at stake to back out now. Branca offered a compromise, and Michael agreed. At the beginning of *Thriller* would run the following disclaimer: "Due to my strong personal convictions, I wish to stress that this film in no way endorses a belief in the occult—Michael Jackson."

Following *Thriller*'s pre-Christmas debut on MTV, weekly sales for the album tripled to over six hundred thousand copies, pushing it back to the number one position. *The Making of* Thriller, meanwhile, was a phenomenon unto itself. Eventually ranking as the biggest-selling music video in history, it quickly sold nearly four hundred thousand copies at $29.95 apiece. Since Michael had financed the project himself, he pocketed the proceeds—an estimated $6 million.

The elders at the Encino Kingdom Hall were not the only ones troubled by *Thriller*. Many worried that the film's more violent scenes might have a negative psychological impact on Michael's younger fans. Dr. Joan Fineman and Dr. Andrea Sakse of the Child Psychiatry Department of the University of Arizona studied forty children who viewed *Thriller* and compared their reaction with that of adults. What surprised the psychiatrists most was the video's addictive appeal to the very young. "It's clear that children are frightened of it, but strangely, they tend to watch it again and again," Dr. Fineman said. "I tend to think there is something in the character of Jackson that makes him more appealing, more compelling, than other entertainers. . . . It is very far-reaching."

Michael shrugged off the suggestion that *Thriller* might be giving millions of children nightmares. The disclaimer had been enough to quiet church elders for the time being, and since the fate of his eternal soul hung in the balance, theirs was the only criticism that concerned him.

But even among the ranks of Jehovah's Witnesses, Michael had his defenders. One breakaway sect went so far as to proclaim that he was the new Messiah. "Jehovah's Witnesses believe that Jesus and the Archangel Michael are one and the same," said Witness and theologian Dr. Gary Botting, "and this cult is saying that Michael Jackson is the Archangel Michael come back to earth."

According to these true believers in Michael's divinity, the year of his conception, 1957, was prophesied to have been crucial in the events leading to the Second Coming. "And at that time," says the Book of

Daniel (12:1), "shall Michael stand up, the great prince which standeth for the children of thy people." A pamphlet circulated by this renegade faction of Michael worshipers warned that by refusing to recognize the pop singer as the new Messiah, Jehovah's Witnesses were damning their souls to perdition.

Church leaders kept up the pressure on Michael, however. Both Michael and *Thriller* were censured in an issue of *Awake,* the official publication of the Watchtower Society: "The performer is seen to transform first into a 'cat person,' then a dancing 'monster,' " read the article. Despite the disclaimer at the start of the video, the author of the article claimed "it was was so realistic that some who saw it admitted they were horrified at first." The church called on its members to "destroy albums and videos with verbal or visual references to witches, demons or devils" and to stop "imitating worldly musicians" in "dress, grooming, and speech by wearing T-shirts or jackets that advertise such performers."

Behind the scenes Michael, still terrified by the possibility of being tossed out of his faith, turned down a number of foreign sales and spin-off deals that would have brought him additional millions from both the *Thriller* video and *The Making of* Thriller. Then, in the same issue of *Awake* that denounced him, Michael vowed that he would "never do it again! . . . I realize now it wasn't a good idea."

No amount of recanting would alter the conviction of devout Jehovah's Witness Samuel Jackson that his grandson was in fact the Archangel Michael—"the great prince who standeth for the children of thy people." Despite his family's enormous wealth, the retired schoolteacher lived in borderline poverty in a run-down section of Phoenix. Over the years Joe's most magnanimous gesture to his aged father was to offer him one of the Jacksons' used Rolls-Royces. "What on earth," replied Sam, "would I do with a Rolls-Royce here?"

Samuel maintained the living room of his cramped house as a shrine to his famous grandson, papering the walls with album covers, publicity photos, and posters of Michael. Just before Michael was to leave for London on a promotional trip, Samuel journeyed eight hours by bus to meet with him in Encino. He then sat Michael down and told him what he had been telling his friends back in Phoenix—that Michael was the new Messiah and that through his music would come world peace.

Michael listened patiently but said nothing. He may have felt there was more than a grain of truth to such talk. While he probably did not see himself as a messiah, Michael often stated that God had a special mission for him on earth. Before Samuel was chauffeured to the bus station for the long trip home, Michael blessed his grandfather and gave him a token of his love: one of his trademark sequined gloves.

11

It brings tears to my eyes when I see any child who suffers.

"I don't know what he has against making money," Joe said of Michael. "You can always need more money. You never get to a point, I don't care how much money you have, where you don't need more. And at that time, everybody in the family, except Michael, needed it."

Indeed, by 1984 the brothers were having considerable difficulty maintaining their lavish lifestyles; a large infusion of capital was needed. Ever since the *Motown 25* television reunion, Jermaine had been pressing for a reunion tour of their own.

Michael resisted the idea. He was exhausted after a year spent desperately trying to complete *Thriller* on time while still working on *The E.T. Storybook.* Nor was he eager to go back to being just one vote out of six; he had fought harder than any of his brothers to carve out a career for himself, and he relished his newly achieved status as the world's number one solo performer.

Joe was right: Michael did not need the money. With his 42 percent royalty on the wholesale price of *Thriller* (the highest royalty rate in the music industry), Michael pocketed a total of $32 million on U.S. sales alone by late 1983—not counting an extra $15 million for foreign sales, at least $2 million in the publishing royalties for the four songs he wrote on the album, and additional millions rolling in from *The*

Making of Thriller. Ultimately Michael's total take from *Thriller* would top $130 million.

At twenty-five Michael was well on his way to overtaking his friend Paul McCartney as the wealthiest man in show business—a fact that did not escape both men as they filmed the video for their "Say, Say, Say" duet in the California countryside. Fittingly, the video, which also featured McCartney's wife, Linda, and La Toya, cast Paul and Michael as two quick-thinking carny dancers out to dazzle the local yokels.

Michael had already fired his father as manager, so turning down his request for a reunion tour would not be difficult. The one person he could never refuse, however, was Katherine. Once Joe made her co-promoter of the tour, Katherine tearfully pleaded with Michael to go along "for your brothers' sake." Ever the good son, Michael relented.

Now that Michael was safely on board, Joe went to the biggest boxing promoter in the world and asked him to help book the tour. Best known for promoting Muhammad Ali's "Thrilla in Manila" bout, Don King easily qualified as one of boxing's most flamboyant characters. With his fright wig hairstyle ("It looks like he stuck his finger in a wall socket," cracked Michael), white stretch limousines, fur coats, and clunky gold jewelry, King looked more like a garden-variety pimp than one of the most powerful figures in the sports world.

Certainly his record was far from spotless. King had started out as a numbers runner in Cleveland, then graduated to murder; he served four years for killing a man in a street fight. After he was released in 1970, he began promoting prizefights, and over the years he would be accused of all manner of shady dealings—scalping tickets, skimming funds, cheating his own fighters.

None of this mattered to Joe, Katherine, and the brothers when King anted up $3 million in cash as a signing bonus to be divided equally among the six members of the group. King had also outlined a forty-city tour that would net $24 million—$1.8 million of that going to Joe and Katherine, $1.8 million to Don King, and $3.4 million to each Jackson brother.

The others were dazzled by the numbers, but Michael neither liked nor trusted King or the loudmouth "I am the greatest" image he had appropriated from Ali. Michael wanted the legendary San Francisco–based rock impresario Bill Graham—or at least someone else with a solid reputation as a rock promoter—to handle the tour. But then King landed a roundhouse punch. Teaming up with corporate deal maker

Jay Coleman, King convinced Pepsi to sponsor the tour for $5 million—a $700,000 bonus for each signing Jackson.

Michael refused. A strict vegetarian and health food fanatic, he only drank water and an occasional glass of juice. "I don't drink that crap," he said, "and I'm sure not going to tell other people to drink it—especially kids."

Once again Katherine stepped in. The deal meant nothing to Michael, she agreed. But what could he lose? Besides, they were being offered the largest endorsement deal in Madison Avenue history—five times Atari's record-setting $1 million contract with Alan Alda for a series of TV commercials.

After weeks of foot dragging, Michael again succumbed to pressure from his mother. He signed, but with the following stipulations: that he not be shown drinking from or even holding a can of Pepsi. Although it was not included in the contract itself, Michael would make it clear that he did not want his face to be shown on screen for more than four seconds.

Not long after the Pepsi deal was signed, Quaker Oats offered to pay $7 million for the privilege of co-sponsoring the tour. Michael, still upset over the prospect of being identified with a sugar-loaded soft drink, wanted King to dump Pepsi completely and sign with Quaker Oats. But it was too late; the arrangement with Pepsi was exclusive. Michael would later discover that two years earlier—long before King represented the Jacksons or anyone even contemplated such a reunion—Pepsi had been approached to sponsor a Jackson tour.

On November 30, 1983, at Central Park's Tavern on the Green, Don King hosted a luncheon press conference to announce that he would be promoting the Jacksons' reunion tour. Outside, 150 police officers and mounted patrolmen held back more than a thousand fans who come to catch a glimpse of the planet's biggest entertainer. Inside, five hundred media types crammed into the Tavern's Crystal Room, a glass-walled pavilion hung with $2 million worth of Tiffany chandeliers.

While the Jacksons waited in the wings for their introduction, King, wearing an electric blue suit and a diamond necklace, expounded on their virtues in his usual, laughably hyperbolic style. But it was hard not to notice that everywhere—on balloons and posters and matchbooks—were representations of King's logo: a crown topped with the letters *DON*.

After ranting for nearly half an hour, the bombastic promoter showed a fifteen-minute documentary—about the legendary Don King. The film was interrupted repeatedly by boos and catcalls. Then, because the true star of the show had not yet arrived, King stalled by introducing sports personalities from the audience who were in fact not even there.

Finally a dais suddenly swung out from behind a curtain and, with a fitting flourish, King introduced the Jacksons. Seated at a long table behind microphones were Tito, Jackie, Jermaine, Marlon, Randy, and Michael. All sat unsmiling behind dark glasses. Lights flashed, cameras whirred. Even normally jaded members of the press, caught up in the glamour and excitement, applauded wildly.

Michael, casting an occasional disapproving glance at King, introduced his mother, father, and sisters La Toya and Janet sitting in the audience. Rebbie was the only Jackson not present; Michael noted that she was working on her first album, *Centipede* (which he, in fact, was producing). Then he sat down and, despite repeated requests from reporters, refused to answer questions.

Had they decided on a name for the tour? a reporter asked.

"They haven't named it yet," blurted King.

"Excuse me, but yes, we have," said Marlon. "We are going to call it the Victory tour."

"That is the name of the tour, ladies and gentlemen!" King boomed triumphantly. "The Victory tour. And what a heck of a name, too!"

All the brothers glared at King. Michael squirmed on his seat, shaking his head in disapproval. Jermaine chose that moment to wax poetic about the tour's significance. "The tour will mean that the brothers are getting together once again," he said. "And unite and work real close with each other. To show the world that we can make everybody happy. And everybody in the whole world will unite as one, because we want to bring this together in peace for everyone."

A photo session followed, and Michael hoisted a delighted Emmanuel Lewis to have his picture taken with the brothers. Then, still carrying Lewis on one arm like the proud father of a three-year-old, Michael slipped out of the restaurant to a waiting limousine.

When they viewed a videotape of the entire debacle at Michael's Helmsley Palace hotel suite that night, all the brothers were outraged. In his clumsy attempt to upstage the Jacksons, King had made a mockery of the tour. "Come on," Michael pleaded with his brothers, "this guy is a joke. I don't like him, I don't trust him, and we can't let him get away with this crap. My . . . our reputation's at stake." Michael instructed John Branca to get rid of King.

It would not be that easy. King was not about to go quietly. It was pointed out to Michael that—blowhard that King undoubtedly was—he did have an ironclad written contract. So Michael wrote a letter to King in which he laid down the law. King was told in no uncertain terms:

1. You will not communicate with anyone on Michael Jackson's behalf.
2. All moneys paid to Michael Jackson for his participation in the tour will be collected by Michael Jackson's personal representatives, not by Don King.
3. You do not have permission to approach any promoters, sponsors, or any other persons on Michael Jackson's behalf.
4. You are not to hire any personnel, any local promoters, book any halls, or, for that matter, do *anything* without Michael Jackson's personal written approval.

"With Michael"—King shrugged—"you always on trial."

Before welcoming in 1984 as part of his annual *New Year's Rockin' Eve* telecast, Dick Clark stated the obvious. "If 1983 wasn't the year of Michael Jackson, it wasn't the year of anybody."

To be sure, *Thriller* was already being hailed as a pop masterpiece. On January 16, 1984, Michael attended the Dick Clark–produced American Music Awards with Brooke Shields, Emmanuel Lewis, and La Toya in tow. Throughout the evening he kept taking out a mirror and staring at his reflection. "How do I look, Brooke?" he asked. "You look great, Michael!" she gushed.

Aware that his dark glasses made him appear somewhat sinister, Diana Ross urged her onetime protégé to remove them. Michael refused, keeping them on even when he took to the stage eight times to accept his awards. Ross was not alone. The following day Katharine Hepburn called and told him to get rid of the "damn sunglasses. You're cheating your fans if you don't let them see your eyes. Besides, Michael, they make you look like a drug addict."

After the awards telecast, Michael and Brooke Shields made an appearance at the lavish backstage party, sitting at the head table with host Clark and Quincy Jones. The entire time, Emmanuel Lewis perched on Michael's lap—much to Shields's consternation. When it was time to go, Michael summoned his bodyguards and, carrying Lewis in his arms like a toddler, once again slipped outside to a waiting limousine. Shields tagged along.

To cap things off, Doubleday announced at this time that it had anted up $300,000 for Michael's memoirs—the culmination of a deal worked out months earlier between Michael and the most celebrated editor in publishing, Jacqueline Onassis.

Michael's star was shining brighter and higher than any in the show business firmament. This was not the time, he was cautioned by his friends Brando, Fonda, Spielberg, and McCartney, to debase his name by doing television commercials.

It was too late now. But if Michael could not back out of the deal, then he would use it to maximize his mystique. To accomplish that, he would exert near total control over the two spots in which he would appear. He picked the music—"Billie Jean"—worked on new lyrics for the spot, persuaded Pepsi to hire Bob Giraldi as director, and did all the choreography. Like his friend Spielberg, Michael demanded—and got—the final cut.

Keeping in mind the four-second limit on showing his face, Michael suggested shots of his socks, his gloves, his sunglasses. It soon became evident that, more than any other pop figure, Michael was less defined by his face than by a whole series of instantly recognizable props.

His artistic control over the project notwithstanding, Michael still waffled about the Pepsi commercial. He had a "strange feeling" about it—a sense of dread that he could not explain away. As the shooting date approached, this free-floating anxiety gave way to nightmares. The night before taping the spot, he woke up feeling hot despite the fact that the temperature inside the house was maintained at a cool sixty-eight degrees. Inexplicably his bedding was drenched with sweat.

The next day Michael, who had just plunked down $163,000 on a new Rolls-Royce, distracted himself with a shopping spree at Beverly Hills' International Gallery of Antiques. "He loved a great many paintings that involved angels and children and picked out one he thought would look good in his home," said store manager Simon Ebrahimi.

Michael also purchased a pair of nineteenth-century French Toussaint bronze statues depicting male nudes in loincloths. Price for the pair: $240,000. After he bought an opal ring surrounded by diamonds for his mother and a few other trinkets, the total tab for the forty-five-minute spree was more than $500,000.

This distraction was short-lived. If he needed another omen, it came only moments before the Jacksons were to begin shooting their highly publicized commercial. Hearing what sounded like a woman's scream, Bob Giraldi searched backstage until he found Michael in a bathroom stall, staring down at his white sequined glove as it floated in the toilet bowl. After a few panicky moments Michael fished out the glove with his hands, stuck it under the hand drier, and slipped it back on. "I dunno, Bob," he said, shaking his head. "I've got a bad feeling about this. . . ."

Michael grabbed his head and screamed. He had been shot—or at least that's the way it looked to more than three thousand fans who were present at Los Angeles' Shrine Auditorium to watch the Jacksons film their much ballyhooed Pepsi commercial. The truth was not much more reassuring: Michael's hair was ablaze.

This all-too-real thriller climaxed nearly four exhausting days of shooting. It was 6:00 P.M. on Friday, January 27. The Jacksons, the crew, even the assembled fans were exhausted and eager to go home. But director Giraldi was dissatisfied with the opening sequence. He ordered a sixth take. Tito, Jermaine, Marlon, Randy, and Jackie all hit the stage the throbbing beat of "Billie Jean." "You're a whole new generation," Michael sang, still out of sight, "you're loving what you do."

There was an explosion center stage, and suddenly Michael appeared at the top of the staircase, striking the signature pose—head cocked, hip jutting out—the stance that *Rolling Stone* described as "a whole physical catechism of cool."

Brilliantly lit, Michael started to descend the stairs. Halfway down, another magnesium flash bomb detonated, and Michael was momentarily lost behind a cloud of bluish smoke. Within moments he began to feel warm—the result, he guessed at the time, of the intense heat emanating from the klieg lights overhead.

Michael reached the stage and did the first of three planned spins when, suddenly, the heat he had felt turned to searing pain. The audience looked on in disbelief as flames shot up from his head. The pyrotechnics had ignited Michael's hair.

"Tito, Tito!" he shouted. Before Michael's stunned older brother could react, Miko Brando leapt on stage. "I tore out, hugged him, tackled him, and ran my hands through his hair," Brando said later. As a result, he severely burned his own fingers.

In a matter of seconds Michael was encircled by bodyguards and crew members. A coat was tossed over his head, smothering the flames. A fan grabbed some ice, wrapped it in a T-shirt, and applied the cold compress to Michael's head. Another quick-thinking bystander sprayed Michael with a fire extinguisher, but according to one crew member, "he was in such a panic, he practically had to be wrestled down. Afterward there was a terrible pungent smell of his burned hair throughout the auditorium. . . . It was horrifying. For a moment he looked like a walking inferno."

Meanwhile Michael's bodyguards, suspecting an assassination attempt, contributed to the hysteria by drawing their guns. Audience members screamed; some ducked for cover.

Michael was still screaming in pain when paramedics arrived and carried him off on a stretcher to a waiting ambulance. But even as he endured excruciating pain, Michael thought of his image. Before he was wheeled into the emergency room at Cedars-Sinai Medical Center, he told ambulance attendants he wanted to keep his jeweled glove on. When news reports of the accident flashed across television screens that evening—"Michael Jackson is severely burned and in serious condition"—they would show a UPI photograph of Michael on a stretcher, his eyes closed but his gloved hand raised in a wan, valiant wave.

Michael had suffered second- and third-degree burns in the mishap, leaving an angry-looking, palm-size wound that nonetheless was easily treated with an antiseptic cream called silver sulfadiazine. "It was quite a shock for Michael, and when I got there he was in a daze," said Dr. Steven Hoefflin, his plastic surgeon. Hoefflin had rushed to his patient's side as soon as he heard the news. "After I examined him and told him he would be fine, he felt a lot better."

At Hoefflin's insistence Michael was transferred two hours later to the burn center of the Brotman Medical Center in nearby Culver City. He was put into room 3307, where nurse Kathy McGrath threw five blankets over him because he was "still pretty shaken up and cold." Still, he managed to stay up until 1:00 A.M. watching a video of one of his favorite films, Spielberg's *Close Encounters of the Third Kind.* Michael was then given a sleeping pill—despite his oft declared distaste for drugs of any kind, he had no objection to sleeping pills—and drifted off.

Meanwhile, fans gathered outside for an all-night vigil. The hospital was also deluged with thousands of cards and letters, while the switchboard fielded calls from well-wishers at the rate of two hundred a minute. Liza Minnelli phoned, as did Diana Ross and Jackie Onassis. Many of the callers were crying. If the president of the United States came here, "said operator Jane Korsi, "I don't think he'd get as many calls."

Dissatisfied with the usual open-at-the-back hospital gown, Michael was issued a green scrub outfit and a knit cap to conceal his scorched pate. "You're going to start a new wave," said nurse Jan Virgil. "The 'net look.' "

"I want to look French," he replied.

Michael was no stranger to Brotman's burn center. At Dr. Hoefflin's request he had visited patients there twice before to boost their spirits. Only weeks earlier he had visited Keith Perry, a twenty-three-year-old mechanic who had suffered burns on 95 percent of his body and had undergone fourteen painful skin grafts. Ironically Michael now occupied the room adjacent to Perry's.

Donning his single glove and white socks, Michael again made the rounds of the burn unit, visiting Perry and seven other patients. An awkwardly posed photo of Michael shaking Perry's hand with his white glove on, taken by *People* magazine's Carl Arrington, ran the next day in papers across the country. Why the one glove? a patient wanted to know. "This way," he said, "I am never off stage."

Less than twenty-four hours after he had checked into the hospital, Michael was released. Wearing hospital whites over his street clothes and a large black fedora, he was taken in a wheelchair to his waiting limousine. Before leaving, he posed for pictures with the hospital staff and signed dozens of autographs for awestruck fans. One fourteen-year-old said he would have broken his arm just to be in the hospital room next to Michael's. "That's nothing," bragged his thirteen-year-old friend, "I would break my neck."

That night in Encino Michael viewed a videotape of the accident. It clearly showed him standing on the staircase behind a grinning Jermaine, his head surrounded by a halo of fire. Michael was furious at Pepsi—particularly over what he saw as bald-faced attempts to shift blame for the incident away from the company and onto him. One theory for the mishap was that Michael used some sort of highly flammable oil on his hair, and this had ignited when he came too close to the lights.

At first Michael insisted to Pepsi executives that the ad run as it was—that the public see, as he put it, "what Pepsi did to me." Instead he settled for releasing a blurry still photo of the accident to the press.

"They knew I could have sued them, and I could have," Michael recalled. "But I was real nice about it. Real nice." In truth, Jackson angrily demanded a cash payment of $1.5 million to forestall such embarrassing litigation. Reluctantly Pepsi paid him the full amount. Jackson then used the money to fund a new burn center at Brotman—in his name, of course.

In the weeks leading up to the Pepsi spot's unveiling—it was to be shown for the first time on the Grammy Awards telecast—newspapers reported every detail of the accident and carefully monitored Michael's recovery. On its cover, *People* magazine promised to tell the story of Michael's "terrifying brush with disaster." Even Jackson was taken aback by the outpouring of public sympathy—unprecedented for a pop star. No amount of money could have brought this kind of publicity—for Michael or for Pepsi.

Scarcely a week after his release from the hospital, CBS threw a party for Michael to celebrate the success of *Thriller*. Invitations for the $250,000 party at New York's Museum of Natural History were printed on white gloves and quickly became the hottest ticket in town.

Michael was flown to Manhattan aboard the CBS corporate jet and checked into the Helmsley Palace hotel on Madison Avenue. Decked out in a gold-braided commodore jacket, jeans, and black fedora, Michael sipped tea in his hotel suite before being whisked to the party. That night hundreds of fans huddled outside the museum on Central Park West, waiting to catch their first glimpse of Michael since his harrowing accident. They would not be disappointed. Michael would venture outside twice to wave his begloved hand at the shivering crowd.

Many of the 1,500 formally attired invited guests inside were as famous as Michael, and all waited eagerly for him to make his entrance. Finally several dancers took the stage and began writhing and pumping to the throbbing beat of "Wanna Be Startin' Somethin'." Michael suddenly materialized in their midst, sauntering down a stairway, and it was hard to imagine that only days before he had, by all accounts, almost gone up in flames. He looked confident, relaxed, healthy. Everyone strained to see if he was wearing a bandage or cap of some sort, but there was no sign of anything out of the ordinary (his scars were concealed beneath a state-of-the-wigmaker's toupee).

The crowd devoutly wished that Michael would sing or at least dance. He did neither. Instead, Walter Yetnikoff began by reading a congratulatory telegram from Nancy and Ronald Reagan. Then Norris

McWhirter of the *Guinness Book of World Records* handed Jackson a hot-off-the-presses first copy of the new edition, which listed him as the best-selling solo artist of all time. McWhirter then presented Michael with a $12,000 Plexiglas globe. "I've only just begun," said Michael.

Then Michael stood smiling as Yetnikoff and a parade of CBS executives sang his praises. "The best-selling album of all time is *Saturday Night Fever* with twenty-five million copies globally," Yetnikoff said. "I have news for you. Today we surpassed twenty-five million copies for *Thriller!* Michael Jackson—the number one artist in the world!" Allen Davis, president of CBS Records International, read a list of "international milestones" for *Thriller:* a total of 140 gold and platinum awards. To commemorate the achievement, Michael was presented with a platinum replica of the *Thriller* album, four feet in diameter. For the grand finale cannons shot confetti over the star-studded crowd.

Standing at his side through all this was Michael's date for the evening, the statuesque Brooke Shields, who, at six foot one inch, towered over her five-foot-ten-inch-tall escort. When it was all over, Michael thanked his family, Yetnikoff, and CBS. "For the first time in my entire career," he said, "I feel like I've accomplished something." Shields then gave him a chaste peck on the cheek, and hand in hand, they dashed up the steps and vanished backstage.

From there, Michael and a chosen few were feted amid stuffed pachyderms in the museum's elephant room—a nod to Michael's oft expressed interest in the Elephant Man. Shields stuck by Michael's side, clearly delighted not to have to share him with Emmanuel Lewis, who was back in Los Angeles on the set of *Webster*. Her spirits fell, however, when she spotted Michael's new "special friend"—a tuxedo-clad eight-year-old Sean Lennon, without his mother, Yoko Ono, but accompanied by a burly bodyguard. Over the next seven months Michael and Sean would develop the kind of close relationship that Shields could only hope for.

Undaunted by Michael's obvious preference for the company of small boys, Shields launched an all-out campaign to win over the world's biggest star. There were obvious parallels to be drawn between Brooke and Michael. At the age of one—three years before the Jackson Five struck gold—Brooke was a professional model and by twelve attracted international attention playing a child prostitute in Louis Malle's controversial movie *Pretty Baby.* The indomitable force behind the Brooke Shields phenomenon that continued with *King of the Gypsies, Just You and Me, Kid, The Blue Lagoon,* and *Endless Love* was her divorced, hard-as-nails stage mother, Teri Shields. Teri had a reputation as a tough negotiator, managing to inflate her daughter's per-film asking price from $27,500 for *Pretty Baby* to $750,000 for *Endless Love*—all of which paled in comparison with the $1 million she received for her famous "Nothing comes between me and my Calvins" commercials. Unfortunately, her most recent film at the time, *Sahara,* was so embarrassingly bad that it did not even make it into general release.

Like Jackson, Shields made it clear that her sexy ads and screen roles had nothing to do with how she comported herself in private. She was a devout Roman Catholic and, as she did not hesitate to admit, a virgin at nineteen. Now a freshman at Princeton University, she was eager for a way to keep her name and face in the public eye while she pursued her studies. Moreover, Teri could think of worse things for her daughter than to have her linked romantically with—or, heaven forfend, married to—Michael Jackson. Brooke's mother stated publicly that she would not mind seeing Michael become her son-in-law. The sentiment was not shared by Joe, who was openly suspicious of whites and violently opposed to his sons marrying outside their race.

Despite professing his undying love for Brooke to Ola Ray, Michael did not, in fact, pursue Shields. Quite the contrary. It was Shields who phoned Michael repeatedly and prodded him to invite her as his date to the American Music Awards and the *Thriller* bash, as well as to the upcoming Grammy Awards. "You are taking me, aren't you, Michael?" she would ask. "Well, of course you are. . . ."

More than once Shields had tried to kiss Michael on the lips, but he always pulled away. She confessed to a friend at Princeton that Michael did not seem to be interested in the opposite sex, but that didn't stop her from actively pursuing him. And when he failed to commit to her over the phone, she dropped by Hayvenhurst unannounced to pressure him face-to-face. Excusing himself, Michael went into the kitchen and told La Toya that he just did not want to take her.

"La Toya, how can I tell her no?" he whined.

"You just have to tell her, Mike," his sister replied. Janet offered to tell "Giraffe Butt" that she was not invited, but Michael restrained his feisty younger sister.

In the end Michael caved in to the determined young woman's request. It was clearly going to be Michael's night, and he would need to share the moment—and the publicity—with someone. Shields would not be alone. To her horror, she discovered when Michael arrived to pick her up in his white Rolls-Royce that Emmanuel Lewis would be meeting them at the Shrine Auditorium, where they would sit together in the front row.

February 28, 1984, was Michael's night of triumph at L.A.'s Shrine Auditorium. He wore more makeup than his date and was attired for the occasion in another Sgt. Pepper blue glitter band jacket, gold sash, white socks, and—of course—the single bejeweled white glove.

Michael was late, and when his Rolls finally pulled up to the Shrine Auditorium, the fans pressing against police barricades went berserk. Michael took Shields's arm and swept into the hall, not noticing that in the process he and his bodyguards had all but shoved aside his old friend Tatum O'Neal. "I'll introduce you to him later," she promised two friends. When they got inside, Michael and Shields were met by an anxious Emmanuel Lewis. "Come on, Michael," he said impatiently. "They're gonna start any minute!"

Flanked by Shields and Lewis, who stood on his chair and was shown on camera whispering into Michael's ear continually, Michael strolled to the stage no fewer than eight times to pick up an award—for Best Rock Vocalist *(Thriller)*, Best Pop Vocalist ("Beat It"), Best R&B Vocalist ("Billie Jean"), Best R&B Song ("Billie Jean"), Best Record Producer, Best Children's Album *(E.T.)*, Best Record ("Beat It"), and Best Album *(Thriller)*.

Each time Michael rose to accept, Lewis jumped up on his seat to "save" it for him. And when he accepted his tie-breaking seventh Grammy, Michael whipped off his dark glasses because, he explained, "my dear friend Katharine Hepburn told me to . . . for the girls in the balcony."

Jacksonmania continued even during the commercial breaks. When Michael's two Pepsi spots flashed on monitors overhead, the audience reacted as if he had just won another Grammy.

One of the Pepsi commercials gave Lewis a glimpse at the competition. In it, a leather-jacketed street kid is moonwalking through his best Michael Jackson impression when suddenly he is confronted with the genuine article. The pint-size Michael was played by twelve-year-old Alfonso Ribeiro, star of Broadway's *The Tap Dance Kid.* After auditioning for the commercial in New York, Ribeiro was brought out to meet Michael, and the two struck up an instant friendship. "Michael talked to me and made me feel at home among his brothers and his family," said Ribeiro, who as a young adult would go on to star on NBC's *Fresh Prince of Bel Air.* "He gave me a few hints on how to be like him. He was beautiful to me. He's my idol, and I've dreamed of meeting him. I got my wish. When he's in New York, I've invited him to look me up." And Michael would.

That night photographers were clamoring for a photo of Michael and his little group. And as they got up to leave, Michael, again hiding behind his dark glasses, held Emmanuel with his left arm, put his right arm around Shields, and smiled for the cameras. Shields felt humiliated. "Let's get out of here!" she said. "Everybody is making fun of us."

As they left, Tatum O'Neal made another futile attempt to get his attention. Once more he ignored her. "We still are friends," O'Neal later said wistfully, "but it's less often, and I can't imagine what it's like for him now. . . . I'm sure we'd still have a good time, and plenty in common. I will always be fond of Michael, and who knows what the future might bring?"

As his Rolls pulled away from the Shrine, with hundreds of fans in hot pursuit, Michael leaned out the back window, waved a Grammy, and shouted for joy. They headed straight across town to the Rex, where Michael was to host a post-Grammy bash attended by two hundred of Hollywood's biggest names. There they sipped Taittinger champagne and dined on caviar, quail, lobster, and salmon.

Paralyzed at the thought of socializing, Michael appeared on a balcony overlooking the dance floor with Shields at his side, and like royalty they waved down at the crowd that included Bob Dylan, Arnold Schwarzenegger, Julio Iglesias, Eddie Murphy, Cyndi Lauper, Tony Curtis, Neil Diamond, and the Beach Boys.

They had been at the party for less than a half hour when Michael asked Shields if he could take her home. When he dropped her and her mother off at their hotel, Shields took him aside. "I guess I have to get used to Emmanuel if I want to go out with you," she said, "but it sure is hard to explain why there are always three of us."

It was clearly not the thing to say. Michael became upset if anyone dared to suggest that he spend less time with children and more with people closer to his own age. Michael waved good-bye and headed home to Encino, where he threw an intimate celebration with his real "friends"—the five loyal mannequins who silently occupied his darkened room.

In his memoirs Michael would describe his relationship with Shields as a love affair. Years later she would deny that it was anything more than platonic. For the moment, however, she encouraged speculation. "Both of us are kind of shy about that," she said when asked if there was anything romantic between them. "Michael is very private. But there is a real boy-girl interest."

It was pointed out that Shields had just come off a similarly high-profile "romance" with John Travolta. "People believe what they want to believe," she said. "But I like mature men, and Michael is very mature, beyond his years. I don't know if I'm his type, or what his type is. . . . But I know he's very flattering, and I can't wait until our next date!"

Seth Riggs, who had been Michael's voice coach since 1978, came right out and asked Michael if he was gay.

"No, it's against my religion," Michael replied.

"Then you sleep with women?"

"No."

It dawned on Riggs that Michael was telling him that at twenty-five he was still a virgin. "You mean to tell me you have never, ever, had a woman?"

"No, I haven't," Michael responded. "Oh, no."

"But what about all those people tearing at you?" Riggs asked. "Those beautiful, beautiful girls. Never?"

"That's not allowed," said Michael, wagging his finger at Riggs. "Not until I get married."

Riggs was astounded. "I can't believe it. Even with Brooke Shields, you're still a virgin?"

"Yes." Michael nodded proudly. "Yes, I am."

Now that he was the toast of Hollywood, Michael turned to Liza Minnelli to show him the social ropes. At literary agent Irving "Swifty" Lazar's annual Oscar party at Beverly Hills' Bistro Garden six weeks after the Grammys, the couple arrived at 1:00 A.M. Again Michael was the undisputed hit of the evening.

"Didn't matter that he has only one movie, a box office flop called *The Wiz*, to his name," cracked writer Jack Curry. "The place went nuts."

Liza steered Michael around the room, showing him off to her famous friends. She drank Scotch and Coke—lots of it—while he nursed a glass of orange juice. Then Liza grabbed Michael's hand and dragged him to the phone in the ladies' room. "Come on," she said, "we're going to call my father." Liza sang "Forget your troubles, c'mon get happy. . ." and did a little dance as she dialed.

"Daddy, I want you to meet Michael Jackson," she said. "He's a wonderful singer and one of my best friends." She pulled Michael to the phone. "Say 'Hello, Mr. Minnelli,' " she instructed him. Which he did.

After ten seconds of silence Liza grabbed back the phone. "Put on your black velvet jacket," she told her famous director-father. "We'll be over in twenty minutes."

The following Mother's Day, Michael returned to the Bistro Garden with the entire Jackson clan to throw a surprise party for Katherine. La Toya would recall that each child and grandchild "did something special: wrote a poem, sang a song, made a speech, anything to let Mother know how much we loved her."

Michael flew out her favorite country-western star, Floyd Cramer, from Nashville to serenade her. Then everyone escorted Katherine to the front of the restaurant, where they had parked her Mother's Day gift: a two-tone burgundy-and-cream Rolls-Royce tied up with a giant bow. They had given her a Mercedes the year before. Throughout the festivities, Joe glowered.

Michael did not spend all of his time in the months before the Victory tour party hopping. Far from it. After eight months without a manager, he decided that he needed someone to help him deal with men like PepsiCo's Roger Enrico and Don King. Diana Ross, who now had her own management company, was among those who approached him for the job. But given the fact that her own career seemed to have stalled, she was hardly her own best advertisement.

Now even the woman he so flagrantly imitated—the woman whose look he was trying so hard to re-create through plastic surgery—worried that Michael was leaving her behind. "We're what you might call kindred spirits," Ross said defensively. "We know what's going on in each other's minds. Our lives have been intertwined for years now, and I don't think that will change. . . . I want to be around when he does work more musical miracles. He's been my friend and my producer and my costar, and I've been his mentor, his pal, his date, his confidante. I know we haven't exhausted our relationships. . . . "

On March 21 Michael had taken a major step by following the advice of Walter Yetnikoff and officially appointing Frank Dileo—whom he called "Uncle Tookie"—as his new personal manager. "I feel thrilled," Dileo told the press, "to be managing the creator of *Thriller* and so many other great works of art."

The pudgy ex-bookie with the gold Rolex, pinky ring, and trademark unlit stogie could scarcely believe his good fortune. Soon Dileo would become not only Michael's most trusted business confidant—with the possible exception of John Branca—but also his constant companion on the road. Within months Dileo would be a multimillionaire, raising horses on a lavish estate not far from Hayvenhurst and driving a new black Rolls-Royce—a gift from Michael (license plate THANXMJJ).

By mid-May of 1984 Michael was immersed in planning the Victory tour—he was in charge of the overall concert concept, including the stage, sets, and special effects—and recording the *Victory* album with his brothers. He was still miffed at having to do the tour at all. He had a new name for the tour that summed up his feelings toward working with his brothers: "The Final Curtain."

Needless to say, the brothers resisted. "It sounds so—final," observed Jermaine, Michael's most outspoken critic within the family. Michael did not force the issue, but he did insist that his participation on the album be limited to one or two songs.

The most memorable cut on the *Victory* album—and its only top five single—was "State of Shock," Michael's hard rock duet with Mick Jagger. The lead singer of the Rolling Stones eyed the phenomenal success of *Thriller* with envy. As an artist he respected Jackson's work. As a businessman he knew that in the hands of the wrong record company, *Thriller* would never have been the epic sensation it turned out to be, regardless of Jackson's talent.

In 1983 and early 1984 Jagger had embarked on the daunting task of hammering out a new distribution deal for Rolling Stones Records. He was also ready to launch a solo career, and there seemed to be no better time to do it. In his own bid for freedom from the constraints of a group, Jackson had succeeded spectacularly. Jagger wanted to know the Gloved One's secret.

"Mick became obsessed with Michael Jackson," said Arthur Collins, then president of Rolling Stones Records. "He wanted to know every detail about Jackson's life, his contract with Columbia, how the *Thriller* singles were selling, who was pulling the strings."

Collins remembered commenting casually to Jagger that Paul McCartney and Jackson had a new hit with their "Say Say Say" duet. "He felt very competitive toward McCartney and toward Jackson, for very different reasons, and it really mattered to him how well their song was doing. Mick is very much a bottom-line guy."

No more than Michael, who had already forged a profitable relationship with McCartney. Their "The Girl Is Mine" and "Say Say Say" were two of Michael's biggest hits.

While Michael admired McCartney as a composer (but not as a

singer), he owed many of his on-stage moves to Jagger, who had grabbed his crotch on stage years before Jackson and Madonna would co-opt this gesture in the late 1980s. "He saw that Mick could wear lipstick, sashay around, and still be thought of as a macho rocker," said a friend. "Michael wanted to find out Mick's secret."

Michael began actively courting Mick for a duet in March of 1984. A summit meeting was held at New York's Helmsley Palace hotel, and throughout the negotiations between the two megastars, little Emmanuel Lewis hovered around Michael, occasionally whispering advice in his ear like, in the words of one observer, "a miniature lawyer." More than once, Lewis hopped up in Jackson's lap and the two often dissolved in giggles, without offering any words of explanation. Jagger found the whole experience disconcerting.

"You've got your family, you don't need me," Jagger told Michael when he asked him to record "State of Shock." Michael insisted, and after several pleading phone calls Jagger relented. With the Jacksons singing backup, "State of Shock" was recorded at the A & R Studio in New York City. Jagger found Jackson limp and boring. "Michael's very lightweight," he said. "He's like froth on beer."

Michael complained that Jagger's off-key singing made their duet practically unreleasable. "How did *he* ever get to be a star?" he asked. "I just don't get it. He doesn't sell as many records as I do."

Michael, who harbored an interest in the occult despite his Jehovah's Witness background, was well aware of Jagger's reputation as a practitioner of witchcraft. "Sympathy for the Devil" was, in fact, a particular favorite of his. Still, when someone warned him that Jagger supposedly had a history of casting spells on competing rock stars, Michael stated solemnly that his personal relationship with God made him impervious to such attacks. "It doesn't matter," he said. "If you are a deeply religious person, evil spells can't hurt you."

As it turned out, Michael's life at Hayvenhurst was weird enough without Mick Jagger. Following his accident and numerous trips to the plastic surgeon (after three rhinoplasties, he would soon have his eyes done and a Kirk Douglas–style cleft carved in his chin), Michael became fascinated with the inner workings of the human body. He ordered up a full medical library (although it is doubtful that he ever cracked a volume), a human skeleton, and a collection of X rays.

With the help of a doctor friend who taught surgical techniques using human cadavers, Michael also obtained a human brain in a jar, which he stored on a shelf alongside his collection of toys, games, and dolls. Whenever one of his special friends visited Michael's room, the brain floating in formaldehyde was invariably a favorite "toy." (Later he added a second brain to his collection.)

Michael also observed several brain operations. "He was not squeamish or reticent at all," one surgeon said. "It really can be a very gruesome procedure, obviously. Even doctors can get a little grim-faced with all the blood involved, but not him. I mean, he was *smiling* through the whole thing."

Other than these infrequent trips to the UCLA Medical Center operating theater, Michael seldom ventured out. When he wasn't tooling around the yard in his electric car, a facsimile of Mr. Toad's Wild Ride at Disneyland, Michael spent hour upon hour holed up with male friends in his darkened room.

Not all were children. "Michael always seemed to be around young men," said his former friend and business partner Bob Michaelson. "On the road, in the studio, he always had some good-looking guy with him, usually somebody between seventeen and, say, twenty. Never a woman. Never."

And the children? "At that time we never really thought that much about all the kids he had with him," Michaelson said. "*All* the people around Michael thought he was gay, no matter what they said publicly. The people who worked for him knew it. His family knew it. It was a real shame, the way they kept talking about his 'romance' with Brooke Shields. But if you asked me or anyone else at the time, we would have said it was young men, not kids."

When Joe took visiting *Time* correspondent Denise Worrell to his son's room one evening, they surprised Michael and one of these young friends. When Joe opened the door, he came upon Michael and a young man "who looked about twenty" sitting side by side in the dark, watching television. "The room is very dark," Worrell said of the scene. "Michael and I shake hands. His hand feels like a cloud. He barely says 'Hi.' His friend extends his hand, which is damp. He seems nervous. Michael stares with his almond eyes for a long minute and turns to the television. There is silence, and I feel that Joe is uncomfortable. It is so dark I cannot see anything. We back out of the room and Joe shuts the door."

Before she left, Worrell was confronted by Michael's mother, who was clearly anxious over what the journalist might have deduced from her impromptu visit to Michael's bedroom. "Michael isn't gay," Katherine told her. "It's against his religion. It's against God. The Bible speaks against it." As Worrell turned to leave, Joe muttered, "Michael isn't gay."

That April, in fact, Michael became increasingly agitated over rumors that he was something other than heterosexual. When he learned that Eddie Murphy's forthcoming CBS comedy album contained a line describing him as "not the most masculine guy in the world," Michael angrily called Walter Yetnikoff and demanded that the offending phrase be deleted. The line remained in the album, but it was deleted from copies given to radio stations for airplay. "When you're as important as Jackson is to CBS," said record industry insider Art Collins, "you pretty much get whatever you want."

Michael even asked his plastic surgeon, Dr. Steven Hoefflin, to help dispel rumors that he was gay, that he had been given female hormones to maintain his high voice, and that he was contemplating a sex change operation. "These rumors torment him and hurt him deeply," said Hoefflin who, in April 1984, used a carbon dioxide laser to remove the five-inch-by-two-inch scar left on Michael's head after his hair caught fire filming the Pepsi commercial. "The people who make up these rumors don't know much about him. His family and closest friends know they're untrue. And who else would know better than his own doctor?

"He is a normal young man," Hoefflin continued, "who is very attracted to girls and loves children. He has never taken female hormones, and his voice is high because of his singing training. He has never had—nor would ever think of having—a sex change operation. He has the normal desires that any man does."

Michael also recruited his vocal coach, Seth Riggs, to offset the stinging one-liners from comics like Murphy, Joan Rivers, and Jay Leno. Riggs described the gossip as "cruel and vicious. We're all fed up with the lies and nonsense about this boy we love so much. Michael is different. . . . He's not of this world. But there is no excuse for the garbage that's been written."

Riggs conceded that Michael's sex life was nonexistent. "Michael is still a monk. He is under God's will," he said. "He has kept all his energies, all his fire, all his power, that the rest of us use in sex, and channeled it into his music. I'm not saying he doesn't like girls or sex, or that he isn't interested. But sex has to come as part of marriage, for that's the way God said it should be."

Riggs also exploded the myth that Michael was either castrated or injected with hormones to maintain his trademark falsetto. "It isn't for real, you know," he said. "He isn't naturally falsetto. His voice is as low as yours or mine. Natural, male, husky. But he doesn't like it. He calls it his 'frog' voice, so for personal reasons, after I had taught him to reach that level and maintain it, he decided to stick with it. But it's just technique—a trick."

The falsetto also made Michael sound more juvenile—hence less threatening—when he talked with his favorite people, small children. "The small voice definitely made him more appealing to kids," a colleague said. "He didn't sound like a grown-up at all, but like one of them. They could talk to him the way they would to a contemporary, and share thoughts they might never share with an adult."

As for his strange friendship with Emmanuel Lewis: "There have been suggestions that there is something sick, unhealthy, and unnatural in his relationship with Emmanuel," Riggs said. "Michael just thinks Emmanuel is wonderful. He adores him. . . . He loves kids very much, loves their fresh minds and open, simple attitudes to life. That's all. The adult world Michael has to live in is so full of sharks and graspers," he added, "it's nice to get away from that, back to being a child again."

12

I think Michael can be hurt very easily. He's sort of like a fawn in a burning forest.

—Steven Spielberg

Tatum O'Neal and her date left the Helmsley Palace hotel, took a cab to Radio City Music Hall, and sat through a Kool and the Gang concert without ever being noticed by the thousands of people in the audience. O'Neal was, after all, no longer the adorable towhead everyone remembered from *Paper Moon,* and the bearded, dark-skinned black man who accompanied her was nobody famous.

Or was he? It may have cost him $10,000, but the disguise concocted by a Hollywood makeup wizard made it possible for Michael to move about the streets of New York undetected. "He was so excited that nobody recognized him," O'Neal said. "At least for a few hours, he could be free and not have people grabbing at him. He could be like everybody else."

Since *Thriller* Michael was no longer merely a star, but a phenomenon. Increasingly he was donning a fake beard, wig, sunglasses, and a hat to venture out alone—sometimes to proselytize as a Jehovah's Witness. "He just knocked me out," recalled his big sister Rebbie of the first time she went preaching door to door with Michael. "He's usually so shy when he meets people, he'll hide behind you. But when he goes door to door, he looks right in the person's eye. He has a very sensible, thought-provoking presentation. Funny thing is, even when he's recognized, people listen to what he has to say."

Rebbie reiterated the family's oft repeated line that Michael's adherence to the tenets of his faith made his being gay inconceivable. "Ours is a clean organization," she said. "Anyone who turned out to be homosexual would be disfellowshiped, cut off right away."

Michael did not confine his forays in disguise to spreading the Word. He often employed makeup tips learned from Hollywood masters so that he could visit pinball arcades or cruise less fashionable parts of the cities he was visiting undetected. Neither did he always choose to dress up as a male. He sometimes slipped on a dress and a black wig to go out on the town. "He put on false eyelashes and more lipstick than usual," said a friend who accompanied him on one of these jaunts. "But other than that, he just wore the same pancake makeup, eyeliner, and mascara that he always did. He was beautiful."

Michael would later opt for a female fashion that offered the added advantage of a complete cover-up, the head-to-toe black chador worn by Muslim women, complete with veil. Michael would act the part, employing his breathless whisper, giggling and batting his eyelashes. His cover was nearly blown several times, however, when the person he was talking to looked down to see his sneakers poking out from beneath the hem of his ankle-length robes.

A few days after his outing with Tatum O'Neal, Michael was invited to the White House as a guest of President and Mrs. Reagan. The visit had originated with a call from Department of Transportation secretary Elizabeth Dole, who had asked for permission to use "Beat It" in a series of anti–drunk driving commercials. Michael reluctantly agreed —but only if he could be received by the president with all the pomp and ceremony of a visiting head of state. The extent of Michael's popularity had not eluded the Reagan administration. Within days the White House issued a press release stating that the president would present Michael Jackson with a public safety award on the White House lawn.

No sooner did word reach Brooke Shields about Michael's impending May 18 visit to the White House than she again began burning up the lines between Princeton and Encino. She had noted with alarm that on his recent trip to New York, Jackson had not contacted her. Even more disturbing, word had leaked out that Michael, traveling incognito, had taken her rival Tatum O'Neal to a concert.

Michael returned to New York and checked into his usual $1,600-a-day triplex suite at the Helmsley Palace. The day before traveling to Washington for the ceremony, Michael returned Shields's call. She once again took charge. "Oh, it will be so wonderful!" she said. "Now, you'll be standing next to the president, and I'll stand with Mrs. Reagan. She'll probably be wearing red, so . . ."

This time Michael put his foot down. Shields was on the guest list along with several members of his staff, including Frank Dileo, Bill Bray, and his publicist, Norman Winter. But she was not to be his "date" for the event. He did not want her to be in the car with him when he arrived at the White House or at his side when he met the First Family.

There was a moment of silence before Shields slammed down the receiver. Michael then told Winter to call the White House and have her name scratched off the guest list. The Jackson party then boarded a private Amtrak car for the trip to Washington.

"Well, isn't this a thriller," quipped President Ronald Reagan as he stood with the world's most famous man on the South Lawn of the White House. "We haven't seen this many people since we left China." In his dull brown suit and rep tie, the elderly Reagan looked less like a commander in chief than his guest, who wore another military getup that sparkled like a Christmas tree. Michael helped the First Lady onto the podium. She wore a Chanel suit with a ruffled blouse and a bemused smile. Throughout his entire visit Michael did not remove his sunglasses.

"At this stage of his career," said Reagan, launching into a speech actually written by Norman Winter, "when it would seem he's achieved everything a musical performer could hope for, Michael Jackson is taking the time to help lead the fight against alcohol and drug abuse." His speech over, the president handed Michael a plaque. And Michael stepped up behind the lectern bearing the presidential seal and uttered a thirteen-word acceptance speech worthy of Calvin Coolidge: "I am very honored," he said. "Thank you very much, Mr. Reagan and Mrs. Reagan."

They loved him anyway. When he raised his bejeweled white glove to wave to the crowd, a roar went up from the thousands of spectators outside the White House gates. At the far edge of the lawn, hundreds chanted "We want Michael!" in unison. Even White House staffers were agog. Peering out of windows and leaning precariously over balcony railings, they waved and cheered like everybody else swept up in Michaelmania. While President and Mrs. Reagan accompanied their guest through the Rose Garden to the Oval Office, a White House staffer in her forties yelled, "I saw his foot!"

Michael and his entourage had to walk through a metal detector before being escorted on a private tour of the White House. Instead of Brooke Shields or even Emmanuel Lewis, Michael had brought along an unidentified young man. When Norman Winter asked who the youth was, Michael told him it was none of his business. But what would they tell White House officials? Winter asked. "It's none of their business," he snapped. Winter improvised; he told anyone who asked that the clean-cut young man was a Secret Service agent.

For Michael, a highlight of the visit was to be a meeting with the children of staffers. But when his party got to the Diplomatic Reception Room to see the president and a few dozen children, there were about seventy-five grown-ups standing around.

"Oh, no," Michael whispered to Winter before dashing into a bathroom just down the corridor from the presidential library.

There was a moment of panic. Winter tried to coax Michael out but couldn't. He had locked himself in. Finally Frank Dileo banged on the door. "Come on, Mike," he said, "let's go. This is crazy." Nancy Reagan looked on, shaking her head in amazement.

Once assured that the crowd had been pared down and that he would meet staffers and their families in groups of ten, Michael sheepishly unlocked the bathroom door and slunk into the reception room. The First Lady shook his hand, then spent the next half hour studying his face for plastic surgery scars. Nancy determined that in addition to operations on his nose, Michael had obviously had some eye-work done. She also murmured under her breath that he was wearing more makeup than half the women in the room and that, in her opinion, Michael not only looked like Diana Ross, he looked *prettier* than Diana Ross. And, Nancy asked, who was the good-looking young man with him? No one knew.

More than two hundred fans waited outside the northwest gate to catch a glimpse of Michael as his limousine pulled away from the White House grounds. Mounted police as well as vans and motorcycle cops formed a wall to protect his exit. But when the limo turned down Pennsylvania Avenue, the fans broke ranks and sprinted after it. Tearing over the antiterrorist concrete block, they pursued Jackson's car, remembered eyewitness Mary McGrory, "hallooing and crying, hurling themselves into the oncoming traffic in a show of reckless courage and devotion that no politician could hope to match."

The heavier social significance of Michael's White House visit was not lost on the Soviets. The Kremlin denounced him as "a singer who sold his black soul for white profit and is serving the Reagan administration by keeping the American public's mind off the country's problems." Michael's music was, of course, banned in the Soviet Union.

Nancy Reagan may have studied Michael's face very carefully during his visit, but the weight-conscious First Lady apparently failed to notice that—under the heavy cosmetics designed to make his face look fuller, beneath the heavy military jacket—Michael was wasting away from his normally svelte 125 to barely 115 pounds. Within a month he would tip the scales at a cadaverous—and medically dangerous—103 pounds.

A year earlier singer Karen Carpenter had become the first celebrity to succumb, at the age of thirty-two, to the effects of anorexia nervosa. Now his inner circle was convinced that Michael suffered from the same life-threatening medical disorder. "He eats barely enough to keep a bird alive," was Katherine's usual refrain about her son's eating habits. And indeed, after becoming a vegetarian in the mid-1970s, Michael fasted every Sunday and ate only what was prepared by his Sikh chef, Mani Singh Khalsa. Tall and bearded, Mani was always clad in his Sikh turban and robes. His accent was rather obvious, but it is doubtful that Michael knew his Sikh chef actually hailed from Brooklyn.

Michael had discovered Mani at Hollywood's Golden Temple Conscious Cookery and Catering Company. And he always prepared Michael's favorite foods—enchiladas, whole-wheat pizza, Oriental salad—often augmenting them personally with cashews, pecans, herbs, spices, seeds, and vitamin supplements. But in the spring of 1984, even Mani could not persuade him to eat.

"Michael is totally, absolutely obsessed with retaining a teenage figure, of appearing to have captured the secret of eternal youth," one CBS executive said. "He will go to any lengths to retain his appeal, which he believes is based on his Peter Pan appearance."

Michael was now exhibiting the classic signs of someone suffering from anorexia. Each morning he weighed himself on the hospital scale that occupied a corner of his cluttered room. Michael called it his "iron judge."

"For a while there," conceded Norman Winter, "it was pretty scary. We all knew Michael was way too thin." Another associate remembered being invited to dinner at Hayvenhurst and watching as Michael ate "only one or two large strawberries."

On June 26 the Jacksons arrived in Birmingham, Alabama, aboard

Michael's private, luxuriously appointed 707 for a week of secret rehearsals. Checking into the Hyatt Hotel, Michael suddenly collapsed. "He just lay there on the floor, quivering like a baby, too weak to get up," said a hotel employee. Bill Bray and another bodyguard helped Michael to his feet and guided him to a freight elevator, where he would avoid the stares of other hotel guests.

The next day Michael collapsed again—this time after returning to the hotel following rehearsals. Again he was leaning on a burly bodyguard for support, and in the freight elevator he suddenly slid to the floor. When his bodyguards reached down to help him, he told them to leave him alone. He sat slumped on the floor with his head in his hands until the elevator arrived at the sixteenth floor.

While those around him worried about his health, Michael found time to brighten the lives of children suffering from life-threatening diseases. When the Brass Ring Society, an organization devoted to fulfilling the dreams of terminally ill children, contacted him about the plight of cystic fibrosis sufferer David Smithee, Michael invited the curly-headed fourteen-year-old from Tulsa to visit him in Encino.

Michael gave Smithee a tour of the mansion and his private menagerie, then taped an interview with his guest. They spent the rest of the afternoon playing video games. Before Smithee left, Michael opened up his closet and pulled out two leather jackets—the two-tone one he wore in the "Thriller" video and the red one from his "Beat It" video. Smithee chose the latter.

"It was one of the most wonderful experiences for the kid," said his stepfather, Steve Melton. At Michael's insistence, a last-minute change was made to the *Victory* album jacket design. Now, in addition to Katherine Jackson and the recently deceased Marvin Gaye, the album was dedicated to the memory of young Smithee.

Smithee was only one of dozens of seriously ill children Michael comforted. And when he read about an Oakland, California, woman who had received a heart transplant from her boyfriend, Michael invited her to spend the day with him and his animals and toys at Hayvenhurst. "It never made the papers," Norman Winter said. "Michael didn't want it to look like a publicity stunt."

According to Winter and others, many if not most of Michael's acts of kindness went unheralded. Winter recalled the case of an eight-year-old boy dying of cancer who was brought to Michael's hotel suite after a show. "They carry the kid's stretcher up to Michael's room, and he can hardly believe he is looking at Michael Jackson," Winter recalled.

"Then he raises his hand from beneath the sheet to touch Michael—and the kid's wearing a sequined glove. Frank Dileo started bawling like a baby. Then I lost it and had to leave. Every adult in the room was crying, but not Michael."

Oddly, no one reported having seen Michael cry or react with emotion when confronted by human suffering. Bob Michaelson, Michael's friend and business associate at the time, recalled being in several situations where seriously ill children—some with only days to live—were brought to him. "Once in Chicago this little kid was brought in in an iron lung. Frank Dileo and I were crying. I had to turn away, it was so moving," he said. "Who wouldn't cry? You'd have to be made of stone. But Michael never broke down. Never. Not even after the kid was taken away. He was all smiles."

When the boy in the iron lung left, Michaelson asked Michael how he managed to maintain his composure under these circumstances. "God, Michael, it's so sad," said Michaelson. "How do you keep from losing it?"

"You don't understand, Bob," Michael replied. "God put me on the earth for this. This is part of my life to do this for kids. I am His special messenger. There's no reason for me to get upset."

"You've got to hand him that much," Michaelson reflected. "He does do wonderful things for sick kids. But it always gave me the creeps. I can understand not wanting to upset the kid by crying when he's there. But *never* breaking down? That always impressed me as sort of, well, heartless."

As controversy concerning the upcoming Victory tour heated up, Michael became more and more concerned about security. With good reason. Threats against his life had increased tenfold. "I'm really scared this time," he confided to Winter. "It has never been this crazy before. I don't want to end up like John Lennon."

Yet one of the most disturbing incidents at Hayvenhurst involved someone obsessed not with Michael, but La Toya. On June 13 a crazed intruder with a knife in his belt scaled the wall surrounding the Jackson estate and fought with guards before being subdued. It was the sixth time Clarence Porter had been arrested for trespassing at Hayvenhurst. "I love her," he said of La Toya, whom he had never met. "We were made to be together. I'd like to marry La Toya. When we get married we'll have a normal married life with kids and everything.... Maybe we'll live at Michael's house for a while."

Not surprisingly, a siege mentality had developed within the Jackson camp. It soon became clear, as one insider put it, that "a bunch of bodyguards who look like Mr. T" would not be enough. This time out, the Jacksons would invade each city in a blur of helicopters, armored cars, vans, and decoys. "In and out," said one security adviser. "Surgical."

In the months leading up to the Victory tour, all was chaos—so much so that for a time many observers were predicting that it would never come off. Everyone knew there had been squabblings within the family, and Michael's disenchantment with the loquacious Don King had been evident ever since the disastrous Tavern on the Green press conference.

But even King, a novice to the world of rock concerts, realized he was in over his head and brought in MCA Records chief Irving Azoff, at a reputed fee of around $500,000, to advise him on such tour details as staging, lighting, and sound. Since the brothers had now returned to their Jackson Five days of rule by consensus, no decisions were being made. No fewer than fifteen lawyers, accountants, promoters, and managers stepped in to fill the void, only adding to the sense that no one was in charge.

"The talent in question is a diamond," said promoter Bill Graham, who as late as May 1984 still held out hope that he might be tapped as national tour director. "But if you saw the way things are being done around this talent, you'd think they were dealing with zircons."

Finally Dileo approached Chuck Sullivan, whose family owned the New England Patriots football team, and San Francisco 49ers owner Edward DeBartolo to promote the tour. They anted up $41 million—an offer the family couldn't resist. DeBartolo changed his mind when he was told the Jacksons expected to collect 85 percent of the ticket price. But Sullivan stuck it out. And to make this arrangement work, tickets would sell for $30 each—double the going rate at the time—and be sold only in blocks of four. A buyer without $120, therefore, was out of luck.

It did not stop there. Even if fans had the money, there was no guarantee that they would be able to obtain tickets. According to the promoters' scheme, the $120 money orders had to be sent to a New York P.O. box with a newspaper coupon. Buyers would then be selected lottery style. Assuming some twelve million fans shelled out for the forty-plus concert dates, that meant $1.5 *billion* in sales. But since only a little over one million tickets were available, the rest of the money—well over $1.3 billion—would have to be returned. That, however, would take about two months—a period during which the Jacksons stood to collect well over $100 million in interest on that money.

Moreover, there were rampant complaints that the Jacksons and their promoters were making unreasonable demands: for free stadium rental, free hotel rooms, free newspaper ads, and breaks on local and state taxes. With no one in command, dates were not booked until the last minute. Tickets went unsold. The schedule dwindled from forty-two to a mere thirteen cities. The legacy of all this avarice and confusion was to be a series of lawsuits that lingered long after the tour itself was finally over.

As star of the family, Michael became a lightning rod for criticism. He was accused of being greedy, callous, and disloyal to the urban black fans who had made him a star but now could not afford to attend his concerts. "It absolutely reeks of arrogance," said *Atlanta Constitution* publisher David Easterly. "I wonder how much the guy and the people around him think of his fans?" It took an open letter in the *Dallas Morning News* written by an eleven-year-old to get Michael's attention. "How could you, of all people," she wrote, "be so selfish?"

At a press conference in the tour's kickoff venue, Kansas City, a bespangled Michael told reporters that he had read the letter in the *Dallas Morning News* and was moved—so moved, in fact, that he had demanded the promoters figure out a fairer way to distribute tickets. And that would include setting aside two thousand free seats at each concert for inner-city youngsters. He also announced that he intended to donate all his earnings from the tour to charity.

The next day—July 6, 1984—the most talked-about, written-about rock tour in history began at Kansas City's Arrowhead Stadium. Everyone held their breath to see if Michael could pull it off.

He did. Spectacularly. In a maelstrom of smoke, fire, lasers, and roaring sound, several giant, Muppet-like "Kreetons" appeared to play the heavies in a space age version of *The Sword in the Stone.* Randy was the Arthur of the moment, taking center stage to yank the sword from the rock and hold it aloft as lasers bounced off the blade. After Randy had dispatched the creatures, a celestial voice boomed as all the brothers materialized: "Arise, all the world, and behold the kingdom."

Then Michael and his brothers (without Jackie, who had injured his leg after his soon-to-be ex-wife Enid accidentally ran over him with the family car) launched into "Wanna Be Startin' Somethin'." With the exception of three songs led by Jermaine, Michael whipsawed, soared, pranced, posed, kicked, and spun his way through fifteen of the concert's remaining seventeen songs—wisely saving his "Beat It" and "Billie Jean" for the end of the show. While Michael wailed the paranoid lyrics of "Billie Jean," a pair of eyes stared from the giant video screen above.

Throughout there were dazzling pyrotechnics—strobes, multicolored laser storms, fireworks. But the most astonishing special effect, according to *Rolling Stone,* was Michael Jackson—"a human hydrofoil gliding through five costume changes and a dance bag of moonwalks."

In one revealing scene that he conceived, Michael writhed helpless on the floor beneath a mechanical spider with helicopter searchlight eyes. His lifeless body was then solemnly laid out on a bier beneath a silver sheet. Another flurry of special effects, and Michael levitated, disappeared, and was resurrected—as the leather-jacketed peace maker from "Beat It."

The Victory tour also served up plenty of oldies from "I Want You Back" and "The Love You Save" to "I'll Be There" and the "Shake Your Body (Down to the Ground)" finale. But because Michael refused to rehearse anything new, there was not a single song from the *Victory* album.

Reviewers in Boston, New York, and Philadelphia would praise Michael's performance. *Time* said the show was "a lot of—quite literal—bang for the buck." *Newsweek* concurred: "The enigmatic star is living up to his reputation as the reluctant Pied Piper of Pop. . . . The crowd gasps and screams, savoring not a fussy high-tech stage set, but the grace and beauty of a brilliant entertainer."

After three nights in Kansas City, the Jacksons rolled into Dallas like an invading army. The logistics were staggering. As soon as they had finished their gig in any given city, over one hundred workers packed up and loaded nearly one-half *million* pounds of equipment—including eleven hydraulic elevators, three stages (two indoor, one outdoor), and thirty-two tons of light and sound equipment—onto twenty-two semitrailers. While Michael relaxed aboard his private jet and his brothers made do in first class, this convoy then drove all night to make it to the next destination.

And so the Jackson juggernaut rolled on for the next six months before finally coming to a halt in December. Meantime, according to

Michael, there were a few fun times reminiscent of the Jackson Five tours—only now the fun times were with Uncle Tookie Dileo, not with his brothers.

On opening night in Kansas City, Michael cracked up when Dileo slipped and fell into the hotel pool fully clothed. In Washington he amused himself by grabbing hundred-dollar bills out of his manager's pocket and tossing them to the crowd below. Not long after in Florida, Michael surprised Dileo, who had a phobia about snakes, with his eight-foot-long boa constrictor, Muscles. Terrified, Dileo grabbed a security guard's gun and threatened to shoot it. Uncle Tookie had to be restrained. Michael laughed.

Michael, trying to recapture those mischievous moments from the Jackson Five days, tossed water balloons off balconies and had food fights in his hotel room—although he now engaged in these high jinks not with his grown brothers, but with Emmanuel Lewis, Sean Lennon, and other "special friends." According to hotel employees, Michael seemed happiest when he was with children or when he was alone. They also noted that even in crowded elevators, Michael made a habit of singing to himself.

In each city he visited, Michael put on one of his flashy band major getups and marched with a contingent from the local police force—all solemn faced and wearing sunglasses identical with his. In addition to cementing relations with the police, who provided additional security during the tour, these marches provide film footage for future video projects and valuable publicity shots.

Michael found other, highly original ways to amuse himself on tour—using his falsetto to impersonate women on the telephone, for instance. He would phone someone from the tour—usually a musician—and whisper in his sexiest Diana Ross voice, "I noticed you with the band tonight, and I thought you were very cute. I would like to meet you." Then he would arrange a rendezvous somewhere within view of his hotel window—usually on a street corner. Using a pair of binoculars, he then watched his victim's facial reactions as he waited in vain for his ravishing mystery woman to materialize.

"So there you are," one victim recalled, "standing right out in the open, waiting for this beautiful girl to come along, and Michael is up in his room laughing his sides off. Later he will get all the guys to his room, and everyone listens to your conversation with this 'girl' on tape, and there sits Michael with this big grin on his face."

Michael was in high spirits when, at one point during the tour, he had his photograph taken with Donny Osmond, a casual friend since the days when the Osmonds tried with some limited success to imitate the Jackson Five. "They were both kid stars at the same time in the late sixties, early seventies," Norman Winter said. "So there was a rapport there."

When they met, Michael asked Osmond, a devout Mormon, if it was true that Mormons look down on blacks. "Oh, no," insisted an embarrassed Osmond. "Mormons aren't prejudiced against blacks."

Then could blacks become Mormons? Michael wanted to know. At the time, blacks could not become elders of the church, Osmond allowed, but they could become members.

The next morning a photo of Michael and Donny Osmond appeared in *USA Today*. Michael was livid—not because of their conversation about the Mormons' policy concerning blacks, but because he did not want people to know he was a friend of Donny Osmond. "Michael hit the roof," Winter recalled. "He'd had sort of a Goody Two-shoes image, and he wanted to get away from it. Now here he was with *Donny Osmond*. Michael told us to destroy all the prints of him with Donny. It was so funny, we started calling the whole thing 'Donnygate.' "

Funny to everyone but Michael, apparently. Not long after Donnygate, Osmond tried to approach Michael for career advice. "Michael had gotten so big, Donny wanted to know how he did it," Winter said. "So he flew from his home in Chicago to Encino." But instead of being greeted by his old friend, Osmond "was kept waiting for hours. Michael never did see him. He stayed upstairs playing computer games with a friend. Donny was really angry, really pissed."

Not long after, Michael did offer Osmond a couple of career tips. He suggested that he distance himself from his wholesome past, and that he exchange "Donny" for a more macho-sounding "Don." According to Winter, "that made Donny even angrier. They haven't spoken since."

More satisfying for Michael was a staged encounter with the other musical colossus who had taken his act on the road in the summer of 1984, Bruce Springsteen. The two crossed paths in Philadelphia, where they met for the first time in the reception room of Michael's hotel suite. The awkward tête-à-tête was treated like a superpower summit. "It felt like history," gushed one witness to the momentous event.

It was, of course, all for public consumption, and cameras were clicking as they exchanged small talk. Michael, clearly nervous, made eye contact only fleetingly as Springsteen sucked on an ice cube. Fidgeting, Michael finally pulled his secretary, Shari, between them and told Springsteen that she wanted him for Christmas.

"What's wrong with Thanksgiving?" Springsteen cracked. Michael seemed not to get the joke. He then expressed surprise that Springsteen told stories to concertgoers between songs. "They like to hear a voice do something besides singing," Springsteen said. They go wild when you just . . . talk."

"Oh, I could never do that." Michael shuddered. "It feels like people are learning something about you they shouldn't know."

Later Springsteen asked, "Don't you ever go out?"

"I can't," Michael replied without taking into account Springsteen's own megacelebrity status. "Too many people would bother me."

Springsteen may have walked away feeling Michael was paranoid, but he was not aware that Michael had been the object of several serious death threats during the tour. "If you think the massacre at McDonald's was bad," read one letter, "you just wait until you see what we've got laid up for you." The letter, titled "A Warning," referred to the murder of twenty-two people at a San Diego McDonald's only a few weeks before.

The Victory tour was a draining experience for Michael. While the brothers were at first delighted that the tour had actually come off without a hitch, petty jealousies began to surface. Chiefly the brothers disliked the fact that Michael was, as usual, grabbing all the glory.

Within weeks tempers were frayed. There had been an agreement among the brothers that only they would ride in the armored van that took them to and from the arenas. When Michael carried Emmanuel Lewis into the van, an argument ensued. From then on each brother drove to and from each concert in his own limousine.

Michael had not hesitated to fire a stage hand during rehearsals back in California. Now he was throwing his weight around, holing up in his room, demanding that a certain publicist he had come to dislike be fired or he would not go on stage. "The pressure on him was tremendous," Norman Winter said. "He had to carry the ball during the tour, then between shows come back to California to work on other things. He resented being in that position."

More than ever Michael was finding solace in the company of children. "Everything was crashing down around him," Winter said, "but there would be Michael in his hotel room, reading a comic book with a kid."

Then there were always fears for his safety. Even when he returned to Hayvenhurst during breaks in the tour, Michael, still receiving death threats, was constantly shadowed by guards. "Oh, if I could only breathe for once," he told La Toya. One day he made a break for it. "That is it!" he declared. "I don't want any security. I'm going for a ride."

With that he sped off in La Toya's black Mercedes 450 SL. But it was only a matter of minutes before he was spotted and followed by two carloads of girls. He made it to Beverly Hills, where he ran out of gas. Michael then leapt out of the car and, with the screaming fans in hot pursuit, sprinted to the safety of Quincy Jones's house.

When the Victory tour landed at Madison Square Garden, Michael spent all his spare time with nine-year-old Sean Lennon, whose father, John Lennon, had been gunned down outside the Dakota in New York four years earlier. Young Lennon had badgered his mother, Yoko Ono, into arranging an introduction, and the two became instant pals.

In addition to making the rounds of video arcades and pizza parlors, Michael and Sean took in several Broadway shows, including *The Tap Dance Kid* (starring his old friend Alfonso Ribeiro) and *Cats*. By the summer of 1984 it was not unusual for Sean to stay with Michael in his Helmsley Palace hotel suite until the early morning hours, when he would be escorted home by Michael's bodyguards.

After Sean returned to his exclusive Swiss boarding school in the fall, Yoko Ono reportedly left specific instructions with the headmaster that the school was to put through calls only from her or from Michael Jackson. Whenever Sean was in the United States, Yoko was apparently so convinced of Michael's good intentions that she dropped her son off at Michael's estate in Encino for up to a week at a time.

There was another welcome addition to life at Hayvenhurst: Bubbles the baby chimp. Rescued from certain death in a cancer lab, Bubbles wore a diaper that Michael changed regularly like any other responsible "parent."

"He was absolutely in love with that chimp," Bob Michaelson said. "Who wouldn't be? We all were. Bubbles was so cute, so *human*. Michael carried him around everywhere." Michael often ate with Bubbles at the dining room table, and the two spent hours playing together in Michael's off-limits room. One afternoon when his mother knocked on the door, Michael threw a full-fledged tantrum. She had interrupted a tea party he was having with Bubbles.

Then there were the perks. Bubbles was assigned his own bodyguard, always rode in a limo, and was assigned his own hotel room whenever he traveled with his owner. Michael even instructed his costume designer to create 20 matching outfits for himself and Bubbles, including a chimp-size tuxedo.

Soon Bubbles would become almost as well-known as his owner—thanks to the efforts of Dileo, Branca, and especially Norman Winter. Since joining Michael in the late 1970s, Winter had been asked to work a number of public relations miracles for his client—beginning in 1979 with Michael's desire, now that he was an adult with a solo career, to be on the cover of *Rolling Stone*. The philosophy at most major publications at the time was simple: When it came to cover subjects, it was often stated at story conferences that "blacks don't sell magazines."

Thus it was no surprise when, after Winter approached *Rolling Stone* founder and publisher Jan Wenner, proposing that the magazine do a story on his client, Wenner wrote back: "We would very much like to do a major piece on Michael Jackson, but feel it is not a cover story."

"Michael was furious at this idea that he wasn't cover material," Winter recalled. "Of course, before long Wenner was writing back begging Michael to cooperate for a cover story. Michael has both letters framed and hanging on his wall."

While the Victory tour would make it into the *Guinness Book of World Records* as the biggest ever, the album fared less well. Even though he did only two songs on the album, Michael controlled every detail—right down to the cover design. Artist Michael Whelan had to redo Michael's photograph four times because "he was not happy with his face. One time, he wanted it painted with a mustache, then changed his mind and had me remove it. Michael also wasn't happy with the way he was positioned. I had him out front of the rest of the brothers, and he said he wanted all the brothers to be depicted as equals. Even after thousands of copies of the record jacket were printed, Michael ordered a recall. He wanted a white dove to be painted on brother Randy's shoulder."

Victory did sell a not unimpressive three million copies (compared with two million for the Jacksons' *Triumph* album). But it was eclipsed in the summer of 1984 by Prince's number one album *Purple Rain*. Perhaps predictably, there developed a not-so-friendly rivalry between the two stars. Michael simply did not like anything about Prince—not his singing (which Michael felt was a pale imitation of his own), not his persona, not his personality. But he was, in the words of a friend, "incredibly jealous" of Prince's success as a filmmaker.

More than just "cute," at age twelve in 1970 Michael Jackson was already a dynamic performer and undisputed star of the Jackson Five.

1

2

Diana Ross took credit for discovering the Jackson Five, photographed with her in 1970. But it was actually Gladys Knight who first brought them to Motown's attention. From left: Jackie, Tito, Marlon, Michael, and Jermaine.

3

Michael tears through "I Want You Back" on the Jackson Five's first television special on September 19, 1971.

America's hottest new group, the Jackson Five, played to sold-out audiences of screaming fans and recorded albums that soared to the tops of the charts.

4

Father and son were all smiles in public, but behind the scenes Joe Jackson terrorized Michael and his brothers both physically and emotionally.

5

6

"He seemed different to me from the other children," Katherine Jackson said of her son Michael, shown here at a Hollywood function in 1975. She withstood her husband's abusive tactics and numerous infidelities to keep the family together.

Michael as the Scarecrow in *The Wiz*, his first—and thus far only—feature film role. His performance got rave reviews, but the film was a dismal flop.

7

8

Michael and Tatum O'Neal celebrated when sales of the Jacksons' *Destiny* album topped the one million mark in June 1979. O'Neal was one of Michael's many high-profile dates in attempts to quell rumors that he was gay.

Backstage at Madison Square Garden during the Jacksons' 1981 *Triumph* tour, Michael wore the single white sequined glove that would become his trademark.

9

10

When he became part owner of Hayvenhurst in 1981, Michael transformed the family estate into a mock Tudor wonderland.

Paul McCartney and Michael recorded the hit duets "The Girl Is Mine" and "Say Say Say." McCartney would later attack his old friend for buying up the rights to the Beatles' songs and allowing them to be used in television commercials.

11

12

13

Jermaine was clearly unaware that Michael's hair was ablaze as he descended a staircase during the filming of a Pepsi commercial in 1984. Moments later Michael bravely raised his gloved hand as he was rushed to the hospital.

14

Diana Ross and her twenty-five-year-old protégé at the 1984 American Music Awards. Still obsessed with Ross, Michael had already undergone plastic surgery to look more like his idol—and to eradicate any resemblance to his father.

Michael's dates for the 1984 Grammys were Brooke Shields and Emmanuel Lewis, twelve. "Let's get out of here!" Shields said. "Everybody is making fun of us."

15

16

Ronald Reagan and First Lady Nancy presented Michael with a presidential award in 1984. Minutes later he locked himself in a White House bathroom and refused to come out.

Fraught with dissension and controversy, the Victory tour in 1984 was supposed to be Michael's parting gift to his brothers. They had lost interest in performing together, and he preferred to focus on his own solo career. 17

This photograph of Michael "sleeping" in a hyperbaric chamber to preserve his youth added to the public's growing perception that he was weird. The tabloids dubbed him "Wacko Jacko," an image he would later try desperately to dispel. 18

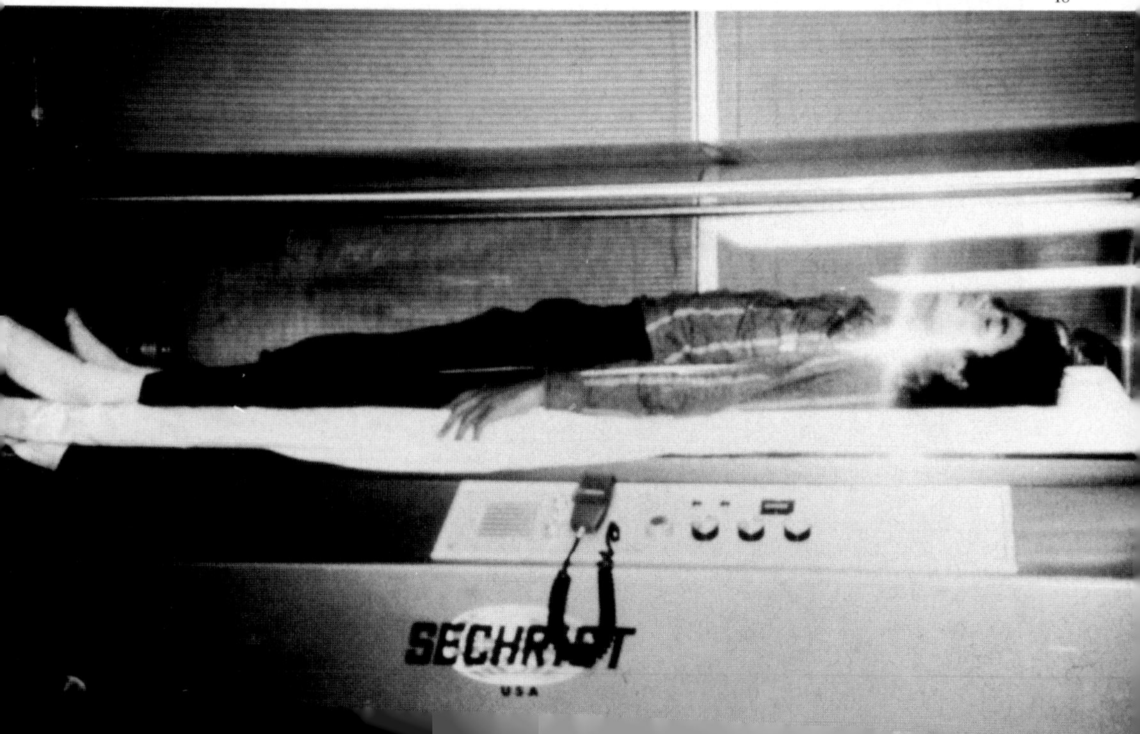

With his sidekick Fuzzball perched on his shoulder, Michael's Captain EO waged an intergalactic war against the forces of evil. The 1986 3-D film adventure, directed by George Lucas, was one of Disney's most popular attractions.

19

Sean Lennon visited Michael in the Brooklyn subway station where he filmed his *Bad* video in 1986. John and Yoko's only child routinely spent a week at a time with Michael.

20

Buckled and zippered, Michael unveiled his *Bad* image in 1987 and could now claim to be the most popular—and highest paid—performer in the world. Mysteriously, he was now adding "1998" to his autograph.

21

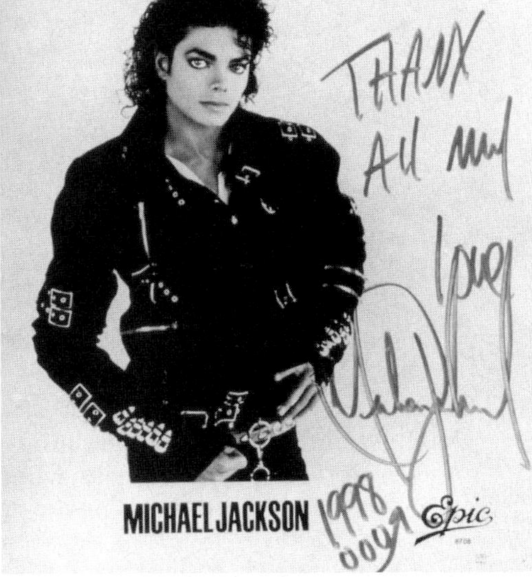

22

Liza Minnelli joined Michael and his then constant companion, ten-year-old Jimmy Safechuck, backstage at *Phantom of the Opera* in March 1988. Michael bought Safechuck's parents a Rolls-Royce.

Despite its remote location, Michael's Neverland ranch was bordered by two schools. A few feet from the main entrance to Neverland was the Family School's playground—complete with treehouse, basketball courts, swings, and sandbox.

23

24

Michael built his own private amusement park at Neverland and lived there in carefully guarded seclusion, some said to re-create the childhood he never had.

Michael with Mark and Faye Quindoy, who worked as housekeepers at Neverland between 1988 and 1990. The Quindoys later told police they had witnessed Michael fondling young boys.

25

Quincy Jones, Michael's musical mentor, and Whitney Houston were on hand in 1988 when Michael received his first degree, an honorary doctorate in humanities, from Fisk University president Henry Ponder.

26

27

Before giving a concert at London's Wembley Stadium in July 1988, Michael presented Princess Diana and Prince Charles with *Bad* tour jackets custom-made for their sons, William and Henry.

Michael on stage in Rome with *Bad* tour backup singer Sheryl Crow, one of several young women he was falsely linked to romantically.

28

29

Michael and his date, Madonna, decked out in $20 million worth of diamonds, caused a sensation at Swifty Lazar's 1991 post-Oscar party at Spago. The outspoken Madonna later said Michael looked like "a space alien drag queen."

30

Sporting his newest affectation—a plaster cast—Michael posed with a leopard to publicize his *Black or White* video. His violent and sexually suggestive actions in the video ignited an international furor.

31

Iman was pharaoh Eddie Murphy's unfaithful queen in Michael's *Remember the Time* video. During the filming, Michael's awkward attempt to kiss Iman proved a major embarrassment.

32

Michael succeeded in steaming up the screen with supermodel Naomi Campbell in his *In the Closet* video. But at age thirty-five he shyly confessed to being a virgin and said he was saving himself for marriage.

33

Macaulay Culkin, shown here with his best friend Michael and Mickey Mouse at Disney World, spent most of his vacations at Neverland. When they were apart, Michael called the child star two or three times a day.

34

Michael arrived in London in March 1992 with ten-year-old Brett Barnes, one of the special friends he introduced as his "cousin."

35

Michael shared an intimate moment with Elizabeth Taylor at a party in her honor at New York's Tavern on the Green in 1992. Cynics said their friendship was for publicity purposes only, until Taylor came to Michael's aid when he was accused of child molestation.

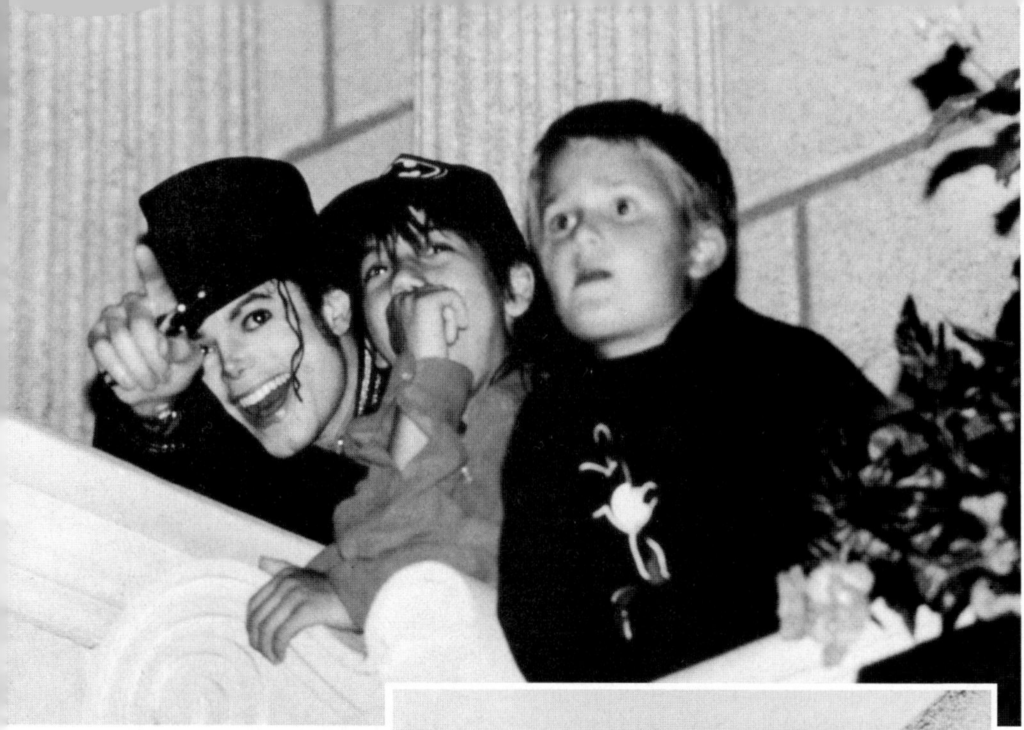

36

Michael took time out from his *Dangerous* tour in 1992 to escort Brett Barnes and nine-year-old Bavarian prince Albert von Thurn und Taxis, one of the richest boys in the world, around Euro Disney.

Fan Eric Herminie clung to the sixth-floor ledge of a building opposite Michael's London hotel in 1992, threatening to jump if he couldn't see his idol. When Michael appeared on a balcony and waved, Herminie agreed to come down and seek psychiatric help.

37

On a break from the tour, Michael sneaked into a Warner Brothers screening of Prince's film *Purple Rain*. Not only was it the sleeper hit of the summer, but the movie went on to win an Oscar for best score—one of the few awards coveted but never won by Michael.

Michael sat unnoticed in the screening room, and when the film was over he did not budge from his seat. This upstart had been on the scene for just a few short years, had scored only a few hits, clearly had negligible acting talent—and already had a box office blockbuster under his belt. What, Michael wanted to know, was Prince's secret?

Not long after viewing *Purple Rain*, Michael invited Prince to Hayvenhurst for dinner with La Toya and Janet. But if he had any hopes of pumping Prince for advice, they were dashed when he discovered that Prince was just as taciturn as he was. Host and guest barely exchanged a word, although the five-foot-tall Prince made several less-than-subtle passes at La Toya. When it was over, Prince handed Michael an unwrapped box and departed. Inside were some leaves, twigs, and a tape that when played backward contained some satanic-sounding chants.

Like Mick Jagger, Prince was known to dabble in the occult. Was he, too, trying to cast a spell on his arch rival? Again Michael claimed that he was far too religious ever to be affected by witchcraft.

According to one observer, Prince was obsessed with his musical arch rival, and at one point wondered aloud if Michael was a "warlock." Prince and his minions would watch Michael's every move—right down to monitoring the many court cases Michael would become embroiled in over the years. At least one litigant in a suit against Michael claimed Prince's aides contacted her repeatedly with offers of information and help in pressing her case.

The similarities between these two eccentric young superstars did not elude the press. "Who rules the music kingdom—Prince or Michael?" asked the teenage magazine *Right On!*. Even *The New York Times* devoted a major piece to the question. Calling them "a perfectly matched pair of alter egos," the *Times*'s Michiko Kakutani went on to point out that "both mix black and white idioms in their music, and both have shattered race barriers in the record business. Both are recluses who refuse to do interviews; and both play coy with conventional racial and sexual definitions." Yet both, she added, were "at two poles": Prince "insidious, threatening, and darkly sexual"; Michael "sunnily upbeat and wholesome."

For his part Michael was particularly irritated by Prince's ability to maintain an image as a "darkly sexual" ladykiller even though he was just as effeminate and wore more makeup and frillier clothes than he did. "I just don't understand it," Michael said. "So he's got some girls in his band. Big deal."

For whatever reason, Michael was once again fodder for comedians everywhere. Joan Rivers, who in 1984 was at the height of her career as Johnny Carson's *Tonight* show heir apparent and the country's hottest stand-up comic, took special delight in ridiculing Jackson's sex life.

"Is Michael Jackson gay?" Rivers quipped in her nightclub act. "*Please,* he's as queer as a three-dollar bill. Ever wonder what happened to Michael Jackson's other glove? It's in Boy George's pocket!" Referring to her own sequined dress, she cracked, "I found this dress in the closet right next to Michael Jackson. Michael Jackson is gay. He makes Liberace look like a Green Beret."

Through intermediaries Michael asked Rivers to quit. But Rivers, whose other favorite target at the time was Elizabeth Taylor, had no intention of easing up. And comics weren't the only ones having a field day with the issues of Michael's sexuality. Lamenting the lack of strong role models for young black males, controversial Muslim leader Louis Farrakhan urged his followers not to follow in Michael's "sissified" footsteps.

The issue reached the boiling point in late August 1984, when the *National Enquirer* reported that Michael and Boy George, the flamboyantly gay lead singer of Culture Club, were having an affair. The story was not true; like Queen's Freddie Mercury and Wham's George Michael, Boy George intrigued Michael as a performer and personality. The two were casual friends.

"One day Michael got on the cellular phone and called me," Norman Winter said. "He really was in anguish over the Boy George story. He felt all these little kids who were barely tall enough to reach the news rack would read this stuff and believe it."

Michael then told Winter that he wanted to respond publicly to the charge. "I was totally against it," Winter said, "but he was so upset, crying, and he insisted."

On September 5, 1984, Jackson called a press conference in Los Angeles. He did not attend, leaving it to Frank Dileo to face an audience of fifty incredulous reporters and read Michael's prepared statement:

"For some time now, I have been searching my conscience as to whether or not I should publicly react to the many falsehoods that have been spread about me. I have decided to make this statement based on the injustice of these allegations and the far-reaching trauma those who feel close to me are suffering.

"I feel very fortunate to have been blessed with recognition for my efforts. This recognition also brings with it a responsibility to one's admirers throughout the world. Performers should always serve as role models who set an example for young people. It saddens me that many may actually believe the present flurry of false accusations.

"To this end, and I do mean *end*—

"No! I've never taken hormones to maintain my high voice.

"No! I've never had my cheekbones altered in any way.

"No! I've never had cosmetic surgery on my eyes.

"Yes! One day in the future I plan to get married and have a family. Any statements to the contrary are simply untrue.

"Henceforth, as new fantasies are printed, I have advised my attorneys of my willingness to institute legal action and subsequently prosecute all guilty to the fullest extent of the law.

"As noted earlier, I love children. We all know that kids are very impressionable and therefore susceptible to such stories. I'm certain that some have already been hurt by this terrible slander. In addition to their admiration, I would like to keep their respect."

When he was finished reading his boss's statement, Dileo left the job of answering reporters' questions to Winter. Winter conceded that he had not wanted Michael to hold such a bizarre press conference but added that his boss was "undaunted. He's fed up with the lies."

Michael's outrage over the Boy George rumors may have had less to do with his pride than with the dollars-and-cents issue of his marketability. He had indeed received a few letters from boys asking how they could go about getting hormone shots so they could sound like him. But most disturbing of all were the hundreds of letters from young girls who begged him to tell them he wasn't gay. Michael knew the power of his female audience. He had seen how his brothers fell from grace as soon as they married and ceased to be the objects of girls' fantasies.

"Now if kids want to grow up and marry Michael Jackson," Winter said after the press conference, "they know they've got a chance." But in reality he thought the whole episode was "comical. I mean, there is Frank Dileo, with his cigar and that gruff voice, reading that statement: 'I don't take hormones. . . .' It was *hysterical.* But I've got to say, in the end everybody, including Frank and Michael, thought it came off well. The rumors quieted down—for a while, anyway."

No sooner had he handled the rampant rumors of his sexuality than Michael was dealt another blow—the elopement of eighteen-year-old Janet with singer James DeBarge, twenty-one. La Toya called her siblings with the news—with the exception of Michael, who had come to regard the quiet, immensely talented Janet as his alter ego within the family.

No one, in fact, had the courage to tell Michael; he only learned of the marriage when Quincy Jones's daughter let it slip out. Michael later conceded that he was "shocked—it killed me to see her go off and get married." Again, there was legitimate cause for concern. The groom, a member of the family group DeBarge, had a history of drug and alcohol abuse. He had been involved with Janet for three years, and their relationship had been a stormy one.

Despite the entire family's opposition to Janet's marriage, the newlyweds moved into Hayvenhurst shortly after their wedding. DeBarge's erratic behavior soon led to the inevitable violent confrontations with Joe, who reportedly more than once threatened to kill his new son-in-law.

Given his own natural flair for the dramatic, DeBarge called Hayvenhurst "the House of Fears," although not just because everyone lived in constant terror of Joe. It seemed to DeBarge, as it did to nearly everyone who spent any length of time there, that a pall hung over the House of Jackson. At one time or another, La Toya would later admit, every single Jackson talked of committing suicide—including Michael.

"It was while I lived there," DeBarge said, "that I came to realize what a sad, lonely figure Michael Jackson is. He was like a ghost wandering around the place looking for friendship. He had Bubbles the chimp on his arm—all dressed up in a diaper so that he didn't mess up the place."

One night the newlyweds were in the passionate throes of lovemaking when an apparition appeared at the foot of their bed. It was Michael, staring intently at his sister and brother-in-law. Unfazed, he then crawled into bed alongside the couple and, DeBarge recalled, "poured his heart out."

"I envy you two," Michael told them, "because you have each other and love each other. But I," he added wistfully, "haven't got anyone."

At other times, DeBarge would say, Michael would tap softly on the door and say, "Is it all right if I come in?" before unloading once more on his sympathetic sister and her frustrated new husband.

Michael's complaint that he didn't "have anyone" was not altogether accurate, according to DeBarge. Michael was spending more and more time with little Sean Lennon—sometimes days at a time in his room, watching television, playing games, roughhousing on the floor.

In a taped conversation with a police informant in 1993 as reported in the British papers, DeBarge revealed that one morning he peeked into Michael's room and saw him in bed with Sean. Asked if he saw Michael and Sean together in a sexual way, DeBarge reportedly replied, "Yes."

DeBarge went on, "My room was next door. I saw them when I was snooping. Michael knew it, too. But he didn't care. I guess he figured I was no threat."

Michael now kept volumes of photographs of child actors and models in his room, and he pored through them in search of children—usually boys aged nine to thirteen—to "audition" for future projects. Over the next several years Michael's bodyguards were instructed, according to court papers filed in Los Angeles in 1993, to smuggle many of these boys into the house at all hours of the day or night. In some instances Michael telephoned in advance to find out if either Katherine or Joe was home or away. If they were home, he asked if they had gone to bed. "If the parents were gone or had retired for the night," the guards recalled, "he would then arrive alone with a young boy typically appearing to be between nine and fourteen years of age. Upon arrival at the grounds, he would drive to an area near his suite in the compound."

They would then enter by a spiral staircase that led directly to Michael's room. From that point, the bodyguards continued, Michael would "disappear with the young boy into his suite sometimes for several hours, sometimes for the entire night." Or longer, in some cases. "All the boys would sleep in bed with him," DeBarge said—a fact later confirmed not only by Michael's own lawyers, but by the boys themselves.

At least once, according to the bodyguards, Michael had them hide "a young Asian boy believed to be somewhere between nine and fourteen years of age in the guard shack until Michael called to say his parents had left the estate."

Because his drug problem made him a virtual pariah within the family, DeBarge said that Michael did nothing to conceal his playmates from him. On one rainy night when DeBarge admitted he "wasn't supposed to be there," he saw Michael "running around naked with a boy."

As for those auditions: "He had all the boys over to the house to audition for his videos," DeBarge said, "more than he needed. If you went near his room when he was with them, he'd say, 'We're practicing.' He didn't want anyone watching." But around DeBarge he made little effort to conceal his activities. "He got away with it so many times, he became comfortable," DeBarge said. "After doing it so many times, you feel you don't have to hide anymore. He did it right in front of me. He knew I saw him and that I knew he was doing it, but he just kept right on doing it. He trusted me."

Michael was right. For nearly a decade—until one of Michael's special friends ignited the biggest show business scandal in history—DeBarge, like so many others, said nothing. By the time he stumbled upon Michael in bed with Sean Lennon, DeBarge claimed to be "unshockable."

Katherine was well aware of her son's visits with Lennon. When the bodyguards claimed in a 1993 lawsuit that one of the children they secreted at the guardhouse had Asian features, Michael's mother inadvertently aggravated her son's situation by confirming that the mystery boy was Sean Lennon. "Sean would come and visit," she said, "and stay about a week." Did Katherine believe that her son might have been molesting these children? "She knows," DeBarge claimed. "Living at that house is a nightmare." Elliot Mintz, Yoko Ono's spokesman and a longtime Lennon family friend, often escorted Sean to Hayvenhurst and claimed the boy was never dropped off at the guardhouse. Mintz described DeBarge's recollections as "nonsense. Sean is a very hip and sophisticated kid," said Mintz. "He had to grow up real fast after his father's death. If anything wrong was going on between him and Michael, he would have reacted appropriately and said something. He never did." Sean Lennon and Michael remain close friends.

However unshockable he claimed to be, DeBarge found Michael's affectionate relationship with Bubbles unsettling. He often watched as Michael changed the chimp's diapers with all the loving tenderness of a new dad. "He'd drop everything to change Bubbles," said another frequent visitor to Hayvenhurst. "He'd talk baby talk to him while he was doing it."

All this child's play stood in stark contrast with Michael's Byzantine business dealings. Over an eight-month period beginning in September 1984 and ending in March 1985, Michael and his shrewd lawyer, John Branca, worked quietly to pull off the biggest deal in music publishing history.

Remembering what Paul McCartney had told him about all the

money to be made simply from owning the copyrights to songs, Michael had already acquired the rights to Dion's "Runaround Sue" and "The Wanderer," as well as the entire Sly and the Family Stone catalog (including "Hot Fun in the Summertime" and "Everyday People"). Now he instructed Branca to keep an eye out for any catalogs that came on the market.

When Branca discovered that ATV Music Publishing and its four-thousand-song catalog was available to the highest bidder, it was as if he had found the Holy Grail. In pop music terms he had, for ATV owned, in addition to the biggest hits of Little Richard and the Pointer Sisters, *all* the Beatles' tunes written between 1964 and 1971. A small sample—"A Hard Day's Night," "Ticket to Ride," "Help," "Michelle," "Norwegian Wood," "Eleanor Rigby," "Penny Lane," "Yesterday," "Strawberry Fields Forever," "Let It Be," "Good Day Sunshine," "Yellow Submarine," "Revolution," "Hey Jude," "The Long and Winding Road," "The Fool on the Hill," "All You Need Is Love."

The only person who lusted after ATV as much as Michael was the man who wrote these classic pop tunes, Paul McCartney. But when he had had the chance three years earlier to buy the catalog for $20 million, McCartney could not convince John Lennon's widow, Yoko Ono, to become his partner in the deal. Now that the asking price was twice that amount, McCartney was definitely not in the running.

Through skill and, in the words of one former ally, "sheer ruthlessness," Branca managed to outmaneuver the competition. A higher bid by music industry wheeler-dealer Charles Koppelman was thwarted when Branca pulled strings to see that Koppelman's financing dried up at the last minute. That cleared the way for Michael to buy ATV—for a record $47.5 million.

Understandably, McCartney was furious over what he viewed as an outright betrayal by his friend. For months after the deal's completion, the former Beatle refused to speak with Michael. But he also blamed himself for having given Michael a crash course on the subject years earlier. "A fish gets caught," he said ruefully, "by opening its mouth." To add insult to injury, as part of the ATV package dating back to 1971, Michael now owned a $5 million policy on McCartney's life.

McCartney would never get over the fact that Michael was paid twice as much for his songs as he was (royalties were split between Michael on the one side and McCartney and Ono on the other). But equally galling for McCartney was Michael's decision to commercialize songs that he—and millions of Beatles fans—regarded as sacrosanct. Over the next few years Michael would license one Beatles song after another for use as commercial jingles ("Revolution" to Nike, "All You Need Is Love" to Panasonic, "Good Day Sunshine" to Sunshine Bakeries). Each time McCartney would lash out in the press.

Eventually Jackson would be fed up with McCartney's whining. "Michael figured Paul had more than enough chances to buy the catalog if it meant that much to him," said a friend, "and at half the price. I think Michael half expected Paul to be proud of him for pulling the whole thing off. After all, when it came to this game, Paul taught him everything he knew. . . ."

As the Victory tour rolled into Los Angeles' Dodger Stadium in December 1984 for its last few performances, major problems persisted. The tour had lost its promoter millions, largely because of the enormous overhead (it cost $1 million a week just to move all the equipment from city to city). But none of that mattered to the Jacksons, who had demanded their money up front.

What did concern Michael was news that the final concert—hyped by Don King as a "historic event"—had not sold out. In fact, it looked as if the Jacksons might be playing to a house that was one-third empty. Michael blamed this snafu on Frank Dileo, who at the last minute had added three extra concerts. Uncle Tookie or no, Dileo learned through the grapevine that Michael planned to terminate his employment if he couldn't fill the stadium. In a desperate last-minute effort, Dileo and everyone else in the Jackson camp gave away thousands of tickets—to family members, friends, neighbors, schoolchildren, even strangers on the street.

While everyone scrambled to fill stadium seats, Michael handled yet another emergency. On December 7 he flew to Chicago to testify in a $5 million copyright infringement case against CBS. A thirty-two-year-old Illinois songwriter by the name of Fred Sanford claimed "The Girl Is Mine" was actually cribbed from a song he wrote in 1981 titled "Please Love Me Now."

As with many future cases in which Michael was the defendant, the appearance of judicial impartiality flew out the window. In this case, while fans lined up outside the U.S. district court hoping to catch a glimpse of Michael, the judge's fifteen-year-old daughter was accorded a front row seat. She then got to meet Michael in her father's chambers. "I'll never wash this hand again," gushed the teenager. "He's so cute. I wish I could take him home. He pointed to a picture on the wall and asked if it was me. He was so shy, he kept turning away."

When he testified, Michael was equally self-effacing. "I woke up from my sleep and wrote the song," he said in a barely audible voice. "And I went over to the tape recorder and sang into it and wrote what was in my head." Michael then launched into a hand-clapping, finger-popping demonstration of how he composed, right down to mimicking the instruments and, of course, tailoring the lyrics to the melody. "It was," said one observer, "an amazing show."

The jury, spellbound and undeniably star-struck, ruled in Michael's favor. It was a courtroom strategy that Michael would employ again and again to counter repeated charges that he plagiarized other people's songs.

Back in Los Angeles, Dileo was relieved that the great ticket giveaway seemed to be working. The press could hardly ignore the bizarre turn of events, however, and the public was left to wonder if perhaps Michael wasn't the biggest star in the cosmos after all. Bruce Springsteen had no trouble selling out his concerts in a matter of hours. Michael vowed that he would never let anything this humiliating happen to him again.

No one else in the Jackson camp attached much importance to the foul-up. King and the Jacksons were already making plans to take the whole extravaganza around the world. Michael said nothing—until the last concert was over. Then he grabbed a microphone and announced to the audience, "This is our last and final show. It's been a long twenty years and we love you all." Period.

That Christmas season shoppers lined up to plunk down $8.95 for Wallaby Books' *Official Michael Jackson 1985 Calendar*. During a session with Los Angeles photographer Matthew Rolston, Michael had indulged his passion for disguises and fantasy, donning a different getup for each month. He was, among other things, a musketeer, a circus clown, a sailor, an animal trainer, and—most revealing of all—a pensive, jewel-bedecked monarch. "Michael is absolutely like royalty," Rolston commented. "There's a princelike air about him."

In keeping with Michael's Jehovah's Witness faith—and his own philosophy of life—the calendar listed not one holiday.

13

You dance till your side hurts and you take oxygen. Then you hide. That's not happiness.

—Jermaine Jackson on his brother Michael

Now that the acrimonious Victory tour was at last behind him—now that he could mark the debt to his family "Paid in Full"—Michael withdrew into his shell. When he was not doting on the newest addition to his menagerie—an eight-month-old giraffe—or playing with Sean Lennon and his other, less famous, young friends, Michael sifted through countless offers.

One he could not refuse came from Harry Belafonte. The calypso singer, movie star, and humanitarian had been so moved by a television documentary concerning the efforts of an Australian physician caring for starving youngsters in Ethiopia that he decided to do something about it.

Belafonte first contacted socially conscious show business manager Ken Kragen, who came up with the idea of doing something along the the lines of "Do They Know It's Christmas?," the holiday record British rockers had banded together to do on behalf of Ethiopian relief. Kragen's clients Lionel Richie and Kenny Rogers were the first aboard, followed closely by Stevie Wonder and Michael.

Belafonte and Kragen dubbed their pet project USA (United Support of Artists) for Africa, and tapped Michael and Richie to co-write the song. Quincy Jones signed on as arranger and conductor. Meanwhile

Kragen corraled the biggest names in the music industry. More than one hundred artists volunteered, but only forty were chosen. Among them were Bruce Springsteen, Billy Joel, Tina Turner, Bob Dylan, Diana Ross, Willie Nelson, Paul Simon, Ray Charles, Cyndi Lauper, Dionne Warwick, and Bette Midler.

Surrounded by the mannequins, dolls, costumes, toys, and medical oddities that littered his room, Michael and Richie wrote "We Are the World" over a one-week period. Much of the time was spent trying to convince Michael that one nonsense lyric he was particularly fond of —"Shalashalingay"—should be deleted from the song (Jones finally succeeded in getting Michael to drop the line during the recording session itself).

On January 28, 1985, the stars, many coming straight from the American Music Awards that were being held that night, filed into A&M studios. A sign was posted at the door: PLEASE CHECK YOUR EGOS AT THE DOOR.

There was no need. The stars proved as star-struck as everyone else. Yet even in this stellar crowd, Michael was a standout. Diana Ross, who ran around collecting autographs, said the other stars were "in awe" of Michael. "Many of them had just been together at the American Music Awards," Belafonte said, "but that was competition, narcissistic and self-possessed. The session really purified them."

The recording session itself started around 11 P.M. Since only a few of the stars present had been chosen to do solos, Jones did the chorus work first. "I knew no one would leave for the solos," he said, "but they might leave for the choir part."

For the planned *We Are the World* video, cameras recorded the all-night session. As they sang, everyone was recorded for posterity—all but Michael. He insisted on being showcased as a star without peer, and that required being shot alone lip-synching his part at a later time. (Prince, who had been invited by Quincy Jones to participate, topped Michael by not showing up at all.)

Released in March of 1985, "We Are the World" was heralded as the musical event of the year. Over the next eight months alone, the song raised nearly $40 million. But already there was controversy. Several of the participants wanted to know why, when they had volunteered their talents gratis, less than one-third of the total had so far actually been dispersed to relieve the suffering of starving Ethiopians.

If he was concerned that the money was too slow in getting to the people who needed it, Michael kept his feelings to himself. "We Are the

World" would go on to become one of the biggest-selling singles of all time.

Now faced with the daunting task of trying to top *Thriller*, Michael began preliminary work on his next album. He was determined that it not only top *Thriller*'s forty million copies, but that it break the one-hundred-million mark in sales. He affixed a note that simply read "100 million" to his bathroom mirror so that he would be reminded of his goal every time he brushed his teeth in the morning. Because of a lack of facial hair, Michael never had to shave.

It would take over two years for Michael to record his *Bad* album—a period during which he carefully fashioned an image to rival that of his arch nemesis in the pop world, Prince. "That whole *Purple Rain* thing bugged Michael beyond belief," said a former colleague. "He figured Prince was getting all this attention because he was this mystery man. There was a dangerous, almost sinister quality about Prince that Michael knew he didn't have. Michael thought his image was too goody-goody. So he set out to change it."

While he decided how to go about altering the public's perception of him, Michael made some lucrative endorsement deals. His on-again, off-again five-year working relationship with veteran entrepreneur Bob Michaelson offered insight into the way Michael did business.

An acknowledged marketing wizard, Michaelson made millions after convincing the NFL Players Association to let him handle the licensing of its name on everything from coffee mugs and pens to T-shirts and helmets. One of Michaelson's clients, New Jersey Generals football star Herschel Walker, had introduced Michael to Michaelson at the infamous Tavern on the Green Victory tour press conference a year earlier.

In late 1984 Michaelson had approached John Branca with an offer to market an off-the-rack line of Michael Jackson clothing. "I offered $1.5 million in cash up front," Michaelson recalled. "Branca said, 'Too late, we've already made a deal for $3 million.' "

"Oh, did I say $1.5 million?" Michaelson said. "I meant $10 million."

Branca gulped. "I'll get back to you," he replied. When he called back, Branca now said $10 million wasn't enough.

"So then I offered $15 million," Michaelson said. "Branca said fine, but then he called back later to say *that* wasn't enough, either." By the time they were finished, Michael had been promised $28 million. For setting up the deal, Michaelson was to receive $1 million, plus a $250,000 annual salary to run the operation for five years.

All that remained to clinch the deal—the largest licensing contract in history—was Michael's approval of the designs. Michaelson knew what Jackson wanted to see. "Michael has such a huge ego, I just told the designers to copy what he wore in the videos—plain and simple," he said. "We took them to John Branca's office at Century City, and Michael was sitting there wearing his sunglasses. He opened up the first box and pulled out a jacket like the one he wore in *Thriller*, then the next was the jacket from the *Beat It* video—basically everything he ever wore, one right after the other."

Michael's reaction? "He went berserk," Michaelson said. "He loved the clothes. He kept yelling, 'You *know* me.' Then he turned to Branca and said, 'Make a deal with this guy now. I love these!' "

But there were delays, and by the time the clothes actually made it into the stores, the market had been saturated with knock-offs. Since Michael would ultimately approve only a few designs for sale, the line fizzled.

Later Chuck Sullivan, former owner of the New England Patriots football team and CEO of Stadium Management Corporation, plunked down $18 million for the licensing rights to the Michael Jackson name for all categories except entertainment. There was another attempt at marketing a clothing line, as well as sunglasses, a doll line, and a unisex "Magic Beat" perfume. With Michael in virtual seclusion, all bombed. By the time the dust settled, promoter Chuck Sullivan had lost $30 million in his dealings with the Jacksons and was driven into bankruptcy. "I'm going to lose the whole works," Sullivan told Michaelson. And he did.

Michael, on the other hand, saw no reason to ameliorate Sullivan's suffering. He kept the nearly $20 million that had been advanced him —including an additional $500,000 in cash paid by a manufacturer of sunglasses who marketed a line of Michael Jackson shades. Lacking support from Michael, that too bombed.

"Chuck Sullivan and I were crushed," Michaelson conceded. But Michaelson tried again—this time proposing a line of plush toys based on Jackson's animals. The line would be called "Michael's Pets." Michaelson also lined up CBS to do a Saturday morning cartoon series based on Bubbles the chimp. The cartoon series was of particular importance —not only because of the revenue it would generate, but also because it would hype sales of the toys themselves.

Michael signed no fewer than sixteen contracts for, among other things, a talking Bubbles and a talking Muscles. "Toys 'R' Us and every other big toy retailer were chomping at the bit for Michael's Pets," Michaelson recalled.

It was at this crucial juncture that Michael decided to pull the plug on the Bubbles cartoon series. Michaelson, desperate now, asked him why he had changed his mind.

"Bob, I'm going to look like a child," Michael complained. "I've got to become a man. No more toys."

Michaelson had his own theory for why Michael nixed the Bubbles cartoon series. Once Michael turned to him and said, "I am tired of seeing Bubbles everywhere. It's Bubbles this and Bubbles that . . . I'm the star, not that chimp!"

"Michael loved his pets—to a point," said Michaelson. "There were times when it was obvious that Michael was intensely jealous of Bubbles."

The intensity of Michael's relationship with his pet chimp was, in fact, the subject of much speculation by visitors to Hayvenhurst. Michaelson and his wife were chatting with Michael in his living room when Bubbles's trainer Bob Dunne brought the chimp by to see his owner.

"I want to play with Bubbles now," Michael told his guests.

"Fine with us, Michael," Michaelson said. "Why don't you play with him here?"

"No, Bob, I want to bring him to my room," Michael said. "Why don't you all go have lunch. . . ."

Michael's guests agreed instead to wait for him in the living room while he played with Bubbles. "I'm sitting downstairs with my wife and Bubbles's trainer for at least an hour," Michaelson recalled. "We all kept asking, 'What's he doing? What can he possibly be doing in a small room for an hour with Bubbles?' "

Finally Michael appeared at the head of the stairs, carrying Bubbles. "At first all you could see was the front of the chimp," Michaelson said. "But all of a sudden they turned and you could see Bubbles's rear end —*totally shaved.*"

"God, Michael," Michaelson blurted, "what have you done?"

"Every time he goes to the bathroom," Michael said sheepishly, "he doesn't know how to wipe himself. It had to be bothering him."

"How could you do this to an animal?" Dunne asked

Michaelson was more to the point. "Michael, if I didn't know better, I'd think you did something to Bubbles."

"Oh, Bob," Michael said, giggling, "you're *crazy*. You say the silliest things!"

Michaelson persisted. "I kept grilling him, but all he'd do is turn beet red and say, 'Oh, Bob, you are so *funny*.'"

"Well . . ." Michaelson shrugged. "Bubbles was a *pretty* chimp. . . ."

Michael's Pets hit toy stores late in 1985, but without the support of the promised CBS cartoon series or a new Michael Jackson album (the *Bad* album was already months behind schedule), they flopped. Once again, the cost of developing, manufacturing, and shipping the line of toys fell to others. Michael lost nothing.

What about the sixteen contracts Michael had signed? "Michael's attitude basically was 'Screw everybody. *I'm* Michael Jackson, and the rest of you are nothing,'" Michaelson said. "Michael is nothing but sleaze. Did Michael know about this? He pretends to be innocent, but he's not. He knows *everything*."

Michaelson blamed himself for being naive in his dealings with the Gloved One. "I fell for it," he admitted. "Like everyone else, I was caught up in Michaelmania—like a real idiot."

This realization did not stop Michaelson from continuing to do business with Michael, however. "One way Michael keeps people on the line is to say, 'I'll make it up later. You'll all make a lot of money,'" Michaelson said. "So you move on to the next thing. . . ."

Michaelson was overseeing certain international arrangements for Michael when—after cancelling the trip six times because of delays recording his *Bad* album—Jackson finally journeyed to Japan in 1987. Upon their arrival in Tokyo, the two men were struck by the fact that Michael Jackson rip-offs were everywhere. There were T-shirts, jackets, lunchboxes, sneakers—all bearing Michael's likeness, and all unauthorized.

After visiting two department stores, Michael turned to Michaelson and said calmly, "I blame you, Bob, You're responsible for this."

"But Michael . . ." Michaelson tried to explain that he had no control over the enforcement of copyright laws in Japan.

"No, Bob, the Japanese are a wonderful people. They would never do anything like this. It's your fault."

At that point, Michaelson blew up—by all accounts the only business associate of Jackson's ever to do so in his presence. "Michael," he said, "you're nothing but an ungrateful, lousy skunk. It's time people like you were exposed." Then he stormed away, leaving Michael with his adoring fans.

On the plane back to Los Angeles, Michaelson wrote a letter outlining point by point all the promises that he felt Michael had reneged on—"all the dirty things he'd done to me and everybody else. I never received a response."

Years later Michaelson and his young son were browsing in a children's bookstore in Los Angeles when someone tapped him on the shoulder. He turned around to see Michael standing there, wearing a hat and his latest affectation—a surgical mask.

"We were hugging and kissing—like long-lost brothers," Michaelson said. "A crowd was gathering, it was wonderful." Michael told Michaelson he wanted to work with him again and instructed him to call Bill Bray to set up a lunch.

When he did, Bray told him solemnly that Michael did not want to see him again—ever. "It's the letter, Bob," Bray said. "He still remembers the letter you wrote him years ago. He will never forgive you. Never."

"I had forgotten that Michael can hold a grudge forever," Michaelson said. "The hugging and kissing in the bookstore was all just an act, so he would look nice in front of my son and all the people in the store."

Still, Michaelson did not stop trying. When he found himself intrigued by the work of local L.A. artist Brett Livingstone-Strong, Michaelson signed him on as a client and introduced him to Michael. "I knew they'd hit it off," Michaelson said. "Brett was very young, very thin, good-looking, blond, soft-spoken—definitely Michael's type."

Michael agreed to sit for a portrait, and when it was completed Michaelson told him he could sell the work for $1 million. "Bob," Michael said, shaking his head, "you're crazy."

A Japanese businessman offered not $1 million, but $2.1 million for the portrait—with the proviso that Michael appear at a press conference announcing the purchase in Los Angeles and at the opening of the businessman's new $20 million entertainment complex on Tokyo's Ginza.

Michael, who reportedly collected an advance of $500,000, was particularly excited that this would once again land him in the *Guinness Book of World Records*. The sale set the highest price ever paid for a portrait of a living person.

When the portrait was unveiled at a celebrity-packed press conference in the Beverly Hilton Hotel, Whoopi Goldberg expressed an opinion shared by many. "Somebody," she gasped, "paid $2.1 million for *that?* Come on . . . you're kidding, right?"

As promised, Michael attended the unveiling. But when it came time for him to appear at the grand opening of the entertainment center in Tokyo, he declined.

"Michael," Michaelson said, "you can't do this to the poor man."

"I'm sick." Michael shrugged. "I don't want to go. That's final."

"So the Japanese guy is literally left standing there in his kimono, waiting for Michael to show," Michaelson said. "Thousands of people were invited to this event, and now nobody believed Michael was ever supposed to be there in the first place. It caused the guy to lose face. The one thing in Japan you cannot afford to do is lose face. So the Japanese guy goes under, goes bankrupt. He considers suicide. Then he disappears completely." On the lam, it was rumored, from elements of the Japanese underworld.

"Michael, what gives you the right to do this to people?" Michaelson demanded. "The poor man is ruined."

"I'll make it up later. You're all going to make a lot of money. . . ."

And the portrait? It vanished, or so reported several newspapers in the spring of 1994, and Michael was searching for it desperately. He did not know that the portrait had been turned over to an American toy manufacturer for safekeeping and was hanging in the office of his midtown Manhattan headquarters. ("I don't think you'd get $100 for it now," Michaelson said in mid-1994 after Jackson's world had been rocked by scandal.)

Brett Livingstone-Strong, meanwhile, had painted yet another official portrait that Michael had posed for at his Neverland ranch in 1994. Coinciding with charges that he was guilty of molesting young boys, the canvas depicted a shirtless Michael communing with several naked nymphs—an obvious attempt by the Jackson camp to show him in a heterosexual light. That painting would also be put up for sale. The asking price: $2 million.

Michaelson claimed that, even compared to the hardened deal brokers he had done business with over three decades, "Michael and his people are vicious. Everybody thinks Michael is a sweetheart, but he is behind it all. And he is ruthless."

By mid-1985 Michael was already worth in excess of $75 million. He could afford to relax, and he did. Michael continued to sneak his young friends into his room at Hayvenhurst and to cruise the streets of Los

Angeles in the new disguises that had been concocted for him by the makeup genius who did *An American Werewolf in London* and *Thriller*.

On July 11, 1985, *Live Aid* was staged at Philadelphia's JFK Stadium before a live audience of ninety thousand and a global television audience of 1.6 billion. Madonna, Bob Dylan, Tina Turner, Mick Jagger, Keith Richards, Ron Wood, Hall and Oates, David Bowie, and just about every pop and rock star in the cosmos showed up for the historic charity event.

Except for Michael Jackson. He did not bother to respond to the invitation from organizer Bob Geldof. Several of the stars would have solos, and Bob Dylan had already been promised the show's grand finale. Without some way of underscoring his stature as the world's greatest entertainer, Michael was not about share the spotlight on a more or less equal basis.

That evening Michael watched the event on television. Ironically, the night belonged to Mick Jagger, who turned his twenty-five-minute portion of the landmark event into a tour de force. Backed by Daryl Hall and John Oates, Jagger sang as he ripped off Tina Turner's skirt in front of a significant part of the world's population. Then Jagger and Turner bumped and ground their way through a sweatily lascivious rendition of "Honky Tonk Women." Jagger's *Live Aid* pièce de résistance: the world premiere of his eyebrow-raising "Dancing in the Streets" duet with Bowie.

Michael merely stared at the screen, shaking his head. "I just don't get it," he said. "The guy is so *old*—and he can't even sing on key."

Jonathan Spence became the focus of Michael Jackson's attention for over a year. An Encino neighbor, the ten-year-old blond actor was with Michael nearly every minute on the set of *Captain EO,* the seventeen-minute miniepic Jackson and *Godfather* director Francis Ford Coppola had undertaken for Disney. Originally titled *The Intergalactic Music Man,* the 3-D film would be shown only at two specially built theaters at Disneyland and Disney World's Epcot Center in Orlando. The film took thirteen months to make and, at a staggering cost of $20 million, would minute for minute easily rank as the most expensive ever made.

To some on the set, Michael seemed oblivious of everything but his ten-year-old companion. Without the slightest hint of self-consciousness, he hugged, cuddled, and generally displayed a considerable amount of affection toward the boy. Spence fetched Michael water and orange juice and sat in his lap between takes.

The project fulfilled a longtime dream of Michael's—to have his own attraction at Disneyland. He was determined to have fun making it, and that meant even more than the usual amount of horsing around on the set. Michael and Spence dueled with water pistols, ambushed crew members with pies, and conducted full-tilt food fights that virtually destroyed the interior of Michael's luxuriously appointed trailer. After filming was over, so, for all intents and purposes, was the friendship.

But Michael was careful not to let another new friendship forged during the making of *Captain EO* fade away. Like Michael, Elizabeth Taylor was one of the few child stars who had managed to sustain their careers as adults. She also clung tenaciously to her celebrity, and like Michael, she had grown accustomed to getting her way.

Yet contrary to published reports at the time, which suggested that Michael and Taylor engaged in the same sort of horseplay he did with his preadolescent buddies, some believed their "close friendship" was largely for public consumption. The two were photographed together at Disneyland, and Michael's publicity machine worked overtime to create the illusion that they were soulmates.

In fact, it seemed that they rarely saw each other privately. "I never saw them together without the press around," said an employee of Michael's. "Not once. It was obvious that they were feeding off each other's fame. And let's face it, it worked for both of them."

One of Michael's criteria for choosing an adult friend was the level of his or her (usually her) celebrity. "Since he's a legend," celebrity photographer and veteran Jackson watcher David McGough observed, "he'll only be seen with other legends."

Michael continued to work on the *Bad* album, and as the deadline approached, there was increasing concern about his state of mind. "I went to see him about some music," one songwriter revealed to journalist Quincy Troupe, "and while I was sitting in the living room waiting for him, I had this sensation that he was in the room somewhere, watching me. Then he came in, we talked, and he just disappeared." A few moments later the songwriter looked out in the yard, "and he was darting in and out among these bushes and trees, chasing these little animals. He was like one of them." Around this time Michael delightedly announced that he had decided on names for his giraffe (Kareem, in honor of basketball star Kareem Abdul-Jabbar) and his new tarantula (Blackula, after one of his favorite horror films).

Two years after Michael swept the Grammys, "We Are the World" won three of the coveted awards, in February of 1986, including the top prize for Record of the Year. After eyeing with envy the hysteria that greeted Prince every time he made a public appearance, Michael wanted to leave nothing to chance. He had read that bobbysoxers had actually been hired to create mass hysteria when Frank Sinatra played New York's Paramount Theater in the 1940s.

"So Michael asked us to do the same," Winter recalled. "He wanted us to find someone who would rush the stage when he went up on stage with Quincy to accept the Grammy. I was totally against it, but he insisted. In the end, it didn't come off anyway. There were so many people standing around backstage that the girl who'd been hired just couldn't get through."

Michael's disappointment was mitigated by the signing two weeks later of another three-year contract with Pepsi. Just two years after Michael had threatened to sue Pepsi into bankruptcy over the famous flaming hair incident, Pepsi president Roger Enrico proudly announced that his company was paying $15 million to Michael for two more television spots and the right to sponsor his first-ever solo tour. It was by far the biggest such deal in history, and—unlike the first $7 million arrangement with Pepsi—Michael would not be sharing it with his brothers. Even so, he objected to use of the word *endorsement,* since he still refused to be seen so much as holding a can of the soft drink. Technically what Michael had was a "relationship" with the company —a $15 million "relationship."

None of this allayed Michael's growing fears that he was gradually being eclipsed—not only by Prince, but by his own little sister. Rising phoenixlike from the charred ruins of her brief marriage to James DeBarge, Janet Jackson exploded on the music scene with her *Control* album in the spring of 1986. Produced by the trench-coat-wearing team of Jimmy Jam and Terry Lewis, *Control* sold six million copies and spawned several hit singles, including "What Have You Done for Me Lately?", the title song, "Let's Wait Awhile," and "When I Think of You." Moreover it unveiled the new Janet—sullen, sexy, and, as she stated frankly in the song "Control," finally free of her father's influence.

The public was also given a look at Janet's newly sculpted facial features. Joe, Katherine, La Toya—the entire Jackson clan with the exception of Jackie—had now followed Michael's lead. Having erased every vestige of his father from his own face, Michael was now confronted with the fact that everyone else in the family—including Joe—had undergone surgery to look more like him.

Michael was wary of Janet's success, and with reason. La Toya, whose room was right down the hall from Janet's and Michael's, overheard her sister talking to someone on her speakerphone. "I'm going to be bigger than Michael," Janet said, "and my album will be bigger than *Thriller.*"

"That's terrible," Michael said when La Toya told him what she had overheard. "How can she be that way?" His concern grew when it looked as if Janet were becoming not just a star, but a *phenomenon.* "Michael was really pissed off at Janet," Bob Michaelson said. "He thought she stole his moves, his sound, his look—right down to the nose."

Janet's stark videos, choreographed by Jackie's mistress, Paula Abdul, had the look and feel of Michael's. "There's an underlying anger in them both," a family acquaintance said. "So much that they do seems to be an expression of rage directed at their father."

Janet was not the only woman Michael now eyed warily. He was shocked to learn that his "sister/mother/lover/friend" Diana Ross had married Norwegian shipping tycoon Arne Naess at her lawyer's office in October of 1985. When they tied the knot again the following February in a fairy-tale wedding at a chapel in the snowy Swiss Alps, Ross pleaded with Michael to be among the scores of celebrity guests in attendance.

In what amounted to a very public and humiliating slap in the face, Michael declined. Nor would he even answer subsequent invitations to the christening ceremonies for the children she had with Naess. It was difficult to believe that this was the same Michael Jackson who only a few years earlier had demanded that his chauffeur call him "Miss Ross" as they tooled around Los Angeles in his Rolls-Royce.

The snub lingered in Ross's mind for years. Michael explained in interviews that he did not attend the wedding because he was jealous of Naess, but Ross must have known that was all an act. He had never had the slightest romantic interest in her, or in any woman, for that matter. He just did not want to compromise his image by appearing with other celebrities—not even at the wedding of his mentor and confidante.

Two years later, when Michael asked Ross to host a Showtime cable television special on his life and career, she turned him down flat. Exercising total control over the Showtime project—an unabashedly self-serving lovefest that included taped raves from Gene Kelly, Elizabeth Taylor, Quincy Jones, Sophia Loren, and even Sean Lennon—Michael saw to it that Ross was virtually edited out of the program. By way of twisting the knife, the show emphasized the fact that Ross had for years falsely taken credit for discovering the Jackson Five.

By mid-1985 Michael had made the conscious decision that he could not afford to squander his celebrity. He had to remain aloof from run-of-the-mill famous people, and that meant shunning contact with the press and public even more—if that was remotely possible.

"The guy never grew up," Norman Winter said. "That doesn't mean he's not bright. He is, but there is so much he doesn't know." During one of those periods when Michael refused to set foot out of his house, Winter said, "So, are you going to pull a Garbo?"

"What's that?"

"It's a person," Winter replied

"Then who is that?"

"You *know,*" Winter said, still half expecting Michael to say he was joking. " 'I vant to be alone' . . . Garbo. *Greta Garbo.*"

"Never heard of her," Michael said, shaking his head.

Winter was flabbergasted that a man pushing thirty who had spent the last quarter century in show business had never heard of Greta Garbo. "I told Michael who she was, and he just sat there soaking it in."

Not long after, several members of Michael's inner circle were meeting at Hayvenhurst when Jackson suddenly turned to Winter. "Tell me more about that woman," he said.

"What woman?"

"Gabor something?"

Winter paused. "Garbo? You mean Greta Garbo?"

"Yeah, her."

Michael listened intently as Winter filled him in on the movie legend who became far more famous for her reclusiveness than for anything she did on screen. "I told him she had a mystique, but then of course I had to explain what mystique meant," Winter said. "Afterward he said, 'I really like that mystique idea.' I bought him a book about Garbo, and then he couldn't stop talking about her. Michael became obsessed with Garbo. He wanted to be the Greta Garbo of his time."

In the coming years Michael would pattern his life and career after three figures: Garbo, billionaire recluse Howard Hughes, and showman P. T. Barnum. "He read all he could get his hands on about each one," Winter said. These biographies were to serve as blueprints for the image Michael slavishly sought to create for himself. And, Winter acknowledged, more than any star he had ever encountered, Michael was "totally focused on his image."

In the months prior to *Captain EO*'s September 1986 Disneyland premiere, Michael carried out a media blitz of his own meticulously crafted design. Borrowing a page from the life of the hermetic Howard Hughes, Michael fed the tabloid press stories about his newfound obsession with hygiene. His fear of germs was so great, it seemed, that he was constantly washing his hands in the manner of a true obsessive-compulsive. Whenever he returned home, "reliable sources" reported, he showered for an hour or more.

Michael had also taken to wearing surgical masks whenever he went out in public—a suitably bizarre affectation that stirred the desired amount of controversy. "Everybody's talking about the mask," he said after his first time wearing it out in public. "Isn't it great?"

Not that it required Michael to give up his innate fashion sense. He was spotted wearing a blue mask getting off a plane in New York, a green one as he checked into his hotel, and a white one as he attended a Broadway show. But his paralyzing fear of germs did not apply at Hayvenhurst, where Michael often kissed Bubbles on the lips and unflinchingly changed his soiled diapers.

Michael employed yet another prop when he visited Disneyland in June of 1986. In addition to wearing his sunglasses, hat, and surgical mask, he now insisted on being pushed around the park in a wheelchair. There he spent two hours in his favorite section of the park—Fantasyland, where he was wheeled to the head of each line, stood up, and went on each ride for as long as he pleased.

"Michael wears his mask because a lot of people turn away real fast when they see a disabled or bandaged person," Frank Dileo explained.

"When he goes to a public place, it's easier for him to look disabled, so that people turn away . . . and the wheelchair made it just that much more credible."

The surgical mask actually served a legitimate purpose that June when Dr. Steven Hoefflin acceded to his patient's wishes and put a masculine-looking Kirk Douglas cleft in Michael's chin. The operation involved drilling two small holes in Michael's jaw to anchor a plastic prosthesis. At the same time, Michael had permanent eyeliner applied. In this procedure, dye is injected into the eyelids, removing the need for daily applications of eyeliner.

Only days before the debut of *Captain EO,* Michael pulled off one of his more memorable publicity stunts when the *National Enquirer* ran a photograph of him sleeping inside a curious-looking device called a hyperbaric chamber. The tubelike device, encased in clear plastic, was originally developed to prevent undersea divers from getting the bends.

Under the headline MICHAEL JACKSON'S SECRET PLAN TO LIVE TO 150, the story accurately stated that Michael had been shown the pressurized oxygen chamber—also used to promote healing in burn patients—by Dr. Hoefflin when he was recovering at the Brotman Medical Center in 1984. It went on to say, however, that Michael intended to buy one for $125,000 so that he could take it home and sleep in it—and thus, theoretically, stave off the aging process.

The story pointed out that the oxygen-filled hyperbaric chamber carried with it a number of hazards, not the least of which was the risk of fire. "Michael's close friends and manager are very worried about his plan to get a hyperbaric chamber to sleep in at his home," Norman Winter was quoted as saying. "His manager and even his doctor have tried to talk him out of it, but Michael just won't listen."

"I'm concerned and confused," Dileo added. "After all, we don't know how safe this thing is. And being responsible for turning the switch on this contraption is something I don't want."

Michael would later dismiss the piece as a perfect example of the nonsense invented by the tabloid press. In truth the entire story was a propaganda ploy concocted by Michael and, over the mild objections of Winter and John Branca, carried out by Dileo.

Michael had posed for the picture, which showed him napping in the futuristic-looking hyperbaric chamber on his left side, and then sent Polaroids to *Enquirer* writer Charles Montgomery. The quality of the photograph was so poor that it had to be reshot, and Michael willingly obliged, climbing back in the chamber for the retake.

The *Enquirer* was given exclusive rights to the photo and the accompanying story under one condition—that it use the word *bizarre* three times in the piece. No problem.

When *Captain EO* premiered at Disneyland on September 21, executive producer George Lucas of *Star Wars* fame was there to participate in the official ribbon cutting, as were director Coppola and Michael's *EO* costar, Anjelica Huston. The star did not take part in the ceremonies—perhaps, as *People* magazine cracked, "he was too tanked to show up."

The premiere, billed as a "nonstop sixty-hour party," attracted the likes of Jack Nicholson, Debra Winger, Jane Fonda, John Ritter, David Carradine, Sissy Spacek, and Whoopi Goldberg—all of whom paid homage to Jackson by tossing aside their egos and riding down Main Street in a *Captain EO* parade. Meanwhile Michael mingled in the crowd, wearing one of his more convincing disguises, and went on the heart-stopping Space Mountain roller-coaster ride—twice.

As the title character of *Captain EO,* Michael played an intergalactic song-and-dance man whose mission was to rescue a planet from destruction at the hands of spiderlike villainess Anjelica Huston. There was also a supporting cast of huggable Disney characters—from Hooter, a tiny green elephant that sneezed music through his trunk, to Captain EO's flying space monkey sidekick, Fuzzball.

Captain EO also featured two new songs: "We Are Here to Change the World" and "Another Part of Me," which became a hit single. But all this merely got in the way of the special effects. The $1-million-per-minute film was a mixed-media event that blended digital sound, computer technology, smoke, strobes, and lasers with the 3-D movie.

In the first scene an asteroid seemingly hurtled off the screen into the face of the viewer. While space battles raged on screen, lasers flashed around the perimeter of the theater itself. The effect was to frighten children as much as amaze them; trying to figure out what was going on, youngsters whirled in one direction and then another as bombs exploded and lasers zapped around them. Eight years later *Captain EO* would remain a major draw at both Disneyland and Epcot.

. . .

The hyperbaric chamber scam concocted to promote *Captain EO* spawned an endless number of tabloid stories in the coming months, some more plausible than others. Charles Montgomery was fed yet another tall tale, this time that Michael had built a shrine to Elizabeth Taylor—an entire room where a giant video screen played her movies twenty-four hours a day "even when no one's there!" And once again the *National Enquirer* lived up to its end of the bargain with Jackson and Dileo, using the word *bizarre* in the headline.

In all these cases Michael chose to plant his stories in the *Enquirer* because it had the largest readership in the country and because it offered instant deniability. He could pooh-pooh these wild tales with impunity. At the same time he could be confident that no one would suspect he was the source of leaks to America's most notorious tabloid.

Whatever the public perception of Michael, it was tame compared to the reality. As he continued work on his *Bad* album, he became more and more inaccessible to those around him; even Dileo and Quincy Jones were now sometimes treated with a sort of imperious disdain.

It did not help that Barbra Streisand turned down his invitation to join him for a duet of "I Just Can't Stop Loving You." Ostensibly she declined on grounds that, given their sixteen-year age difference, nobody would buy it. More accurately, Streisand still regarded herself very much as "the greatest star by far." She was not about to be outdivaed by Michael Jackson. Neither was Whitney Houston, who also turned him down.

The next most logical choice was Diana Ross, but Michael was still angry with her for having married Naess. "Why should I do *her* a favor?" he asked Winter. Rather than risk being rejected by another star with an ego as big as his, Michael instead recorded the ballad, which would go on to be a huge hit, with unknown Siedah Garrett.

An antidrug rap with Run-D.M.C. fell through when, after a recording session at Hollywood's Westlake Studios, it was abundantly clear to all involved that there was absolutely no chemistry between the streetwise rappers and the ephemeral pop star.

It was also clear that Michael was not about to make his original deadline and have the *Bad* album completed in time for a January 1987 release. CBS needed another Michael Jackson hit. Walter Yetnikoff, who was counting on *Bad* to help boost his company's profits after a comparatively lackluster year, blamed the star for taking precious time out of his schedule to work on *Captain EO*. When Yetnikoff learned that Michael had actually written and performed two songs for the movie, he threatened to sue—until Branca and Dileo calmed him down.

The self-imposed strain of trying to top *Thriller* was beginning to manifest itself in extreme ways. More and more Michael was beginning to resemble the "bizarre" creature described in the tabloid stories he planted. "He has a split personality," explained one member of his staff. "He is very bright and self-destructively brilliant. He has an extremely high IQ and certain quirks and personality disorders. He might have six or twenty sides to him, and they're all competing against each other."

One of those personalities devoutly wanted to be white, according to La Toya. Michael would claim in a 1993 interview with Oprah Winfrey that for years he had secretly suffered from vitiligo, a skin disorder that robs the skin of pigment. His dermatologist, Dr. Arnold Klein, confirmed that Michael had been diagnosed with the disease in 1986.

La Toya doubted the story, pointing out that in the Jacksons' large family there was no history of any skin disorders whatsoever. In fact, La Toya said that Miko Brando would cart over cases of skin bleaching cream to the house in Encino every week, and Michael religiously applied it to his skin—even after La Toya warned him that it might be carcinogenic.

"I read the label and checked out the ingredients," she recalled. "I said, 'Michael, this could give you cancer.' " He shrugged off her concerns and, according to her, continued using the cream to make his face, limbs, and torso lighter than that of many Caucasians. It was all part of his ongoing crusade to make himself as little like his father as humanly possible.

Another of Michael's many personalities—that of Pied Piper to young boys—went on behind closed doors at Hayvenhurst. The bodyguards continued to bring young boys into the Encino compound at all times of the day and night. According to La Toya, whose own bedroom was adjacent to Michael's, he spent nearly every night with young boys between the ages of nine and fourteen—at least fifty over a three-year-period.

"There was *always* one boy at the house," she said. "He would spend the night with Michael in Michael's room for a night, or he would stay a week, a month, or longer. These little boys were sleeping with him." None of these boys, as far as she could recall, was African American.

The door to Michael's bedroom was always locked, and the staff was instructed never to disturb him. It was made clear that any employee who violated this rule risked immediate termination. Even family members were loath to knock on the door. "He loved his privacy," said La Toya, "and hated to be disturbed by any member of the family. Not even Mother."

Michael would phone down to the kitchen and order up meals, instructing the cook to leave the food on a tray outside the door. Once the coast was clear, Michael would furtively stick his head out his bedroom door, then reach out and pull the tray inside. When he and his "special friend" were finished eating, he placed the tray back out into the hallway.

According to La Toya and Michael's longtime personal maid, Blanca Francia, Michael stayed in his room with one little boy for three full days without ever coming out. The length of time a boy spent with Michael apparently depended on how infatuated Michael was with him. "Some boys were invited back many times," La Toya said. "Others bored Michael after just a few visits. It was pathetic when they kept phoning to see him."

Some boys fell out of favor merely because they reached a certain age or because they looked older than their years. "When they got too old," said La Toya, "he'd drop them."

Francia, a single mother with a young son, had emigrated from El Salvador in 1975. From March of 1986 until she quit ("I saw too much") in June of 1991, she worked as Michael's personal maid. Every day for more than five years Francia cleaned up after Michael—and not just at Hayvenhurst. She also went backstage when Michael was on tour. And when he moved to Neverland, Michael brought his trusted Francia along with him. He even trusted her to feed the animals he kept caged inside the house.

Not long after going to work for him, Francia says she was confronted with the fact that Michael spent nearly every night alone in his room with a young boy. He made no effort to conceal his preferences from her. Most of his guests preferred not to sleep on the floor, so they slept with Michael in a Murphy bed that pulled out of the wall. "It became routine," she said. "It was normal for him to sleep with boys—the two of them together in bed."

At times Michael and his friend wore pajamas. "His pajamas were really feminine," Francia said. "Always silk, trimmed with little rhinestones and pearls." But sometimes she would enter the room to find

Michael and a boy in bed together, naked from the waist up. She also says it was not unusual for her to come upon Michael and one of his special friends in the Jacuzzi together, their underwear lying crumpled on the tile floor.

Francia had been working at Hayvenhurst for only a few weeks when Michael confronted her. "What do you think about me?" he asked her.

"Pardon?" Francia replied, nonplussed.

"You know," Michael pressed, "if somebody asked you what you thought about me, what would you tell them?"

"Well," she said, "it's none of my business."

"What do you think about what you've seen?" he continued. "What do you think about these boys coming to my house?"

"None of my business," she repeated, shaking her head.

Michael studied her face for a few moments. "Good," he said. "Good. I like that."

Not long after that conversation, Michael grilled her again. "I like you, Blanca," he said. "Just remember that whatever you see is none of anybody's business. If you are ever asked by anyone, don't tell them anything about me."

Francia received cash and gifts, which she believed were rewards for her discretion. Michael would frequently hand her a $100 bill and tell her that he was pleased with the job she was doing, that he appreciated her loyalty. "It was obvious what was going on," Francia later recalled. "I didn't want to lie for Mr. Jackson. But I wanted to keep my job. I was going to keep the secret all my life. But it bothers me. . . ."

It also began to bother La Toya, who, like the other members of the family, outwardly pretended not to notice anything unusual. One day when Michael was away from the house, La Toya passed by his room and noticed that the door was ajar. She stepped inside and out of the corner of her eye caught her mother, standing in Michael's closet.

"Mother was *frantic,*" La Toya would recall. She had gone into Michael's closet and found a pile of checks.

"That fucking faggot," La Toya claims Katherine said, shaking her head in disgust. "La Toya, look at this."

She handed La Toya a canceled check; there were others beneath it. La Toya looked at the check her other had given her. "Yes, so?" she said.

"La Toya, *look*—look at the amount. This is *one million dollars!*"

La Toya said nothing.

"Look who it's made out to," La Toya recalled her mother saying. La Toya recognized the name. It belonged to the father of one of Michael's most favored special friends, who was employed as a garbage collector.

"Mother, you don't know what the money is for," La Toya said. "Maybe the man is in financial trouble. . . ."

"La Toya," Katherine went on, "this is one million dollars! And look at these others," La Toya claims she said, pulling out one check after another. "Michael is a *fucking faggot.* He's always been that."

According to La Toya, from then on Katherine often used that term to refer to her son. "She called him that all the time," she said. " 'That faggot,' " she'd say, " 'that damn fucking faggot. . . .' "

La Toya had seen the evidence that Michael was already making huge payments to the families of some of the boys who participated in what he called "pajama parties." For now La Toya, like everyone else in the family, publicly chalked it all up to Michael's overriding love of children. But behind closed doors, she warned Michael that he was setting himself up for a scandal. "Don't be silly!" He laughed. "We're just friends. We're just having fun. You know how I love kids. . . ."

Michael was not entirely oblivious of the danger he was courting. One night when he was out of town, he called the house in Encino repeatedly and asked to speak to a specific security guard—one who had worked for the family for years and in whom he had complete confidence. After numerous attempts to locate the trusted guard failed, he asked Leroy Thomas, a relatively new member of the Jackson security force, to undertake a "special assignment" for him.

On Jackson's very specific orders, Thomas says he went into the kitchen at Hayvenhurst and fished around under the refrigerator for a special key. He found the key and, again following Michael's instructions, went into his room and used the key to enter Michael's private bathroom.

When he flicked on the light switch, Thomas was shocked by what he claims he saw taped to Michael's bathroom mirror: a Polaroid shot of a naked young male—Caucasian or possibly Asian—between the ages of ten and fourteen. The profile shot clearly showed the boy's genitals and buttocks. "Jesus," he muttered to himself. Thomas would later say that given the number of times he had smuggled boys into the house for Michael, he should not have been surprised. But he was.

According to Thomas, Michael had ordered him to destroy the photograph, and Thomas called his boss and told him he had done so. (Years later Thomas passed a lie detector test when he recounted this episode. He apparently flunked the test, however, when he claimed to have destroyed the photo.)

Katherine's alleged anger over her son's fondness for young boys notwithstanding, the need to protect Michael from scandal became an overriding concern at Hayvenhurst. "The Jacksons were seen as a happy, loving family," La Toya recalled. "In the black population, we were like the Kennedys. People would say 'Gosh, I wish we could be like that.' But we were *never* that kind of family."

14

He's the oldest man I know, and he's the youngest kid I know.

—QUINCY JONES

Wherever he looked within the family, Michael saw the unmistakable signs of his father's bitter legacy. Even after Jackie's tempestuous marriage to Enid Spann ended in August 1987—in large part because of his steamy affair with Paula Abdul—the eldest Jackson son was arrested for harassing his ex-wife.

Meanwhile Jermaine followed Joe's less-than-sterling example and started a family with another woman right under his wife Hazel's nose. Jermaine often invited the little boy he'd fathered by his mistress Margaret Maldonado to family gatherings, reducing Hazel—herself pregnant with their third child—to tears. In October 1987 Hazel filed for divorce. Ten months later she would accuse Jermaine of attempting to rape her while he was visiting the children.

Although he had not been subjected to as much abuse as his older siblings, Randy would marry Eliza Shaffe in May 1989 and proceed to abuse her physically throughout her pregnancy. She learned that Randy was having affairs with several women, and that one of them was also pregnant. After eighteen months of marriage Eliza filed for divorce and at the same time lodged a criminal complaint against Randy. He, in turn, would end up pleading no contest to wife-beating

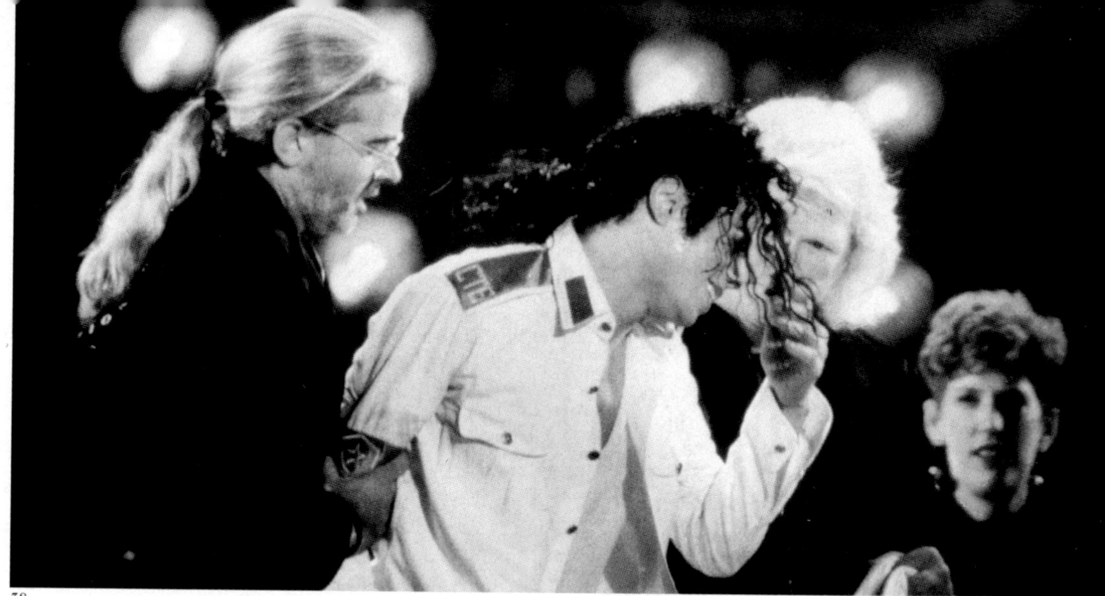

38

Suffering one of his frequent anxiety attacks, Michael was helped to his feet after collapsing on stage at London's Wembley Stadium in August 1992. The crowd of seventy-two thousand included Prince Charles.

Hillary and Chelsea looked on as President Clinton joined Michael and Stevie Nicks in a chorus of "Don't Stop" at the inaugural gala in 1993.

39

At the peak of his fame, Michael was all dazzle and flash during his Super Bowl halftime show in 1993. In the grand finale he surrounded himself with thirty-five hundred children singing "Heal the World."

40

41

42

Oprah Winfrey was treated to an impromptu performance—and confessions about his unhappy childhood and his skin condition—during her landmark interview with Michael in February 1993. It was the fourth most watched entertainment show in TV history.

Brooke Shields was stunned when Michael told Oprah that they were romantically involved. Two weeks later the couple kissed for the cameras as they left a post-Grammy party. The diamond ring on Brooke's finger was a gift from Michael.

43

On February 24, 1993, Janet Jackson, now a star in her own right, presented her brother with a Lifetime Achievement Grammy. Both transformed by plastic surgery, they looked more alike than ever.

45

46

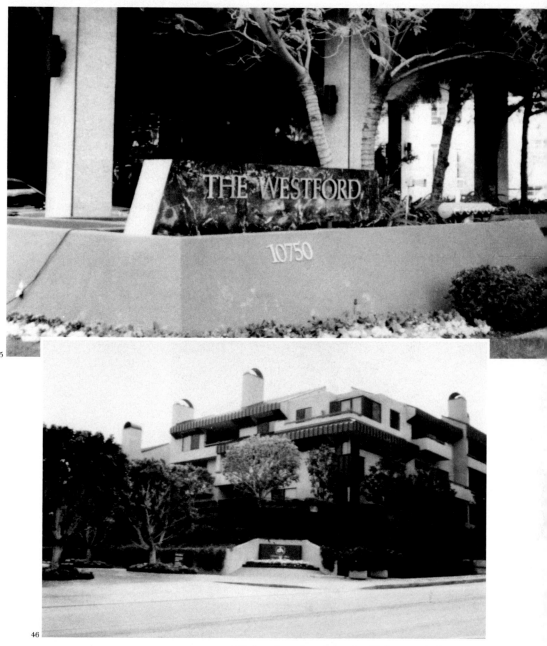

Michael took several of his special young friends to The Westford, the top-secret Wilshire Boulevard address he called "the hideout," and to his Century City condo.

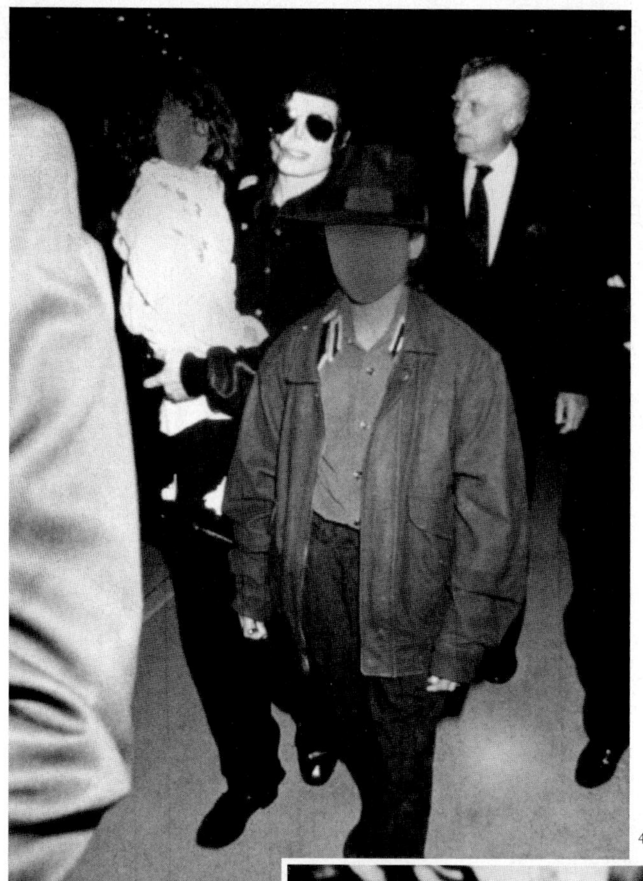

47

Michael with another special friend, "Joey Randall," and Joey's sister, "Molly." When his parents became alarmed by the relationship, Joey charged Michael with child molestation and lifted the lid on his astounding secret life.

48

The day after the child abuse scandal broke, Michael's criminal attorney, Howard Weitzman, read a statement in which his client maintained his innocence. Private investigator Anthony Pellicano, right, then falsely claimed that Michael had been the victim of a blackmail attempt.

49

Michael greeted his hosts when he arrived in Bangkok in 1993 on the Asian leg of the *Dangerous* tour. Hours later he was reeling from allegations of child abuse.

50

Apparently undaunted by the scandal that raged around him, Michael continued to grab his crotch on stage as the *Dangerous* tour moved on to Moscow.

51

Michael and traveling companions Eddie and Frank Cascio looked down on fans from the balcony of their Tel Aviv hotel room. Not long after, they were driven from the Wailing Wall by angry crowds.

In a bizarre act of defiance, Michael stuck his arm out the window of his Buenos Aires hotel room and waved a copy of *Child* magazine at the crowd below.

52

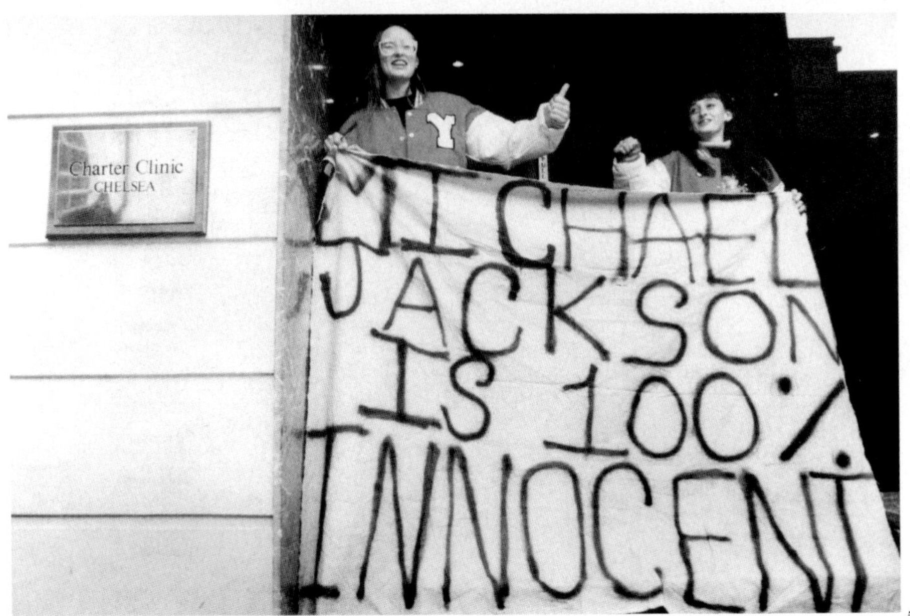

53

Abruptly canceling his *Dangerous* tour, Michael disappeared to undergo treatment for addiction to painkillers at a London clinic, where loyal fans proclaimed his innocence.

With husband Jack Gordon at her side, La Toya called a Tel Aviv press conference in December 1993 to announce that she had seen evidence her brother Michael was guilty of child molestation.

54

55

Back in the United States and live from Neverland, Michael, wearing false lashes, lipstick, and heavy makeup, took the offensive and pleaded his innocence in a national telecast on December 22, 1993.

56

Dressed like an Arab woman, Michael paid a New Year's Eve 1993 visit to the MGM Grand theme park in Las Vegas with convicted junk bond king Michael Milken. Whatever else they may have had in common, both were fallen idols—and both were multimillionaires.

57

Over his advisers' objections, Michael invited one hundred disadvantaged children to a Martin Luther King Day party at Neverland.

58

On January 25, 1994, Michael's attorney, Johnnie Cochran, announced the settlement of the civil case against his client. "Randall's" lawyer, Larry Feldman (second from right), listened intently. Standing between Cochran and Feldman: the author's researcher, Wendi Rothman.

59

After the "Joey Randall" case was settled out of court for a reputed $26 million, Michael showed up in Las Vegas to honor Elizabeth Taylor and Berry Gordy, Jr., as part of the televised *Jackson Family Honors*. The ill-timed show was an unqualified disaster.

The civil suit was settled, but the criminal investigation against Jackson continued. He angrily denounced prosecutors when his mother, Katherine, shown here talking to son Randy, was called to testify before a Los Angeles grand jury in March 1994.

60

61

Beset by financial worries, marital discord among the children, and scandal, Joe and Katherine Jackson were the centerpiece for this revealingly glum family portrait.

62

In spite of a growing chorus of allegations about his bizarre behavior, Michael received the 1994 Children's Choice Award.

In a stunning turn of events, Michael Jackson became Elvis Presley's son-in-law on May 26, 1994, when he secretly wed Lisa Marie Presley in the Dominican Republic. Wearing less-than-convincing disguises, they honeymooned at Disney World with her two children (right).

63

64

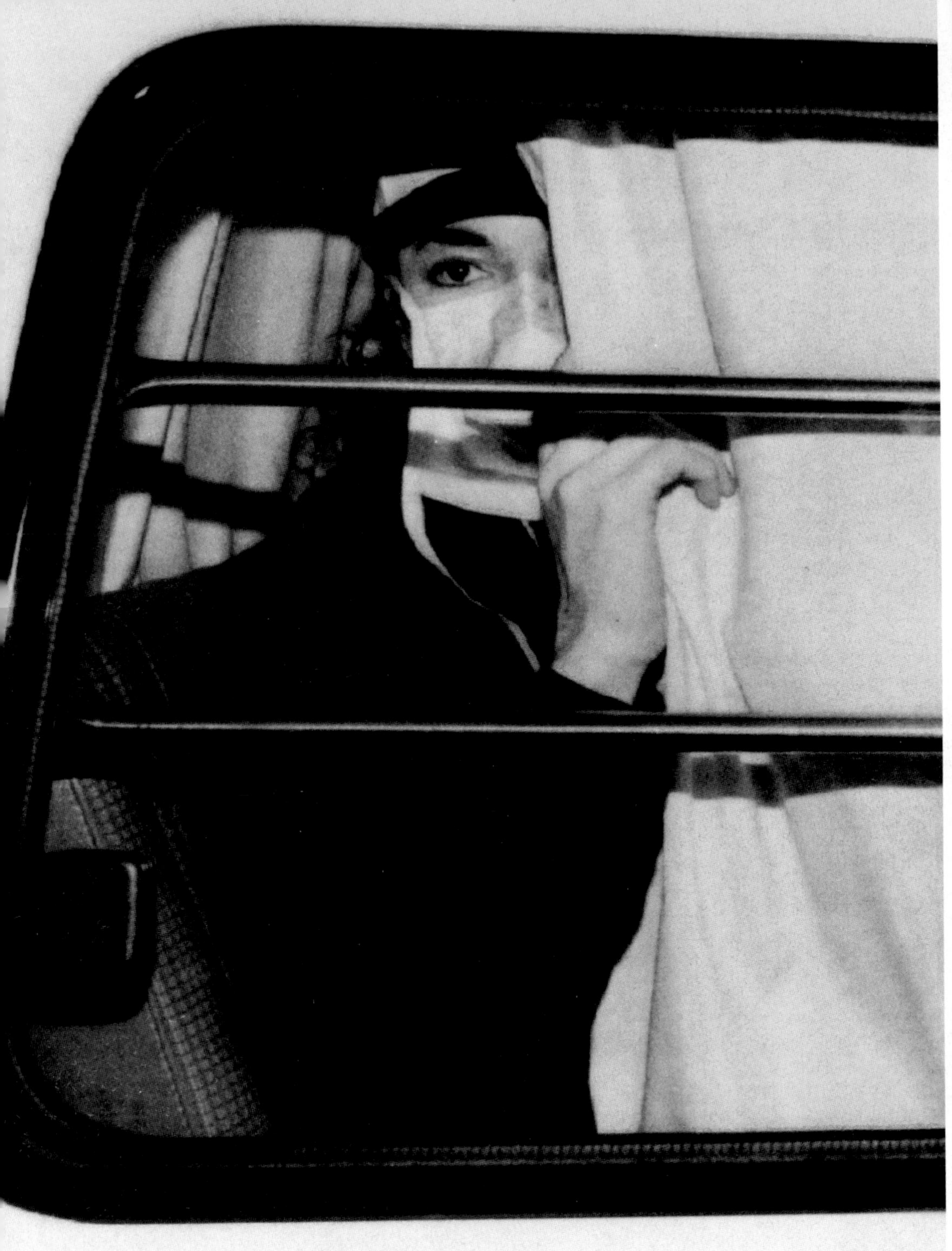

His career on hold and still facing the possibility of criminal prosecution for child molestation, the embattled icon faces his uncertain future.

charges for which he was put on two years' probation and later sentenced to thirty days in jail for violating probation.

Even Tito would live up to his father's example. In 1990 DeeDee would end their eighteen-year marriage after learning that Tito had also been cheating on her. The horrific details of his brother's private lives did not make headlines, however. Michael's weird personal habits did—thanks, in large part, to his own relentless efforts at self-promotion.

Inevitably, Michael's increasingly "bizarre" (his word) lifestyle led to an official break with the ultraconservative Jehovah's Witnesses. As recently as February 1987, Michael had been going door to door with the grandnieces and grandnephews of Katharine Hepburn who were themselves Witnesses. But in May an official of the Woodland Hills, California, Kingdom Hall attended by Michael issued a statement saying that Michael "no longer wants to be known as a Jehovah's Witness."

"He took the initiative," said Watchtower Bible and Tract Society spokesman William Van De Wall. "We didn't take any action. We were informed of his wishes."

There was obviously no love lost between Michael and church elders. They were still upset over the *Thriller* video, the suggestive nature of his dancing, the tabloid stories about hyperbaric chambers, and the story that he had attended a birthday party for his friend Elizabeth Taylor in direct violation of Witness rules against celebrations and gift giving.

Being "disfellowshiped" was bad enough, but for a Witness to *choose* to leave the faith was even worse. Were she to follow the strict tenets of her faith, Katherine would never have spoken to her son again. She was not, however, about to disown Michael. Despite her declarations of piety, she had ignored Witness rules and regulations when it suited her purposes. She had, for example, no problem accepting the expensive jewelry and gifts lavished on her by her children ("My favorite gift from Michael is a burgundy Rolls"). Her solution was to not discuss the matter with him, to pray for her son and carry on as usual.

"Michael left for his own reasons," Katherine said of his decision to resign from the church. "Who knows? One day he may come back. But it isn't true that I can't speak to him because he has left. We still speak, and we still hug each other. All that stuff about my children not speaking to each other isn't true. . . . We haven't got room for big heads in my family."

Michael, meanwhile, was taking time to cultivate Hollywood's old guard. Although he was far too fragile emotionally to attend relatives' funerals, he made a point of being there for Liza when her father,

Vincente Minnelli, was buried. And at various times Michael invited Elizabeth Taylor, Sophia Loren, Jane Fonda, Liza Minnelli, the Gregory Pecks, and the Charlton Hestons to dinner. One of the most memorable such occasions was an "Italian night" arranged by Frank Dileo. The guest list included Robert De Niro, Joe Pesci, Martin Scorsese, Marlon Brando, Dileo, and assorted girlfriends and wives. "Bob De Niro and I were both friends of Frank's," said Pesci, "and we really wanted to meet Michael. So Frank set it up."

Surrounded by the godfathers and punks of the silver screen, Michael was speechless. He spent most of the evening giggling into his napkin.

His identification with Disney notwithstanding, Michael also harbored an unalloyed interest in the underworld. He was "absolutely *obsessed* with the Mafia," said his then business partner Bob Michaelson. "That's why he loves Italians. He surrounded himself with them—he thought they were all 'connected.' Look at Frank Dileo, John Branca, Marlon Brando, and Marlon's son Miko, just to name a few. In his next life, Michael either wants to be Peter Pan—or Al Capone."

The hyperbaric chamber had generated so much valuable publicity for *Captain EO* that Michael was determined to do the same as the release date approached for *Bad*. Reviving his old interest in the "Elephant Man," on a trip to England Michael arranged with officials at London Hospital Medical College to view the skeleton of John Merrick. Instantly recognizing the possibilities for more "bizarre" publicity, he then authorized Frank Dileo to announce that he intended to buy the bones of the Elephant Man for an undisclosed sum. "Michael Jackson has a high degree of respect for the memory of Merrick," Dileo said in a press release. "He has read and studied all material about the Elephant Man, and has visited the hospital in London twice to view Merrick's remains.

"His fascination with their historical significance increased with each visit, along with his hope of adding them to his collection of rare and unusual memorabilia at his California compound. He has no exploitative intentions whatsoever and cares about and is concerned with the Elephant Man as a dedicated and devoted collector of art and antiques."

Hospital officials entrusted with John Merrick's remains saw things differently. When Dileo called them with an official offer of $1 million for Merrick's remains, they replied that the Elephant Man was not for sale at any price—and especially not to satisfy Jackson's lust for "cheap publicity."

Cheap indeed. Without investing a nickel, Michael had reaped a million dollars' worth of publicity. Every major newspaper and magazine in the world dutifully reported that Michael had a plan to buy the bones of the Elephant Man. "Michael was thrilled," Bob Michaelson said. "Everybody was talking about how weird and mysterious he was just before the new album was about to come out—he could not have been happier."

There were, however, long-term consequences to this form of helter-skelter self-promotion that Michael would come to regret. Like the sorcerer's apprentice, he had unleashed forces that he simply could not control. Now that he was universally pegged as a weirdo, a certain segment of the press declared open season on Michael Jackson.

On the subject of his friendship with Elizabeth Taylor alone, there were reports that he had sent her an inflatable doll of himself for her birthday; they had a "bizarre pact" to share one another's homes; he had asked her to marry him ("I can't live without you, Liz. I worship and adore you like no man has ever loved a woman. Please, please, please say you'll marry me!"); he had tried to convince her to stay eternally middle-aged by sleeping in his hyperbaric chamber.

Then there was the story that he wanted his mother to undergo plastic surgery to look like Liz. In truth, after Taylor lost fifty pounds and underwent a face-lift, Michael suggested to Katherine that she might follow suit. Other articles claimed Michael bathed only in Evian and that every week he frolicked with his "own private harem" at Hugh Hefner's Playboy mansion.

No more plausible were other stories that linked him with several beautiful women during 1987. All of these rumored romances were sanctioned by Michael, who was still eager to dispel the persistent public perception that he was gay.

Siedah Garrett's duet with Michael on the number one hit "I Just Can't Stop Loving You" certainly put her in proximity with the superstar. Siedah (real name Debra Christine) first attracted Michael's attention when Quincy Jones played one of her compositions for him. The song was called "Man in the Mirror," and, in Jones's words, Jackson was "blown away." Michael called her up and, days later, invited her to perform the duet with him.

Garrett also bore a striking resemblance to Michael, leading to the inevitable headline MICHAEL JACKSON & LOOK-ALIKE TALKING MARRIAGE.

But aside from playfully tossing nuts at her in the recording studio and bringing in his new pet boa Crusher to terrorize her (the three-hundred-pound, twenty-foot python actually had to be carried into the studio by three men), Michael made no overtures whatsoever. Still, Siedah claimed bravely, "I treat him like a normal guy and he behaves like one."

During the filming of the *Bad* video in Harlem that January, Michael was said to have fallen for blond makeup artist Karen Faye. Michael and Faye, who had also done his makeup for *Captain EO*, huddled together for warmth between takes. In one of the stories that Michael willingly fed to the *National Enquirer*, he supposedly held her around the waist and hugged her. But on one occasion, while Michael waited to go before the cameras and Fay opened her overcoat and wrapped it around the shivering superstar, to one observer it looked as if Michael, taken by surprise, was "paralyzed with fear."

Michael fanned rumors of romance. "We love each other deeply," he was quoted as saying to a friend. "I've never felt this way before. She's turned my life around!" One photo, of Michael stiffly embracing Faye, was taken to confirm the "romance."

Backup singer Sheryl Crow, who was to accompany Michael on his upcoming *Bad* world tour, was also touted as "the girl of Michael's dreams." Michael took the slender blonde to Disneyland, threw a small surprise birthday party for her, and was supposedly telling everyone that Crow would make "the perfect mother for my baby."

Certainly the two did generate heat on stage. And Crow told one reporter, "I'm still pinching myself because I can't believe all this has happened to me. I love him. He's a wonderful person. I never thought we would be this close. You dream about these kinds of things, but you never really think they'll come true."

In Michael's case they didn't. Florida-born dancer Tatiana (full name Tatiana Thumbtzen) arrived in Los Angeles in the summer of 1987 to audition for the video *The Way You Make Me Feel*. More than two hundred girls showed up, but the minute Tatiana walked in, Michael jumped out of his seat, pointed at her, and shouted, "She's the one!" The next day Tatiana's agent called to tell her that she had been hired to star opposite Jackson in the video. The shoot would take four days, for which she would be paid $5,000.

In the video Tatiana was cast as a miniskirted seductress. During one scene Michael chased her through an old car. Tatiana's heel got stuck, and when Michael helped free her, he brushed his hand across her rear end. "I was shocked," she recalled, "but it felt good and kind of sexy."

Convinced that Michael was interested in her, she flirted with him outrageously. Over the next eighteen months, in fact, she waged a one-woman campaign to land him in bed. She would put on a "skintight black dress, black stockings, high heels, the works. I wanted to get him going. . . ."

She waited by the phone for him to call, but he didn't—although several of his aides and a crew member did. "I'd wonder, What's wrong with me? His people would always make excuses for him." They told Tatiana that Michael was exhausted from rehearsing for the *Bad* tour, that he had business to conduct. But they also told her that no other woman had affected him the way she had.

On the set Michael was every inch the macho street kid: his hands grazed Tatiana's body and lingered, he would wink, press his body against hers. Yet when the cameras stopped rolling, he made his excuses and vanished.

Still, Frank Dileo encouraged her to keep trying. Even Katherine took her aside and, her eyes welling with tears, told Tatiana that Michael loved her but had no idea how to go about letting her know. She was told constantly by those around Michael that she was the first woman "to even remotely stand a chance of a heterosexual relationship with Michael Jackson." Katherine urged her son, "Just tell the girl!"

When Michael invited her to accompany him on the *Bad* tour, Tatiana was convinced that it was his way of letting her know they had a future together. Even though she had been warned by Dileo and others not to kiss Michael—that he shied away from such intimate contact with women—she spontaneously kissed him on the cheek during a concert at New York's Madison Square Garden. Michael did not seem to mind. So the next night she went a step farther, grabbing Michael and kissing him full on the lips. "I regretted it instantly," she recalled, "because his body went rigid."

In the coming years Katherine and the family would call on Tatiana to step forward and claim that she had had a romance with Michael. In 1993, when a thirteen-year-old boy accused Michael of molesting him, Tatiana appeared on several television programs to offer firsthand testimony that Michael was heterosexual. "He wanted people to think," Tatiana later said, "that he was an all-American red-blooded male, that one day he'd get married, have kids. But deep down in his heart, he knows he never will."

Ironically, at the same time Tatiana was relentlessly pursuing Michael, a Chicago woman named Lavon Powlis was filing a $150 million paternity suit against him, claiming he was the father of her three children. Calling herself "Billie Jean Jackson," Powlis said she first met Michael at Hayvenhurst in 1975 and that each of her three children was conceived after sessions of torrid lovemaking in the backseat of his blue Rolls. She even renamed her children—Lanhej (born in 1976) to Tina Jean, Ansar to Michael Joseph Jackson II, and Lanelle to Michael (pronounced "Michelle") Josephina Jackson. Ansar and Lanelle were twins born in 1982.

Powlis bombarded Michael with love notes and letters and over the years managed to sneak onto the grounds at Hayvenhurst. In 1985 she was arrested for trespassing at the estate with her children in tow. And soon after, custody of her children was awarded to Powlis's brother and sister.

The paternity suit was dropped, but that was little comfort to Michael. Of all the crazed fans who had stalked him over the years, Lavon Powlis appeared to frighten him the most. Katherine shared his concern. "Something has got to be done about that woman," she said, "before somebody gets hurt."

Michael, never truly comfortable around women his own age, unwound only in the company of his special friends. June Scott, whose cousin was a neighbor of Michael's, said she was sometimes invited into Hayvenhurst when she was a teenager in the late 1970s. Then, in July 1987, Scott was visiting Disneyland with her daughter when she spotted Michael. "He was with a pretty little white boy with dark hair and beautiful eyes," she recalled. "He appeared to be about twelve years old. He was very happy and excited to be there with Michael. While we were walking down the path leaving the park, I saw Michael grabbing at and fondling the little boy's butt while he frolicked in front of him. I thought it was strange, but I didn't give it much thought since the little boy didn't seem to mind. He was so thrilled just to be in Michael's presence."

Without an on-screen love interest like Tatiana to distract him, things had gone much more smoothly for Michael during the filming of the *Bad* video in the subways of New York. In an attempt to land a grittier quality to Michael's image and work, Frank Dileo had persuaded his client that neither George Lucas nor his friend Steven Spielberg should direct the video from the title track. Instead Dileo's friend Martin Scorsese of *Taxi Driver* and *Raging Bull* fame was given the job.

"Your butt is *mine.*" Those were the first words in the title song from Michael's new album. "Bad" was his answer to "Beat It," a hard-driving rock number that cast Michael as the tougher-than-tough, black leather–clad leader of a subway-prowling gang. Once again Michael, in all his buckled, zippered glory, seemed almost comical in the role—leaping over turnstiles, turning back knife-toting felons with a sneer. For the part of an urban outlaw, he wore heavy pancake makeup, eye shadow, and lipstick. Shooting was held up briefly one day because one of Michael's artificial eyelashes had fallen off. ("Weird Al" Yankovic capitalized on the silliness of both of Michael's gang-banger videos, turning *Beat It* into *Eat It* and *Bad* into the hugely popular *Fat.*)

Coincidentally, while Michael was shooting the *Bad* video at the 125th Street subway stop in Harlem, Madonna was nearby shooting her *Who's That Girl?* video. She dropped by to spy on the master of the medium and was particularly impressed by a new dance move Michael was trying. She watched as Michael reached down in the middle of the song, grabbed his private parts, and—for all intents and purposes—fondled himself while staring defiantly into the camera. Madonna's reaction was no different from that of others who witnessed the crotch grab for the first time: "Did you see that? Is he *grabbing his balls?* Oh, my God. . . ."

With that one crass in-your-face gesture—which almost certainly would have imperiled the career of any other mainstream star (if it didn't land him in jail)—Michael telegraphed a startlingly defiant message to his father and the stiff-necked elders of his former church. For the benefit of those who still doubted his masculinity, he was also making a statement of another sort. But there was an unmistakably adolescent quality to the gesture. Boys around the age of Michael's special friends were often cautioned by their parents that publicly scratching or touching their genitals was considered uncouth. Michael's brazen message to America's youth seemed to be that Mom and Dad were wrong.

Starting with the *Bad* tour, Michael would grab his crotch frequently and with more ferocity; next to his signature moonwalk, it became his most identifiable on-stage move. But in mid-1987 Walter Yetnikoff was screaming at Michael over the phone to finish *Bad*. He refused. He claimed to be dissatisfied with the quality of the album, but it was doubtful that anything would have satisfied him. He was postponing the release as long as humanly possible because, quite understandably, he feared the inevitable comparisons to *Thriller*.

In July 1987, after the fourth of six surgeries on his nose, Michael invited fifty record industry honchos to Hayvenhurst for a dinner party. It was an evening none of them would forget. Arriving in a fleet of stretch limousines, the executives roamed freely about the Tudor-style estate with its twinkling white Tivoli lights and theme park ambiance.

This was undeniably Michael's world—from the nearly life-size statues of David slaying Goliath and Louis XIV on horseback to the mechanical bull in the game room and the trophy room practically upholstered in gold and platinum records. Perhaps no room impressed Michael's guests more than the gallery above the garage. There, surrounding a life-size wax figure of Michael, were all the talismans of his fame—the glove, the sequined white socks, the Liberace-goes-to-war military jackets, all displayed in bulletproof glass cases rigged with alarms.

Michael was upstairs with Bob Michaelson, looking down at his guests milling about in their expensive suits, drinks in hand, pinkie rings flashing. He was balancing Bubbles, decked out out in sequined suspenders, on his hip. "Just look, Bob," he said, "I've got half the Mafia in my backyard! Isn't it exciting?"

"He was caught up in the whole thing," Michaelson recalled. "I really thought he was getting a physical charge out of it."

Then Michael turned to Michaelson and said, "You're Italian, aren't you, Bob?"

"With a name like Michaelson?" he replied. "No, Michael, I'm Jewish."

Michaelson would later recall the "real look of disappointment on Michael's face" when he told him about his ethnic background. "I guess because I look and talk like those guys, he thought I was one of them. But it was obvious he thought of me differently after that."

Michael's guests had been there about an hour and were about to be summoned to the dining room when the host and La Toya made their entrance, looking, in the words of one guest, "frighteningly" alike in their all-black outfits. "They were so much alike in every way," Norman Winter said half jokingly, "you'd almost forget which one you were talking to."

. . .

While Michael posed for pictures with the recording industry bigwigs he giddily referred to as "half the Mafia," his wheelchair-bound grandfather Samuel Jackson was alone and on welfare at the Tanner Chapel nursing home in Phoenix. A stroke had left him with slurred speech, but it hardly mattered. The other welfare recipient who shared his tiny room suffered from Alzheimer's and spent all day every day staring into space.

Unlike other patients at the home who received monetary support from their families, Samuel Jackson could not afford to buy even a small black-and-white television for his room. Nor could he afford the better meals that were served privately funded patients. Like his roommate, Samuel spent his days in lonely silence—gazing at the signed posters that had been sent him by La Toya and Janet. Michael had not taken the time to send him a picture. Samuel proudly hung a poster of his most famous grandchild on the wall only after it was given to him by a photojournalist.

Every Sunday Samuel, who still believed Michael was the new Messiah, dressed up and waited for a visit from his grandson that never came. In fact, during Samuel's first two years at the nursing home, Michael reportedly did not visit, call, or so much as send a card. "I can't understand," said one angry nurse, "how a man with all those dollars can allow his grandpa to spend the last of his days on state aid." Thomas Dickey, the nursing home's executive director, even appealed directly to Jackson in an interview. "I don't think Michael can have any idea," Dickey said, just how much pleasure his grandfather would get from a visit."

When his grandfather's plight was brought to his attention, Michael sent him an autographed eight-by-ten glossy and went back to promoting *Bad.*

Katherine's mother—Michael's maternal grandmother—was left in even more dire straits. After suffering a series of strokes, she too wound up in a run-down L.A. nursing home that catered primarily to welfare recipients.

Semicomatose but still able to recognize people, Martha Bridges apparently was almost never visited by members of the Jackson family, despite the fact that she lived in nearby Panorama City. Instead she lay vegetating in a tiny room without a television or so much as a photo of a single family member on the wall. "Michael's chimp, Bubbles," said one observer, "lives better than his own grandmother."

The family would rush to Panorama Community Hospital when it appeared Bridges might die in April 1989. Allegedly refusing to pay extra for a private room and a private nurse, the family had relegated Michael's grandmother to a ward crowded with welfare cases. Once she recovered from that crisis, the Jackson family—by any reckoning collectively worth well in excess of $150 million—supposedly balked at paying the 20 percent of her hospital bills not covered by Medicare. The wealthiest man in show business did not spend a penny on his grandmother's care. "It's not," he reportedly said with a shrug when La Toya suggested they care for her at home, "our responsibility."

When the *National Enquirer* carried a story on Martha Bridges' plight in December 1989, the family finally sprang into action. Michael's grandmother was moved to a comparatively luxurious room with round-the-clock nursing care. Michael sent dozens of flowers, several family members visited—and everyone denied that there had ever been a problem.

But within days of her transfer to the private room, gangrene set in, reportedly as a result of infected bedsores and poor circulation. Bridges was transferred to Valley Hospital Medical Center, where her foot was amputated.

When Martha Bridges died in April 1990, Michael and all his siblings except La Toya attended the funeral. She complained that the rest of the family, stung by her criticism, had neglected to inform her that her grandmother had died.

By any measure other than *Thriller*, *Bad* was a glistening, state-of-the-art pop confection. In addition to the pulsating title song, there was the exuberant "The Way You Make Me Feel," "Another Part of Me" from "Captain EO," and Jackson's trembling "I Just Can't Get Over You" duet with Siedah Garrett. On the serious side there was a hard-edged indictment of groupies called "Dirty Diana," an obvious swipe at Michael's old mentor (although he denied it); "Smooth Criminal," a chilling account of a bloody crime; and the stirring "Man in the Mirror." For this last, inspirational cut, Michael was backed up by gospel stars Andrae Crouch and the Winans.

The album was released in August 1987, but not before a last-minute change in the cover design. Instead of a portrait of Michael shot through lace à la Gloria Swanson, CBS used a photograph of Michael looking pretty but surly in his black leather *Bad* attire.

To ensure a proper send-off, CBS aired a half-hour prime-time special, *The Magic Returns,* featuring the full-length, twenty-four-minute *Bad* video interspersed with footage of Michael's career. The critical response was, as Michael had feared, less than ecstatic. But while it did not top or even equal the success of *Thriller, Bad* debuted at number one and would go on to sell more than twenty million copies worldwide, making it the *second* biggest album in history. It also achieved the distinction of being the only album to spawn five number one singles: "I Just Can't Stop Loving You," "Bad," "The Way You Make Me Feel," "Man in the Mirror," and "Dirty Diana."

In September 1987 "Typhoon Michael" swept into Japan on the first leg of his eighteen-month Bad world tour. *"My-ke-ru, My-ke-ru!"* shrieked the forty thousand fans at Korakuen Stadium as Michael emerged from a trap door to the beat of "Wanna Be Startin' Somethin'." Performing without his brothers for the first time, Michael whipped through hit after hit as the audience was dazzled by piercing lasers, throbbing strobes, and a pair of two-story-high video screens that carried the action overhead—all at a cost of $500,000 per show. Pandemonium erupted when Michael put the white glove back on and moonwalked through "Billie Jean."

When the glove came off, Michael sported a brand-new gimmick. Having been informed that the germ-obsessed Howard Hughes sometimes wrapped his fingers in surgical tape so they would not touch any contaminated surface, Michael sported tape on three fingers of his right hand.

Behind the scenes, Michael oversaw every detail of the ninety-member tour, from costumes and special effects (including a magic trick that had him levitating across the stage) right down to the issuing of backstage passes.

It was while Michael was performing before sold-out crowds in Tokyo that a five-year-old Japanese boy named Yoshhiaki Ogiwara was kidnapped and murdered. Michael's publicist Ginny Buckley informed the press that Michael was so "horrified and upset by the whole thing" that he gave the boy's grieving family $20,000. "Michael loves children," Buckley told reporters. "Anything mean or harmful to a child really upsets him."

Meanwhile, back home tabloid stories were beginning to spin out of control, and Michael dispatched his minions to quell some of the rumors. "Michael is overwhelmingly sane," Quincy Jones told reporter Rick Skye, "despite all the oddball rumors flying around. He's far from crazy—and I should know. I've been around him for a long time. He's one of the smartest and most together people I know.

"But he's vulnerable," Jones continued. "When people make out he's some kind of freak, it really hurts him because he's not."

For a *People* magazine cover story that bluntly asked, "Is this guy weird, or what?" Frank Dileo was authorized by Michael to knock down one story after another. Hormone shots? "Ridiculous." Chemical or surgical skin lightening? "Preposterous." The hyperbaric chamber? "He has a chamber. I don't know if he sleeps in it. I'm not for it. . . ." The Elephant Man's bones? "Well, everyone has a skeleton in their closet."

The net effect was, of course, merely to fan the flames of controversy. Michael was particularly upset with the flip manner in which Dileo responded to journalists' questions. Now that he was featured posing with Michael on the *Bad* jacket, Uncle Tookie fancied himself Michael's equal. Michael was going to have to do something about that.

After just a couple of weeks in Japan, Michael cracked under the strain. The fact that he had actually planted many of the rumors—and that some of these wild stories were indeed accurate—mattered little. Convinced of his own martyrdom, Michael sat down in his room at Tokyo's Capitol Tokyu Hotel and scribbled a two-page note. Written with little regard for punctuation, spelling, or penmanship, the note revealed that he was not only in a fragile state of mind, but that his writing skills were scarcely above those of a ten-year-old:

like the old Indian prover SAYS
DO NOT judge a Man until you've walked two moons in
his Moccosins.
MOST people don't know ME, that is WHY they write
such things in wich MOST is not true
I cry very very often Because it Hurts and I wory
about the children all my children all over
the World, I live for them.
If a Man could SAY nothing AGAINST a character but
what he can prove, HISTORY COULD NOT Be Written.
Animals STRIKE, not from Malice, But because they
want to live, it is the same with those WHO
CRITICIZE, they desire our BLOOD, NOT OUR pain.
But STILL I MUST Achieve I MUST seek Truth in all

things. I must endure for the power I was sent
forth, for the World for the children
BUT HAVE Mercy, for I've been Bleeding a LONG TIME
NOW.

The note, signed at the bottom with a tiny, barely legible "MJ.," was intended to fend off his critics. Certainly it spoke volumes about Michael's troubled, childlike mind. But if he was in pain, Michael, who had managed to conceal so much of himself from the public, hid that from them as well. The note would also mark one of the last times Michael signed his name without appending "1998" to it. A numerologist had told him that the number, in combination with his signature, had some spiritual significance. Michael became convinced that if he did not add the "1998" to his name when he signed, he would die.

Whatever his state of mind, going through his dark night of the soul had its compensations. The Japanese leg of the tour alone grossed more than $20 million. And in November Michael moved on to Australia, where he received another unpleasant bulletin from the home front. John Branca phoned to tell him that two old family friends from Gary, Robert Smith and Reynaud Jones, had filed suit in U.S. district court, claiming that their music was stolen for use in the singles "The Girl Is Mine," "Thriller," and "We Are the World." They were demanding $500 million in damages.

Jones had played a role in the original Jackson Five, writing the opening number for the group's very first public appearance at the Roosevelt High School Talent Show. Jones and Smith had teamed up as songwriters and had journeyed to California to play some of their tapes for Joe. They told him they wanted $20,000 for the songs, and Joe arranged a meeting with Michael.

According to Smith and Jones, at the house in Encino, they sang a few of their compositions for Michael, who asked to keep their tapes for a few hours so he could listen to them carefully. The tapes were not returned as Michael had promised, but Smith and Jones went back to Indiana confident that they had a deal with Michael.

As it turned out, there was no deal, and the tapes Smith and Jones gave Michael were never returned. Joe had refused to listen to their complaints so after a decade they had filed suit. "Why are they doing this to me?" Michael squealed. "Those are *my* songs. Why won't everyone just leave me alone!" Outrage was quickly replaced by benign resignation. He knew what he would have to do—go before another star-struck jury and dazzle them with a performance from the witness box. It had worked in Chicago, and it would work again, and again. . . .

Michael suffered yet another blow to his pride in February 1987 when *Rolling Stone* readers voted him the worst artist in no fewer than eight separate categories, including worst male singer, worst dressed, worst album (*Bad*), worst video (*Bad*), worst single ("Bad"), worst hype, and most unwelcome comeback.

Michael wasted no time in getting even. On March 2 he sang "Man in the Mirror" on the Grammy Awards Show—his first live television performance since 1983's *Motown 25*. The awards, held at New York's Radio City Music Hall, featured performances by Whitney Houston, Aretha Franklin, and Billy Joel. But it was unquestionably Michael, backed by a gospel choir, who stole the show.

While he performed on four continents over the next year and a half, Michael made a point of making as many trips home to California as possible. Unknown to his family, he was actively house hunting.

Michael had been in love with the lush Santa Ynez Valley ever since he'd filmed the *Say Say Say* video there six years earlier. During that shoot he had stayed with Paul and Linda McCartney at their rented country home—the awe-inspiring, 2,700-acre Sycamore Ranch. When the property came on the market for $35 million furnished ($32.5 million unfurnished), Michael offered the owners less than half that amount. After weeks of haggling, he prevailed in March 1988 and acquired the ranch—fully furnished with European antiques—for the bargain price of $17 million. He promptly renamed the Sycamore Ranch "Neverland."

Michael did not bother to tell his parents about the purchase, and when they saw on television that he had paid $28 million for the property, they phoned. "Is it true, Michael?" Katherine asked. "Did you buy this ranch for twenty-eight million dollars?"

"Of course not, Mother," Michael replied. And, since he had not actually paid $28 million for the property, he was technically telling the truth.

A few weeks later he moved into his new estate ("I was waiting for Michael to come to us and say something, but he never did," Joe said) and celebrated with a housewarming party. His brothers and sisters and their families were invited. Conspicuously absent were Joe and

Katherine. He had snubbed both his parents because he could not face confronting them with the truth—that as he approached his thirtieth birthday, he was leaving home. Still, Joe admitted, "That hurt us."

But not nearly as much as the fact that Joe remained totally frozen out of Michael's affairs. He and Katherine were particularly suspicious of Michael's ultraloyal inner circle. "The one thing I know is that [Michael's managers] don't want me anywhere around," Joe said at the time. "I'd love to know if Michael is aware of what his people are doing, which I don't think he is. We're talking about millions and millions of dollars."

Michael had put up with his parents' interference for years, but it took a dramatic incident to hasten his departure. During a family barbecue at Hayvenhurst, Joe suspiciously eyed the handsome young blond man Michael had invited. Suddenly he called Michael aside and —within earshot of his siblings and their children—asked, "Well, is it true what everyone says about you—that you're gay?"

"Don't you have any trust in me?" Michael reportedly shouted back. "I'm not gay!"

"It's hard for me to believe you're not," Joe retorted. "You spend a lot of time with so many young guys." Then he suggested to Michael's young friend that it was time for him to leave. He did, and Michael went with him. The following day Michael dispatched a van to Hayvenhurst to collect his things.

With its lushly beautiful landscape and remote location at the foot of the San Rafael Mountains, Neverland—just a twenty-five-minute helicopter ride from Los Angeles—seemed the perfect retreat for the world's most reclusive superstar. And there were additional factors that set Neverland apart from other properties Michael had considered. Not only was the isolated property situated directly across from a nursery school and adjacent to a prep school—putting Michael in close proximity to scores of children from the ages of three to eighteen—it was only minutes from another favorite spot of Michael's: the tiny town of Solvang.

Familiar to most Californians but virtually unknown outside the state, Solvang had been settled by Scandinavian immigrants at the turn of the century and throughout the decades retained much of its ethnic charm. By the late 1980s this quaint collection of inns, restaurants, and bakeries was booming. With its windmills, blue-and-white Copenhagen decor, candy shops, toy stores, and twinkling white Tivoli lights,

Solvang was a particular favorite of children. Michael would bring his special friends there often, to sight-see and shop for toys. None of that could compare, however, with Michael's plans for Neverland.

While battalions of workers began on Michael's private amusement park, he brought his tour home, once again kicking off the U.S. leg of his tour in Kansas City. Michael's *Moonwalk* autobiography was about to be published, and he had invited both the book's editor, Jacqueline Onassis, and her daughter to be in the opening-night audience. When illness kept them both home in New York, Michael arranged for a special phone hookup so they could listen to the concert live. Whenever there was a break, he would dash into the wings and shout, "How'm I doing?" into the phone.

Some three hundred thousand copies of *Moonwalk,* which was ghostwritten by Doubleday editor Shaye Areheart, hit bookstores in April 1988. Michael's memoirs featured a brief introduction by Jackie Onassis and were dedicated to Fred Astaire. In the book, he attacked the press for printing vicious lies about him, sang the praises of his large, warm, and caring family, insisted that he would one day marry and have a child of his own, and extolled the virtues of Frank Dileo—"my shield of armor, my other half. We dream together and achieve together."

Ironically Jackie was as curious as everyone else when it came to Michael's peculiar habits and, more particularly, his sexual preferences. Book designer J. C. Suares, who worked on *Moonwalk* and accompanied Jackie to meetings with Michael at Hayvenhurst, claimed Jackie "couldn't figure out what made him tick. His house was kitschily furnished with paintings of clowns, kind of a la-la land. She kept asking me if he was gay." Indeed, according to Suares, each time they left Hayvenhurst they would "get in the car and she'd say, 'Well, do you think he likes girls?' She was really fascinated by his sexual orientation. She never quite figured it out."

Moonwalk reached number one on *The New York Times* best-seller list just as Michael embarked on the European portion of his tour. No matter. Since worldwide sales figures made it clear that the *Bad* album would not even approach the mark set by *Thriller*, Michael vowed to fire his entire staff once the tour was over. Frank Dileo included.

15

I haven't slept with a woman.
I don't believe in sex before marriage.
I am still a virgin.

In Leeds—the English city where he had met his onetime phone pal Terry George more than a decade earlier—Michael stood center stage while one hundred thousand fans sang "Happy Birthday." He was thirty years old, and he would celebrate his birthday in the company of his current special friend, nine-year-old Jimmy Safechuck.

Not since Emmanuel Lewis had Michael been so infatuated with one of his young playmates. The blond, blue-eyed California boy had appeared as one of the adoring youngsters in a Pepsi spot Michael filmed in early 1988. And once the shoot was over, he had asked Safechuck to tag along on the tour. During much of 1988 and 1989 Michael spent every available hour with Safechuck. He had his costume designers duplicate his stage getups in Safechuck's size so the two could go out in public dressed identically. They even appeared on stage together in matching leather "bondage" suits of the sort that Michael wore in the *Bad* video.

They hugged and whispered behind the tinted windows of Michael's bus, held hands as they took in the sights, and went on buying sprees in Europe. Michael and Safechuck spent tens of thousands of dollars on toys, games, and gadgets in a single outing. Michael even paid

$20,000 so that they would have an entire amusement park to themselves for one day.

Tongues wagged, but it did not seem to bother Safechuck's parents. Michael put them on the payroll and gave them the keys to a sparkling new 1989 Rolls-Royce. The price: $180,000. Later they would be given matching Mercedeses, his and hers.

Michael's publicity machine, meanwhile, worked overtime to create the illusion that he had fallen for backup singer Sheryl Crow. In Rome Crow reportedly went along with Michael when the Vatican gave him a private look at the Sistine Chapel, then accompanied him to Florence to see Michelangelo's *David.* She did, in fact, go with Michael—as did some two dozen others who were part of the tour. Crow, like all other members of the tour—and, for that matter, anyone who worked for Michael—was required to sign a strict confidentiality agreement vowing not to utter a syllable about any of her experiences while in his employ. Crow would go on to a major career of her own as a solo artist.

During their stop in Paris, the Louvre also closed its doors to the public so that Michael could stroll in private through its masterpiece-lined halls. Still, he was never that comfortable solely in the company of adults. In Rome, Italian director Franco Zeffirelli threw a celebrity-studded bash in Jackson's honor. Michael spent the entire evening away from the other guests in a back room, playing on the floor with a half dozen pajama-clad children.

If he seemed wary of adults, Michael made an exception in the case of Princess Diana. He admired her quiet style, grace, and fashion sense —so much so that at one point he had dressed up one of his mannequins in a gown, tiara, and blond wig. In the solitude of his room, Michael and his plastic Princess Di had lengthy conversations about their mutual love of children, their painful shyness, and the unrelenting pressures of coping with the ravenous media.

Moments before taking the stage for his third sold-out concert at London's Wembley Stadium, Michael proudly presented Princess Diana and her husband, the Prince of Wales, with the proceeds from the event—a check for £300,000 (about $450,000). The money went to the Prince's Trust, a charity for disadvantaged children. "He's the most famous person," Diana later told friends of her encounter with Michael, "I've ever met."

Michael also handed Princess Diana two tour jackets for her sons William, then six, and three-year-old Harry. Disappointed that the boys were not on hand to receive their jackets personally, he asked the royal couple why they had not brought William and Harry to the concert. "How did you learn to dance so well?" asked Charles, awkwardly changing the subject. "Could you teach me to dance?"

When it was time for the concert to begin, Michael told the crowd, "I'd like to welcome our royal guests." Then he waved up at the box and yelled, "How're ya doin'?"

"Michael's my favorite pop star," Princess Diana would admit, "but I'm not so sure about my husband." While she bounced and clapped to "Dirty Diana," which Michael seemed to be singing directly to her, Charles glowered in obvious disapproval.

Wherever Michael went in Europe, celebrities turned out to pay homage. In addition to the royal couple, Joan Collins, Ava Gardner, and Harrison Ford were among those who cheered Michael from their VIP seats at Wembley; in Geneva his soulmate, Elizabeth Taylor, and Bob Dylan were in attendance; in Rome Sophia Loren and Gina Lollobrigida, Placido Domingo in Hamburg. Michael would pose for pictures after each concert. His friend Sophia Loren and her onetime rival Gina Lollobrigida had not spoken in years before he brought them together for a photo—but only for a few awkward moments before he rushed off with Jimmy Safechuck.

For all the celebrity encounters on the road, Michael would nonetheless pick as a high point of the tour his visit with Charlie Chaplin's widow, Oona, at Chaplin's home in Vevey, Switzerland, overlooking Lake Geneva. Oona, daughter of the Nobel Prize–winning American playwright Eugene O'Neill, took Michael on a tour of the house. At one point she told her guest that he and her husband had "a lot in common: you were born poor and had to strive to achieve all that you have."

Stunned, Michael replied that in visiting Chaplin's house and speaking with her, he had fulfilled his "biggest childhood dream."

Michael was often in the headlines during the tour, and he made news once again in the fall of 1988, when on a stopover in Ireland he refused to kiss the Blarney Stone—not because of a specific phobia about AIDS, as was widely reported, but because of his phobia about germs in general. The AIDS issue reared its head again in November 1988, when Michael returned to Japan on the final leg of the *Bad* tour. Before Japanese officials would grant members of the tour visas, they had to be tested for AIDS. Four out of the ninety tested HIV positive and were thus unable to obtain visas for the trip. Again it was then rumored that the decision to test had been Michael's and not that of the Japanese government.

Michael was upset enough to call Elizabeth Taylor, founder of AMFAR and an active crusader on behalf of AIDS research, to reassure her that the rumors were untrue. Michael was not, in fact, more afraid of the AIDS virus than he was of any other serious communicable disease. He did, out of concern for any number of serious ailments that could be transmitted through tainted blood, travel with a frozen supply of his own—just in case.

In January 1989, as the tour rolled into its final three weeks, Michael unleashed *Moonwalker* on an unsuspecting public. A ninety-four-minute, eight-segment montage of file footage documenting his twenty-four-year career, clay animation, and several superbly crafted music videos, *Moonwalker* was as slick as it was ambitious.

In "Badder," Michael's *Bad* video was reenacted by a gang of children (the actor playing "Baby Bad" Michael, Brandon Adams, became one of Michael's special friends). "Speed Demon" had Michael eluding fans by undergoing a variety of chameleonlike transformations via claymation. And in "Leave Me Alone," one of *Moonwalker*'s most imaginative segments, Michael spoofed his own manic celebrity by viewing his life as a carnival ride—complete with the Elizabeth Taylor shrine, the Elephant Man's bones, and dog-faced paparazzi.

The centerpiece of *Moonwalker*, however, was a forty-minute film version of Michael's exquisitely sinister song "Smooth Criminal." And once again Michael was playing with children—in this case Sean Lennon, Brandon Adams, and Kelly Parker—when he was suddenly plunged into the lair of the nefarious "Frank Lideo." Frank Dileo's anagrammatic screen persona, played by his friend Joe Pesci, was out to enslave children through drugs, and, as always, it was up to Michael to stop him. Smooth as silk in his spats and mafiosio outfit, Michael again indulged his ongoing fascination with the realm of the criminal underworld.

USA Today claimed that *Moonwalker* "tripped the hype fantastic." Accusing Jackson of being his own "special effect" in the film, *Time* pointed out that *Moonwalker* was "heavily shrouded in fantasy—of persecution, of reprisal, of reclaiming lost innocence—but compromised by its own willful and slightly desperate flash."

Still, within two weeks *Moonwalker* had sold five hundred thousand copies, surpassing Michael's own *Thriller* to become the biggest-selling home video ever. It would go on to gross around $30 million. Unfortunately Michael had bankrolled the video to the tune of $27 million, leaving him with the net profit of $3 million. For Michael, accustomed to eight-figure sums, it was a major disappointment.

He blamed the shortfall on the fact that Dileo had failed to arrange a theatrical release for *Moonwalker* in the United States (it was released theatrically in Europe). Dileo had, in fact, negotiated an $8 million deal, but at the last minute Michael had rejected it.

However upset he may have been over the failure of *Moonwalker* to turn a huge net profit, Michael was desolate over the final numbers on the *Bad* album. Selling a paltry twenty million copies—again, making it second only to *Thriller*—*Bad* fell woefully short of the mind-boggling one hundred-million-copy sale Michael had predicted.

On January 27, 1989, Michael stood on stage at the Los Angeles Sports Arena and bade an emotional farewell to his fans. In the last three days of his tour, Barbra Streisand, Sylvester Stallone, and nearly every other star in the Hollywood galaxy showed up to see him. Bathed in sweat and adulation, an exhausted Michael embraced his backup singers and band members, then stretched out his arms in a Christ-like gesture as the applause washed over him. This had been his first solo tour, and, he pledged, it would be his last.

Playing before a record 4.4 million people in fifteen countries, Michael grossed $125 million—making the *Bad* musical tour the biggest in history. Along the way he had donated millions to orphanages, hospitals, and charities—almost exclusively for the benefit of the young. During his Madison Square Garden stint, for example, he donated $600,000 to the United Negro College Fund. The fund's Michael Jackson Scholars program paid tuition and board for seventy-eight students enrolled at predominantly black colleges around the country.

"His goal was to establish himself as the world's biggest solo artist," Frank Dileo said. "He's done that. He's got the biggest gross and has played to the most people. What are we going to do next time? Play for two years? That would kill *me.*" In the course of the *Bad* road show, stress resulted in Michael losing ten pounds. Dileo had gained forty.

Michael was now determined to pursue the goal that had eluded him since *The Wiz*—screen stardom. When the *Bad* tour stopped in London, Michael had dropped in at Elstree Studios, where Steven Spielberg was filming *Indiana Jones and the Last Crusade* with Harrison Ford and Sean Connery. Jackson had heard that Spielberg was likely to direct the screen version of Andrew Lloyd Webber's hit musical *The Phantom of the Opera.*

"Steven, I want to play the phantom," Michael said, tying on his surgical mask to make his point. "I can do it. Nobody understands him like I do." Michael's undeniable empathy for the tortured character aside, Spielberg knew that he lacked sufficient weight—physically and emotionally—to carry it off.

One member of Michael's inner circle who had been put to work on finding him the right screen vehicle was entertainment tycoon David Geffen. But after three years he had failed to come up with a movie project suitable for Michael. "It's my failure, not his," Geffen was quick to explain. "I just wasn't interested in doing a bad movie."

Likening Michael to his idol Fred Astaire, Geffen pointed out that a movie would have to be specially tailored for him—that he wasn't suited to heavy dramatic roles or even standard comedy ones. "You can't cast him in just anything. Don't bet against him. He's very single-minded and he's a very hard worker. He'll get it done."

Dileo insisted, somewhat disingenuously, that Michael was in no rush. "There are a lot of artists who have chosen to do scripts that they shouldn't have done," Dileo said. "It's like a good poker game. You can afford to wait it out till it's right."

Meanwhile, Dileo was basking in his bizarre (and here the word was appropriate) friendship with Michael. In a you-say-either, I-say-either interview with *Los Angeles Times* writer Paul Grein, Dileo described himself and Michael as the music industry's oddest couple. "You couldn't find two more different people. He won't eat meat; I'll run out to get a cheeseburger. I'll take a drink; he won't touch the stuff. I'll sit and watch football; he'll go crazy if I'm doing it. Just look at us—he's skinny; I'm fat. If we stand next to each other, we look like the number ten." And yet, Dileo went on, "we have a ball."

After nearly eighteen months on the road, Michael was drained physically and emotionally—and still reeling from the "Wacko Jacko" stories that had trailed him throughout Europe. Returning to Neverland—an Elba of his own creation—Michael now had the time to seethe. "I know him when he gets like that," Bob Michaelson said. "If something goes wrong, it is never Michael's fault. He has to find someone to blame. He needs a constant supply of scapegoats."

As the decade drew to a close, Michael became increasingly aware that his chief rival was not Prince, but Madonna. Madonna and Jackson had actually been fascinated by each other for some time. They were, after all, pop icons nonpareil and as such could empathize with each other in ways that few others could. Michael was intrigued by Madonna's uncanny ability to continually refashion her image and by her own shrewd handling of the "suits" who ran the entertainment industry.

In truth, she had been emulating his business savvy all along. Just as her career was getting off the ground back in the early eighties, she had hired Freddy DeMann as her manager—not knowing that he had just been fired by Michael. Unlike DeMann's relationship with Michael, the DeMann-Madonna business marriage thrived as long as DeMann was willing—as one business associate put it—"to put up with her endless shit. It's 'Freddy do this, Freddy do that—now!' Madonna treats him like dirt."

Michael may have respected Madonna as a businesswoman, but he was also jealous of her. "She isn't that good," he complained to an associate after she was named Artist of the Decade by Warner Records in 1989 (at the award ceremonies, Madonna had expressed her gratitude by licking her trophy). "Let's face it: She can't sing. She's just an okay dancer. What does she do best? She knows how to market herself. That's about it."

Michael called Dileo to complain that Madonna didn't deserve her award, pointing out that it made him "look bad." It was then suggested that he ask MTV to name him Video Vanguard Artist of the Decade—a notion that appealed to him. "That'll teach that heifer," he was quoted as saying. Madonna harbored no such resentment of Michael. She was in awe of his talent, his legendary weirdness, and most of all his business acumen.

Michael had also complained frequently to Dileo that he was tired of hearing people praise Elvis Presley. "Why do they call Elvis the King?" he demanded to know. "He wasn't even that talented. Why don't they call *me* the King?"

Dileo would listen to Michael's Elvis tirade, then sigh. "I'd have to explain," he said. When it became clear that explanations wouldn't do, Michael's people arranged for Elizabeth Taylor to proclaim him "king of pop" at one of the many awards ceremonies at which they both appeared. From then on it was understood that she would remind the world of his regal stature whenever she mentioned his name in public.

Michael did not make his feelings about Elvis known to his daughter, Lisa Marie, in late 1988. The heir to Presley's $100 million-plus fortune had become friends with Michael around the time her brief marriage to musician Danny Keough was breaking up. Lisa told Michael that she was expecting a baby, and in Keough's absence he kindly offered to be a surrogate father to the child. At her mother Priscilla's urging, Lisa Marie politely declined his offer.

Kenny Rogers knew both Elvis and Michael, and he recognized the parallels. "Michael is the Elvis of his generation," Rogers said, "and he, too, is locking himself away from the real world. That's an extremely unhealthy way to live. I know what it's like to be mobbed by fans every time you go out. It can be terrifying. . . . But he's seen out so rarely that when he's spotted, it's a major event, and he gets mobbed. He's got to learn to get out more."

Michael often seemed to want it both ways. He wanted to get out and mingle with people, but he could not bear being ignored; he needed to be noticed without being recognized. Thus he often selected disguises that were calculated to conceal his identity and at the same time attract attention.

More than once, these absurd getups got him into trouble. Julie Andrews (a clerk at Zales jewelry store in suburban Simi Valley, not the singer) immediately became suspicious when she noticed a man wearing an obviously fake mustache, glasses, red polyester clothes, a red baseball cap, and false buck teeth. The tall stranger had a boy with him and kept looking in the mirror to adjust his mustache as a sales clerk showed him a case of rings. Stopped by a security guard as he left the store, he was asked why he was wearing a false mustache. "I have to, I'm in disguise," the odd-looking man said. "I'm Michael Jackson."

"My first thought was that this guy had gotten off the elevator between floors," said the guard—until Michael whipped off the mustache and removed the teeth. Within minutes three squad cars arrived and Michael was mobbed by autograph seekers. Then Michael and his young companion zipped off in a brown Mercedes with the few things they had managed to buy at a gift shop before their cover was blown: a $4.99 toy figurine and a pair of heart-shaped sunglasses.

Once, Michael's mother was confronted by a portly man standing in her kitchen. When she demanded to know who he was, the stranger squealed, "Mother, you don't know who I am! "

"That," Katherine said, "was my introduction to Michael's fat suit."

According to Katherine, it was around this time that police in the suburb of Van Nuys spotted a young black man driving a blue Rolls-Royce and ordered him to pull over. "This looks like a stolen car," the officer said. When the young man turned out to have inadvertently left his driver's license at home, a check was run on the car and it turned out that there was an outstanding traffic ticket.

Even though Michael was not wearing a disguise, the officer refused to believe this skinny young man in the sunglasses and broad-brimmed hat was who he said he was. Michael wound up in the holding cell at the Van Nuys jail until someone could bail him out.

"Michael was not only not put out by the experience," his mother claimed, "he professed to be happy." "I got to see how it felt to be in jail!" he told her.

No matter what disguises he wore, Michael could not escape the never-ending Jackson family melodramas. La Toya, once considered the most docile of the Jackson offspring and the only one still living at home, now complained bitterly that her father's mismanagement had cost her a chance for any career of her own. She wanted to fire him, but Joe proffered a compromise. While their contract remained in force, he brought in Jack Gordon, a shadowy character with underworld connection, to devote himself full time to managing the career of the nettlesome La Toya.

Joe had intended for Gordon, a former Nevada brothel owner who had served time in prison for attempting to bribe state gaming officials, to be nothing more than his puppet. Instead La Toya ran away with Gordon in March 1988. They would be married the following September in Reno, although La Toya would insist that the marriage was a strictly platonic arrangement. Charging that her parents had hired "goons" to kidnap her and drag her back to Hayvenhurst, La Toya claimed that Gordon was her sole protector.

Her fears were not entirely unfounded. Joe and Katherine had reportedly considered the possibility of having their rebellious daughter committed to a mental hospital—a move they could conceivably accomplish as La Toya's legal next of kin. Once she married Gordon, he became La Toya's next of kin, effectively eliminating her parents as a threat.

Why were Joe and Katherine so frantic to lure La Toya back home? There, they stood at least a small chance of controlling her. Under Gordon's influence La Toya was becoming more outspoken about what had really transpired behind the stone and stucco walls of Hayvenhurst.

In a move that shook the entire family down to its foundation, La Toya was paid a reported $1 million to pose nude for *Playboy*. Katherine in particular was mortified by the photographs which, among other poses, showed a voluptuous La Toya lounging about with her pet boa constrictor in a rather compromising position.

Once the issue hit the stands, Jermaine assumed the role of the family spokesman and condemned his sister on *Entertainment Tonight.* Then he telephoned her directly and, according to La Toya, called her "a piece of shit. You've degraded our family, and you've made us all look bad!" Janet also phoned and harangued her sister—not for posing nude, but for neglecting to tell her what she had done. Years later, Janet herself would pose nude on the cover of *Rolling Stone,* her boyfriend's hands cupped over her breasts.

Michael, who had gotten wind of the nude layout weeks before publication, had tried unsuccessfully to have La Toya's nipples airbrushed out of the photos. But even then—weeks before the *Playboy* issue hit the stands—he called La Toya to praise the pictures. "You know," he said, "you're going to sell more copies than any other issue in *Playboy* history."

La Toya would also claim in her memoirs that Michael told her he knew the reasons why she'd posed for the explicit pictures: to get back at both their parents and at the Jehovah's Witnesses. "I know," he said, "because that's why I wrote *Bad.* And that's why I wiggle the way I do and grab myself . . . it's to get back at Joseph and tell them I do what I want, and they can't control me."

La Toya took solace from her brother's words of support, but they rang hollow when he cautioned her not to tell anyone. Michael then went back to his parents and said that he shared their sense of disgust and moral outrage. From now on, he told them, he would no longer speak to La Toya. "As much as I love Michael," La Toya said, "recently he always seemed to play both sides of the field."

For all its Sturm und Drang, La Toya's defection was by no means the biggest crisis facing Joe and Katherine. Years earlier Joe had teamed up with real estate developer Gary Berwin to build a $7.9 million entertainment complex in Los Angeles. When that deal soured in 1988, Berwin won a $3 million judgment against Jackson for breach of contract. Now, unable to raise the $3 million in cash, Joe and Katherine faced nothing less than financial ruin.

Neither Michael nor Janet, whose collective worth was well in excess of $185 million, came to their parents' aid. A glimmer of hope appeared from an unexpected source: the Moonies. As an envoy of the Reverend Sun Myung Moon's controversial Unification Church, a South Korean businessman named Kenneth Choi arrived in Los Angeles to offer the family $15 million if they would play a series of four concerts in Korea. Aware that Michael was estranged from the Jehovah's Witnesses, Reverend Moon sought to marry the interests of his cult to the world's most celebrated person.

After two trips to Seoul to hammer out the details of a contract with the Moonies, Joe and Katherine were still unable to talk Michael into going to Korea. So the Moonies put a price on Michael's head: anyone who could persuade him to sign up for the four concerts would receive $1 million in cash. The Reverend Moon's emissaries eventually decided their best hope lay with Katherine and paid her the million dollars—on condition that she could land Michael within two weeks.

In the coming months the Koreans would lavish millions of dollars' worth of gifts—mostly cash and cars—on anyone who had the faintest chance of securing Michael's signature on a contract. Katherine had to return her $1 million. Still, Korean money would continue to flow in the Jacksons' direction. As a down payment, Michael's parents were given $90,000 in cash and the keys to a new black Rolls-Royce Corniche. Michael, for his part, did not turn down their offer of a white Rolls.

Ultimately, according to Jerome Howard, former president of the Jackson family companies, the Koreans paid $5 million to Joe—including the Rolls, gold statuary, and gold coins. Joe repaid $3 million but reportedly kept the remainder. In return, Joe pledged that Michael would not only perform in Korea, but that he would do so dressed in native garb.

When it became clear to Kenneth Choi that Joe could deliver Michael's brothers but not Michael, he told the Jacksons that he would rather commit suicide than lose face back home. He went to Hayvenhurst and again pleaded with Katherine to intervene. With Choi in the room, she placed a call to Michael. When he still balked at even meeting with the Moonie, Choi grabbed the receiver. "Please come to Korea," he begged Michael, crying hysterically. "Please perform—or else I'll kill myself and my family!"

"Family?" responded Michael. Choi, he learned, had a wife and an infant son, Elbert. Michael relented, agreeing to meet with Choi at the *Soul Train* awards. When a decidedly relieved Katherine brought her Korean benefactor backstage, Choi literally fell to his knees, clasped his hands together, and begged Michael to come to Korea. To avoid any further embarrassment, Michael grudgingly agreed.

One of the few people who did not take advantage of the Moonies' largesse—he had flatly turned down Choi's $1 million offer—was Frank Dileo. Choi had visited Dileo while he was in North Carolina trying to shed pounds at Duke University's famous reduction clinic. Dileo, wanting to make sure his client was aware of all that was going on behind his back, briefed Michael over the phone. When they ended the call, Dileo remembered, "everything was hunky-dory."

Three days later John Branca phoned Dileo. "Michael," Branca said, "doesn't want to work with you anymore."

Jackson's publicist Lee Solters issued a brief statement: "Michael Jackson and Frank Dileo have announced an amicable parting. Jackson said, 'I thank Frank for his contribution on my behalf during the past several years.' "

Dileo was crushed. After five years together Michael did not even think enough of his uncle Tookie to fire him personally. "It was a cowardly thing to do," Dileo told friends. "He should have told me how he felt himself."

Dileo's firing sent shock waves throughout the music industry. Speculation ran rampant, but there seemed little doubt that David Geffen had played some role in Dileo's ouster. Certainly Michael had his own reasons for dumping Uncle Tookie. Dileo had become accustomed to treating him like a surrogate son—pushing him to meet his record deadlines, scolding him when he tried to duck out of social obligations. As a thirty-year-old man, Michael had now come to expect the kind of deferential treatment afforded few mortals, and Dileo wasn't giving it to him. Tookie—part power broker, part court jester—had forgotten who was king.

"They always had a casual relationship," a colleague said. "Michael likes that sort of thing—food fights, practical jokes, horsing around. In some ways—not all—he's got the mind of a twelve-year-old. No, make that a nine-year-old. But there's also that fifty-year-old businessman inside who's thinking Don't forget who makes the money. You work for *me.* Frank just got too close to Michael, too comfortable. He stepped over the line without knowing it. Frankly I'm amazed he managed to hang in there as long as he did."

Dileo was also entirely too visible. Since Michael had cast himself in the role of recluse, it was left to his manager to talk to reporters, and he was worried that Dileo was getting cocky, that he was gradually assuming the mantle of a Svengali. But most important, Michael was still peeved that *Bad* had not outsold *Thriller.*

Once he had given the order to dump Dileo, Michael refused even to speak to the man he had called "my shield of armor, my other half." To complicate matters, Michael balked at Dileo's demand for $5 million in severance—a not unreasonable figure considering the fact that Michael had amassed a $150 million–plus fortune during the period Dileo managed his career. Dileo threatened to sue and, worse, to spill some of Michael's darker secrets to the press. He got the $5 million.

A year later Dileo confessed that his abrupt and unexpected dismissal "still hurts plenty." Yet he took some consolation in the fact that while Michael still searched for a film role, he, Dileo, was already acting opposite his friends De Niro and Pesci, playing tough guy "Tuddy" in *GoodFellas.* "You'll never guess," he joked with his fellow screen mafiosi between takes, "who's number one on my hit list."

Less than a week before summarily axing Dileo, Michael had paid a visit to the Cleveland Elementary School in Stockton, California, where a crazed gunman dressed in battle fatigues had killed five children and wounded thirty others. Although he wore a blue military-style uniform and was flanked by armed bodyguards, Michael comforted the children with his reassuring presence. He walked through classrooms, handed out Michael Jackson T-shirts and tapes, signed autographs, and chatted with several children one to one. He also visited a church where several children who were too afraid to return to school were gathered, and the San Joaquin General Hospital, where two students were recovering from their wounds.

"When Michael came, he looked right at me and waved," said eight-year-old Thahn Tran, whose brother was one of those massacred. "I didn't want to go back to school, but Michael made it all right again."

As his limousine pulled away from the waving students, Michael suddenly turned silent and began shaking his head. "Why?" he muttered to himself. "Why? Why?"

16

My best friends, in the whole world, are children. I wish people wouldn't lie so much and just come out and say what they mean. Children and animals haven't learned those things yet, and they can't hurt you.

"There was a big change after he moved to Neverland," Michael's long-time personal maid, Blanca Francia, said. "It was 'Now I get to do what I want to do.' "

To ensure his privacy, Michael required all Neverland employees to sign a confidentiality agreement. They were also instructed not to discuss anything they saw at Neverland with one another. "It was like a police state," said Charli Michaels, who worked as a member in good standing of Neverland's security force for three years. "Employees were not supposed to talk to each other. It was all a game of manipulation and control to keep you on the edge."

Yet over the next six years they would look on as Michael played enthusiastic host to scores of "special friends." While some of these young boys were just friends, others had a more intimate relationship with Michael. For many the drill seldom varied. The little boys whose company Michael craved were usually dropped off at the front gate by their parents. They rode to the main house in a carriage pulled by a Clydesdale, and then an aide would take them directly to Michael's bedroom.

"Adult guests were always announced," said Johnny Ciao, who worked as a cook at the ranch for eight months in 1988, "but the kids arrived in a hush-hush manner, off to the side. Suddenly they just appeared. . . . We members of the staff would be called and told that there was a kid in Michael's room."

The initial response of each child was predictable: "These little boys were awestruck when they arrived at Michael's mansion—they thought they'd died and gone to heaven." Ciao described the boys as aged seven to fourteen and "of a certain type: angelic faces, brown hair, and big eyes."

Neverland boasted a lavishly appointed four-bedroom guest house and another ten bedrooms in the stately main residence. Nonetheless, virtually all of Michael's little visitors stayed in their host's second-floor bedroom—for anywhere from one night to several weeks.

To ensure total privacy, Michael's bedroom was strictly off-limits, as was what some Neverland employees referred to as the Secret Playroom, located in the building adjacent to the main house. Only Blanca Francia and Neverland's Filipino housekeepers, Mark and Faye Quindoy, had keys to these rooms.

The master suite itself was dominated by a king-size bed. And adjacent was the Shirley Temple Room, for guests. A virtual shrine to the mop-topped child star of the Depression era, the Shirley Temple Room included movie posters, dolls, and an eerily lifelike Shirley Temple mannequin wearing a pink dress, a matching pink hair bow, and patent-leather Mary Jane shoes. Pictures of Temple papered the walls along with childhood snapshots of Michael; on one end table was an autographed photo of Temple with Franklin Roosevelt.

The housekeeping staff had strict orders to change guests' bedsheets every day, just as if they were at a hotel. Yet in all the years Francia worked at Neverland, she says she never had to make up the bed in the Shirley Temple Room. Nor was it ever made up by the maids who succeeded her; there was never any need. "No one ever made up that guest room," said Neverland manager Mark Quindoy, "because there was no sign that it had ever been slept in. Not once."

In the master bedroom there were mirrors everywhere—for one overriding purpose: Michael always put on full makeup before leaving his bedroom. After affixing his false eyelashes, he always applied the same cosmetic brands: Fashion Fair, Honey Glow, and Lancôme eye shadow, mascara, and eyeliner. The layers were so thick, said Mark Quindoy, that Michael appeared to be wearing "full stage makeup at all times around the house. No one ever saw him without makeup. No one." Mark's wife, Faye, who also prepared meals for Michael, concurred. "When I took him his breakfast, he'd already have his makeup on."

The headboard of Michael's king-size bed contained controls for the giant-screen television—which raised from the foot of the bed with the press of a button—the VCR, stereo, and a number of other electronic gadgets. One of these was a surveillance system that monitored footsteps in the hallway outside the room. The steps were magnified on loudspeakers in the room so that they grew increasingly loud as someone approached Michael's door. When the steps came within a few feet of the door, a small alarm bell sounded in the room. There was also a peephole in the door.

Whenever a boy was with Michael in his bedroom or the Secret Playroom, he called Ciao to order meals at any time of the day or night—nearly always vegetarian pizza or tacos, Ciao said, "even for breakfast." The cook would bring the tray to the room, knock on the door, and wait while Michael checked him out through the peephole. Instructions were the same as they had been at Hayvenhurst: "Just leave it outside."

Once, while Michael was inside the Secret Playroom with a special friend, Ciao delivered a tray and then turned back to see Michael wearing nothing but a pair of white BVD briefs. "I was shocked," he said. "Michael quickly picked up the tray and went back to the room. He never acknowledged me."

The Secret Playroom was scarcely six feet wide and ten feet long, with a sofa and a thirty-inch Sony Trinitron TV that provided the only illumination. There was a single phone in the room, rigged to make outgoing calls only, so that Michael and his companions would not be disturbed. Whenever he managed to glance inside, Ciao saw the same thing. "There was always a young boy," he said, "reclining on the sofa."

What Ciao did not know was that there were other "secret" rooms to which only Michael had access. His special friends were amazed when Michael walked over to one of his bedroom walls, pressed in one spot, and—open sesame—a concealed door swung wide to reveal a narrow passageway. Michael then led his friends down the ten-foot-long corridor and unlocked the door of a room to which only he had the key.

This was Michael's Treasure Room, the windowless, flagstone-and-stucco-walled fourteen-foot-by-ten-foot bombproof bunker where he horded some of his prized possessions. In one bulletproof glass case glittered over $1 million worth of jewels. More than one hundred antique dolls were displayed in the room, as well as an autographed photo of Michael and Elizabeth Taylor, a snapshot of Michael at the hospital bedside of courageous AIDS victim Ryan White, and framed personal letters from Presidents Gerald Ford and Ronald Reagan.

Under a glass bell jar, there was a one-of-a-kind $50,000 porcelain figurine depicting Michael in the company of several Disney characters. Above a small fireplace hung an oil portrait of the Jackson Five in their early 1970s heyday appraised at $100,000. And hanging over the room's narrow maple bed was the pièce de résistance of Michael's collection: a $200,000 oil painting commissioned by him depicting Michael among his "equals": Albert Einstein, George Washington, Abraham Lincoln, the Mona Lisa, and E.T.—all wearing his trademark sunglasses and white sequined glove.

Not even Mark Quindoy, who had keys to every other room at Neverland, was allowed inside the Treasure Room without Michael's permission. With that exception, they were given total access and had an insider's view of life at Neverland accorded few others.

Quindoy and his wife, Faye, got their first glimpse of Michael's peculiar brand of quirkiness when he interviewed them for the jobs of estate manager and cook in May 1989. "The place took our breath away," recalled Quindoy, who had practiced law in the Philippines before emigrating to the United States. "Everything was so lavish and spectacular."

The job interview began in Michael's office, where a huge Indian chief's headdress hung on the wall alongside three London bobbies' helmets and two full suits of armor. Michael did not look either Quindoy in the eye during the interview but, as Quindoy recalled, "just stared into space as he spoke to us. Suddenly he sat up and said, 'Would you like to see the ranch?' "

During the twelve-hour personal guided tour of Neverland, Michael pointed out to the Quindoys that he spent $300,000 a year on new bulbs because it made him cry when flowers died. All thirty of the ranch's gardeners had strict instructions to replace a flower as soon as it started to wither. "He turned to me with tears in his eyes," Quindoy recalled, "and he said, 'You know, I hate to see pretty things dying. I wish they lived forever, like in the movies.' "

Michael took the Quindoys to the Treasure Room. "This is my monument," he said before opening the door. "I want you to see it and to love it." As they stared in amazement at the painting over the bed, Michael suddenly turned to them and asked, "Do you love me?"

"Why, yes, Michael, we love you," the Quindoys answered in unison. They got the job.

As manager of Neverland for the next two years, Quindoy oversaw a staff of thirty groundskeepers, fifteen armed guards, ten maids, two zookeepers, and the estate's own one-man fire department. Michael had become so terrified after a small fire broke out near his animals that he built his own pump station on the premises.

Faye Quindoy replaced Ciao as the cook. Michael insisted her dishes be given the names of Disney characters. So when she prepared each day's menu, it would feature such fare as Goofy Salad, Mickey Mouse Cake, a Minnie Mouse Milkshake, Seven Dwarfs Pizza, and Cinderella Ice Cream. They always served Elizabeth Taylor's favorite meal whenever she dropped by: Peter Pan Hot Dogs (Taylor would eat two or three), Pluto Pie, Donald Duck chocolate drinks (she downed four in a row). Taylor was especially fond of Quindoy's Chicken Littles, chicken wings formed to resemble lollipops. She ate twenty-two at a single sitting.

Most of the time Faye Quindoy found herself in the same position as Michael's mother—trying desperately to get him to eat and worrying about his health. "We were terrified that he never cared for food," said Mark Quindoy, who believed Michael was anorectic. "He would only drink Evian water or orange juice every day."

The Quindoys would encounter new eccentricities with each passing day. Whenever he was inspired, Michael pasted song lyrics on the bedroom walls or scrawled them on his $1,000 sheets. Once Mark Quindoy came upon Michael sitting cross-legged on the floor of the living room, tearing up $100,000 in $100 bills and laughing as he tossed them into the air. "Oh, Mark," he told the startled Quindoy, who pleaded with him to stop, "it's only money. Isn't it pretty? Money makes the best confetti."

Perhaps no one was more intimately familiar with Michael's strange personal habits than Blanca Francia. Michael was no less messy at Neverland than he had been at Hayvenhurst. Beds were rumpled, toys left scattered about, and clothes dropped on the floor right where they had been taken off.

But there had been one noticeable change. "Now the little boys were staying weeks at a time," Blanca said. "Sometimes the parents came with the kids, and they would sleep in the guest house or a guest room, and the boys would sleep with Michael. The parents just looked the other way. They were getting money, getting things. . . ."

Some of the parents, however, were clearly upset about what they discovered at Neverland. As early as 1988 one boy's parents reportedly argued with Michael when they arrived to pick up their son one Sunday morning. Michael anxiously told Johnny Ciao to "get them anything they want." The parents were in the living room, and when he walked in, Ciao told writers Tony Brenna and Alan Braham Smith, "I immediately felt a frost. It was obvious something was up and Michael wanted me to appease the parents in some way."

The thirteen-year-old boy was slouched in a chair, looking, in Ciao's words, "very glum."

Ciao asked the parents if he could get them anything.

"No!" they snapped. "We're leaving!"

"It was obvious they were very unhappy and that words had been exchanged between them and Michael." According to Ciao, Michael "looked very disturbed, didn't call me for food that night, and didn't come out until noon the following day."

Blanca Francia also eventually became concerned when she saw Michael's increasing interest in her son. Meanwhile Francia kept quiet about what she saw and, she freely admitted, understood she was taking cash and gifts in exchange for her silence. There were little notes —"For a charming person," Michael would scribble, or "a competent person"—usually accompanied by two or three $100 bills. In the course of her employment, Francia estimated, these tips amounted to at least $5,000. Since Michael was not overly generous with other members of the staff, many of whom complained bitterly about their wages, Francia had strong suspicions about why she was being treated so well.

Usually when she arrived in the morning to tidy up Michael's room as best she could, Michael would be lying in bed in his frilly silk pajamas while a special friend stretched out beside him. Before long Francia, the Quindoys, and the rest of the staff became accustomed to the sight of the young boys walking about unself-consciously wearing nothing but cotton briefs.

On occasion, Francia would walk in while Michael and a boy sat in bed together, both naked from the waist up. As he had in Encino, Michael took baths with some of the boys. He did not seem to mind when Francia saw him in the water with a nine- or ten-year-old guest, their underpants clearly visible atop a heap of towels alongside the Jacuzzi. She assumed that beneath the swirling water they were nude.

Once when Francia came in to clean up, Michael was nowhere to be seen. She heard squeals coming from the bathroom and went to investigate. Peeking into the bathroom, she saw Michael and one of his special friends in the shower together, laughing and "moving around."

She glanced down and saw their underwear on the floor. "Oh, my God," she said to herself, backing slowly out of the room, "he's going to get mad because I got into the room." Later she confessed to being "embarrassed. I feel like I got in there, and I shouldn't do it. I shouldn't just walk in and see what I can see."

Francia would later claim that she learned far more than she ever wanted to know about Michael's habits. One day she found him rummaging through his dresser drawers for a pair of underpants. Francia joined in the search and promptly found piles of BVD briefs—as many as sixty pair—that she had folded neatly and placed in a drawer.

"No, not those," Michael said, still searching. "You know, the special kind."

Michael had run out of the underwear she says he preferred—briefs with a small pocket in the front—and told her to go out and get him some. When she returned with a new supply, Michael asked her what she thought of them.

"I don't know." Francia shrugged.

"Well," she remembers Michael replying, fingering the pocket located just above the genital area, "it's just that I use it for a special dance."

After the "special dance," the underwear would often disappear. Michael told Francia that he had thrown them away.

There was more. According to Francia, Michael seemed to have decided that he did not have to abide by the rules of polite society. If he felt the need, he would not bother to find a bathroom—he simply would relieve himself in his pants. "Don't be surprised if you see any dirty underwear," Francia recalled him saying. "Sometimes I can't hold it, so I just go in my underwear."

Michael's toilet habits sometimes spilled over into his vocabulary. He went through entire days speaking in "doo-doo." He called himself and everyone around him "doo-doo head," managing to work the infantile term into nearly every sentence—much to the consternation of his staff. "This is doo-doo," he said of a television program he and a friend were watching. "I'm hungry. I wonder what I'll have. Maybe some doo-doo."

More revealing and disturbing was the "special name" he now gave his young friends. To Michael they were all "Rubba." Why Rubba? From "rubbing boy against his body," Francia surmised. "He had boys sitting in his lap, rubbing them." Quindoy reached the same conclusion: "He called them Rubba because he was always rubbing up against them."

In return, one of the boys called Michael "Daddy."

Michael's bedroom featured two large walk-in closets. One was papered with sixty or more photographs of children. Hidden inside was yet another closet within a closet that contained his large collection of videotapes and photo albums from agencies representing child models and actors. Just as he had done at Hayvenhurst, Michael would sit for hours in his room, poring over these books of publicity pictures, looking for boys.

He often did some picture-taking of his own. With a Polaroid camera he kept in his room, Michael took photos of his special friends. Francia spotted one such snapshot lying on a table in Michael's room. Francia said it showed a particular favorite of Michael's sitting on the edge of his bed apparently nude, with only a sheet draped over his genitals. Beneath that photo were more Polaroids—close-ups of the boy's lips, his open mouth, his face. Francia placed them back where she found them.

Jolie Levine had been in the record business for seven years—first as an executive at Qwest Records, then as a production coordinator on the *Bad* album—when Michael hired her to be his secretary in mid-1987. For the next two years Levine kept track of his schedule and his appointments, took his phone calls, served as his liaison with accountants, attorneys, managers—in short, all the duties of any executive secretary.

Levine was also called upon to run personal errands for Michael—to buy him clothes, household items, and, frequently, gifts for his friends. Levine would later recall picking out a present for Elizabeth Taylor, but far more often she was dispatched by Michael to buy toys for the young boys he had befriended. A card was always attached, and no matter whom the gift was for, it was addressed to "Rubba."

Every two weeks or so, Michael himself would take his special friend on shopping sprees. Typically, they would arrange to visit a Toys 'R' Us or other toy store after hours, then run up and down the aisles, picking out toys and games at whim. The tab during one such outing exceeded $25,000.

As his private secretary, Levine had accompanied Michael on most of the *Bad* tour. Whatever city they were in around the world, Levine said, she would walk into Michael's hotel room and find her boss in bed with his young friend. There was always a second bed in the room, and it was, according to Levine and other witnesses, never slept in. When she saw Michael at the end of the day, her pajama-clad employer would be back in bed in his hotel room—again with his young companion.

At Neverland Levine was not surprised to see Michael continue the pattern with a constant stream of special friends. As they got older, Blanca Francia said, "he'd just drop one and get another one." Away from the ranch, Michael's then private secretary referred to him as a "chicken hawk"—slang for pedophile.

In June 1989 word leaked out to the press of a "bachelor pad" that Michael presumably kept somewhere in Los Angeles. "Friends say he's a late bloomer who recently 'discovered' the opposite sex," wrote one columnist, "and has taken to partying and entertaining pretty girls at the hideaway."

According to Francia and others, "the Hideout" was what Michael called his fourteenth-floor condominium at The Westford, a decidedly upscale building at 10750 Wilshire Boulevard. "Don't tell anyone where the Hideout is," Francia recalled Michael instructing her, "Don't tell *anyone*—including Mother. If Mother asks, tell her you don't know."

"That was Michael's favorite phrase," Francia said. "*'You don't know.'*" Michael also told her not to tell Katherine that he had relocated his office at the same time.

The three-bedroom corner condominium at The Westford boasted a balcony with a sweeping view to the Pacific. But for the most part, Michael kept the drapes drawn. Inside there was no furniture except for a big-screen TV and a sleeping bag. Francia cleaned the Hideout on a daily basis whenever Michael stayed there. "The first thing he asked me to bring him," she recalled, "was his sleeping bag and his blue blanket."

Michael brought several boys to the Hideout over the years, and they always shared the one sleeping bag. Invariably, whenever she arrived at the Hideout, Francia encountered the same scene she normally did at Neverland. Michael would be inside his sleeping bag with a boy beside him. Sometimes they both wore pajamas; Michael's were getting increasingly frilly.

Just as often, they were naked from the waist up and the sleeping bag covered the rest. There was no way Francia could tell if they were at least wearing briefs, "and sometimes it would be so dark that I couldn't even see what was going on."

Most of the parents who dropped their sons off at Neverland had no idea that they would be taken to the Hideout. "Michael made me lie to the boys' parents," Francia said. " 'If somebody asks you about the Hideout on Wilshire Boulevard, don't tell anyone,' he kept saying."

There was a full-blown crisis at Neverland when one mother arrived to pick up her son. A series of frantic calls were made—to the Hideout, to Michael's office—but neither Michael nor the boy could be located. The boy had been missing for twenty-four hours when Michael finally turned up with him at Neverland. Rather than face the distraught mother, who had been persuaded by his staff not to call the police, Michael handed the boy over to an aide and went back to his room.

What should I tell his mother? the aide asked. "Forget it," Michael said, waving him away. "I'll take care of her."

Francia turned a blind eye to all of this—until Michael moved in on her own son. In 1991 she would discover them together in the darkened Hideout. Unable to make out what they were doing, she admitted to being "nervous"—a feeling that intensified when she checked her son's jeans pocket and discovered three crisp $100 bills. Not long after, fearing for her son's welfare, Francia quit.

Ever since 1987 Michael had been confiding in friends that he intended to become a single father. He was willing to spend up to $2 million for a surrogate mother to bear his child—by means of artificial insemination. The woman would have to combine the physical and intellectual traits of the three women he admired most besides his mother: Diana Ross, Elizabeth Taylor, and Jacqueline Onassis.

Meanwhile a screenwriter told journalist Maureen Orth that he had been asked to sign a release form shortly after his wife gave birth at a Santa Monica hospital. "It's from Michael Jackson," the nurse told him, adding that Jackson often visited the maternity ward to "stare into the eyes of newborns. He feels then that he can really see their souls."

Their son, Elbert, was three months old when, in the midst of negotiations in 1988 concerning the proposed Moonie concerts in South Korea, Michael first met Kenneth Choi and his wife. When Elbert turned one hundred days old, Michael's "interest in the infant really peaked," said one of his staff members. I don't know the significance of one hundred days, but all of a sudden Michael was having these people down to stay with him."

Soon after, Michael asked the Chois if he could adopt Elbert. Choi was stunned but aware that it was important not to offend Michael at this delicate juncture in their talks. "No, we can't let you do that, Michael," he said, "but you can be a second father to him."

From then on Michael was obsessed with the Choi baby. Choi wanted to come to Neverland to discuss business, but Michael insisted he bring Elbert. "Only if you bring Elbert," he said. "You'll bring Elbert, okay?"

Over the next three years Michael doted on Elbert. "We were invited to the ranch many times, Choi said, "and Elbert was the love of his life." Whenever the Chois visited Neverland, Michael insisted that Elbert stay in one of the "secret rooms." When Elbert turned three, Michael gave him four dolls from his $200,000 antique doll collection with the handwritten note, "To Elbert Choi, I love you, Michael Jackson."

As long as there was still hope of luring Michael to Korea for a concert series, the Chois publicly maintained that he was, in Kenneth Choi's words, "a very loving second father to Elbert. I think that with Elbert he was clinging to the love of a child and playing the fatherly role he never saw in his own crowded home of superstars.

"We always felt very safe leaving our son with him," Choi insisted, adding somewhat cryptically, "Michael was a very disciplined man, and I felt Elbert could learn discipline from him." Since the Chois and Jacksons parted company before Elbert turned four, that statement seemed particularly odd.

For the record, at least, Elbert's mother, Mirae, agreed. "Michael was a wonderful adopted daddy," she said. "He loved our son so much, I think he wanted to keep him. He used to baby-sit whenever we went to visit the ranch, and he even asked if he could care for him when we went on holiday."

Privately Kenneth began to question why Michael insisted that Elbert spend the night in one of the "secret rooms" to which only he had access. Choi's concern intensified when one of Jackson's most trusted lieutenants warned him not to leave his son alone with Michael.

Michael's handling of Elbert over the months the Chois stayed at Neverland actually made several staff members queasy. "It worried us all," Mark Quindoy said. "When the kid arrived he was a baby, and everyone cuddles babies—that's only natural. But the way Michael did it gave us all the creeps. He would lay the kid down and stroke the whole length of his body, from top to toe, with the tips of his fingers."

Three years later Michael was more smitten with Elbert than ever, and vice versa. "Michael treats him like his own," Choi said. "Elbert runs around our home shouting, 'Mikey, Mikey!'" But it was also around this time that it began to dawn on the Chois that all was not right at Neverland. Mirae was sobbing and begging her husband to return to Korea. "I wanted to kill myself," Choi told a British journalist, "because I suspected my child was in some kind of danger, and yet I left him alone at the ranch."

Choi, who according to staffers "practically lived" at the ranch for a time, claimed that Michael developed an intimate friendship with him as well. Choi and Michael sat on Jackson's bed and, said Choi, "cuddled each other, laughed, and cried. I told him I loved him, and he said he loved me."

It was during one of these "cuddling" sessions in Michael's bedroom, Choi said, that Michael confided in him the reason he could never be intimate with a woman. "Only a woman," Michael claimed, "can destroy me."

No woman or girl ever stayed in Michael's room, either at Hayvenhurst or at Neverland. Neither were any females allowed into Michael's "secret rooms." But Michael did not restrict his private quarters exclusively to boys and a select few young men. Occasionally Bubbles, wearing a diaper, would spend the night in Michael's room.

It began to bother Michael that Bubbles, now five, was becoming increasingly hard to handle. "Once they were horsing around and Bubble just hauled off and clobbered Michael," Bob Michaelson recalled. "Of course Bubbles didn't know what he was doing, but adult chimps can really do some damage. . . . Michael was furious."

Another time Michael was recovering from the fifth operation on his nose when Bubbles playfully ambushed him as he lay on his bed. The chimp pounced onto the bed and right onto Michael's bandaged face. Michael reportedly grabbed Bubbles and tossed him to the floor. Shrieking, the animal sprinted down a hallway and cowered in fear behind a door.

"Come quick," Michael cried, "I think I've killed Bubbles! I didn't mean it. I didn't mean it! Bubbles, come here. Please don't be dead." When he finally found the terrified chimp, Michael reached down to hug him, and Bubbles fled again. Michael burst out in tears.

For advice on how best to deal with Bubbles, Michael invited the world's foremost expert on chimpanzees, Dr. Jane Goodall, to Neverland. "The first thing he said to me," Goodall recalled, "was he knew I didn't approve of him having a chimpanzee for a pet."

Goodall changed her mind after touring Michael's private zoo, which in addition to chimps also housed deer, antelopes, and giraffes. "With the money and space he has," she said, "he can create conditions on a par with any zoo. Of course, in an ideal world, no chimps should live in captivity, but I think Michael's are very well off and should stay with him."

Goodall did persuade Michael to fire one of his trainers for using cruel methods and told him Bubbles craved the company of other chimps. Michael then bought two new baby chimps—Alex and Max—ostensibly to keep Bubbles company.

Out of gratitude, Michael agreed to show up at a celebrity function in Los Angeles to raise money for Goodall's pet project, the Gome Stream Research Center in Tanzania. "I found him," Goodall said of Jackson, "very shy, but sweet."

Like all visitors to Neverland, Goodall was impressed with Michael's obvious devotion to animals. But not *all* animals. Afraid of dogs, he banned employees and guests from ever bringing them onto the property.

Unfortunately Michael had grown tired of Bubbles, who by now was —perhaps next to Cheetah—the world's most famous chimp. "Bubbles just isn't that cute anymore," he said to Michaelson.

From that point on Michael banished Bubbles to live with trainer Bob Dunne at Dunne's zoo in Sylmar, California. There Bubbles, who once inspired a line of plush toys, wore designer clothes, rode around in limousines, and had his own bodyguards, now shared a cage with twenty-two other chimps.

Whenever children visiting Neverland asked to see Bubbles, Michael told them he was at Hayvenhurst. In truth Michael was no longer interested in his famous pet. Photographs of the chimp were even removed from the walls at Neverland. "Bubbles," a Neverland insider said solemnly, "is persona non grata."

"Michael treats animals and people the same way," Michaelson said. "When they get too old, he gets rid of them and moves on to the next."

Michael doted on Alex and Max. He made sure they were washed at least three times a day by their handlers, and diapered and dressed in designer baby togs that he personally selected. When one of his special friends was not staying with him, Michael usually asked Mark Quindoy to bring Max to his room for the night.

Within a year Max was replaced as Michael's favorite by an even younger chimp, five-month-old A.J. When he wasn't playing with his owner, A.J. sat in front of his own television set and watched as a tape of Walt Disney's animated feature *The Jungle Book* was played over and over again.

Kenneth Choi, who was in his early thirties when he sat cuddling Michael on the edge of his bed, was apparently not the only adult male who got close to him at Neverland. Chef Johnny Ciao surprised Michael and a famous New York artist as the two sat together on the floor of the video room. The two jumped to their feet, "clearly disturbed," and the artist started fastening his belt as he beat a hasty exit. The man, whose clothes were disheveled and whose hair was mussed, looked "embarrassed and guilty," Ciao said. "I'd walked in on something that was not quite right."

Ultimately Michael—because of his devotion to Elbert—agreed to do the concerts in Korea. But by the time he did, Choi's bosses in Korea were no longer willing to pay the $15 million they had offered originally. The deal unraveled, and in 1991 the Reverend Sun Myung Moon filed suit in U.S. federal court charging Michael, Joe, and Katherine with racketeering and fraud. Moon claimed that of the $5.5 million paid up front for the concerts, only $3.5 million was returned. The rest, he charged, was spent on cash gifts, luxury cars, and expensive gifts for the Jacksons and their pals.

In the flurry of suits and countersuits that followed, a wounded Michael would claim that the white Rolls-Royce Corniche and the cash given to him by Choi were "gifts from the heart." From that point on, the gates to Neverland were shut to the Chois—including little Elbert.

If Katherine had suspicions about Michael's predilection for young boys she kept them to herself. But there were those within the family who began to voice their concern. La Toya remembered standing with Michael one day and studying his face as he watched a group of children play. "He would single one out, and he'd stare at him," La Toya said. "He had this glazed look—a predatory look. I'd ask him, 'Why, Michael, are you looking at him like that?' He'd smile and say, 'I'm just looking—I enjoy it. What's wrong with that?' That's the boy who stays there for a month or more. Then you'd see this boy who was laughing and running around, and now he was sad, with a terrible look—this sad, vacant, frightened look. They change. . . ."

La Toya never saw Michael fondle or molest a child, but she had no doubts that "he is a pedophile. I don't blame him. He's sick. He needs help."

La Toya knew all too well the root of Michael's problem—that he had been not only beaten by their father, but molested by a relative as well. When she signed a book contract with Putnam, word got to Michael that she intended to tell the world that he had been abused as a child.

Frantic, Michael threatened to sue if she said anything about the brutal childhood incidents that may have shaped his sexuality. According to conflicting reports, either Michael offered La Toya $12 million not to publish the book or La Toya and her new husband, Jack Gordon, demanded millions not to publish. Either way, no money ever changed hands.

When she did finally publish her memoirs in 1991, they did not contain the explosive revelation that Michael had been sexually abused as a child. They did, however, portray Joe as a physically and emotionally abusive parent and Katherine as his enabler. For his part, Michael was shown to be a loving, caring, and wildly misunderstood brother.

The Jackson family was up in arms when the book was published. Both parents called the allegations of abuse a "pack of lies." Katherine said, "Our kids could not have gone to school, become entertainers, or raised kids themselves if we had beaten them like that." Joe agreed: "We never punched [La Toya] or any of the kids." They also denied La Toya's charges of sexual abuse made by her while she was promoting the book.

The public, meanwhile, remained blissfully unaware of the games Michael really played behind the iron gates of Neverland. If he blamed Frank Dileo for the tabloid stories that had depicted him as a freak prior to the *Bad* tour, there were never more wild rumors than *after* Uncle Tookie's departure.

With Michael back in virtual seclusion throughout 1989, the rumors flew fast and furious about the man the British had dubbed "Wacko Jacko":

* Unable to buy the Elephant Man's remains, Michael now wanted to buy Marilyn Monroe's and display them in his home.

* Michael hired a team of Nobel Prize–winning scientists for $1 million to develop a potion that would make him invisible—"so he and

Bubbles could go out to a shopping mall and have a great time without people staring at them."

* Michael wanted to have him himself frozen when he died, along with Bubbles, so they could be revived in the next century.

* Bubbles had been run over by a Jeep and killed.

* Michael was leaving Bubbles $2 million in his will.

* God often appeared in a cloud of smoke while he performed on stage, and Michael would reach out to touch his robe.

* Elizabeth Taylor was visiting the ranch for treatments in Michael's hyperbaric chamber.

* Michael believed he was the reincarnation of an Inca god, had purchased $150,000 worth of pre-Columbian art, and was planning an Inca-inspired clothing line.

* Rather than see a doctor, Michael slept with a small glass pyramid over his head to treat a cyst on the back of his throat.

* Michael had become a Muslim.

* Paula Abdul had left Jackie and moved in with Michael at Neverland (Michael still hated her).

* Michael was scouring the South Seas and the Mediterranean for an island "kingdom" where his animals could run free (later it was reported that Michael was building a futuristic city in the Paraguayan jungle with "robot-controlled space cars to whiz people across town").

* Michael was convinced that the world was coming to an end in 1998. . . .

That last rumor carried in it a kernel of truth. With the release of the *Bad* album, Michael had begun adding "1998" to his signature, reportedly at the suggestion of a numerologist who told him it was the numerical "equivalent" of his name. Now he offered a different explanation. He was obsessed with the idea that he would turn forty in 1998. Believing, as he often said, that he was divinely inspired, he became convinced that his fate was linked to the fate of all mankind.

Michael reminded friends that many biblical scholars believed forty was the "number of Judgment." The Great Flood was the result of forty days and forty nights of rain; Moses wandered in the wilderness for forty years. Michael told friends that he expected to face God's judgment on his fortieth birthday. It remained to be seen if that meant Michael would die at forty or if that date would coincide with the Apocalypse predicted by the Jehovah's Witnesses. As his obsession with the number *1998* grew, Michael tried dropping his name from correspondence altogether—replacing it with 1998 followed by a baffling series of arrows, circles, and symbols.

Whatever form it took, Michael's remained the most coveted signature in show business—particularly if it appeared on a contract. In the summer of 1989 Michael told John Branca he wanted to strike a deal with his old boss Berry Gordy for the purchase of Jobete, the Motown catalog. If he could acquire Jobete, Michael would then own the copyrights for thirty thousand titles, including all the great Motown hits by the Supremes, the Temptations, Smokey Robinson, Stevie Wonder, the Four Tops, Marvin Gaye, and many more.

Gordy held firm to his price of $200 million. Michael offered as much as $135 million, but Gordy wouldn't budge. It had become a contest of wills that Michael was no longer interested in playing. He withdrew the offer.

Next he told Branca he was interested in endorsing a line of athletic shoes. In September he appeared at a $50,000 press conference that featured a fog machine and a Hollywood set dotted with palm trees to announce that he was replacing basketball star Kareem Abdul-Jabbar as the new spokesman for L.A. Gear.

Behind Michael was emblazoned the giant logo for Unstoppable, the line of footwear that he was to design and promote in exchange for a multimillion-dollar signing fee and a piece of the company—amounting to not less than $20 million over the next two years. Michael read a prepared statement that lasted ten seconds, and when reporters began to bombard him with questions, he whimpered to a company executive, "Protect me. Don't let them ask me any questions."

With that, he left. When asked why L.A. Gear picked a spokesman who refused to speak, company chairman Robert Y. Greenberg replied, "I've spoken with him, and he speaks very well."

The success of L.A. Gear's Unstoppable line hinged on the release of a Michael Jackson greatest hits album in time for Christmas 1989. The album, appropriately titled *Decade,* was to include cuts from *Off the Wall, Thriller, Bad,* his "State of Shock" duet with Jagger, and several new songs. For this he was to be paid more than any artist for a single album—$18 million, more than three times what the previous record holders, the Rolling Stones, were paid per album.

Michael would collect the $18 million—and considerably more—but not for *Decade.* Urged by David Geffen to concentrate on an album of exclusively new material, he dropped *Decade* altogether. And without the promised support of the album, Michael's shoe line fizzled and L.A. Gear demanded its money back. An initial settlement was reached, but in 1993 the company claimed Michael reneged on his deal to refund some of the money and sued him.

Around the same time their brother signed his contract with L.A. Gear, Jackie, Randy, Jermaine, and Tito released *2300 Jackson Street* to commemorate the twenty-fifth anniversary of the brothers' first stage appearance back in Gary, Indiana. (Marlon had dropped out of the group to pursue an ill-fated solo career of his own.) Without Michael's participation the album bombed, and not long after, CBS dropped his brothers' contract.

For its end-of-the-decade special issue, *Vanity Fair* dubbed the 1980s the "media decade" and assigned Annie Leibovitz to photograph the epoch's most influential media movers and shakers for its Hall of Fame. Inside were "power portraits" of, among others, CNN founder Ted Turner (shot in black and white and colorized), Diane Sawyer of CBS, and, of course, Oprah Winfrey. The cover was reserved for the biggest media star of them all: Michael Jackson, white silk shirt open to the waist, black hair flowing, frozen in the middle of yet another gravity-defying dance move.

There were more honors. In January 1990, a star-studded audience crammed into the Beverly Hilton to see Michael receive the American Cinema Award as Entertainer of the Year. In typical fashion he waited until well after honorees Elizabeth Taylor and Gregory Peck had picked up awards for their movie work to make his dramatic entrance. Wearing his usual black military garb and flanked by six bodyguards, he marched to the podium to accept the evening's top honor from Sophia Loren. Later Taylor claimed she was "happy to be honored with my beloved Michael, whom I would have loved and admired if I had never seen him dance or heard him sing."

The White House was not about to be left out of the act. In this year of congressional elections, President George Bush sought to make political hay just as his predecessor had by inviting Michael to the

White House in April—this time to formally proclaim him "Entertainer of the Decade." First Lady Barbara Bush and the presidential dog Millie looked on.

That same day Michael was whisked north to Atlantic City for the opening of Donald Trump's new Taj Mahal Casino. The pair posed to exchange smiles, handshakes, and compliments for the benefit of the press, then Michael vanished to his quarters for the night: the fiftieth-floor Alexander the Great penthouse suite.

That spring there were other, more sobering ceremonies to attend. After battling AIDS for five years, Ryan White succumbed to the disease in April at Riley Children's Hospital in Indianapolis. White, a hemophiliac who had contracted the HIV virus after receiving a tainted blood transfusion in 1984, had become a symbol of the AIDS movement. Michael had invited White to spend time with him at Neverland and had given him a red Mustang sports car for his sixteenth birthday.

As soon as he learned of White's death, Michael and Donald Trump flew in Trump's private jet to Indiana, where they comforted Ryan's mother, Jeanne. At the funeral Michael sat next to Jeanne while Elton John performed "Candle in the Wind." Michael would include his own tearful tribute to White, "Gone Too Soon," on his next album.

Several weeks later, Michael was mourning again—this time the death of his grandmother Martha Bridges. A week after that, on May 16, 1990, another blow: the throat cancer death of Sammy Davis, Jr., at age sixty-four. "The stress," Michael's spokesman Bob Jones would later recall, "was really mounting."

Michael also felt the pressure to stay on top. After dominating the 1980s by sheer force of his talent, energy, and—perhaps most importantly—his mystique, he was more determined than ever to surpass the success of *Thriller.* And toward that end he relied more and more heavily on David Geffen for advice.

Starting out in the William Morris mailroom at twenty-one in 1964 (a job for which he forged a letter from UCLA saying he had a college degree), Geffen was soon the protégé of Atlantic Records' flamboyant founder, Ahmet Ertegun. In 1970 he started his own record label, Asylum, and over the next twenty years pyramided his holdings into a formidable entertainment conglomerate bearing his name. Geffen produced movies *(Risky Business, Beetlejuice),* backed Broadway musicals *(Dreamgirls, Cats),* and recorded blockbuster heavy metal groups like Whitesnake and Guns N'Roses.

Geffen sold his record company to MCA for ten million shares of

MCA stock in the spring of 1990. When Matsushita bought MCA several months later, Geffen's share of the company was worth a cool $660 million. Since he retained his filmmaking and theater companies, he would be worth nearly $1 *billion* by 1994. On his way to the top, the slightly built, boyishly good-looking Geffen had earned a reputation as one of the industry's most shrewd, ruthless, and at times vengeful figures. "David," said a top agent who had engaged him in numerous screaming matches over the phone, "knows how to get what he wants. He knows how to play hardball, and he knows how to get even. Believe me, you don't want to cross him."

Geffen, who had carried on lengthy and public affairs with Cher and Marlo Thomas, among others, was also outspokenly bisexual. "I date men, and I date women," he proudly declared. Not surprisingly, as Geffen's influence over Michael grew, rumors abounded concerning the true nature of their relationship. "Who knows?" said an industry insider. "I suppose if Michael is having sex at all, Geffen is as good a bet as any. They're two peas in a pod."

Certainly Geffen sought to make the most of their friendship. His record company was handling the sound track for the upcoming Tom Cruise racing saga *Days of Thunder,* and he wanted Michael to do a single for the film. Michael was not up to contributing a new song, but he did agree to let Geffen use an outtake from the *Bad* album, his version of the Beatles' "Come Together."

CBS Records president Walter Yetnikoff, however, nixed the idea. Yetnikoff and Geffen had been at odds for years, and now the CBS chief was going so far as to wisecrack about Geffen's sexual preferences. After Geffen was asked by Yetnikoff to give his girlfriend some tips on how to perform oral sex, he launched an all-out campaign to lure Jackson away from CBS.

While he whispered into Michael's ear that he was not being fully appreciated by the CBS brass—Jackson had sold seventy-seven million records for the company—Geffen also pushed Michael to appear at the opening of the new Universal Studios theme park in Orlando. Geffen had a vested interest; he still owned $700 million in MCA stock, and MCA owned Universal. Michael agreed, but Disney chairman Michael Eisner viewed this as nothing less than an act of treason. If he did appear, Michael was warned that his long-standing association with the Disney organization would be irreparably compromised.

On June 3, 1990—just a few days before the scheduled Universal Studios opening—Michael was practicing a dance routine in his room at Hayvenhurst when he suddenly felt a sharp pain in his chest. The pain persisted, and soon he felt dizzy and nauseated. "Oh, my God, I'm having a heart attack!" he screamed. "I'm going to die!"

Before Dr. Steven Hoefflin arrived, Michael had vomited, then collapsed. Hoefflin detected an irregular heartbeat and, now somewhat alarmed, rushed Michael to Saint John's Hospital in Santa Monica. Clutching his chest and wearing his ever-present black fedora (and more makeup than any of the nurses), Michael was wheeled on a gurney into the emergency room and given oxygen. "Please don't hurt me," he pleaded with a nurse who hooked him up to an IV. He then asked to be given a room across from Elizabeth Taylor, who had been hospitalized with serious respiratory problems.

Not surprisingly, Michael's "heart attack horror" made international headlines. While he remained in the hospital to undergo tests—including a test he requested for the AIDS virus, which came back negative—every detail of his stay was duly chronicled. Taylor dropped by in her wheelchair with a bunch of African violets. President Bush phoned to wish Michael well, as did Elton John and Liza Minnelli. Jermaine and Janet visited, while La Toya, who was touring in London, sent him flowers: a dozen black roses. "I think they are beautiful," she insisted. And once again, the self-described "Billie Jean" Powlis (now Lavon Muhammad) was arrested for violating a court order by trying to sneak onto Michael's floor. Even more disturbing, a twenty-eight-year-old man was arrested at the hospital after saying he was there to kill Michael.

When the dust had settled, doctors determined that what the papers were calling Michael's "mystery illness" was hardly that. In the course of his particularly strenuous dance routine, he had suffered an attack of costochondritis—an inflammation of cartilage where the ribs join at the sternum.

Stress over the deaths of Ryan White, his grandmother, and Sammy Davis, Jr., may have also contributed to Michael's collapse. Yet even more significant seemed to be the timing of Michael's illness. During his hospital stay—prolonged to a week after an unexplained "setback"—Michael missed the Universal Studios grand opening altogether. He would not (thank God) have to choose between Disney and Geffen.

Geffen had convinced Michael, however, that his trusted lawyer, John Branca, was too close to Yetnikoff. In fact, Branca had long been one of Yetnikoff's cronies and almost by definition an enemy of Geffen. For his efforts on Michael's behalf, Branca had been rewarded with a cut of the Pepsi deal, 5 percent of the *Bad* tour profits, and a new Rolls-Royce (when he learned that Elvis gave his "people" cars, Michael bestowed Rolls-Royces on both Branca and Dileo).

If by 1990 Michael was the king of pop, then, as industry observer Jane Birnbaum put it, Branca was the king of pop lawyers. Michael had always resented the fact that Branca had other clients. Indeed, as a partner in the powerful firm of Ziffren, Brittenham & Branca, he boasted a client list that included Stevie Nicks, Dan Fogelberg, David Lee Roth, and the Rolling Stones. Branca's firm even represented Michael's arch rival, Prince.

The fact that Branca was intimately involved with the Rolling Stones' *Steel Wheels* tour was particularly irksome for Michael. *Steel Wheels* broke the records set by Michael's *Bad* tour to become the biggest rock tour in history. Still, Branca now claimed that he was devoting so much time to Michael at the expense of his other clients that he should also be given a percentage of Michael's royalties from music publishing as well. Geffen would use this request to portray Branca as grasping and cocky.

Meanwhile Geffen pointed out to Branca that under California law contracts could not be held enforceable for more than seven years and that Michael's original contract with CBS was far older than that. Why not use that loophole to leave CBS? Geffen asked. It was obvious that Geffen wanted Michael for his record company, and Branca made it clear that he was not about to go along with the scheme. Besides, any label that signed Michael under these circumstances was sure to spend years in litigation because Jackson still owed CBS four albums.

Michael shared Geffen's view. He saw no reason to be shackled to CBS—despite the fact that those shackles were pure platinum. Scarcely a week after Michael's release from the hospital in June of 1990, a messenger arrived with a letter from Michael's accountant, Richard Sherman, informing Branca that Mr. Jackson no longer wished to work with him. It was pure Michael.

That letter was withdrawn immediately, but at a tearful and stormy meeting Geffen made it clear that he no longer trusted Branca to keep Michael's best interests at heart and wanted Branca's firm off the team. When Branca's partner Kenneth Ziffren pleaded with Geffen and Jackson to change their minds, Michael started crying. As he left the room Michael slipped a note to another partner of Branca's. It read: "Tell John and Karen [a paralegal] I'm sorry and I love them." By July Branca was out.

Although he described himself as being "scared shitless" when he was fired by Michael, Branca rebounded quickly. Soon he had even signed one of Geffen's biggest acts, Aerosmith, as a client.

Branca was replaced by Sandy Gallin, who had been Dolly Parton's manager, and three lawyers: Bert Fields (Geffen's attorney), Lee Phillips (also Geffen's attorney), and Allen Grubman. Of these, the most strikingly obvious choice was Gallin, who just happened to be Geffen's closest friend.

By now even Geffen had come to realize that trying to break Michael's CBS contract was unrealistic. But with Branca gone he now eyed another prize: ATV Music Publishing Company. EMI had administered the ATV song catalog for years; before long MCA honcho Geffen had persuaded Michael to replace EMI with MCA Music.

While Geffen divvied up the spoils, Branca's firing had a domino effect at CBS. With Geffen's power over Jackson growing and Michael's relationship with CBS strained, it was only a matter of months before Yetnikoff's ouster.

As the power brokers jockeyed for position at his court, Michael consorted with his special friends at the Hideout. There he played king to the hilt, parading around in a crown and flowing red cape, holding a scepter. "You won't say anything?" he asked Blanca Francia when she saw him in his royal robes.

"No, Mr. Jackson"—the maid sighed—"I won't say anything."

17

A lot of times you had to see and not see, hear and not hear.

—ORIETTA MURDOCH,
FORMER EXECUTIVE ASSISTANT
TO MICHAEL JACKSON

"The first time I heard the rumor that Michael was gay was back in the seventies," Katherine Jackson wrote in her autobiography, *The Jacksons—My Family*. "All I can say is, Michael is not gay!"

Katherine's book, published in October 1990, was just as forthcoming when it came to the stories of her children's abuse at the hands of Joe, her own assault (with the helping hands of Janet and Randy) of Gina Sprague, their endless financial difficulties, the Korean mess, the brothers' marital woes, the clan's collective make-over via plastic surgery, and other embarrassing details of Jackson family life.

In December 1990 Michael's paternal grandmother, Chrystal (shortened from Chrystalee) Jackson, died in Phoenix at the age of seventy-six. She and her husband, Samuel, then ninety-seven, had lived in one of the poorest sections of town. "Nobody would ever have guessed," said a neighbor, "that their grandson was one of the richest men in music." When Chrystal became too ill with diabetes to care for herself, she had moved into the same welfare case nursing home where Samuel was living out his last years. Their neighbors were understandably taken aback when their son Joe arrived at the funeral in his black Rolls-Royce.

At the Jehovah's Witness church where funeral services were held,

Michael arrived with a bodyguard and was seated in the front pew next to his father. They did not acknowledge each other. Instead Michael chatted with his nieces and nephews. "Michael only wanted to speak to the kids. He seems far more relaxed with them," said a mourner. "It was as if his father weren't even there."

Afterward everyone drove the ten miles to the cemetery and stood at the graveside in the ninety-degree heat. Michael rode out in a white stretch limousine with vanity plates reading JET SET 7 but did not get out, preferring to watch the final interment from the air-conditioned comfort of his car.

Michael was visibly upset by his grandmother's death, but his mood brightened when he received his Christmas present from Elizabeth Taylor—an Asian elephant named Gypsy.

No one was more taken with this seven-thousand-pound arrival than Michael's new best buddy Macaulay Culkin, towheaded star of the blockbuster *Home Alone* film series. When *Home Alone* was released in 1990, Michael, like much of the world, was utterly captivated by Culkin's impish charm. So much so that, alone in his private theater at the ranch, he screened *Home Alone* over and over again.

Michael invited Culkin to Neverland, and the two hit it off instantly. Culkin's appeal was twofold. Not only was "Mac" an adorable, mischievous kid, but he was now one of the biggest name-over-the-title stars in Hollywood, commanding in excess of $5 million per film.

"Macaulay spends all of his vacations here," Michael would later say. And with good reason. Shortly after their first raucous weekend together at Neverland—mostly spent playing Nintendo and pinball and practical jokes on the staff—Michael bought Mac a $50,000 red Corvette, then spent another $10,000 to have it converted into a bed. And to accommodate their mutual taste for pitched battles fought with squirt guns, hoses, and water balloons, Michael built an elaborate three-story "water fort" where he and "Mad Mac" doused each other for hours with water cannons.

If Mac and Mike felt like something less strenuous, they repaired to the one-hundred-seat movie theater at Neverland with its free candy counter and the original E.T. displayed in a glass showcase in the lobby. Michael had two beds placed on either side of the theater ostensibly so that terminally ill children could be brought in for special screenings. More often Michael and Macaulay Culkin would sit propped up in each of the beds, munching popcorn as they watched movie after movie.

Whenever he returned to his home in New York, Michael would keep in constant touch with Culkin over the phone, calling two or three times a day. "He calls every night, usually," Culkin said. "He's cool. He's a lot like me. We go to video arcades, we like animals, carnivals, and four-wheeled motorcycles. We like goofing off."

Michael sometimes flew to New York to spend time with Culkin. "We kinda plan out our daily schedule," Culkin said. "We say, 'Hey, let's go shopping at eleven, but then we'll sleep in and not go until one o'clock." Every day included an expedition to Toys 'R' Us, where Mac and Mike would each grab a shopping cart and then run up and down the aisle, picking up whatever struck their fancy. "Michael pays," Culkin said, smiling. "He's cool."

Culkin's manager father, Kit, himself a former actor, had a reputation as one of the toughest and, some said, most difficult show biz dads ever. Yet he and Mac's mother, Pat, were not in the least bit hesitant to let their eleven-year-old son stay alone with his thirty-two-year-old prankster-loving friend. They even let Macaulay's little brother, Kieron, then eight, tag along a couple of times. "I feel perfectly happy when they visit Michael," Pat said. "I know they are safe with him. He is the perfect gentleman."

The publicity did not hurt, either. The pairing of Mac and Mike, that powerhouse show business duo, made for irresistible copy. Elizabeth Taylor was another star who clearly appreciated how valuable a "friendship" with Michael could be. Even though she hadn't had a hit film in over twenty years, Taylor still commanded plenty of attention at Michael's side. She, in turn, lent him some credibility as a member of Hollywood's old guard.

Jackson's publicity machine worked overtime to create an image of Michael and Liz as two wacky kids who, when they weren't ambushing each other with water pistols, engaged in rowdy food fights and tickle fests. "It's not unusual," one unnamed source was quoted as saying, "to see Mr. Jackson grabbing Miss Taylor around her waist and tickling her until she begs him to stop. Sometimes she'll sneak up behind him and smack him over the head with a water balloon. . . ."

Some believed that in truth theirs was primarily an arm's-length business relationship. Away from the cameras, they rarely socialized. Even when she was a guest at Neverland, they seldom ate together; Taylor dined alone while Michael and a special friend had tacos and pizza brought up to his room.

"Liz—so funny. Poor lady," Blanca Francia said. "[Michael] was just playing with her. Everyone knows they're not close." Mark Quindoy agreed: "I think Michael's relationship with Liz Taylor is pure farce. They are using it to promote each other. She was at Neverland two weeks, and they only had dinner together once."

In Culkin's case, however, the friendship was genuine. So too was Michael's affection for several other boys during this period—not celebrities, but often children whose parents devoutly wished them to become stars.

In late 1990 Norma Staikos was hired to serve alongside Bill Bray as Michael's majordomo at Neverland. A dark-haired, soft-spoken, matronly Greek immigrant, she nonetheless ruled the staff with an iron fist. "Nobody went to Michael without first going to Norma Staikos," said Michael's executive assistant, Orietta Murdoch. "Norma is very motherly. Michael likes that. Michael needed a mother figure, and she gave it to him. A match made in heaven."

Theirs was not the traditional mother-son relationship, however. Staffers remember the time when, after a particularly well-endowed statue of the Roman god Mercury was installed at Neverland, Staikos gave the order for all employees to clear the area. Then Michael and Staikos drove over in his Blazer to scrutinize the statue close up.

Behind their boss's backs, the staff began to call Neverland "the Golden Cage" and to decry what they described as Neverland's "Gestapo" atmosphere. According to Charli Michaels, when Norma Staikos drove through the front gate she would give the staff a Nazi salute and nod "Yes, yes" as the guards shouted "Heil Hitler!"

It was under Staikos that employees were told they would be fired if they spoke to one another. Borrowing a page from *The Caine Mutiny*, Staikos also peppered the staff with strange memos. No staff member was to ask to have his photo taken with Michael. No pizza deliveries. A staff favorite: "Don't be too nice" (either to visitors or to one another).

Staikos forbade employees from speaking to guests altogether—although she hobnobbed freely. She became friendly with Elizabeth Taylor and sometimes shared a hot tub or sunbathed on the grass with a Speedo-clad Marlon Brando.

There were more substantive orders under her reign that several staff members found disturbing. Prior to 1991 guards at the gate had been ordered to look into the backseat of any car—Michael's included—before it was allowed onto the property. But beginning in 1991, guards at the front gate were ordered not to check the back of Michael's car. In addition, they were often radioed and ordered to "go mobile"—

which meant that Michael was about to drive in and that the guards were to leave immediately so they would not see him arrive.

On one occasion, however, Staikos forgot to give the "go mobile" order when Michael arrived. Charli Michaels looked into the car and spotted a young boy crouched down in the back behind Michael, wearing a Michael Jackson hat. "It was a very odd and peculiar situation," she recalled, adding that when a child did arrive on the premises—typically between 10 P.M. and 2 A.M.—it was "always a boy, never a girl." Staikos deridingly called them "Michael's little boyfriends."

Things got even odder. At about this time the guards, who had always been urged to keep meticulous records of individuals' comings and goings at the gate, were instructed never to enter a child's arrival into the log. What did Staikos know? According to Orietta Murdoch, Michael's top assistant at MJJ Productions and the mother of a ten-year-old boy, Staikos said to her, "Never leave your son with Michael. It's not a good idea."

By the estimate of staffer Gayle Goforth, Michael was now spending fully 40 percent of his nights at Neverland sleeping with his special friends. One boy's mother was known to staff members as "Michael's mother-in-law."

In exhaustive accounts later given to Los Angeles police investigators—accounts backed up by prodigiously detailed diaries kept by both himself and his wife—Mark Quindoy claimed to have seen Michael molest several of his special friends. One, whose mother actually lived for a time in a cottage on the grounds, was only seven and slept each night with Michael in his bed. Michael often took his little friends on short excursions up to Solvang, and one day he asked Quindoy if he would drive him and his seven-year-old friend there in the four-wheel-drive Chevrolet Blazer.

At Solvang Michael took the boy to see a huge dollhouse that he was thinking of duplicating at the ranch. Driving back after sunset, Quindoy glanced back in the rearview mirror and was astonished to see Michael embracing the boy "like a lover," kissing him passionately. "It was just like a boy kissing a girl in the backseat," Quindoy said. "The boy wasn't protesting—but he just sat there stiffly, without moving, while Michael kissed him on the lips."

Then, according to Quindoy, "Michael began kissing him everywhere—his neck, head, arms, shoulders, and body. I was utterly stunned—appalled that he could do that to a seven-year-old boy," said Quindoy, who believed Michael didn't realize he was clearly visible in the rearview mirror. Not only did he have plenty of time to look into the mirror at stoplights, Quindoy said, but illumination from passing streetlights made it easy for Quindoy to see clearly what was going on.

The seven-year-old stayed for three weeks, and no sooner did he leave with his mother on vacation than a nine-year-old took his place. According to the Quindoy's diaries, this boy spent up to nineteen days at a time at the ranch. More than once, Michael spent two full days holed up in his bedroom with the boy without ever venturing out. They would place their first call for food shortly after getting up around two P.M.

One of the favorite games Michael played with this and other boys was to wait at the bottom of the stairway and catch them after they slid down the banister. At the special water park Michael had constructed with its fort, pirate ship, and suspension bridge, Michael also rigged up a special harness for the boys so they could slide across a man-made pond. He waited at the other end to catch them.

Whenever Michael announced that he planned to spend time in the spa with a special friend, it was understood that the staff was not to disturb him. But once Quindoy violated that standing order and spied on his boss from a window. "Perhaps I shouldn't have done what I did," he said, "but my curiosity got the better of me. Both were wearing white underpants and sat on the edge of the hot tub with their feet in the water. They were talking, and then I saw Michael lean over and put his hand down the front of the boy's underpants. He kept it there for as long as I watched. The boy didn't protest or try to stop Michael. I was utterly shocked."

Quindoy went on to observe that Jackson and the boy "acted like lovers. They threw food at each other, and even had screaming rows over toys or games." The boy's parents were separated at the time, but both visited the ranch. They, too, were each given a Mercedes by Michael.

Why did they tell no one what was going on? It was a question many of Jackson's employees would eventually ask themselves. "All I feel now is regret that we didn't have the courage to speak out at the time," Faye Quindoy later admitted. "But we were just employees, and Jackson was a superstar, seemingly above suspicion."

To be sure, while stories concerning the strange happenings at Neverland were gradually being leaked to a handful of journalists, Sony was signing him to the biggest entertainment contract in history. For nine months Michael's cadre of lawyers and managers had played hardball with CBS and its parent company, Sony. Presumably at Geffen's urging, Michael threatened to leave CBS if it did not come up with some imaginative ways to make him happy.

"He doesn't need the money; this is the guy who owns the Beatles' music catalog," said communications analyst Emanuel Gerard. "What we're dealing with largely is his ego. And from Sony's standpoint, no matter what, they could not afford to have Michael Jackson signed away from them."

The Sony deal: Michael was to receive an $18 million cash advance for his next album, *Dangerous,* plus 25 percent of the *retail* price on every copy sold—the highest for any artist. He was also to receive a $5 million bonus for each of his next five albums. In addition, Sony agreed to bankroll Michael's own label, Nation Records, and pay him an annual salary of $1 million to run it. Moreover, Michael would establish the Jackson Entertainment Complex for the production of music video, television projects, and feature films. This was a fifty-fifty deal with Sony Software—the first time a pop star had signed a contract with the company's software division.

Michael was being paid $60 million up front, but Sony predicted that the arrangement could ultimately gross $1 billion for the company. This figure was based on the fact that the *Thriller* and *Bad* albums alone had racked up $650 million in sales.

How big a role did Michael, so busy working on his upcoming *Dangerous* album and playing with his special friends, play in hammering out the megadeal? "He was involved," said Sony Music president Tommy Mottola, "either on the line or behind the scenes because he knew exactly what he wanted to accomplish. Michael is very intuitive, and he's real smart. He knows exactly what he's doing and exactly where he's going. Michael has always dreamed of himself as more and more a multimedia artist."

The announcement of the Sony deal was delayed to eclipse sister Janet, whose $50 million deal with Virgin Records was—at least for a week—the biggest package in music history. In fact, following the tremendous success of Janet's *Rhythm Nation 1814* album, Michael was determined to sign her up as the first artist on his new label. When she declined, he took some small satisfaction in claiming Nation Records as his own.

Michael had other matters weighing on his mind as well. As the Academy Awards approached, he faced the classic dilemma. Who was big enough to escort him to the show? The field quickly narrowed down to one person: Madonna.

A week before the March 25, 1991, awards—and just before the Sony deal made headlines—Michael and Madonna met at a trendy Los Angeles restaurant called the Ivy to plan their impending big date. Jackson wore his trademark dark glasses, and the moment they sat down at their table, Madonna leaned over, yanked off the glasses, and nonchalantly tossed them across the room. "You're with me now," she said. "I want to see your eyes." When Jackson kept eyeing her cleavage, Madonna grabbed his hand, placed it on her breast, and held it there for several seconds.

As they left, the maître d' angrily shooed away photographers, shouting, "No pictures!" Recalled celebrity photographer Vinnie Zuffante: "No pictures? *Both* Madonna's people and Michael's people called us to say they'd be there! Eight photographers showed up. It was a madhouse —exactly what they were hoping for."

It was only a few years earlier that Zuffante had watched as fans chased Michael's Rolls down Century City's Avenue of the Stars as he giddily tossed autographed pictures out the window. "Nothing had changed," Zuffante said. "He was still the king all right—the king of publicity."

At the Shrine Auditorium the night of the Academy Awards ceremony, the biggest names in Hollywood strained to get a good look at Madonna and Michael as they took their front-row seats on the aisle. They had made certain to coordinate their outfits. Michael wore gold-tipped cowboy boots, a white sequined jacket, a huge diamond brooch, and, for this special occasion, not one but two gloves. Madonna wore a glittering white strapless Bob Mackie gown, an ermine wrap, and $20 million worth of diamonds on loan from Harry Winston. She went on stage later to vamp her way through Stephen Sondheim's "Sooner or Later" from her film *Dick Tracy*. It won for Best Song.

"I can't believe all this," Madonna whispered to Michael. "It's so unbelievable. What a night! I'm having such a good time." They were, of course, the focus of everyone's attention. "They almost looked like caricatures," Barbara Walters said of Jackson's two-on-the-aisle act with Madonna. "They seemed untouchable, larger than life."

The new oddest couple moved on after the awards to literary agent Irving "Swifty" Lazar's annual Oscar bash at Spago. Columnist Army Archerd asked Madonna how she got Jackson to attend the party. "Michael's coming out more," she said, smiling. But once inside and away from the cameras, they split up—the Gloved One to pose with Diana Ross, the Material Girl to flirt with ex-love (and *Dick Tracy* costar) Warren Beatty.

Madonna invited Michael back to her Hollywood Hills home, where they snacked on her favorite food—popcorn—and watched old movies until dawn. Asked what the two superstars did when they got together, Madonna cracked, "We exchange powder puffs, powder our noses, and compare bank accounts."

The pair actually had business to discuss—they were planning a duet for *Dangerous.* But Madonna had stipulations. Arguing that "nobody's going to buy a stupid ballad or love duet," she told him, "Look, Michael, if you want to do something with me, you have to be willing to go all the way or I'm not going to do it."

All the way? To begin with, Madonna was determined to change Jackson's look. "I would like to completely redo his whole image," she said, "give him a Caesar—you know, a really short haircut—and I want to get him out of those buckley boots and all that stuff."

Madonna, a favorite of gays who had done little to conceal her own bisexuality, was also peeved at Michael for being coy about his own preferences. She told Michael, "I'd love to turn José and Luis [the two gay dancers who taught her to vogue] loose on you for a week. They'd pull you out of the shoebox you're living in. Anybody who's in a shoebox in the closet cannot be in one after hanging around with Luis and José for a while." To all this, she claimed, Michael "keeps saying yes."

Michael tolerated Madonna's not-so-vague references to his sexual orientation as long as it looked as if she would work with him on a song. He went back to Neverland and, keeping what she had said in mind, wrote a duet for them entitled "In the Closet." Her reaction was not what he'd expected. He played a tape of the song for her, and when it was finished she blurted, "Are you kidding? I'm not singing that piece of shit." Michael ran out of the studio, and when he came back, she had left.

Michael, not surprisingly, cancelled plans to accompany her to the opening of her film *Truth or Dare.* Said Madonna, shrugging, "No one cares. He's an even bigger wimp than I thought." Not long after, Madonna learned that Michael had called her a "heifer"—a term he often used to describe women. "I'd rather look like a cow," Madonna shot back, "than a space-alien drag queen."

Still intent on topping *Thriller,* Michael again was working to the point of exhaustion during recording sessions for the *Dangerous* album. After countless retakes for the song "Keep the Faith," studio technicians were stunned when he began sobbing uncontrollably. "Pull yourself together," album co-producer Bruce Swedien told Michael. "We are not going home until you have sung this all the way through." Recalled Swedien of the breakdown, "This was scary, but he did it. He didn't leave the studio until dawn."

On Sunday, May 5—Mother's Day—Evangeline Aquilizan was going about her business as a maid at Neverland when she heard a strange sound coming from the dining room. The mother of one of Michael's special friends was sitting at the dining room table, sobbing. "I'm so sad," the woman told Aquilizan. "It's Mother's Day, and here I am all alone." She knew where her son was: spending the day with Michael in his room. Although the boy's mother had asked to at least stay near her son in the main house, she was told there was "no suitable room" for her and banished to a guest cottage.

Although Michael was with the boy that entire Mother's Day, they did not confine themselves to Michael's bedroom. Security guard Charli Michaels was working that morning and was told to take the boy's mother on a "barn run" to see all the animals on the estate. "I took her in my truck and drove her to the barn," Michaels recalled. "She was crying. She hadn't seen her son all day and appeared very nervous and concerned." After she took the mother to the barn, Michaels was summoned to pick up food at the snack bar and deliver it to Michael and his special friend in the private theater.

As she headed for the snack bar, Michaels passed the mirrored dance studio. There was giggling coming from inside. Glancing into the studio, she saw Michael in the mirror, "draped over the back" of the boy, she said, "with his arms fully around the front and crotch of the little boy, holding his hand and genitals and moving them up and down, while moving to the rhythm of the music that was playing. They shouted 'Whee!' repeatedly each time he pulled the boy's genitals up.

"Michael was around him in such a way that it scared me, it shocked me," she later said. "Here he was giving the famous Michael Jackson crotch grab to this little boy—over and over again. I didn't know what to do or what to say. All I could think of was, I've got to get out of here. I can't get caught. I'll lose my job."

Later she tearfully reflected on the plan to separate the children from their parents. "It's not right," Michaels said. "Where was the mother?"

She claimed she and others wanted to tell the mothers and fathers what was happening, but "the employees were instructed to keep the parents away."

Even when the parents found out, of course, Michael had ways of mollifying them. Charli Michaels was standing in a breezeway area just ten feet from Michael's room when she heard a boy crying. "I was told the boy [a frequent guest at Neverland] said Michael 'touched him funny,' " she recalled. "The odd thing is that when the family came back, they came back in a brand-new white Mercedes, then a brand-new black Mercedes."

The little boys also availed themselves of Michael's generosity. In addition to the toys and games he invariably showered on them, they would call Michael's executive assistant, Orietta Murdoch, directly with requests for gifts ranging from concert tickets to gold jewelry.

When it came to parents inquiring about their sons' whereabouts, Michael evinced little sympathy. Murdoch remembered the day a boy's mother and father called, upset that their son was not at Neverland where they had left him. But the staff stalled until Michael contacted them that afternoon. A cardinal rule, Murdoch explained, was that "you don't bother Michael in the morning." Employees didn't call Michael; he called them.

A select few parents were clued into the existence of the top-secret Hideout. They were sometimes put up at what was then a Holiday Inn across the street. It was routine for boys to walk over to the Hideout in the evening and back to the Holiday Inn the next morning.

Once when Michael seemed to have vanished, he finally called Murdoch from the Hideout to say he was having too much fun to leave. He told her to cancel a meeting with Donald Trump. "Just tell him," he said, "that I'm not feeling well."

Michael took a break from work on *Dangerous* in June and headed for Bermuda with Macaulay Culkin and his mother and dad. Macaulay and his parents checked into a sixth-floor room at Hamilton's luxurious Princess Hotel, but Mac spent virtually all his time with Michael in the hotel's $1,000-a-day penthouse.

Mike and Mac toured the island and attracted crowds when they tried scuba diving. But most of the vacation was spent in the penthouse suite, zapping unsuspecting hotel guests with toy laser guns or bombing them with water balloons. As they dropped the balloons down, soaking passersby, Michael kept shouting, "Desert Storm! Desert Storm!" while Culkin dissolved in laughter. When room service arrived the pair would jump out from behind the drapes and shoot the startled waiter with squirt guns.

Michael also arranged for a private performance of a musical revue at the hotel, and during the performance he periodically leaned over to Culkin and gushed, "Isn't this the greatest? I just love being here with you." Before they left the island to continue their vacation at Disney World, Michael was overheard saying to Culkin, "I just want you to know that I'll remember this holiday forever."

The high jinks continued on the set of *Black or White,* the first video from *Dangerous* and definitely its most ambitious. Hoping to stir things up as he had done with the *Thriller* video, Michael again hired John Landis to direct. Throughout the arduous filming, Landis and the crew had to steel themselves against a relentless onslaught of practical jokes from Mike and Mac. The two eventually grew bored tossing water balloons and firing squirt guns; toward the end of the shoot they were setting off stink bombs on the set.

The climactic attack was anything but for the long-suffering Landis, who tried gamely to act surprised when Mike and Mac plastered him with cream pies. One crew member said most of his co-workers found the whole thing "infantile. With Culkin it's one thing—he really is only a kid. But Michael is thirty-three, for Christ's sake! But they're the stars, and you gotta humor them."

At Neverland the staff had seen how easily Michael could become infatuated with a young boy. But in Macaulay Culkin's case, it seemed to many that after the Bermuda trip Michael's interest had turned to obsession.

Philippe LeMarque worked as a cook at Neverland with his wife, Stella, for ten months in 1991 and 1992. They watched as Michael and his special friends jet-skied on his private lake, went on every ride in his private amusement park, watched movies, and played video games (thirty-five in all) until, in the words of one staffer, "the kids barely knew where they were."

At two o'clock one morning, after the adults in the house were asleep, Michael called LeMarque on the phone and told him to bring French fries to the video game room. "I called security and asked, 'Where is Blue Fox [Michael's code name]? They said, 'Oh, he's in the arcade.' " Rather than use the main door to the room, LeMarque decided to use the private entrance on the opposite side—a direction from which Jackson would not expect him to approach.

LeMarque claimed that as he quietly nudged open the door, he clearly saw Michael groping Macaulay Culkin with his free hand as the boy was engrossed in a video game. Shocked, LeMarque, like the other employees who feared for their jobs, backed away without saying anything. "He did not see me," LeMarque recalled, "so I tiptoed back and reentered through the other door." Michael suspected nothing.

According to LeMarque, the local fire department arrived at Neverland when an alarm was sounded at the ranch. "When the chief fireman arrived, Stella and I were there, and Jackson came downstairs," he recalled. "The fireman was trying to account for everyone, and he asked where Macaulay was sleeping. Michael snapped at him, 'What does that matter? What has that got to do with you? Why are you asking me that?' "

There would later be unsubstantiated rumors that the Culkins discovered what was reportedly going on between Michael and their son, and that he agreed to give them $1 million. That money, the rumor continued, was to pay for the long-term psychotherapy the boy was now forced to undergo as a result of being molested by Michael.

Kit Culkin strongly denied these stories, insisting that his son and Michael "were just friends—nothing more." Unfounded rumors aside, the LeMarques stuck by their story and would later repeat it in graphic detail to Los Angeles police investigators. Claiming that what he saw in the video game room that night made LeMarque "sick—he couldn't believe his eyes," attorney Arnold Kessler insisted LeMarque "knows in his heart what he saw."

Certainly the LeMarques did not made the most ideal witnesses. They had been fired by Norma Staikos and were trying to sell their story for $300,000. But they had first approached reporters with their story two years earlier—long before Michael became the subject of a police investigation. Given Michael's popularity, the press had been reluctant to pursue these leads. And the LeMarques were apparently not the only ones at Neverland who harbored suspicions about the nature of Michael's friendship with Culkin. His name also turned up on the list of "special friends" submitted to the police by Mark and Faye Quindoy.

Stella LeMarque claimed she also saw "Blue Fox" groping another boy in his private theater while the child's mother sat three rows in front. "Everyone always says, 'Oh, Michael, he loves children,' " Stella said. "I say that's bullshit." "Everybody knows what's going on at the ranch," her husband added. "Everybody knows, but nobody talks."

By all accounts this was one of the happiest times of Michael's life—

until he learned that Joe was about to become the father of yet another love child. During the *Bad* tour in 1987, Michael had wanted total control of all merchandising and actually paid his mother $1 million not to interfere. She used that money to buy a house in Las Vegas. It was there—on May 4, 1991, Katherine's birthday—that Joe began an affair with a buxom, blond model named Kristen Knight. "He answered the door completely naked," Knight said, "and led me right to his bedroom. He took his time, pleased me like I'd never been pleased. I was in heaven."

Was he worried that Katherine might get wind of the affair? "Yes," Joe allegedly told Knight. "But what can she do about it?" Knight learned she was pregnant in July.

Michael was furious, and his anger manifested itself in a number of ways. At Neverland he threw a full-fledged tantrum when someone left open the gate around his helipad. Several animals strayed onto the pad, and the pilot of Michael's chopper circled for thirty minutes while they were rounded up. "If this happens again," he reportedly shrieked, "I'll fire you all!"

He also became more paranoid than usual, ordering that birdhouses around the grounds be outfitted with surveillance cameras. Certain that he could hear footsteps outside his door, he ordered his bodyguards, guns drawn, to search the entire house. They turned up nothing, but he was still not convinced. To ward off whatever it was that lurked in the hallway, he had a pair of mannequins dressed as bearded, menacing-looking Sikh guards stationed outside the door to his bedroom.

The most obvious expression of Michael's rage toward his father would be on display for all the world to see with the release of his special effects–packed *Black or White* video in late October. Meanwhile, he was pleasantly distracted by the October 6, 1991, wedding of Elizabeth Taylor Hilton Wilding Todd Fisher Burton Burton Warner to twice divorced (and twenty years younger) construction worker Larry Fortensky. The couple had met while undergoing treatment for their respective drug dependencies at the Betty Ford Clinic, and Taylor's "beloved Michael" had agreed to have the wedding at Neverland. A grateful Taylor asked Michael to join with her eldest son, Michael Wilding, Jr., in walking her down the aisle.

To accommodate the 160 guests, Michael constructed a huge tented pavilion and ordered his gardeners to dig up thousands of colorful flowers and replace them with only white blooms. For protection against the hordes of prying paparazzi, Taylor's longtime bodyguard, former Israeli army officer Moshe Alon, headed up a one-hundred-man special security force to augment Neverland's own. Locals called these grim-faced commandos the "Israeli Mafia."

That didn't stop a dozen press helicopters from hovering overhead on the day of the wedding, and one enterprising photographer parachuted in and actually landed twenty feet from the bride and groom as the ceremony was taking place. Unfortunately for the photographer, the camera malfunctioned.

It had been rumored for weeks that Bubbles would be the ring bearer; the public was unaware that he had long since been banished from Neverland by his disenchanted boss. Michael himself did not disappoint, wearing two black gloves (it was a formal occasion, after all) and a fist-sized diamond brooch fastened at his throat.

With Michael standing at Taylor's side, pop guru Marianne Williamson performed the ceremony. Among the guests: Michael's Neverland neighbor Nancy Reagan, Gregory and Veronique Peck, Quincy Jones, Merv Griffin, Eva Gabor, and Taylor's ninety-five-year-old mother, Sara.

The wedding was lavish but low key, and after the bride and groom took a turn on the dance floor to Stevie Wonder's "Overjoyed"—Michael's suggestion—Michael and his date, Brooke Shields, cut in. Throughout the festivities, Michael's lieutenant, Norma Staikos, hovered on the periphery and managed to get her picture taken with Taylor.

Mr. and Mrs. Fortensky stayed at Neverland for the next two nights before heading back to work. The ceremony—a wedding portrait of Liz, Larry, and Michael graced the cover of *People* magazine—just so happened to coincide with a promotional campaign for Taylor's new perfume, White Diamonds. Michael was a major investor in her thriving perfume business.

The fairy-tale nuptials at Neverland would be all but forgotten in the headline-making wake of the eleven-minute, $4 million *Black or White* video a month later. Ostensibly the song's theme was racial harmony, and in the video Michael was shown dancing exuberantly with African tribesmen, Balinese dancers, and Native Americans. It also included a shot of adorable infants, wearing environmentally correct cloth diapers, sitting on a giant globe.

In one of the more ego-gratifying scenes, Michael, singing from his perch in the Statue of Liberty's torch, looms over Big Ben, the Taj Mahal, the Eiffel Tower, and the Acropolis. But the single most striking effect (at the cost of $10,000 *per second*) was called "morphing"—a sophisticated computerized process that made it appear as if faces transmogrified one to the other before the viewer's eyes.

In making the video, special effects were only half the battle. With Sony's $1 billion man under pressure to deliver, the tension had been palpable throughout the grueling shoot. Claiming to be felled by the flu, Michael lost several days' work, returning when only forty-eight hours remained before Landis was due to depart for Rome and another film commitment.

Showing up at night in a run-down section of Los Angeles to shoot one scene for the video, Michael climbed out of his limousine in a cape and slunk toward his trailer. When he did emerge at one A.M. to go before the cameras, he seemed scarcely up to the task. "He clings to the shadows, as if afraid of being spoken to," observed *TV Guide*'s Stephen Galloway, on hand to witness the filming. "Landis leads him to the spot where he must move like a panther, and for a few brief takes, Jackson suddenly comes alive. He arches like a wild cat, crawls forward, unfurling as if he is about to take off. Then it's over. The energy is gone, and the near invisible man is back again. Jackson disappears into his trailer, locking the door behind him."

The *Black or White* video also contained a prologue and an epilogue that were wildly contradictory to the song's basic message of tolerance.

In the opening scene, Macaulay Culkin is playing hard rock when his father (played by *Cheers* star George Wendt) tells him to turn it down. For this Culkin blasts him through the roof in his BarcaLounger.

In the epilogue, a black panther prowling a deserted city street suddenly "morphs" into Jackson, who then launches into a frenetic a cappella dance routine to a chorus of grunts, howls, and screams. He tap-dances, grabs his crotch repeatedly (he touches his genitals no fewer than thirteen times during the video), and, now armed with a crowbar, leaps onto the roof of a car and smashes its windows to smithereens. There's a close-up shot of Michael's hand lingering on his crotch, simulating masturbation.

Still howling, Michael hurls a garbage can through a store window, rubs his torso in anguish, and falls to his knees in a rain puddle as a neon sign topples in a hail of sparks. Then, apparently satisfied with the effects of his rampage, he becomes a panther once again.

The video ends with Homer Simpson telling Bart to turn off the set—a scene Michael worked directly with *Simpsons* creator Matt Groening to produce. "Michael called me on the phone to talk about what Bart would say at the end of his video, and I didn't believe it was him," Groening said. "You can see that he's human. Most people perceive him as a special effect."

Few could argue with John Landis's assessment of the final result: "It's phantasmagoric, an extravaganza, a real lollapalooza." To hype the *Dangerous* album, a thirty-second commercial directed by David Lynch had been airing for weeks. The eerie montage featured fire, spooky-looking trees, and a sinister close-up of Michael's hypnotic eyes.

On November 14, 1991—two weeks before the album's release—the eleven-minute *Black or White* video premiered right after the popular animated series *The Simpsons* on the Fox network, Black Entertainment Television, and MTV. In exchange for the right to get in on the action, MTV contractually agreed to instruct all its on-air personnel to refer to Michael as the "king of pop" at least twice a week for the next two weeks.

Beamed abroad, the *Black or White* premiere was seen by an estimated five hundred million people in twenty-seven countries. *The New York Times* said that it had been "longer awaited, it seemed, than anything without theological implications."

Around the world, Michael's truly bizarre, overtly sexual video rampage was treated as a major news event. At home, public reaction was swift and visceral. Fox was flooded with thousands of calls from angry viewers condemning Jackson's lewd and violent behavior—particularly since it included cameos by Homer and Bart Simpson and was aimed squarely at children. "People couldn't believe he did that," one Fox executive said. "He wasn't just grabbing his crotch—he was rubbing it." Said one parent: "If my six-year-old grabbed himself in public as much as Michael Jackson did, I'd be sending him off to a shrink."

A flurry of editorials pondered the video's underlying message. "Is the destruction an assertion of masculinity?" asked Jon Pareles in *The New York Times.* "Mr. Jackson looks as fragile, even feminine, as ever. Is it an outpouring of pain and frustration? A desperate cry for attention from one of the world's most famous people? Or is it simply a noisy self-indulgence?"

All of that—and more. "Michael's crotch-grabbing reveals his lack of sexual experience," theorized psychiatrist and noted media consultant

Dr. Carole Lieberman. "His frustration explodes and then turns into rage, violence, and aggression." Lieberman was aware that Michael had since childhood bitterly resented the fact that his father cheated on his mother. "On the one hand," she said, "he would like to identify with the stereotype image of his sexually charged father. On the other, he's scared, and remains a man-child. The video is a safe way to combine his rage and mixed feelings."

"The family situation is so sad," Landis said by way of explanation. "Michael has a very difficult life. Granted, he does strange things . . . but you see it is ultimately up to the public, and it doesn't matter what the media says."

Of course, with the possible exception of Madonna, no one knew better how to exploit the media to his own ends. Barring the occasional media circus—Elizabeth Taylor's wedding, for example—Michael had been in virtual seclusion since 1989. He now needed to reclaim the spotlight and give the *Dangerous* album a properly explosive send-off.

At that, he succeeded brilliantly. The day after the video's premiere, a contrite Michael apologized and promised to cut the offending four-minute rampage. "It upsets me to think that *Black or White* could influence any child or adult to destructive behavior, either sexual or violent," he said in a press statement. "I've always tried to be a good role model and therefore have made these changes to avoid any possibility of adversely affecting any individual's behavior. I deeply regret any pain or hurt that the final segment of *Black or White* may have caused children, their parents, or any other viewers."

Actually, the offending portion was excised only for television; anyone who bought the video would be treated to the unexpurgated version. And a separate *Dangerous* video documentary would not only highlight the offending portion, but include footage of dozens of U.S. and foreign broadcasters covering the controversy as if it were an earth-shattering event.

Privately Michael could not contain his glee. In every sense of the word, *Black or White* was a smash. "Wow! This is great! Everybody's going *crazy*," he was overheard telling an aide. "And Madonna thought *she* knew how to shock people!"

Jermaine quickly proved that Michael wasn't the only Jackson who knew how to pull a publicity stunt. The release of his solo album *You Said* just happened to coincide with *Black or White*. What's more, a bootleg copy of Jermaine's "Word to the Badd!," a stinging indictment of his brother's persona, was mysteriously leaked to radio stations.

In "Word to the Badd!" Jermaine tells Michael to "get a grip" and slams his attempts to alter his appearance with plastic surgery and bleaching creams: "Reconstructed / Been abducted / Don't know who you are. . . . Once you were made / You changed your shade / Was your color wrong? / Could not turn back / It's a known fact / You were too far gone."

The lyrics to *Black or White* aside, Jermaine had a point. To Michael, color—at least his own—clearly mattered. When he heard "Word to the Badd!," he went to his bedroom and wept.

Michael was so impressed with the street saga *Boyz N the Hood* that he hired its twenty-four-year-old wunderkind director, John Singleton, to oversee the making of his next video, *Remember the Time.* The setting was ancient Egypt because, Singleton said, "Egypt has never been done right. I've seen movies on Egypt, and everybody looks like they don't come from Egypt."

For this production a special set was constructed on a Universal Studios sound stage. The players: Eddie Murphy as the glowering pharaoh, model Iman as Queen Nefertiti, and in a cameo as a royal slave, Magic Johnson. (Although Michael was delighted to see the former basketball star on the set, one tabloid would report that he was leery of getting too close to him because he was HIV positive.)

The plot was simple enough. Nefertiti is bored. A juggler is sent to entertain her, then a fire swallower. Both fail and are beheaded. Then Michael materializes and entertains the queen—a little too much. Pharaoh Murphy orders his guards after Michael, and a chase through the marketplace ensues.

While everyone in the thirty-plus member cast is suitably clothed in period attire, only Michael wears black trousers beneath his Egyptian skirt. Since adulthood Michael nearly always kept his legs covered, presumably for one overriding reason. From the neck up his skin was almost ghostly white, but his legs remained a dark brown. He was not eager for the public to see the startling contrast between his pale face and his original skin color.

Michael was supposed to look sexy in the video, and toward that end there was a scene in which he was to give his first screen kiss to the strikingly alluring Iman. But during the filming he froze. And the obviously forced, painfully chaste result—perhaps the most utterly unconvincing kiss ever filmed—was instantly evident to everyone on the set. Singleton wanted another take, but Michael ran to his trailer and locked the door. There he remained closeted for much of the rest of the shoot, watching *The Little Mermaid* over and over again.

"The video tries to make Mr. Jackson look sexy," wrote one reviewer when *Remember the Time* was released. "With his pallor, his frightened eyes, and his mechanical motions, he doesn't."

Singleton became somewhat friendly with Michael over the two-month period they worked on the video. Between takes they sometimes sat in Singleton's car, listening to the radio. Still, Singleton had to concede, "Nobody really knows the real Michael. He's truly an enigma, but he's a very nice man. . . ." When he was finished with *Remember the Time,* Singleton went to work on his next film, *Poetic Justice,* starring Michael's little sister Janet.

Rather than commute from Neverland, Michael stayed at the Universal Studios Hotel while he worked on *Remember the Time.* When he checked out of room 1901, the maids found that he had signed his name on everything—the sheets, the pillowcases, the walls, the mirrors, on countertops, dressers, inside drawers and closets, even in the shower stall and bathtub.

"He was in the room for hours, signing his name over and over and over and over again," said photographer Vinnie Zuffante, who occupied room 2001 just one floor above. "When he left they had to overhaul the room. They never billed him—for the room or the damage."

Still determined to be sexy, Michael tried again—this time opposite another sexy "supermodel," Naomi Campbell.

For the video of *In the Closet,* he hired as his director Herb Ritts, who had filmed steamy black-and-white videos for Madonna and Janet Jackson, among others.

For four weeks prior to the filming, Michael worked with a personal trainer to build up his upper body. The cast and crew then headed out into the desert outside Palm Springs. Wearing black pants and a T-shirt, with his hair slicked back and tied in a ponytail, Michael engaged in a sizzling, suggestive mating dance with a scantily clad Campbell. When Campbell wrapped her bare legs around his waist and ground herself against him, Michael again went rigid. But this time there was a playful chemistry between the two that lent some credence to a British headline: MICHAEL'S DESERT STORM OF SEX.

After wrapping the *In the Closet* video, Michael appeared to greet the winners of an MTV "My Dinner with Michael" contest at a tented bash outside Palm Springs. Out of 4.1 million entries, thirty-four lucky fans were flown to this exotic location in the desert to party with Michael.

In an uncharacteristically gregarious mood, Michael chatted with the winners and even joined a conga line led by barely clad Brazilian dancers. There were carnival games, a magic act, stilt walkers, and a palm reader, but Michael was clearly most interested in the animals that had been brought in to liven things up: an elephant, a black panther, a lynx, and a camel. His favorite: a spider monkey that drank virgin daiquiris.

On February 4, 1992, Michael, dressed in a black leather uniform festooned with medals and a red armband, descended the dramatic art deco staircase in the lobby of New York's Radio City Music Hall to the accompaniment of *Black or White.* He then joined Pepsi executives to announce the *Dangerous* world tour and the establishment of his Heal the World Foundation to benefit children's charities around the globe. His goal: to raise $100 million for the foundation by Christmas 1993.

How much would Jackson receive on top of that amount? Pepsi vice president Peter Kendall smiled and would only say, "A lot." To be more precise, around $20 million.

"The only reason I am going on tour is to assist the children of the world and the ecology," Michael insisted. "This tour will allow me to donate time to visiting children throughout the world and spread global love. I want to tell the children of the world, 'You're all our children, each one of you is my child, and I love you all.' "

Throughout early 1992 Michael's spin machine went into overdrive, manufacturing romances for the superstar. SPARKS FLY BETWEEN "DANGEROUS" DUDE AND CASINO CUTIE shouted one headline, which showed Michael in Las Vegas cavorting with showgirl Shoshana Hawley.

Michael actually spent nearly all of his time in the company of Brett Barnes, an Australian ten-year-old he had invited to Neverland the previous year. Michael was now telling everyone Barnes was his cousin, and in press report after press report over the coming months, that was how Barnes would be identified. Barnes did his part; when asked his name, he replied dutifully, "Brett Jackson."

"Just say you went to a toy shop," Barnes said of his new pal, "and saw a toy you wanted. He'll buy that. And if he's wearing a piece of jewelry and you say, 'Oh, that's nice,' he'll give it to you! He's a great friend to play with, to love. He's like your best friend, only big."

During his Las Vegas sojourn, Michael stayed with Barnes in his video game-stocked suite at the Mirage Hotel-Casino, where he was an investor. They also caught the act of magicians Siegfried and Roy and dueled with plastic swords at the Excalibur.

On a five-day trip to London with Barnes in late February, the pair visited comic Benny Hill in the hospital, where he was recovering from a heart attack. Michael compared him to Chaplin and suggested they team up for a television special. Elated by Jackson's visit, Hill was released from the hospital—but died a short time later. Michael later made a bid to buy his scripts and sketch notes.

As he always did with his special friends, Michael escorted Barnes on a tour of London's most expensive toy stores, buying thousands of dollars' worth of games they would use for just a few days in their hotel room. Pandemonium erupted when they were set upon by fifty frenzied fans outside the Dorchester Hotel. Terrified, Michael was pushed to the ground and almost trampled before bodyguards came to his rescue.

Michael and his "cousin" Brett stayed in a $2,000-per-night ninth-floor suite at the Dorchester while the twenty-six members of his entourage took over the entire eighth floor at a daily cost of $10,000. By the time they departed on the Concorde, it was estimated that Michael had spent $200,000.

It was only the beginning of a whirlwind eleven-day promotional tour that covered thirty thousand miles, eleven time zones, and four continents. The highlight was to be his tour (with Barnes along for the ride) of five African nations. A camera crew came along to tape the triumphal journey for a planned *Return to Africa* video.

Nineteen years after his first visit to Africa, Michael was greeted at the airport in Gabon by a screaming crowd of more than one hundred thousand. His arrival the next day in the Ivory Coast capital of Abidjan sparked a full-scale riot. From the window of the hotel room he shared with Barnes, a terrified Michael watched the pitched battle between police and thousands of fans below. When it was over, 37 people had been injured and 143 arrested.

Later Michael traveled to the Ivory Coast village of Krinjabo, where, sitting on a gilded throne in full tribal regalia, he was crowned "King of the Sanwis." In Gabon Michael attracted bigger crowds than Nelson Mandela; in the Ivory Coast he drew more people than the pope.

It might have been one of the biggest public relations coups in Michael's career, if not for one annoying habit. Throughout the visit, Michael, seemingly offended by the smells of Africa and its people, kept holding his nose. Not surprisingly, some Africans took offense. "The American sacred beast took it upon himself to remind us that we are underdeveloped and impure," read an editorial in Gabon's leading newspaper. "And this re-created, bleached being who is neither white nor black, neither a man nor a woman—is too delicate, too frail, to inhale it."

"Under no circumstances," protested Michael's spokesman, Bob Jones, "would we be here if we thought your country smelled. You are our roots. The air here is as fresh as it is everywhere."

There was another theory to account for Michael's nose fussing. Although his lawyer, Bert Fields, would deny it, yet another plastic surgery—his sixth—had left Michael with what appeared to be a hole in the side of his nose. Plastic surgeons theorized that his nose had been packed to keep it from sagging and that stitches inside may have been causing his nose to itch.

One doctor went so far as to suggest that Michael's nose had been operated on so many times that it was in danger of collapsing. "There is a chance," he said, "Michael could end up with a plastic nose." Whatever the condition of his nose, Michael took care to conceal it under what now amounted to a thick paste of makeup.

Back home and supposedly reeling from what was now being called the African tour "fiasco," Michael passed up Elizabeth Taylor's much ballyhooed sixtieth birthday party at Disneyland. Instead he holed up at New York's Helmsley Palace hotel with his "cousin" Brett.

The day before Taylor's televised party, Michael decided to visit an indoor amusement arcade called Sportsworld in Paramus, New Jersey, and had it cleared out on the spur of the moment so that he and Barnes could have the place all to themselves. At 10:00 P.M. an announcement was made over the park's loudspeaker: "A situation has arisen, and we must close immediately!" Patrons were refunded their money as they left. "Police were astonished," said the complex's co-owner Allan Mekles, beaming, "that we could empty the park in fifteen minutes." Thrilled that they had the run of Sportsworld's 150 video games, Michael and Barnes stayed until 1:30 A.M. They had such a good time that they returned the next day.

Meanwhile, back at the Enchanted Kingdom, Disney chairman Michael Eisner played host as Michael's billionaire confidant David Geffen and dozens of the biggest names in Hollywood celebrated Elizabeth Taylor's birthday. But everyone noticed that she seemed oddly distracted. "Michael *is* coming, isn't he?" she whispered to Geffen. "He's just going to surprise me at the last minute . . . right?"

18

I am just like a hemophiliac who can't afford to be scratched in any way.

"He's got me concerned," said Liz Taylor when Michael failed to show up at her Disneyland birthday extravaganza. "He really has." Taylor had been told that Michael, whose latest affectation was a plaster cast he strapped onto his right forearm each morning, was seriously depressed over all the bad publicity generated by the trip to Africa.

If the so-called African fiasco bothered Michael at all, it must have been because it rekindled speculation concerning his plastic surgeries—specifically his apparent attempts to look anything but African American.

While making *Dangerous,* Michael confided to producer Terry Riley that he regretted having had the extensive plastic surgery. "If Michael could do it all over again," said Riley, who spent months in the studio with Jackson working on the new album, "he probably wouldn't have done it. But when you do things like that, you can't turn back. . . ."

Precisely how much plastic surgery had Michael undergone? In addition to reports of six rhinoplasties, the cleft inserted in his chin with a plastic implant, and the tattooed permanent eyeliner, he was now said to have several face-lifts, fat suctioned from his cheeks, his upper lip thinned, bone grafts on his cheeks and jaw to add definition to the contours of his face, a "forehead lift" to smooth his skin and raise his eyebrows, and several eye jobs to remove the bags and crow's-feet. All this in addition to supposed skin peels and the bleaching creams he used to lighten his complexion.

Michael tolerated this rampant speculation in the American press. But before long he would take action against a British tabloid that, he claimed, had gone a step too far. But more often these days, he was on the receiving end of litigation. L.A. Gear was preparing its $10 million fraud and breach of contract suit, claiming its line of Michael Jackson Unstoppable footwear had flopped because he had not produced an album in time to promote it, as promised.

In April the Cleveland Orchestra joined the fray. It sued Michael for $7 million, charging that he lifted sixty-seven seconds of its recording of Beethoven's Symphony no. 9 for "Will You Be There?" (a cut from the *Dangerous* album).

Michael took full credit on the album for writing and producing "Will You Be There" (later used in the hit save-the-whales film *Free Willy*), with no mention of Beethoven or the Cleveland Orchestra. "Mysteriously," cracked the orchestra's lawyer, Brad Rose, "one minute and seven seconds of the symphony as performed by the Cleveland Orchestra appears in the first minute and seven seconds of the song."

Fortunately Sony owned the rights to the Cleveland Orchestra recording, and the issue was quickly settled. Not, however, before Bert Fields issued an indignant denial on Jackson's behalf. "He's no music thief," he said. "Michael doesn't steal anything from anybody."

Denver songwriter Crystal Cartier added her name to the list of composers and lyricists who strongly disagreed. Cartier wrote a song entitled "Dangerous" in 1985 and had performed it for hundreds of people around Denver for years. In October 1990 she recorded it, registered the copyright, and published it with BMI. She released her song "Dangerous" as part of an album entitled *Love Story* in July 1991, and it was played repeatedly on radio in Denver.

When she first heard Michael's song "Dangerous" played over radio station KS104 in late November 1991, she immediately called the disc jockey. "Damn," the DJ said. "It's the same song. His is just slower." The songs not only possessed the same title, but according to Cartier, they sounded virtually identical. In June 1992 Cartier filed a $40 million suit against Michael, claiming he had stolen her song.

The "Dangerous" lawsuit would consume Cartier's life for the next two years, but Michael barely took notice. Instead he was busy planning his upcoming tour and making a new special friend.

He had first encountered Joey Randall* in 1984 at a Los Angeles restaurant. Joey, then four, was there with his mother, Anne, a stunning dark-haired model, and his stepfather, David Schwartz, the owner of the trendy Rent-a-Wreck car agency. Schwartz had made millions catering to celebrities who supposedly sought to avoid the limelight by tooling around town in nondescript cars. Joey was Anne's son by her first marriage to Adam Randall, a Beverly Hills dentist and aspiring screenwriter.

When Michael was burned filming the Pepsi commercial a few months later, Joey sent him a get-well note and Michael phoned him personally from Brotman Medical Center to thank him. Four years later during the *Bad* tour, Joey wrote Michael a fan letter and sent him a picture. Michael sent him free VIP tickets to one of his L.A. concerts.

They would not meet again until May 1992, when Michael's car broke down and he stopped in at Rent-a-Wreck for a replacement while his was being repaired. Schwartz called Anne at home and told her to bring Joey, then twelve, to the office to meet Michael.

Was the meeting sheer coincidence? "Get real," said one of those who would later become involved in investigating child abuse allegations against Michael. "First of all, Michael Jackson's car just happens to break down in L.A., then instead of calling one of his one hundred or so lackeys, he personally goes to a rental agency, and it just so happens to be the one where Joey is? Pretty farfetched."

It did not escape Michael's notice that the diminutive Joey Randall, fine-boned with dark skin, hair, and eyes, was a ringer for Brett Barnes. From the day of their meeting in May 1992, he bombarded Randall with phone calls. "From the very beginning," said a Jackson staff member, "he was totally obsessed with that kid."

In July Michael gave Randall a copy of his *Dancing the Dream*, a slim coffee-table book of poetry, photographs, and "reflections" published by Doubleday. As with *Moonwalk*, Jackie Onassis oversaw the project, although the actual editing was done by Shaye Areheart.

"When I hear the name *Michael Jackson*," Elizabeth Taylor wrote in the book's introduction, "I think of brilliance, of dazzling stars, lasers, and deep emotions . . . one of the most gifted music makers the world has ever known . . . intense caring and love . . . alarmingly bright . . . unearthly, special, innocent, childlike . . . a wise man, one of the sharpest

* In the interest of protecting the alleged victim's identity, pseudonyms are used not only for the boy but also for members of his family—with the exception of David Schwartz, whose name has been widely published. All other names in the book are real.

wits, so giving . . . an incredible force of incredible energy . . . one of the finest people to hit this planet. . . ."

But a poet? In "Quantum Leap," Michael wrote, "I looked for you on hill and dale / I sought for you beyond the pale." Then there was "Planet Earth": "Cold as a rock without a hue / held together with a bit of glue. . . ." More interesting were the photographs, including stills from the *Black or White* video, and full-page color portraits of Michael as Napoleon, Henry VIII, and Julius Caesar.

And in case all this might have appeared too effete, photos of Michael firing off an Uzi-like TEC-9 automatic handgun at Neverland were leaked to the press. "Forget his reputation for wimpy weirdness," read the caption in the *Star*. "When Michael Jackson grabs a gun, he turns into a tough-talking terror."

The Jackson camp was careful not to let anything leak about Michael's new plan to create a tax-exempt "Neverland Zoo Foundation for the Preservation and Breeding of Endangered and Other Species." On April 13, 1992, incorporation papers for the Neverland Zoo Foundation were filed stating that the Foundation was "organized and operated exclusively for charitable, religious, scientific, literary, and educational purposes within the meaning of Section 501 (c) (3) of the Internal Revenue Code." Although Michael has not publicly divulged his plans, Neverland Zoo, if part of the "nonprofit public benefit corporation not organized for the private gain of any person," could become a multimillion-dollar tax write-off.

As of September 1994, the application to the IRS for tax-exempt status was still pending. If granted, the startling fact is that some or all of Michael Jackson's private 2,700-acre Xanadu could be run at the expense of the American taxpayer.

Dangerous was obviously not going to top *Thriller*—it was hard to imagine what could—but by now it had sold nearly five million copies. It was a blockbuster by any standard other than Michael's. But he was determined that *Dangerous* match *Bad*'s sales of twenty million; he could not afford to look as if his popularity were slipping.

He needn't have worried. Taking along the hugely popular twelve-year-old rappers Kris Kross as his opening act, Michael premiered the *Dangerous* world tour in Munich that June 1992. To *really* launch the tour Michael appeared to strap on a jet and—for his grand finale—rocket two hundred yards out of the stadium. Of course, the spectacular exit, worked out by master illusionist David Copperfield, was actually executed by a stunt double.

For the rest of the year Michael would play to sold-out venues in thirty-two European cities before moving on in 1993 to Asia, Australia, and Latin America. After that he would probably tour the United States in 1994—barring any unforeseen developments.

During the tour, every spare moment was spent in the company of children. Outside Paris Michael visited Euro Disney with Brett Barnes and nine-year-old Bavarian Prince Albert von Thurn und Taxis, son of high-living "punk princess" Gloria von Thurn und Taxis and one of the wealthiest young men in the world. They went to the Phantom Haunted House, on a space flight simulator, then on the Thunder Mountain roller coaster—twice. Wherever they went within Euro Disney, the trio stayed within a square of rope held by a dozen guards.

In London Michael played to 360,000 fans and grossed $13 million during just three days at Wembley Stadium. But when London's *Daily Mirror* ran a particularly ghastly photo and described him as "Scarface" and a "cruelly disfigured phantom" whose face was about to fall off, Michael was livid. The accompanying story claimed that he had a hole in his nose "like an extra nostril," an "oddly sagging chin," and one cheek "higher than the other." The British tabloid went on to say that he regularly wore a mask to conceal the scar tissue on his hideously deformed face. "Michael now looks like a grotesque burn victim," wrote the *Mirror*'s Rick Skye. "His nose is so deformed it looks like misshapen plastic."

"I am incensed, furious," Michael said, and he ordered his attorney, Bert Fields, to sue the tabloid for libel. "Normally people in my position ignore these types of stories. But this has been going on too long, and somebody has to stand up and fight for the truth against this newspaper."

It was not going to be easy. After examining hundreds of pictures that he had taken of Michael from 1977 on, photographer Russell Turiak told Fields, "There are definitely some photographs that reveal scars. I mean, you're gonna have a tough time proving the case."

Distraught, Michael stayed sequestered in his Dorchester Hotel suite with Brett Barnes. "Don't worry about that picture," Barnes told his sobbing friend as they played with toy trains on the floor of their hotel room, "you're still handsome." Several weeks later Michael and Barnes graduated to a larger model. For one stretch of the tour, Michael reserved the entire *Orient Express*.

Also along for much of the European tour was Dr. Deepak Chopra, author of *Quantum Healing: Exploring the Frontiers of the Mind.* Chopra was spiritual guru to a number of celebrities, including Michael's friend Jackie Onassis.

His own fragile condition aside, Michael had been called upon to save someone else's life during his London stay. An obsessed fan, a twenty-eight-year-old unemployed decorator named Eric Herminie, climbed up a fire escape and stood on a narrow sixth-floor ledge across from the Dorchester Hotel, threatening to kill himself if Jackson didn't make an appearance. "I want to see Michael!" he screamed over and over. "If I don't, I'll jump."

A crowd gathered below. Meanwhile Herminie, a Jackson look-alike dressed in Michael's trademark black attire, tossed his jacket to the ground and balanced precariously on one leg as the crowd below gasped. He became increasingly agitated, screaming, "Michael! Michael!" over and over again.

Finally Michael walked out onto the balcony of the Dorchester with Bill Bray, waved to the weeping Herminie and the crowd below for two minutes, then did an impromptu dance. After Herminie came in off the ledge, Michael called him on the phone. "He basically saved my life," Herminie said. "If he hadn't come out, I obviously would have jumped. He told me not to do it again—to stay together. Of course, I am going to."

That night Michael, who had inexplicably lost ten pounds over the previous few weeks, apparently suffered another serious anxiety attack and collapsed on stage at Wembley in front of Prince Charles and seventy-two thousand fans. After he'd been helped to his feet by stage hands, he managed to finish the show, but, claiming another bout with the flu, he cancelled the following night's performance.

Throughout the grueling tour and despite Brett Barnes's companionship, Michael phoned his other young friend Joey Randall in California nearly every day from the fifteen countries he visited. These conversations would last for up to three hours. "Michael and I talked," Randall recalled, "about video games, the Neverland ranch, water fights, and famous people he knew." Someday, Michael promised, he would introduce Joey to Princess Di, Elizabeth Taylor—and E.T.

According to *Forbes* magazine, Michael earned $55 million in 1992 alone. A sizable chunk of that came from HBO, which paid $18 million to broadcast the final performance of his European tour in Bucharest. The figure was nine times what HBO had paid for the finale of Madonna's *Blonde Ambition* tour.

The actual concert was preceded by yet another fifteen-minute tribute to Jackson full of fawning celebrity endorsements, shots of hysterical fans, and a four-minute opening ovation with Michael standing frozen at center stage. New York *Daily News* critic Jim Farber called the HBO broadcast "the most terrifying spectacle of a rampaging star ego since Diana Ross appeared last." *Newsday* worried, "His current technique of pulling on his genitals has evolved from choreographic cliché to genuine mental health dilemma. If you saw his costume, you had to wonder why someone didn't tell Jackson that you wear an athletic supporter *inside* your pants."

HBO wasn't complaining. Once again Michael demolished all records. His concert was the highest-rated HBO program ever.

A month later Michael returned to the airwaves with the five-hour ABC miniseries *The Jacksons: An American Dream.* Again Michael was giving the rest of the family an opportunity to make some money—in this case $1 million for the rights to the Jackson story. In exchange for letting Jermaine and his wife, Margaret Maldonado, produce the miniseries, Michael demanded approval of the director, the writer, the script, and the three actors chosen to play him at various ages.

He also asked for "someone beautiful" to play Katherine, and he got his wish: Angela Bassett (who later received an Oscar nomination for portraying Tina Turner in *What's Love Got to Do with It?*) was cast as Katherine, with Lawrence Hilton Jacobs as Joe, Vanessa Williams as Suzanne de Passe, Billy Dee Williams as Berry Gordy, and Holly Robinson as Diana Ross.

Understandably, the project had hit its biggest snag a year earlier, when Jermaine's derisive "Word to the Badd!" came out. Back then an angry Michael had showed up unannounced at Hayvenhurst to pull the plug on the miniseries. In a closed-door session in the Trophy Room, Jermaine—with Joe and Katherine looking on anxiously—had told Michael that he had not written the lyrics of the song but had been forced by his record company to say he had (the label, Arista, heatedly denied this). Michael was satisfied, and the miniseries went ahead.

If it wasn't a whitewash, *The Jacksons: An American Dream* came awfully close. Joe was depicted as a driven stage father who sometimes "whupped" his kids, but the extent to which he had abused and terrorized his children was scarcely hinted at. ("Our father got a bad rap," said Jermaine. "My father is rough. He beat our butts, but he didn't abuse us.") Michael's early insecurities—his acne, the pressure to achieve—were also touched upon, but little more. There was no mention of plastic surgery or the lingering tensions between Michael and the rest of the family. No matter. Despite tepid reviews, *The Jacksons: An American Dream* was a ratings blockbuster for ABC.

All three of the young actors Michael approved to portray him at different ages in the miniseries were black. So it came as a surprise when, after picking a black actor to play him as a youngster in an Australian Pepsi commercial, he changed his mind and hired a white one instead.

Wade Robson was only five in 1987 when he won a Michael Jackson dance contest in Australia and Michael invited him on stage to perform with him. Four years later, at Michael's urging, Wade and his parents moved to California, where he promptly became one of the most frequent visitors to Neverland.

The two grew so close, in fact, that Wade's mother Joy was reportedly put on the Jackson payroll and given a Rolls. "I just want to be big in the industry and try to touch people in the world of all ages," said the boy, "just like Michael."

Wade's father left his wife and returned to Australia, apparently in disgust.

Michael's nickname for Robson was "the Little One." And he had already cast him in small parts in three of his videos by the time the Pepsi spot came along. In the sixty-second commercial, the adult Michael is playing the piano and singing "I'll Be There" while the ten-year-old Robson, portraying the young Michael, watches him in the background.

To play the part, the light-skinned Robson put on an Afro wig, his skin color was darkened using computerized colorization, and a top artist was hired to superimpose the real Michael's childhood features over Robson's for the close-ups. The result: a younger Michael whose features seemed to correspond with the more delicate-boned, Kabuki-white Michael of 1993.

While the press had a field day with the fact that a white child was playing the young Michael in a Pepsi commercial, Michael returned home in December from a series of *Dangerous* concerts in Japan. When he arrived at Neverland, he was amazed to find the place decorated from top to bottom for the holidays—courtesy of his friend Elizabeth Taylor. "It was wonderful," he recalled. "I'd never celebrated birthdays or Christmases before. Not one. It was always, Work! *That's* why I believe in Neverland."

Michael's newfound Christmas spirit faded quickly. By January 1993 he was desperate. In the year since *Dangerous* had forced him out of his self-imposed exile, it had become clear that the "Wacko Jacko" image he himself helped forge with hyperbaric chambers and Elephant Man bones had backfired. *Dangerous* had stalled, and in a *Los Angeles Times* survey of music industry executives, Jackson was ranked fourteenth on the list of marketable stars. The problem? By design, Michael no longer seemed of this earth. "His career went stratospheric," *Time*'s Richard Corliss observed, "and he went extraterrestrial. For some imaginary Madame Tussaud's, he transformed himself into his own waxed, blanched figure."

Michael was now determined to win back his fans—to pull himself down to terra firma and reclaim his humanity. "Michael's going to be more receptive from now on," Bert Fields said. "The nineties demand more reality and accessibility."

Following an appearance at the NAACP Image Awards, Michael performed at the Clinton inaugural gala on January 19. Flanked by the president and an ecstatic first daughter Chelsea, he led a stirring all-star chorus of his "We Are the World" anthem. Then it was on to the American Music Awards, where Michael won three out of five nominations for *Dangerous,* including Best Album. Performing the title track live on stage, he grabbed his crotch a dozen times—including several two-handed yanks that took even his fellow musicians aback.

At the Super Bowl Garth Brooks sang the national anthem while Oscar-winning actress Marlee Matlin signed for deaf viewers. But the main event—aside from the game—was Michael headlining the half-time show with a razzle-dazzle act featuring lasers, blazing pyrotechnics, a 750-member choir, and a 98,000-person flashcard stunt to promote his Heal the World Foundation—all displayed on two JumboTron screens. For the grand finale Michael surrounded himself with 3,500 children singing "Heal the World." Some critics were disappointed with Michael's performance, but no one contested the fact that his sheer presence helped boost the viewership to more than 120 million—the largest U.S. viewing audience ever.

The biggest coup was yet to come. Three months earlier, *Oprah Winfrey Show* producer Debra DiMaio had approached Michael about appearing on one of Winfrey's prime-time specials. It did not hurt that Quincy Jones and Steven Spielberg, with whom she had worked on the film *The Color Purple,* were mutual friends. She was also far and away the most popular talk show host on television, with a 1992 income to prove it—at $88 million, she had made $33 million more than Jackson.

Michael admired Oprah for other, less tangible reasons. She reminded him of his mother in younger days. There were also the obvious similarities in their rags-to-riches stories. As two of the richest, most influential, and most beloved people of any race, they served as an inspiration to millions of their fellow African Americans.

What Winfrey did not know was that they may have shared another life-altering experience. If La Toya and others were right about her brother, then both Winfrey and Jackson, as children, had been sexually abused by a relative. Winfrey, however, had been open in discussing her personal experience and had become a crusader against child abuse in the process.

Winfrey was surprised when Michael called her directly at the offices of Harpo (her anagrammatically named production company) to say he was interested in appearing on her program. Elated, she immediately contacted ABC president Brandon Stoddard with the news.

No one was more acutely aware of the ratings possibilities than Winfrey and Stoddard. When it was announced that she was interviewing Michael Jackson in prime time on February 10, it was as if, as one wag put it, "pop culture fire alarms had gone off all over the world." In promos for the show, Winfrey talked to the camera with her hand on Michael's leather-clad shoulder while Jackson, turned away from her, was visible only in silhouette. Intoned the venerable *Boston Globe:* "The great Oz will speak. The mouse will roar."

There were no restrictions placed on what Winfrey could ask—she was not, like MTV, contractually required to call Michael the "king of pop"—but her staff was clearly nervous. They had ninety minutes of prime airtime to fill—*live*—and Michael Jackson was not known for being loquacious. Who knew if he could speak more than a few halting words?

Michael, too, was wary. Not one to leave important matters to chance, he personally orchestrated the media event. There would be never-before-seen video clips from his private archives, a live nighttime tour of Neverland, and—taking full advantage of the prime-time audience—the world premiere of his new music video: *Give in to Me* from *Dangerous.*

The one-on-one interview was conducted in the baronial living room of the main house at Neverland. Elizabeth Taylor was waiting in the wings to once again sing Michael's praises. And unknown to Oprah, Michael had also invited a new special friend—Joey Randall—to occupy a ringside seat. "Joey was in the house at the time," an investigator would later say. "Michael wanted to get him all excited about what was going on. That was how he operated. She never knew, of course, but he was basically using Oprah to pimp the kid."

More than ninety million people tuned in to Winfrey's Michael Jackson interview, dwarfing the audience for the Academy Awards and making it the highest-rated show in six years—and the fourth most-watched entertainment show in history (after the final episode of *M*A*S*H,* the "Who Shot JR?" episode of *Dallas,* and the nuclear holocaust scenario *The Day After).*

In case anyone was not fully aware of Michael's supremacy in the pop universe, the show began with the usual video tribute. Then Michael made his entrance, looking every bit as fragile and otherworldly as anyone could have imagined. Sitting in a brown leather chair opposite her subject, Winfrey then managed to get Michael to deliver one revelation after another in his frail voice.

Not all his answers were completing forthcoming. Michael debunked the notion that he ever slept in a hyperbaric chamber ("an absolute lie") or attempted to buy the Elephant Man's bones ("Another stupid story. Where am I gonna put some bones, and why would I want them?"). Both, of course, were stories that Michael himself had planted. The plastic surgery? "Very little," he said. "You can count it on two fingers."

When asked about his ever-lightening complexion, Michael dropped a bombshell. Claiming that he was "proud to be a black American," he vehemently denied that he had asked that a white child portray him in a Pepsi commercial. In a voice choked with emotion he then revealed that he suffered from a disorder that robs skin of its pigment. "It's a problem for me," he whispered, "I can't control it." (His dermatologist, Dr. Arnold Klein, later confirmed that Michael had been diagnosed in 1986 with vitiligo, a genetic disease that can be treated with ultraviolet rays in conjunction with a number of oral medications and topical creams.)

Janet Jackson later claimed that Michael had first told her about the vitiligo in 1990 and had grown more panicky as the disease worsened. But by then, according to La Toya, he had already been using bleaching creams for years. Michael also said nothing during the interview about reports that he had recently begun having collagen injections to smooth out the wrinkles in his face.

Then there were his answers to Winfrey's questions about his stolen childhood ("I'd look out and see all the children playing, and it would make me cry"). In his mid-thirties, Michael said, he was still making up for what he missed most: "slumber parties."

"Did your father ever beat you?" Winfrey asked.

"Yes," Michael replied softly, acknowledging that Joe still upset him so much that he sometimes vomited if he had to see him. He then turned to the camera and spoke directly to Joe. "I'm sorry. Please don't be mad at me." Not only had his father beat him, Michael elaborated, he had routinely called him "ugly," turning adolescence into "very sad, sad years. I used to always cry from loneliness," Michael said. "I would cry every day."

As for the crotch grabbing, Michael said it "happens subliminally.... I'm a slave to the rhythm."

Who was he dating now? Winfrey asked. "Right now," he responded, "it's Brooke Shields." He added that he had also loved another woman but declined to name her.

Winfrey pressed on: Was Michael a virgin? "I'm a gentleman. You can call me old-fashioned, if you want." Then he giggled and said that she had "embarrassed" him.

Elizabeth Taylor stepped out of the wings to say that Michael, who eyed her warily, was "the least weird man I've ever known." Then Michael escorted Winfrey to his private theater, with beds on either side for seriously ill children. There he sang an a cappella snippet of "Who Is It?" from the album. And so strong was the reaction to those few brief notes that radio stations across the country clamored for it to be played the next day.

While Michael gave Winfrey the royal tour of his own magic kingdom, a young girl from Germany was huddled in a culvert beneath the road that led to Neverland. She had lived there for months. Each day, she walked the five miles into town for food and water, then returned to wait for her idol. Eventually she vanished. "We all were very worried about her," said one local resident who brought her food and blankets. "It was so sad, really. I wonder what ever happened to her...."

The girl in the culvert was not the only fan to make the pilgrimage to Neverland. According to residents of the area, no one paid much attention to local celebrity ranch owners like Ronald Reagan, Bo Derek, and action-adventure star Steven Seagal. But every week hundreds of fans from all over the world made the trek to catch a glimpse of the king of pop.

Reaction to the Winfrey interview was unprecedented. Under the headline PETER PAN SPEAKS, *Time* described it as "great TV: live, reckless, emotionally naked." In its "Can You *Believe* This Guy?" cover story, *Entertainment Weekly* concluded that "in a single evening of TV, the Genius Weirdo had repositioned himself as the Genius Victim—abused and melancholy, yet strengthened and redeemed by extraordinary talent."

"He exposed himself to the world," Michael's agent, Sandy Gallin, said. "He showed the world that he's a very articulate, normal, loving human being." Still, writer Ken Tucker acknowledged that there was "a creepy subtext in a crotch-grabbing guy who hangs out with children. . . ." Cracked *Tonight Show* host Jay Leno: "You've got to admit, Michael looked a little strange. The Elephant Man called and wanted to buy *Michael's* bones."

The interview certainly had the desired effect at the cash register. The *Dangerous* album, which had slipped over the previous year to number 131, shot back to number 12 in a single week—a resurgence, said *Billboard* magazine's Timothy White, of "truly historic proportions."

The day after the interview Michael sent his father a peace offering: a $100,000 Range Rover with a note attached to the windshield that read, "I'm sorry, Daddy." Michael also gave Elizabeth Taylor a $250,000 diamond necklace as a token of his affection.

For Brooke Shields the interview also paid off handsomely. Swamped with calls from reporters, her office issued a formal statement: "Michael was brave to do the show, and he was quite the gentleman. I hope he's as proud of himself as I am."

Privately Shields's reaction was less restrained. Michael had phoned her weeks earlier to tell her she would probably be mentioned in some way. But she was hardly prepared to hear him declare his love for her before ninety million viewers. Glued to the television at her home in Princeton, Shields burst out laughing when Michael spoke her name. "She thought it was hysterical," a close female friend said. "The next day she and her mother, Terry, were still laughing their heads off about the whole thing. Brooke cares for Michael a lot, but trying to pretend there was something romantic going on between them? Even Brooke thought that was too much. She thought it was all very, very funny."

As a fellow child star–turned–perpetual–virgin icon, Shields did empathize with the psychic pain Michael expressed. "It is very hard when your own family turns against you and outwardly hurts you," she said. "When anybody you ever befriended inevitably uses you and turns around and slaps you in the face. . . . You get callous in this business after years. People hurt him all the time. He allows it to eat away at him. So of course he wants to be surrounded by kids. The light in their eyes is what he wants to keep alive in his own soul."

A month later Michael, whose stringy hair now hung over his eyes in a bizarre wet shaggy dog look, showed up at the Soul Train Awards in Los Angeles to pick up three awards. He had graduated from surgical masks and bandaged fingers to a wheelchair. Claiming that he had sprained his ankle while dancing, he sat in a chair performing "Remember the Time" while dancers swirled around him. Michael Bolton had also sprained his ankle, but he hobbled in on crutches. And when a disbelieving Eddie Murphy was asked backstage about Jackson's condition, he said, laughing, "You'll have to check with Michael's physician."

By now Michael's seduction of Joey Randall was in full swing. Beginning with a weekend visit in February, Randall, his five-year-old half-sister, Molly, and his mother, Anne, spent nearly every weekend at Neverland. During this time all three stayed together in the guest house where the other mothers and fathers stayed, far from the main residence. On one of these very early visits, another boy sat in Michael's lap so they could hug one another. Joey later confessed to his mother that it made him jealous.

Anne Randall, who had been estranged from David Schwartz for some time, watched as Michael showered presents on her children. The local Toys 'R' Us reopened after store hours to let Michael, Joey, and Molly have free run of the place. The children were allowed to get anything they wanted, and they did—up to $10,000 worth in a single visit.

On an official trip to Disneyland in late February, photographers crowded around the van carrying Michael and his entourage through the park. During the five-minute trip Anne sat in the backseat, staring out the window, while Michael sat in front of her with Joey in his lap. Once away from the photographers, Michael "wrapped his arms around the youngster," one witness said. "He began nuzzling the boy's ear and running his fingers through his hair. It made my skin crawl."

Pulling a piece of candy out of his pocket, Michael offered it to Joey, then pulled it away at the last minute. Eventually he placed the candy in Joey's mouth. "When the candy was gone . . . he lovingly looked at the boy and began kissing him on the face . . . then on the forehead, hairline, and temple. He sighed as he buried his face in the boy's hair." A Disney employee riding in the van reportedly observed: "They were soft and lingering kisses. If those two were a man and a woman, you would swear they were on a honeymoon."

As soon as the van stopped and they were once again encircled by photographers, Joey hopped off Michael's lap and Michael grabbed little Molly's hand.

On March 15 Michael appeared at the Grammy ceremonies to pick up a Lifetime Achievement Award. When Janet, now remade by plastic surgery to look uncannily like her brother, presented Michael with the award, he pulled her alongside him and said, "See, me and Janet really are two different people!" Actually, the resemblance between Michael and La Toya was even stronger.

Later that evening Michael took his date, Brooke Shields, to a party being thrown in his honor by Sony. For the benefit of photographers he leaned over in the back of their limousine, grabbed Shields's hands, and planted a kiss on her cheek. The pained expression on her face and the fact that Michael was wearing more makeup than she was undermined the intended effect.

Shields was careful, however, to make sure that photographers got a clear shot of the $100,000 diamond ring that she held up to her face as they kissed awkwardly. Michael had given her the ring over a year before. It was not an engagement ring, but Shields allowed that it "would be interpreted by the world as 'I am asking you to marry me.' He just simply said, 'I want you to have this to appreciate it to let you know how much I love you and smile when you look at it.' " Immediately after the Winfrey interview, however, Michael had given Shields a $200,000 necklace for, said a friend, "being a pawn in his little game."

Several days later, between weekends spent with Joey Randall, Michael flew to Winnetka, Illinois, to visit Macaulay Culkin on the set of *Home Alone 2.* Culkin was on the cover of the current issue of the children's magazine *Disney Adventures,* and Michael wanted to tell him in person that he had agreed to pose for the cover—the first time he had posed for a magazine cover since *Vanity Fair*'s decade-end issue in 1989. Michael was particularly excited about the star who was appearing with him on the cover—"You aren't going to believe this, Mac, but I'm gonna be on with Pinocchio!"

Since most of Michael's special friends went to school during the week, he spent much of his time alone (with the exception of the staff) at Neverland. His neighbors at Midland School knew when he was alone because he turned up the music that spewed forth from speakers hidden in Neverland's flower beds and trees until it echoed off the hillsides. "It's not what you'd expect at all," a resident teacher at the school said. "In the middle of the night he's playing show tunes, Julie Andrews stuff—Muzak, really. It's quite annoying."

These were the times when Michael, his Magic Kingdom ablaze with lights, rode the Ferris wheel and roller coaster alone. "I do it," he had confided to Winfrey, "all the time."

It was difficult to believe that this same man-child was negotiating with junk bond king Michael Milken to start an educational and entertainment cable TV network aimed at children. Jackson and Milken, who had just been released after serving two years in prison for securities fraud, had, in fact, been friends for seven years. After paying fines of $1 billion, Milken still had $500 million left over—a figure that impressed even Michael, whose own personal fortune now hovered around $350 million.

When word leaked of his plan to go into business with a man described in newspapers as "America's biggest crook," Michael issued a statement: "Michael Milken is my friend because he has been through the fire, as I have, and emerged better for the process. He has been misunderstood, as I have been, and harshly judged by those who had no right to assume they knew this man without ever spending even an hour in his company."

By mid-March Joey Randall's mother, Anne, was no longer always in the picture. Michael had purchased a condominium on Galaxy Way in Century City, around the corner from the ABC Entertainment Center, the Century Plaza Hotel, and former president Ronald Reagan's office. Here Michael and Randall played video games for hours on end and tossed water balloons from the balcony at motorists and unsuspecting pedestrians.

The third weekend in March, Joey Randall joined Brett Barnes and New Jersey's Cascio brothers—Frank, thirteen, and Eddie, nine—for a nonstop session of fun and games with Michael at Neverland. The Cascios' father, Dominic, had managed New York's Helmsley Palace hotel, and Michael asked to meet his sons after noticing a photo of them on the wall of his office. They were babies at the time. And Michael's interest in the Cascio brothers had continued even after Dominic left the Helmsley Palace in 1986 to start his own restaurant.

On March 28 Anne, Joey, and Molly Randall flew with Michael on his private jet to Las Vegas and checked into the $3,000-a-night Michael Jackson suite at the Mirage for a week. That first night Michael rented *The Exorcist* and sat in bed, watching it with Joey. A devout fan of horror movies and the occult, Michael had already seen the R-rated movie with its graphic language and stomach-turning scenes (in one, the nine-year-old heroine violates herself with a crucifix). And he was all too aware of its impact on young children.

Joey was understandably terrified, and Michael suggested that he sleep with him that night. Joey wore sweat pants, Michael his silk pajamas. There was no physical contact between the two that evening. But when Anne walked in the next morning to discover Joey and Michael in bed together, she confronted Michael. He started crying and shaking uncontrollably. "This is about family, not making judgments," he pleaded. "This is not about sex. This is about truth, honesty, and love."

Anne was made to feel guilty for ever doubting Michael. She agreed to let him continue sleeping with her son. The next day she received a ruby-and-diamond bracelet from Cartier's. All told, she would receive $40,000 worth of jewelry, including rings, earrings, necklaces, and a Cartier watch.

For the next few days Michael and Joey slept together, but without physical contact. They swam with dolphins in the hotel's dolphin pool, caught Siegfried and Roy's act and the Cirque du Soleil. Twice they dined alone at the Mirage's Moon Gate Chinese restaurant, giggling and teasing each other with chopsticks. Just as he had with Brett Barnes, Michael introduced Joey as his "cousin."

In April Michael essentially moved into the family's cramped, three-bedroom home in Santa Monica Canyon, sharing Joey's bed with him each night while Anne and Molly stayed in their respective rooms. According to Michael's chauffeur, Gary Hearne, during one period Michael slept over with Joey thirty nights in a row.

Randall's small room was already brimming with presents from Michael—a Michael Jackson doll was buried beneath thousands of dollars' worth of videos, compact discs, Nintendo and Sega game cartridges, and expensive gadgets from the Sharper Image. An Everlast punching bag hung from the ceiling and posters of Batman and the X-Men superheroes decorated the walls.

A photograph taken by Joey's father when he dropped by one day showed Michael sitting in the boy's room on a wicker chair next to Joey's double bed. Michael was wearing his blue-, white-, and pink-striped silk pajamas, a black hat, full makeup (including lipstick and eyeliner), and a Band-Aid on his nose.

Over the next three months Michael and Randall slept together every night almost without exception. "At Neverland I would always sleep in bed with Michael Jackson," said the boy, whose mother and sister still stayed in the guest house. "I also slept in bed with Michael at my house and at hotels in New York, Florida, and Europe. . . . During our relationship," the boy added, "Michael Jackson had sexual contact with me on many occasions."

It had begun innocently enough, with hugs and the occasional brief kiss on the cheek. "There was genuine affection for the boy, absolutely," Joey's lawyer, Larry Feldman, would later concede. "It started out as a tender, loving relationship." Michael then began cuddling with the boy and kissing him on the lips, kisses that lasted longer each time. They kissed when they were in bed together.

Joey did ask Michael if their kissing in this manner was wrong. "People are just conditioned to think it's wrong," he recalled Michael telling him. "I'm an unconditioned person." Throughout their intensifying relationship, "conditioning" would be a key word in Michael's lexicon. Michael kept drumming into Joey's head the notion that he would have to fight being "conditioned" like everybody else. "People who aren't conditioned," Michael said, "are the ones with magical powers."

"It's cosmic," Michael said of their relationship. "We're just meant to be together."

One night in bed, according to Joey, Michael pushed the stakes higher by sticking his tongue in the boy's mouth. "I said, 'Don't do that,' " Joey later recalled. Stricken, Michael started crying. "I guess he tried to make me feel guilty," said the boy.

Again, Joey would say, Michael insisted there was "nothing wrong" with what he was doing. "Just because most people believe something is wrong," he said, "doesn't make it so. Todd [a pseudonym] lets me do it, Rubba," Michael told the confused boy. "He kisses me with an open mouth, he lets me put my tongue inside. I guess you don't love me as much as he does. . . ."

Joey relented. Another time in bed, Michael grabbed him by the buttocks and stuck his tongue in his ear. "I told him I didn't like it," Joey recalled. Once more, the wounded Michael began to weep.

During daylight hours and frequently around other people, Michael would "rub up against me quite often," Joey said. Sometimes, he later told a Child Services caseworker, he could feel that Michael had an erection. Joey also said that at night they began lying on top of each other with erections.

The publicity campaign to promote the new, accessible Michael was still in full swing with the publication of a *Life* magazine photoessay on Neverland. Reveling to his newfound popularity, Michael ordered his management team to begin renegotiating his contract with Sony.

Veteran photojournalist Harry Benson, perhaps best known for his pictures of the Beatles during their first trip to the United States, was the first photographer ever given entree to Michael's world of carousels, Ferris wheels, steam trains, free candy counters, and the zoo inhabited by "everything from alpacas to wallabies." In addition to giraffes, pythons, alligators, lions, and Gypsy the elephant (Elizabeth Taylor's seven-thousand-pound Christmas present), Michael's menagerie boasted such Lilliputian wonders as Cricket the thirty-four-inch-tall stallion, Petunia the potbellied pig, and Linus the two-foot-tall sheep.

Under the headline MICHAEL IN WONDERLAND, *Life*'s opening spread showed Michael as a pop Pied Piper, head held high and arms outstretched as he led an impromptu parade of ten youngsters—the children of his seventy full-time employees—across his Rose Bowl–size backyard. Although they were seldom seen at Neverland unless they were the siblings of his special friends, Michael made certain that only girls were shown in the foreground.

Michael revealed to the magazine's writer, David Friend, that he had seen Disney's *Aladdin* no fewer than six times, that his favorite toys were "jack-in-the-boxes, rocking horses, and Peter Pan—anything Peter Pan," and that Macaulay Culkin "spends all his vacations here." Friend noted that Jackson occasionally broke into song as he zipped around the grounds in a golf cart and that he wore one yellow sock and one orange.

In a touching aside, Michael told Friend that his fondest memory was the night when "we had a houseful of bald-headed children. They all had cancer. And one little boy turned to me and said, 'This is the best day of my life.' You had to hold back the tears."

Over the years Michael had unquestionably spent millions of dollars for a wide variety of children's charities and had spent countless hours with children in orphanages and hospitals around the world. Yet there were those who claimed that most of these gestures were meticulously orchestrated for press consumption. Longtime Jackson bodyguard Charli Michaels used to help out at the well-publicized parties Michael threw for the DARE antidrug program and the Make-A-Wish Foundation for seriously ill children. "They were only half-day parties," she said, "and this is the last day that these children will remember in their lives."

While the children repeatedly cried, "Where's Michael?" Charli Michaels and other Neverland employees were told to give the kids a tour and feed them lunch. Still the children, several of whom were in wheelchairs, begged to see their hero.

Finally Michael would make his appearance, pick up a little girl on the fringe of the crowd, and then disappear. "It was the most heart-wrenching experience with young children," Michaels recalled. "Michael spent five or six minutes at the most, then went back and waited for one of his little boyfriends to show up for the weekend."

Charli Michaels was described in her last job evaluation as "an honest, hardworking, intelligent employee—a team player." But after three years at Neverland she left in disgust in 1993. "When people come up to me and ask me what I think, I can't say anything nice," she stated. "I can't tell them what they want to hear. They want to hear that this magnificent superstar who gives to everybody is wonderful, and I just can't say that. . . . "

To the outside world, however, Michael remained a savior to children—an image further bolstered by the adulatory *Life* piece. That issue of *Life,* along with an earlier issue featuring Jackson on the cover, rated among the magazine's all-time top sellers.

As usual, Michael could count on some family melodrama to bring him crashing down to earth. In the predawn hours of April 21 in New York, Jack Gordon punched La Toya in the face so savagely that she was knocked down, splattering blood across the white marble floor of the couple's luxury apartment. As she tried to flee, he smashed a heavy dining room chair across her back.

Michael called La Toya at Lenox Hill Hospital, where she was being treated for cuts and contusions, and begged her to leave Gordon. Fearing her family—and particularly her father, Joe—even more, she refused. She explained to her brother that Gordon was suffering from inoperable cancer, and that his violent behavior was due to the effects of pain medication. Michael was skeptical, but La Toya returned to Gordon rather than be left to battle the Jackson clan alone.

Around the same time, brother Randy, thirty-one, was abducted by rebel guerrillas while visiting a friend in Colombia. When they saw the name in his passport, the machine-gun-toting terrorists asked if he was Michael Jackson's brother and threatened to cut off his fingers if he didn't tell the truth.

By reportedly pretending to be a Rastafarian evangelist with no money, Randy left his captors convinced that he couldn't possibly be one of the famous Jackson brothers. They ripped off his shirt, tied him to a tree, and left him to die. By the time he was rescued two days later, Randy was covered with insect bites and suffering from exposure—but alive. Had they known he was Michael Jackson's brother, one government official said, "they could have ransomed him for enough money to finance an entire war."

Michael again boarded his private jet in mid-May and flew with what many people were now calling his "adopted family" to join such fellow international stars as Tina Turner, Rod Stewart, and Luciano Pavarotti at the World Music Awards in Monaco. Michael was there to pick up three awards, including one as the "World's Best-Selling Record Artist of the Era."

When Michael introduced his friends to Prince Albert and Princesses Caroline and Stephanie, "it was as if he were introducing his own family," a bemused Monacan said. "It seemed very odd." But not as odd as what transpired at the awards ceremony itself. For more than two hours, before a VIP audience and five hundred million TV viewers around the world, Joey Randall sat in his lap, giggling as Michael cuddled, stroked, and nuzzled the boy without restraint. One observer watched in amazement as Michael reportedly ran his hand up and down the boy's leg.

The two were dressed identically in black outfits and red armbands, matching black hats, and mirrored sunglasses. To most in attendance it appeared the boy was no more than nine. Had they known he was thirteen, the reaction would probably have been even stronger. "It was really very shocking," said British journalist Piers Morgan, who sat just a few yards from Jackson. "Monaco was talking about it for days."

To add to the surreal scene, Michael, who sat next to Prince Albert at the royal table, consumed only Evian poured by his bodyguard—and even then wiped the glass before drinking. He also kept touching his nose throughout the evening, fueling speculation that he was indeed suffering from one too many rhinoplasties.

Prince Albert managed a feeble smile but later confided to his father, Prince Rainier, that it was one of the most perplexing spectacles he had ever witnessed. One of the male singing stars present called the scene "disgusting." When Anne Randall grew bored, Michael sent her off in a limousine with carte blanche to buy whatever she wanted in Monaco and charge it to him. Observed journalist Morgan, who followed Michael and his friends around Monaco for five days: "He could hardly take his hands off Joey. . . . I found the whole thing extremely uncomfortable."

It was in Monaco, Joey later said, that "the whole thing really got out of hand." Michael and Joey caught colds, and much to Princess Caroline's consternation, Michael used this as an excuse not to show up at a private dinner she was giving in his honor. He might have made the effort had Princess Caroline not made the mistake of inviting Pavarotti and a few others to join them. "Michael was supposed to have dinner with the royal family *alone*," sniffed Jackson spokesman Lee Solters.

Monaco's royal family and their celebrated guests waited for Michael to appear, growing more impatient—and angrier—by the minute. He never showed up. Michael had agreed to pay his own way to the World Music Awards out of his admiration for the late Princess Grace. But he apparently had no qualms about standing up her children on this particular night. He had other plans.

Michael and Joey had stayed behind in the $2,000-a-night Winston Churchill suite at the Hotel de Paris all day while Anne and Molly went sight-seeing. It was there that Michael, according to a Child Services report, told Joey that his "cousin" and several of his other "special friends" often masturbated in front of him and that masturbation was a "wonderful thing."

Joey said Jackson had been urging him not to close the door when he took a shower, and now he persuaded Joey to take a bath with him. It was the first time they had seen each other naked. According to Joey, Michael then masturbated in front of him. "When you're ready," he told the boy, "I'll do it for you."

Later, while lying alongside each other in bed, Michael put his hand over Joey's penis. "This is going to be great," he said as he slid his hand under the boy's underpants and, again in the explicit words of a Department of Child Services report, "masturbated minor until minor had orgasm."

"Wasn't that good?!" Michael said as he cleaned up the semen with a tissue. Later he no longer bothered with the tissue; he began eating the boy's semen. Then, the boy continued in graphic detail, Michael began "masturbating me with his mouth."

They returned from Monaco with stopovers at Euro Disney outside Paris and at Orlando, Florida, where after a day of fun at the Magic Kingdom, Michael had his special friend "suck on one of his nipples and twist the other while he masturbated." There was no sodomy, according to the boy.

"If you tell anyone," Michael warned Joey, "you will go to juvenile hall, and we'll both get in trouble. I've done this with other boys, but I didn't go as far with them."

According to court reports, Michael's seduction of Joey continued. Seizing on Joey's normal adolescent resistance to parental authority, Michael took every opportunity to undermine his parents' and stepfather's authority. He would tell Joey that he had the right to make his own decisions, that the adults were just trying to control him, that Michael had chosen him because he was special—not them. No one, Michael kept saying, could understand Joey as he could.

"He tried to make me hate my mom and dad," Joey himself would later say, "so that I could only go to him." Michael kept up the attack on "conditioning," and when he told the boy, "I love you," waited until Joey replied "I love you, too."

Michael had also devised "Six Wishes a Day"—a sort of mantra that he required Joey to recite with him at least once every day:

* No wenches, bitches, *heifers*, or ho's (whores).
* Never give up your bliss.
* Live at Neverland with me forever.
* No conditioning.
* Never grow up.
* Be better than best friends forever.

Another frequently repeated slogan of Michael's: "Kids have the right of way."

The wooing continued. Wherever they went, Michael splurged heavily on the Randall family. In addition to the trips and the jewelry for

Anne, there were $20,000 worth of computer equipment, a $1,500 carousel horse, a $700 telescope, a remote-control toy car, high-tech clocks, leather jackets, and toys and games of every conceivable kind. By the time he was finished, Michael had spent over $150,000 on Joey, his half sister, and their mother.

After a time the shopping sprees seemed to become almost counterproductive as Michael and Joey began to squabble over toys. When New York's famous FAO Schwarz toy store opened its doors to Michael and Joey after closing time, the two dashed about in a frenzy. A similar scene with another boy was captured on the store's security camera two days before Christmas 1989. That night, an unidentified boy in a baseball cap was being shown a $1 million solid gold Monopoly set by a clerk when Michael put his arm around the boy to leave. Rather than go along, he shoved Michael away roughly and continued looking at the Monopoly set. After viewing the tape, psychologist Joyce Brothers observed that in that outburst of temper, they were displaying a significant degree of intimacy. "Here's a little boy with real power in the relationship," she said. "He is not in awe of the superstar. There is more on the scale than meets the eye." That night alone, Michael spent $62,000 on his little friend.

It was difficult to imagine that Anne would ever tire of Michael's largesse. Relations with her current husband, David Schwartz, had cooled to the point where they now led separate lives. And Joey's biological father had never paid her child support. He was behind $68,000.

Michael's strategy to make himself the center of Joey's world had worked. The boy cut off all contact with his father and six-year-old half brother completely and stopped playing with kids his own age.

In the meantime, Adam Randall's Beverly Hills dental practice was thriving. Yet he longed to be a full-time screenwriter. Thanks to his son, Randall already had one feature film credit. Joey had come up with an idea for a spoof on Kevin Costner's much ballyhooed hit *Robin Hood,* and Randall sold his script for *Robin Hood: Men in Tights* to veteran comedy director Mel Brooks. The film bombed, but Randall was more encouraged than ever to follow his dream—and to encourage Joey in his dream of becoming a director.

Adam Randall, who had since remarried and had another son, often boasted of Joey's friendship with Michael Jackson. Understandably, he was delighted at the prospect of Michael coming to spend five days at his three-bedroom house during one of Joey's court-ordered visitations.

The visit coincided with yet another milestone in Michael's career. On June 13 he officially launched his new MJJ/Epic label with the sound track for *Free Willy.* The movie was a sleeper hit, and its "Will You Be There?" theme an overnight best-seller.

Randall was swept up in the excitement that surrounded practically everything Michael did. Yet as someone trained in medicine, he recognized that there was something strange about Michael's behavior. He began to wonder whether the yellow overnight bag Michael carried everywhere might not contain drugs.

A revealing incident occurred one evening at Randall's when Michael complained of a headache. Randall gave him a shot of an Advil-like liquid called Toradol. It had no effect, so a second dose was administered. And as Randall would later report in his diary, he was amazed at how Michael "got so high."

Randall became more and more uneasy when Michael spoke of his undying affection for his son. Randall told Michael he knew—as did everyone else in the entertainment industry—that several of his key advisers were gay. Was Michael gay? he asked. "No," Michael said, and giggled.

When he discovered Michael and Joey in bed together, Randall grew suspicious. Both his son and their famous houseguest were dressed. Joey was curled up in a fetal position. According to Randall, Michael was behind him, his arm stretched across Joey's torso, his hand on the boy's crotch.

The following night Randall secretly taped them from the adjoining bedroom. What he heard he said was so upsetting that he made the difficult decision to confront his son and ask him if he was being sexually abused by Michael Jackson.

Michael, meanwhile, had invited Joey to accompany him on the continuation of his *Dangerous* world tour in the fall. Anne made plans to pull Joey out of L.A.'s exclusive St. Matthew's School and hire a tutor so that they could all go along.

When he got wind of this, Adam Randall became desperate. Michael, he was now convinced, had essentially robbed him of his son. While working on a patient, Beverly Hills attorney Barry Rothman, Randall began to cry. He told Rothman that his once congenial relationship with his ex-wife had turned bitter over Joey's disturbing involvement with Michael Jackson. The only way to reclaim his son, Randall decided, was to fight her for custody. Rothman agreed to take the case.

Randall spoke to his ex-wife, and as he became more and more insistent that they meet to discuss their son's future, Anne phoned Michael for help. Michael ordered his high-priced entertainment lawyer, Bert Fields, to intervene. Fields, in turn, brought in flamboyant, highly controversial private investigator Anthony Pellicano. For all intents and purposes the "ultimate problem solver," as Pellicano liked to call himself, would now be running things for the Jackson camp.

Christened Tony Pellican (he added the "o" in his twenties to stress his Sicilian heritage), Pellicano grew up in Cicero, Illinois, was expelled from high school, and got a job as a bill collector for the Spiegel catalog company. Starting his own private detective agency in 1969, Pellicano was appointed to the Illinois Law Enforcement Commission but was forced to resign in 1976 when it was discovered that he had borrowed $30,000 from the son of an underworld figure.

Ironically, Pellicano's first celebrity case involved Elizabeth Taylor—or, more accurately, the missing corpse of Taylor's third husband, Mike Todd. The remains of the famed producer, who was married to Taylor when he was killed in a 1958 plane crash, disappeared from a Forest Park, Illinois, cemetery in 1977. Pellicano called police, saying the grave robbers were after a ten-carat diamond ring Taylor had given Todd—a ring the thieves believed was in the coffin with him. What's more, Pellicano knew where the remains could be found and brought along a local TV news team to be on hand for the unveiling.

Sure enough, Todd's bones were concealed under a pile of leaves two hundred feet from the cemetery. Police determined that two mob figures had pulled the crime off and Pellicano became Elizabeth Taylor's hero. He also got plenty of press in the bargain.

In 1983 he moved his practice to Los Angeles, where he was taken under the wing of Fred Otash, the legendary Hollywood private investigator who allegedly bugged President John F. Kennedy having sex with Marilyn Monroe. Almost immediately Pellicano was hired by criminal attorney Howard Weitzman to help former auto tycoon John De Lorean beat cocaine-selling charges. He did, and with the help of a grateful Weitzman and Bert Fields, Pellicano quickly built a list of celebrity clients that included Kevin Costner, Roseanne Arnold, and even the *National Enquirer*.

By the 1990s Pellicano was wearing $1,000 suits, collecting million-dollar fees, and driving a black Lexus with a baseball bat in the trunk. The music that played on his office telephone answering machine was the theme from *The Godfather, Part III,* and his walls were covered with corny photos of Pellicano in a variety of Sam Spade poses.

Variously described as a "bully," a "shark," and a "junkyard dog" by his detractors, Pellicano was viewed as nothing less than a savior by those he helped extricate from one messy situation after another. "You always," said client Don Simpson, producer of the film *Top Gun*, "want to be on the right side of Anthony Pellicano." A favorite Pellicano phrase: "This is war!"

The prize thoroughbred in Pellicano's stable was, of course, Michael Jackson. Given Michael's long-standing admiration for Italians and what he wrongly perceived to be their mob connections, the tough-talking PI fit into Jackson's organization perfectly.

Seizing upon what he rightly saw as an opportunity to make himself into a household name, Pellicano went on the offensive in the matter of Joey Randall. He would set out, as he usually did, to dig up as much dirt on the opposition as possible, then paint them as wanton extortionists. "If they dish it out," he liked to say, "they better be able to take it."

Joey's father and stepfather had long been on friendly terms, so David Schwartz called Adam Randall to discuss Jackson's relationship with Joey. Schwartz secretly taped the conversation. "Michael is using his age, experience, money, and power to great advantage over Joey," Randall said. "The problem is he is also greatly harming him for his own selfish reasons. He is not the altruistic kind of human being he appears to be."

"Jackson is an evil guy," Randall continued. "He is worse than that. I have the evidence to prove it. . . . If I go through with this and blow the whole thing wide open, I win big time. I will get everything I want. She [Anne] is going to lose Joey, and Michael's career will be over."

"And does that help Joey?" Schwartz asked.

"That's irrelevant to me," Randall replied. "The bottom line is, yes, his mother is harming him, and Michael is harming him. I can prove that, and I will prove that . . . and I will be granted custody and she will have no rights whatsoever.

"It cost me tens of thousands of dollars to get the information I got, and you know I don't have that kind of money," Randall said. "I'm willing to go down financially. . . . It will be a massacre if I don't get what I want."

"Do you think that's going to help Joey?" Schwartz asked again.

"I believe," Randall said, "Joey's already irreparably harmed."

Randall went on to promise that "this man is going to be humiliated beyond belief. He will not believe what will happen to him . . . beyond his worst nightmare. He will not sell one more record. The facts are so overwhelming, everyone will be destroyed in the process."

Two days later, on July 9, Schwartz played the tape for his wife, Pellicano, and Bert Fields at Pellicano's Sunset Strip office. Then Pellicano went straight to Michael's Century City condo, where Joey was staying with Michael, and grilled the boy alone for forty-five minutes.

"He said it never happened," Pellicano would later report. "I asked him point-blank, did Michael ever molest him? He said, 'No, never.' I asked him if he had ever seen Michael naked. He said: 'No, he was too shy. He always wore pajamas and socks and a hat in bed."

Pellicano then asked Michael to come down from his room and, with Michael and Joey side by side on the couch, went over the same questions. Did they masturbate together? Did they talk about masturbation? Both claimed total innocence.

When Michael was told that Randall might have secretly bugged their room when they visited his house, Michael shrugged. He told his lawyers that he had nothing to fear, that he had done nothing wrong.

While Pellicano was interrogating his son, Adam Randall did not stand idly by. He consulted Beverly Hills psychiatrist Dr. Mathis Abrams and, without identifying the principals involved, asked him for a hypothetical opinion. Pointing to the adolescent boy's relationship with "an idolized male who is more than twenty years his senior" and to the fact that the boy's mother had accepted gifts from this mystery celebrity, Abrams delivered a written opinion: "The child has on many occasions spent the night in the same bed with the adult male, though separate beds are available. The child and the adult male have been observed in the same bed under the covers, by the child's mother and father on separate occasions. Based on the above the child appears to be at risk."

Armed with the psychiatrist's opinion, Randall insisted on a meeting with Jackson. On July 11, 1993, Fields agreed to allow Joey to stay with his father for a week. The next day Anne was forced to sign a court order agreeing not to take Joey outside L.A. County without his father's written consent. She was also instructed to "not allow the minor child to have any contact or communication in any form, directly or indirectly, including, but not limited to, telephone communication, with a third party adult male known as Michael Jackson."

Randall used the time with his son to confirm his suspicions once and for all. On July 16, 1993, after extracting one of Joey's teeth, he started asking the boy questions as soon as the anesthetic wore off. Had

Jackson ever touched his penis? "The longest couple of seconds of my life went by," Randall later wrote in his diary.

"Yes," Joey replied softly.

Randall stepped up the pressure, threatening to go public unless he could meet with Michael directly.

Michael's team moved swiftly. Bert Fields set in motion legal efforts for Anne to get her son back. Pellicano, according to Randall's lawyer, Barry Rothman, approached Rothman with a settlement offer. Michael would pay Randall enough money so that he could shut down his dental practice and devote himself full time to writing screenplays with Joey. Pellicano claimed that this idea was first introduced by the Randall camp.

Randall, Joey, Pellicano, and Michael met in the penthouse of the Westwood Marquis Hotel on August 4. At this session Randall began reading the psychiatrist's letter and portions of the criminal statutes as they pertained to reporting child abuse.

Pellicano stopped him midsentence. Randall then got right to the point and asked Michael if he had molested Joey. "Michael looked his weak little victim straight in the eyes, smiled, and denied it," Randall wrote in his diary. "It was a chilling smile, like the smile you see on a convicted serial killer who perpetually declares his innocence despite the mountains of evidence against him. I knew it right then: Michael Jackson had not only molested my son, but he was a criminal."

That evening Pellicano and Rothman met, and Pellicano learned what would satisfy Joey's father: $20 million. Joey's camp says the money was for a trust fund to be placed in Joey's name. Pellicano says that the father wanted four movie deals at $5 million apiece. In any event noting that Randall and Joey might strengthen their father-son bond by working together on a project, Pellicano countered with $350,000 for one screenplay. That offer was summarily rejected.

"Pellicano was convinced they'd go for some kind of offer," Bert Fields told *Vanity Fair*'s Maureen Orth, "and then we'd have them." In a taped conversation with Rothman on August 17, Pellicano tried to get the lawyer to make some reference to the $20 million. If he could, any such reference could be made to look like a blatant attempt at blackmail.

Rothman wasn't biting. Besides, Anne's attorneys had that very day managed to persuade the court to return Joey to his mother, citing that she had somehow been misled into signing a document that would bar contact between Michael Jackson and her son. Without a deal to silence Randall, and without any overt evidence of extortion, Michael's fate was precarious. Events were rapidly spinning out of control.

Yet, typically, Michael found complete escape from reality in the company of another young boy. With Brett Barnes and lawyer John Branca, who was slowly working his way back into his good graces, Michael went house hunting in Beverly Hills.

The trio was most impressed with an $11.5 million, 37,000-square-foot château complete with bowling alley, elevator, marble ballroom, and a dining room with a glass floor that looked down on the indoor pool. Michael and Brett were so giddy as they ran from room to room that Michael apologized to the real estate agent. "We've got a case of the giggles today," he said, then offered $10 million for the house on the spot (the offer was later withdrawn). Whether his actions were the result of arrogance or denial, Michael seemed oblivious of the dangerous nightmare ahead.

Even as Pellicano was trying to get Rothman to say something incriminating, Adam Randall had taken his son to see Dr. Mathis Abrams—this time to tell the whole shocking story. Three hours later Dr. Abrams did what California law compelled him to do: he reported the allegation of child abuse to the proper authorities.

Ann T. Rosato of the Los Angeles County Department of Children's Services interviewed Joey, as did a police sergeant. All three—Rosato, the sergeant, and Dr. Abrams—agreed that Joey was telling the truth.

No longer oblivious of what was happening, Michael prayed it would never come to this, but for weeks he had expected the worst. At a power dinner thrown by his manager, Sandy Gallin, such industry heavyweights as Michael Ovitz, David Geffen, and Ron Meyer gathered to talk about ways to rejuvenate Michael's long stalled movie career. For much of the dinner Michael sat at one end of the table with his head in his hands, sobbing.

19

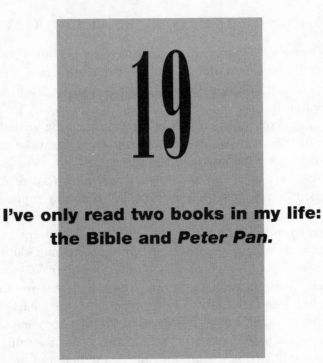

I've only read two books in my life: the Bible and *Peter Pan*.

PETER PAN OR PERVERT? shrieked the front page of the August 25, 1993, *New York Post. Newsweek* asked IS HE DANGEROUS, OR JUST OFF THE WALL? In the two or three days immediately following the lightning-swift police raids on Neverland, Michael's condominium in Century City, and his suite at the Mirage in Las Vegas, the world press reveled in the breaking scandal. Television news programs led off with the story and illustrated it with one of Michael's many available crotch-grabbing clips.

The investigation—at this stage, at least—moved quickly. In seducing him, Joey said that Michael had repeatedly talked of other "special friends" who let him "do things." Joey gave the names of four boys to the police, and all four were questioned immediately—including Macaulay Culkin.

Alleged eyewitness accounts from Philippe LeMarque and Mark Quindoy aside, Culkin denied that anything inappropriate had ever transpired between himself and Michael. Macaulay's manager-father, Kit Culkin, reiterated, "Michael and my son are friends—just friends. Any suggestion that Michael was anything but a friend is completely untrue."

Yet the senior Culkin could hardly have been unaware of the devastating impact any such innuendos could have on his son's status as one of Hollywood's few bankable, name-over-the-title stars. Privately the Culkins made the decision to keep their son away from Jackson for the foreseeable future. With the controversy still raging in November, Macaulay stayed out of the reach of the media, doing virtually no promotion for his film version of *The Nutcracker* in the wake of a dispute with the studio over the movie.

The police were to face similar obstacles. After that first question-answer session on August 19, investigators would try repeatedly to reinterview young Culkin, even on the set. Kit Culkin angrily told them to stay away from his son or he would sue for harassment.

Pellicano and company offered up some of Michael's other special friends to speak in his defense—a ploy that backfired spectacularly. Brett Barnes, Wade Robson, and even twenty-two-year-old Corey Feldman, who had been a buddy of Michael's eight years earlier, stepped up to say they all slept with Michael on numerous occasions.

"He kisses? Yeah, like you kiss your mother," Barnes said. "We slept in the same bed? Yes! I was on one side of the bed and he was on the other. It was a big bed. It's not unusual for him to hug, kiss, and nuzzle up to you? Yeah, just the fun stuff.

"It's like I've known him all my life, and in a past life," Barnes added. "He loves you like he is your own father or brother or sister or mother. He hugs and kisses, but nothing more."

"Michael is a very, very kind person, really nice and sweet," Wade Robson said. The ten-year-old actor now wore a close-cropped, dyed blond punk hairstyle and sported an earring. "Sure, I slept with him on dozens of occasions. But the bed we shared was huge. He sleeps on one side, I sleep on the other. We just go to sleep. . . ."

Wade Robson's sister, Chantal, fourteen, claimed that she also slept with Jackson. "I've slept in the same bed with Michael, too," she said. "But he never laid a finger on me. The bed is very big, and you don't get anywhere near each other. It's just like two buddies sleeping together."

Corey Feldman claimed his childhood relationship with Michael was also strictly platonic. "One time I went to shake his hand and he hugged me," he said. "There was no sexual connotation. We talked every day. And we slept in the same room and hung out.

"I was molested as a child, and I know the difference," he added. "Maybe if we were watching TV, we fell asleep in the same bed. Michael never said we couldn't sleep together. . . ."

Even Pellicano, once touted as "the Big Sleazy" in a *GQ* profile, conceded that Michael slept with boys, explaining that they were always fully clothed at the time. "Michael goes to bed with his hat on, I'm serious," he said. In a statement that summed up the Jackson camp's view of the case, he stated: "If it's a thirty-five-year-old pedophile, then it's obvious why he's sleeping with little boys. But if it's Michael Jackson, it doesn't mean anything."

One week after the story broke it seemed as if Michael's spokesmen were gaining ground. On Michael's home turf, the *Los Angeles Times*, acknowledging that it had been pressured by the Reverend Jesse Jackson to use "restraint" in its coverage, gave Pellicano's extortion charges (which were later officially discredited) the same play as it did the child abuse charges themselves. Michael was the subject of "twenty-five to thirty" such blackmail schemes a year, Pellicano was quoted as saying. No one asked him to prove this claim, and he never did.

After a few bland stories in September, the *L.A. Times* would not run a single piece on the unfolding scandal throughout the entire month of October. A number of other important publications also decided to tell the story from Michael's, not Joey's, perspective. In its first story on the Jackson affair—which ran in the paper's "Style" section—*The Washington Post* stressed the "extortion" angle over the police investigation. *Newsday*'s first headline—JACKSON: NO!— also gave the story a decided pro-Michael spin.

During the entire first week of the scandal, *The New York Times* carried only a single article and buried it inside. "If nothing else," began the peculiarly lighthearted piece, "this summer is keeping Hollywood's gossip mills churning. First it was the uproar over Heidi Fleiss, the alleged madam to the rich and famous. Now it's Michael Jackson, the childlike pop singer who has tongues wagging."

Even the *New York Post* hedged its sensational PETER PAN OR PERVERT headline with an accompanying piece by Lisa Robinson titled "Don't Believe the Dirt! This Is a Guy Who Doesn't Even Swear." Normally ferocious television shows like *A Current Affair* and *Inside Edition* began to portray Michael as the tortured innocent. Even those children speaking in Michael's defense unflinchingly admitted that he slept with them. The next logical step would have been to interview psychologists on how "inappropriate" it was for thirty-four-year-old men to sleep with children.

Why wasn't even this done? No sooner had muckraking television programs and the print media jumped on the story than tens of thousands of outraged fans leapt to Michael's defense. Networks and editorial offices were flooded with indignant letters and threats to cancel subscriptions. In poll after poll, the vast majority of respondents made it abundantly clear that they gave no credence to the charges leveled against Michael. In a poll taken by *Entertainment Weekly* days after the case broke, only 12 percent believed the allegations against Michael, and 55 percent believed that he was the victim of extortion. Some fans were so overwrought that they placed flowers, lit votive candles, and held prayer vigils at Michael Jackson's gold star on the Hollywood Walk of Fame.

Almost certainly it was Michael's sense of vulnerability—of what *Newsweek*'s Jonathan Alter called "ineffable" sadness—that made it believable to most people that he had been framed. "From James Dean and Marilyn Monroe to Elvis Presley, all the really big ones had it," Alter wrote. "It even makes credible the idea," he added wryly, "that there's nothing wrong with having slumber parties with twelve-year-olds."

The possible economic consequences of pursuing the Jackson story too vigorously were very clear to management. Newspapers did not want to see their ratings decline after their viewer surveys showed overwhelming support for Michael. They made the conscious decision to suppress their natural journalistic instincts and back off—at least for the time being.

Michael was winning the public relations war handily. Pledging Michael its "full support," Sony Music cited his "exemplary fund-raising for children's charitable organizations around the world. . . . We applaud his work on behalf of children everywhere." Pepsi was more cautious. While stating flatly that its contract with Jackson remained in place, Pepsi spokesman Ken Ross added, "These are serious allegations. . . . in the absence of any facts, our place is most appropriately on the sidelines."

Behind closed doors at both companies, there must have been panic in the boardroom. "When a celebrity under contract has negative publicity," said David Burns of Burns Sports Celebrity Service, "a corporation immediately makes plans to pull out. They announce that 'Absolutely, we're behind Blah Blah 100 percent.' But believe me, backstage, they're scurrying around, running for their lives."

Sony executives took the public stance of sitting out the crisis, but privately they were already making contingency plans. Under the generous terms of their deal, Michael had been paid $40 million from sales of the *Dangerous* album alone. Now Sony executives were debating whether their money wouldn't be better spent pushing the careers of less controversial artists like Mariah Carey and Michael Bolton.

Pepsi brass was even more concerned. As soon as they were made public, the company launched its own investigation of the charges against Jackson. It must have been studying ways to get out of its contract with Michael. "Sexual abuse is a parent's worst nightmare," said Gerri Shaftel, vice president of the Celebrity Endorsement Network, a California firm that matched stars with advertisers. "Even if nothing is ever proven, people will doubt what they believed about Jackson. Advertisers are not willing to take that risk."

For the moment only one deal would have to be aborted. Michael abruptly pulled out of an agreement to write and perform the title song for the movie *Addams Family Values.* (When the movie was released in time for Christmas, one of its more memorable scenes had an Addams Family child look up at a Michael Jackson poster and cringe in terror.)

In the headline for its front-page story, *USA Today* proclaimed KING OF POP UNSHAKEN BY INVESTIGATION. Despite the outpouring of public support, nothing could have been farther from the truth. Michael, who had just started the Asian leg of his *Dangerous* tour in Bangkok when police raided his homes, had already canceled two shows after collapsing. No sooner did his doctors announce that their patient was suffering from acute dehydration than local Coca-Cola bottlers saw an opportunity to tweak Pepsi. They began running ads in Thai newspapers that simply read: "Dehydrated? There's always Coke."

Michael, now teetering on the brink of a complete nervous breakdown, waited anxiously for Elizabeth Taylor to join him in Singapore. Only weeks after Taylor had nearly succumbed to pneumonia, she and husband Larry Fortensky donned sweat suits—Larry's was white, hers pink—and boarded a jet for Singapore.

During the nineteen-hour flight Taylor chatted with reporters. "This is the worst thing that could happen to a man like Michael, who loves children," she told one. She told another journalist on the flight that she believed in "Michael's integrity, his love and trust in children. I know it will come out all right. Michael is a very proud man, and he has good faith. He's a very spiritual and a very religious man."

To yet another journalist: "Michael is one of my best friends in the whole world, and I can't think of anything worse that a human being could go through than what he's going through now. You can imagine how he feels. How would you feel if you had these allegations against you? He's a very sensitive, very vulnerable, very shy person. I believe totally that Michael will be vindicated." Asked about the motive for the allegations, Taylor said, "Well, I think all of that is becoming quite clear—extortion." Before she had set foot in Singapore, Taylor was leading a one-woman cavalry charge in Michael's defense.

It was a familiar role for Taylor, who had stood by such old friends as Montgomery Clift and Rock Hudson in times of crisis. Clift and Hudson were peers and co-workers, however. It was almost impossible to imagine what Michael and Elizabeth had in common save for a childhood lost to stardom and mutual love of publicity. In Michael's case Taylor was probably motivated as much by her desire to defy the tabloid press as she was by maternal concern.

At one-thirty on the morning of August 29, Taylor and Fortensky checked into a penthouse suite directly across from Michael's at Singapore's famous Raffles Hotel. Taylor walked straight to Michael's room, and when he opened the door, they embraced. "Michael, it's going to be fine," she told him. Michael was sobbing. "I'm here and I love you," Taylor said.

The next day she threw a thirty-fifth birthday party for Michael in his hotel room. For the first time, Michael, who had lost nine pounds since the scandal broke, ate something other than milk and bread—two slices of his favorite dessert, carrot cake with butter frosting. That evening, midway through a show at Singapore's National Stadium, forty thousand fans serenaded a beaming Michael with "Happy Birthday."

The following day Michael, who complained of missing his pet chimps, repaid the favor by hosting a tea party on Raffles' poolside marble terrace for Taylor. The only other guests at the party: six orangutans Michael had brought in from the Singapore Zoo.

Michael seemed almost back to normal when, only minutes before his next show in Singapore, he began crying uncontrollably. He vomited, then collapsed completely. This would be the third canceled concert since the scandal erupted. The next day Michael's physician ordered an MRI brain scan. After the test revealed no physiological abnormalities, Dr. David Forecast determined that Michael was suffering from acute migraine headaches. When he returned to the hotel, a shaken Michael was literally leaning on Taylor for support.

Back in Los Angeles, a press conference was held to announce plans for a special "Jackson Family Honors" concert at the Atlantic City Convention Center in December. Some twenty members of the Jackson clan were present, and they used the forum to declare their support for Michael.

"I would like to let the world know," Katherine said, "that I am behind my son. I love him. I have talked to him several times. . . ."

"We want to state our collective and unequivocal belief," Jermaine added, "that Michael has been made a victim of a cruel and obvious attempt to take advantage of his fame and success. We know, as does the whole world, he has dedicated his life to providing happiness for young people everywhere. . . . Our entire family stands firmly at his side."

The next stop on Michael's itinerary was Taiwan, and it was there that Katherine, Joe, and four Jackson siblings finally joined him. As soon as they arrived, Katherine hosted a family-only lunch to which Taylor and her husband were not invited. The next day they returned to California.

"I'm very surprised my mother didn't go to Michael sooner," La Toya said. "I felt she should have been there before Elizabeth Taylor because, after all, she is his mother." La Toya went on to say on NBC's *Today* show that she supported her brother "One hundred percent," but then conceded that when she lived with him in Encino he often spent the night in his room with "lots of little boys. I honestly don't think he'd do anything like that . . . but we don't know."

While all this was going on, Michael went on a $4,500 shopping spree at a Tapei Toys 'R' Us, causing a small riot in the process.

That evening, during the MTV Awards in Los Angeles, actress Sharon Stone clearly spoke for most of the celebrities in attendance when she lashed out at Joey's father. "I firmly believe," she said, "that if this family has—or ever had . . . evidence of abuse, it would have surfaced by now. All I know is that if a child of mine had been abused, I would not have been making deals."

Only k. d. lang offered a reasoned assessment. "I think this whole thing is very scary," she said, "and I pray that Michael is innocent. I think he is, but it goes without saying that if he's not, then my support is with the boy."

Randall's side appeared to score its first major victory when high-profile women's rights attorney Gloria Allred agreed to take Joey's case. At a packed conference, Allred declared that her thirteen-year-old client was "ready, willing, and able" to testify in court against Jackson. "Up until today there has been a largely one-sided view portrayed," she told reporters. "There has been a feeding frenzy, with the media getting their food only from one side of the table. No one has spoken out on behalf of the child until now."

Forcefully Allred described how Jackson had "devastated" her young client, how he had turned Joey's life "upside down. Many people love and trust Michael Jackson. Our client loved him and trusted him as well. Unfortunately, that trust has been destroyed. Now the question is, 'Should Mr. Jackson be held to the same standards of conduct as any other person, or does he think, and do his assorted wise men, that Mr. Jackson should be above the law?' "

Allred went on to slam the public figures who had rushed to Michael's defense: "These celebrities do not know many of the key facts, have never spoken to the child in question, and were not present to witness what occurred." The pivotal question, according to Allred: "Why is Michael Jackson, an adult, repeatedly sleeping in the same bed with a young boy?"

Most significant, she raised for the first time the broader social implications of the case. "It is important to note that children everywhere are watching," she said. "They may be fearful about what will happen to them if they come forward to make a charge against a celebrity or other powerful person. . . . Will their voices be heard?"

A few days later Allred was off the case. Joey's parents, who had now combined forces, wanted reparations from Michael. They were not interested in making their son the object of a holy children's rights crusade.

"What it boiled down to," said a member of the Randall team, "was that Allred was not as interested in going after money as she was seeing Jackson prosecuted criminally." Another insider claimed Allred "wanted to run the show. She burst in there and said, 'Okay boys, I'm taking this over.' She didn't want to press the civil suit. She said it looked too money grubbing."

Allred was replaced by the less flamboyant but competent Larry Feldman. "The point is not money," Feldman said. "It's to make Jackson talk."

On September 15, 1993, former Neverland employees Mark and Faye Quindoy held a news conference in Manila. Reading some of the more shocking excerpts from their diaries, they announced that they had seen Michael molest several boys and would testify to that in open court. A few days later the Quindoys were interviewed in Singapore by two detectives from L.A.'s Sexually Exploited Child Unit. The information they gleaned would be shared with Santa Barbara law enforcement officials, who were conducting their own criminal investigation.

Pellicano instantly called the Quindoys' credibility into question. They had a $283,000 back pay dispute with Michael, and they had tried to sell their story. Yet by cooperating fully with the police and offering to testify in open court, the Quindoys had effectively ended their chances of ever securing a settlement with Jackson. Nonetheless, Pellicano promptly labeled the couple "cockroaches and failed extortionists." They, in turn, threatened to sue him for slander.

Pellicano's bluster was strictly for public consumption. Behind the scenes, he was also scrambling to discredit Joey Randall. In a taped phone conversation, he reportedly hammered away at the boy, badgering him mercilessly about places and dates as if he were a hostile witness. In a timid voice, Joey tried to answer the questions. "It's a painful recording to have to sit through," said a woman who worked in Pellicano's office at the time.

Pellicano then supposedly took the taped conversation to four of the country's top child sex abuse experts for analysis, confident they would be willing to offer expert testimony that the boy was lying. It was reported that all four experts believed Joey's testimony, and that ultimately some within the Jackson camp decided that the only way to handle this was to try to take the four experts off the market. Each was allegedly put on a $5,000 retainer and guaranteed hourly fees as an expert witness, ensuring that they would not be compelled to testify on the boy's behalf. Pellicano would later deny both that he had taped a conversation with Joey and that he had played it to therapists.

Pellicano and Jackson's legal team of Bert Fields and criminal attorney Howard Weitzman, meanwhile, continued their media campaign to paint Randall as an extortionist. Intending to show that Joey's father was out to soak Michael for money, they released to the media the tape of his phone conversation with Joey's stepfather, David Schwartz. Again, the tactic backfired. Full of gaps and clumsily edited, the taped conversation showed an angry father out for revenge, but there was no hint of extortion.

Jackson's side also produced the tape of Pellicano trying to get Randal's attorney, Barry Rothman, to mention a $20 million deal for four screenplays. But on the tape it is Pellicano who offers Rothman $350,000. "I was trying to set him up with the extortion," Pellicano confessed. "I wanted to see if he would take it."

Enter Chicago private investigator Ernie Rizzo, on the side of Adam

Randall. Rizzo, a former Chicago police detective, had also had his license suspended temporarily for illegal wiretapping. But he was uniquely well equipped to counterbalance Pellicano's bullying style. "He supposedly has all kinds of guys out there he can make phone calls to and they'll break heads," said Rizzo of Pellicano's supposed penchant for thinly veiled threats and outright intimidation. "That's just a complete farce. He tries to scare people with that stuff, but he's a joke."

And what about Pellicano's oft-repeated claim that he was a martial arts expert? "The guy," scoffed Rizzo, "never even ate Oriental food." Pellicano shot back by branding Rizzo a "numb-nut," a "fruit fly," and an "ambulance-chaser" (his hyphenated description for Feldman as well).

Over the next six months Rizzo worked tracking down leads for the Randall camp. He also proved an unlikely but relatively effective advocate for Joey in the media arena. While he was by no means the family's official spokesman, Rizzo appeared on television talk shows—almost always outnumbered by Jackson supporters and in the face of hostile audiences—to give the boy's side of the story. On one talk show Rizzo was stunned when one woman got up in the audience and proclaimed that she would be "proud" to have Michael Jackson molest her son.

On September 14, 1993, Feldman filed suit in Santa Monica on behalf of Joey Randall against Michael Jackson. Charging Michael with six counts of sexual battery, the seventeen-page document spelled out how Jackson "seduced" Joey into a "despicable sexual relationship through sordid manipulation of trust and friendship." The suit went on to claim Jackson "feigned despair and grief" when Joey rejected his sexual advances.

After spelling out the specific acts—"orally copulating plaintiff, masturbating plaintiff, having plaintiff fondle and manipulate the breasts and nipples of defendant Michael Jackson while defendant would masturbate," etc.—the suit charged Jackson's actions were for the "sole purpose of satisfying his lust and sexual desires."

All in all, the suit accused Michael of "sexual battery, battery, seduction, willful misconduct, intentional infliction of emotional distress, fraud, and negligence." And as is often the case in such sky's-the-limit actions, it sought an unspecified amount in damages.

The day the suit was filed, Michael was performing for the first time to enthusiastic if rain-soaked crowds in Moscow. He marched with grim-faced Russian soldiers for yet another video shoot—by now he had been filmed leading dozens of army and police units around the world—and was mobbed wherever he went.

Public sentiment in what used to be the Soviet Union was squarely behind him. "I don't think anyone in Russia believes in this," said Nina Rugina, who came from St. Petersburg with her fourteen-year-old daughter for the concert. "You look at his face and know he wouldn't do this. He loves children so much, he would never do this." In Red Square a banner was unfurled: "Siberia Loves You, Michael!"

The reception was decidedly chillier in Israel. Michael, wearing bright red lipstick and once again accompanied by Eddie Cascio, nine, and his thirteen-year-old brother, Frank, tried to visit Jerusalem's Wailing Wall. Instead Michael and his special friends were driven back by dozens of angry worshipers. "Go home, Michael Jackson," shouted one yeshiva student, "you are an abomination." Israel's spiritual leader, chief rabbi Yisrael Lau, just happened to be nearby when the ruckus occurred. "I am delivering a lecture on atonement," Rabbi Lau commented. "Maybe he should attend."

Although the American Friends of the Hebrew University had already announced that they were giving Michael the organization's prestigious Scopus Award, they abruptly withdrew the honor and gave it to George Burns instead. Invitations to the event had already been sent out depicting Michael—much to the embarrassment of the event's organizers—at the Wailing Wall.

Righteous indignation aside, eighty thousand fans packed the first of two sold-out concerts in Tel Aviv. "Nobody can excite people like Michael," said Tel Aviv university student David Eizenstaadt. "Not Rabin, Peres, or Arafat. Michael's so electrifying, we think he may even be the Messiah."

Strangely, Michael seemed determined to flaunt his preference for the company of adolescent boys—even as he battled for his professional life. During a break in the tour, he flew with the Cascios to Elizabeth Taylor's chalet in Gstaad, Switzerland. The first day there, Michael went out and spent thousands of dollars on ski suits, CDs, and video games for the boys. Later, ten fans were allowed inside to meet him, and wound up in the middle of a pillow fight between Michael and his traveling companions.

. . .

Flames licked at Neverland's perimeter as the most devastating fires in Southern California history raged out of control the last week of September 1993. Planes swept down, spewing orange fire retardant over the hillsides, and in a last-ditch effort backfires were set. As firefighters battled round the clock, it appeared that Michael Jackson's storybook paradise would not be spared. The zoo was evacuated, and Neverland's staff was in the process of doing the same.

At the very last minute, the wind shifted. And when the smoke cleared, thousands of scorched acres surrounded Jackson's property, but Neverland itself was miraculously unscathed. "It seemed that the fire authorities," said one neighbor who suffered devastating damage, "made an extra effort for Michael." It remained to be seen, however, if Michael's own battalion of firefighters could extinguish the flames that threatened his career—not to mention a possible jail term for child molesting.

As Michael romped with the Cascio brothers in Switzerland, a document surfaced that was purported to outline the terms of a $600,000 payoff agreement between Michael and the mother of one of his young friends. The money was supposedly to buy the mother's silence. In its story on the so-called cover-up, the *Globe* obtained a letter from the office of Bert Fields and had an expert compare it to the alleged payoff agreement. The expert concluded that they had been typed on the same typewriter.

Subsequent press accounts wrongly speculated that Macaulay Culkin's name was on the agreement. The name on the document, whatever its authenticity, belonged to someone else.

Fields angrily denounced the document as a fake. On October 7 he filed a libel suit against the tabloid, demanding $10 million in damages.

Once reporters in Gstaad realized that Michael was holed up in their backyard with two young boys, they ran a story updating their readers on the case. The next day an outraged mother stood outside Taylor's house, waving a newspaper in the air and shouting, "Go home! We don't want you here!"

Feeling the heat, Michael boarded his private red-winged 747 and flew to Buenos Aires to resume the tour. On the huge marble terrace of his $10,000-a-day mansion—part of the city's Park Hyatt Hotel—he paraded around with the Cascio boys in his pajama top and trousers. After playing to the crowd below, he went back into the room with the boys. A few moments later Michael and Eddie Cascio returned, both wearing surgical masks.

Later Michael greeted photographers gathered outside the hotel by sticking his pajama-clad arm out the window and waving a copy of the parenting magazine *Child* at the incredulous crowd. The magazine showed the photo of a toddler with the headline 46 FUN BABY GAMES.

The Cascio boys' parents seemed unconcerned. "Some people who don't know Michael may say my sons should not be there—that they are at risk," Dominic Cascio conceded. "They can say what they want. I trust Michael, and so does my wife."

Michael's in-your-face gesture in Buenos Aires was in stark contrast with the quiet agony of Joey Randall. The boy, asked not to return to his private school until things died down, now spent most of his time in the company of therapists, detectives, and lawyers. Angry at Michael for what he had done, and at his parents for allowing him to become the center of a global sideshow, Joey drew a picture of himself committing suicide. A stick figure stands on the roof of a five-story building shouting, "No!!" then jumps, splattering on the pavement below. "Don't," reads the caption, "let this happen."

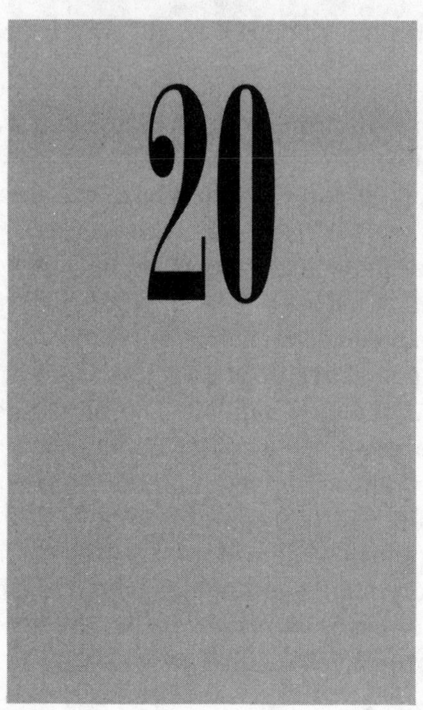

"Anthony," one of Pellicano's assistants blurted in frustration, "he did it. He's *guilty*. You *know* he's guilty."

"I don't care if he's guilty or not," Pellicano reportedly shot back. "You do what I tell you—or you can go work someplace else!" That must have been why Michael paid Pellicano a monthly retainer of $100,000. What Pellicano didn't realize at the time was that one of his short-term employees would later go to the tabloids with this and other stories about the private detective. Pellicano would later characterize these allegations as "lies."

Bert Fields's next step was to file a motion asking that the case be delayed six years—time enough for the statute of limitations to run out on any criminal charges.

"Innocent people," Larry Feldman responded, "do not ask the courts to postpone until the year 2000 the case that will supposedly prove their innocence." He continued to press for a March 1994 trial because his thirteen-year-old client (whom he referred to repeatedly as a "little boy") needed "closure" so that he could "get on with his life."

The motion would ultimately be denied, but it proved to be an effective delaying tactic. It gave Michael and his inner circle time to plan their next move.

Michael worried that he would be arrested if he so much as set foot on American soil. To cope with his mounting anxiety, he took more and more pills—specifically the painkillers Percodan, Demerol, and codeine and the tranquilizers Valium, Xanax, and Ativan. When Samuel Jackson, who once told his grandson that he believed he was the Messiah, died in Phoenix at the age of one hundred, Michael did not return home for the funeral.

He did find time, however, to meet with Mexican president Carlos Salinas as soon as he arrived in Mexico City on October 24. Three days later Bert Fields, Howard Weitzman, Elizabeth Taylor, and Michael's dermatologist Arnold Klein flew to Mexico City for a strategy session.

Why Dr. Klein? There had already been reports that Joey Randall could identify markings on Michael's genitals. And it was rumored that police might force Michael to undergo a strip search to determine whether he was telling the truth.

There was widespread speculation that Klein was summoned to Mexico City to see if he could alter or disguise those identifying marks on Michael's genitals to discredit the boy.

According to one top plastic surgeon, by using an ultraviolet light and prescription drugs, a skilled physician could alter or even erase the markings caused by vitiligo. It would take six to eight weeks. "If an alleged witness drew a picture of what he saw," the surgeon said, "and it was compared to a photograph of the area treated, you could convince a jury that the testimony of the alleged victim was fictitious."

It remained to be seen whether Klein's assistance would be sought in this department. For the moment, the principal purpose of the summit was to persuade Michael to return home and face the charges. They could not promise him he wouldn't be arrested, but Fields and Weitzman told him bluntly that the longer he stayed away, the guiltier he looked.

At one of these sessions, a shouting match ensued when Michael's longtime confidant Bill Bray openly attacked Fields for mishandling the case. Specifically Bray criticized Fields for appointing Pellicano the team's principal spokesman. Bray was not the first inside the Jackson camp to express such concerns. There had been a constant flow of advisers down to Mexico City, and most of them expressed dismay that Fields had given Pellicano so much leeway.

Bray wanted Michael to hire Johnnie L. Cochran, a criminal lawyer widely respected in the black community, to head up his legal team. Earlier, Sandy Gallin and Howard Weitzman had called from Elizabeth

Taylor's home and persuaded Michael to appoint Weitzman as official spokesman for the team. But now that they wanted Michael to hire Cochran, Taylor objected. Michael was in too fragile a state, she told them, to be worrying about such personnel matters now.

It was at this critical juncture that, according to writer Kathleen Tracy, Pellicano phoned Michael from Los Angeles. "Well, you've really done it this time," he said. "You're really in deep. It doesn't look good. But we've been through this before and I'll get you out of it."

On the road, Michael had been insulated from much of the ugliness at home. After talking with Pellicano, he was furious with the others for not leveling with him. There was a real possibility that on the tour's next stop in Puerto Rico—U.S. territory—Michael could be hauled off the plane, handcuffed, and dragged back to Los Angeles to stand trial. The prospect terrified him.

"Fix it," Michael reportedly told his senior advisers after the call from Pellicano. "Fix this mess or I'll fire you all and find somebody who can!"

The last thing Michael needed now was a toothache, but at Mexico City's ABC Hospital, he went under general anesthesia to have an abscessed molar extracted. The local dentist prescribed two more drugs: an antibiotic and the painkiller Dolacet. Michael was also compelled to give a deposition in one of the copyright infringement cases pending against him. He did not want to return to Los Angeles to testify, so attorney Howard Manning flew to Mexico City to videotape his deposition.

Throughout the nine-hour session, Michael slurred his speech and at times seemed about to nod off. Although Manning would later claim Michael was "alert and answered questions . . . he performed well as a witness," he seemed to be under the influence of some substance.

The criminal investigation took another surprising turn on November 8. While the family was attending Samuel Jackson's funeral service in Phoenix, police raided their Encino compound. The sixteen officers scoured every inch of Hayvenhurst, focusing on Michael's bedroom. A locksmith had to be brought in to gain entry.

Once inside, they shook their heads in disbelief at the costumed mannequins, dolls, and toys that still cluttered Michael's room. Like many parents whose children leave the nest, Katherine had kept his room exactly as Michael had left it. His leather outfits were there, and the police searched the pockets carefully.

Katherine rushed back from Phoenix by plane and watched in tears as investigators combed through the house. That evening they carted off fifty boxes loaded with photographs, videotapes, magazines, and notebooks.

Once word of the Hayvenhurst search—and his mother's emotional reaction—reached Michael, he phoned Taylor in Los Angeles and begged her to return to Mexico. "I need you here so badly," he reportedly told her. "I'm drowning." Within hours Taylor and Larry Fortensky were aboard a Learjet bound for Mexico City.

Before Taylor could get there, however, Michael overdosed on Percodan. In combination with the Valium and other drugs he had been taking—not to mention his precarious state of mind—it first triggered a full-blown psychotic episode.

Michael went berserk. Crying uncontrollably, he began banging his head against the wall so hard it left an impression in the plaster. Then he became violently ill, throwing up all over the white carpets. "Why? Why are they doing this to me?" he kept asking as he stumbled into his bedroom. "This is hell. I don't want to be alive. . . ."

Michael took a pen and—just as he had done when he was taping *Remember the Time*—began scrawling all over the walls and furniture. But this time, instead of signing his name and the number *1998,* he wrote gibberish. And after covering virtually every surface of the bedroom in ink, Michael fell on the bed, curled up in the fetal position. Arriving shortly before two A.M., Taylor kept a vigil by his bed until he pulled through the crisis.

Michael was in the throes of a nervous breakdown. And he had taken an overdose. Whether he was, in fact, addicted to the painkillers remained open to question. Doctors who examined Michael shortly after his dental surgery said he showed no sign whatsoever of a chemical dependency, and attorney Howard Manning insisted that off camera Michael seemed "very bright and completely normal."

When Taylor arrived, however, her instant diagnosis was that he was addicted to painkillers. It was the diagnosis one would expect from Elizabeth Taylor, who had been very candid about the fight with her own addiction that led her to the Betty Ford Clinic.

"That's where you belong—Betty Ford," she told Michael. But, of course, that was out of the question; Michael had no intention of returning to the United States at that point. So Taylor called her friend and fellow ex-addict Elton John for advice. John, in turn, referred her to Beauchamp ("Beechy") Colclough, the therapist he credited with helping him overcome his addictions to alcohol, drugs, and food. Taylor called Colclough and told him that Michael was suicidal and in urgent need of help. Colclough instructed her to get him to London immediately.

Whether or not Michael was a bona fide drug addict, the claim that he was allowed him to buy even more time for himself as he sought treatment for his "addiction" outside the United States.

On November 12, 1993—the day he had been scheduled to fly to Puerto Rico—Michael made his final concert appearance in Mexico City, with Taylor and Fortensky sitting in the wings. After taking his final bows, Michael rendezvoused at midnight with Taylor and her husband, Bill Bray, and Taylor's personal bodyguard, Moshe Alon, in an underground reception area. From there they rushed to the airport, where Michael, swathed in a blanket, was spirited onto an MGM Grand 727 chartered by Taylor.

After refueling in Canada and Iceland, the plane was scheduled to land in Shannon, Ireland. On board, however, they received word that the press had been tipped off. In a last minute maneuver, they flew instead to a deserted runway at Luton Airport outside London.

At one A.M., British bodyguard Steve Tarling, whose mission was to hide Michael from the media, boarded the plane to meet Jackson and escort him to a waiting van. Michael was curled up beneath a blanket, his face hidden beneath his large black hat. Elizabeth Taylor and Michael's personal physician, Dr. David Forecast, were trying to shake him awake while Taylor's husband, Larry Fortensky, looked on.

When Jackson's hat fell off, Tarling recoiled at what he saw. "He looked like a transvestite who'd had the same makeup on for a couple of weeks," Tarling said. "What shocked me most was the tip of his nose—it was jet black. His whole face was white except for his nose, which was like an open cut when it congeals over into a scab. It looked awfully painful."

Jackson, heavily sedated, struggled to his feet, but slumped back into his seat. Tarling had to carry him from the plane, just as an identically dressed decoy was smuggled on board. Checking the flight again, British immigration officials saw what they believed to be the real Michael Jackson still dozing under a blanket.

The remarkable cloak-and-dagger operation continued, according to Tarling. Taylor, riding in the van with Michael, was clearly annoyed when Tarling told her there had been a last minute change in plans. Instead of going straight to the Charter Nightingale Clinic, where reporters were already milling about, Tarling drove them to the home of Elton John's manager, John Reid.

Once at Reid's house, they opened the door to the van and Michael tumbled out "like a corpse," Tarling recalled. "Thankfully, we caught him before he hit the ground." Taylor demanded that he be loaded back into the van and taken directly to the clinic. He was.

Five hours after Jackson's party landed at Luton, the private jet took off again, this time, according to Tarling, headed for Switzerland with Taylor, Fortensky, and the Jackson lookalike on board. When it landed, only Fortensky and Taylor, clutching her Maltese, Sugar, got off.

At San Juan Airport, U.S. officials who had been waiting to detain Michael for questioning were told that he might have been spirited out of Mexico to parts unknown. Meanwhile, back in London a white ambulance backed up to the laundry entrance of London's Charter Nightingale Clinic in the predawn hours of November 13. A mysterious figure was met by doctors and hustled inside.

As far as the world at large was concerned, Michael Jackson had vanished. In a taped statement released by his publicist on November 12, Michael announced that he was canceling the *Dangerous* tour to seek treatment for an addiction to painkillers.

"My friends and doctors advised me to seek professional guidance immediately in order to eliminate what has become an addiction," Michael said, claiming that the painkillers were first used "sparingly" after scalp surgery seven months earlier. The surgery was supposedly done to repair damage done when his hair caught fire during the Pepsi taping in 1983.

"I realize that completing this tour is no longer possible, and I must cancel the remaining dates. I know I can overcome the problem and will be stronger for the experience.

"As I left on this tour," he continued, "I had been the target of an extortion attempt and shortly thereafter was accused of horrifying and outrageous conduct. I was humiliated, embarrassed, hurt, and suffering great pain in my heart. The pressure resulting from these false allegations, coupled with the incredible energy necessary for me to perform, caused so much distress that it left me physically and emotionally exhausted.

"I became increasingly more dependent on the painkillers to get me through the days of the tour." He concluded his statement with a grateful nod to Taylor, "a source of strength and counsel as this crisis came about. I shall never forget her unconditional love and encouragement in helping me through this period. . . . I love you all. Good-bye."

Trying to head off the skeptics, Bert Fields and Howard Weitzman held a press conference that was carried live on CNN. Michael would return to the United States in six to eight weeks after completing a drug rehabilitation program, Fields explained. His client, Fields added, was now dependent on "heavy-duty painkillers . . . to kill not only the pain in his body, but the pain in his heart and mind."

Police investigators took note of the time Michael would be undergoing treatment: six to eight weeks. It seemed more than coincidental that six to eight weeks was the length of time the experts said it would take to disguise any incriminating markings on Michael's genitals.

Claiming Michael was "barely able to function on an intellectual level," Fields insisted that "the very last thing in the world he would want would be the humiliation of admitting that he has become an addict, a man who has hated drugs all his life. If we wanted a smokescreen, we would have stayed on tour. That was the perfect one."

Weitzman was characteristically abrupt when asked about reports that Joey Randall had provided police with a detailed description of Michael's genitals. "You've got to be kidding," Weitzman huffed. Any suggestion that Jackson might be fleeing from the law was, Weitzman said, "ludicrous and untrue." "If Michael Jackson wanted an excuse to stay out of the United States," Fields repeated, "all he had to do was stay on his tour."

One nagging question was why Michael continued to travel around the world with two young boys. "His buddies are kids," Fields said with a shrug. "It's always been that way."

The press conference, ill conceived and awkwardly executed, raised more questions than it answered. What, exactly, was the state of Michael's mind? John Branca, who was rapidly regaining the power he'd once enjoyed before being deposed by David Geffen, clipped out a newspaper article on the press conference and sent it to Michael. Branca circled Fields's comment that Michael was "barely able to function on an intellectual level." Michael was not pleased.

For his part, Larry Feldman claimed that the whole painkiller addiction story was just a scam, a transparent ploy to gain Jackson sympathy —and time. "Poor Michael," he cracked. "This terrible boy drove him to drug addiction." As for Jackson seeking treatment outside the United States, Feldman stated, "If he can fly from Indonesia to South America to Russia, he can fly to the U.S. to testify."

For Pepsi, the cancellation of the *Dangerous* tour was something of a godsend. They would not have to fire Michael; he was, in effect, firing himself. "Our deal," said a Pepsi spokesman, "was to sponsor this international concert tour. If the tour is over, that would end our sponsorship."

Once again, reaction from Michael's fans was swift. One bumper sticker read PEPSI—IF YOU'RE DUMPING MICHAEL, WE'RE DUMPING *YOU*. Michael's supporters in the black community were also speaking out. "I can't believe," said Von Alexander, director of entertainment for the National Political Congress of Black Women, "this is being done to such a humanitarian."

Sony, with $1 billion riding on Jackson, felt it had only one way to go. On the same day Pepsi made its announcement, Sony pledged Michael its "unwavering and unconditional" support. Understandably, NBC announced that the *Jackson Family Honors,* scheduled originally for December in Atlantic City, was being postponed indefinitely.

That night CNN's *Crossfire,* which usually dealt with national policy issues, devoted its entire program to the Jackson affair. Although she was officially off the case, Gloria Allred said that the best thing Michael could do "for himself and the children of the world is to confront the issue. He could talk to police, take a lie detector test. When he is circling the globe . . . there is the appearance that he is trying to obfuscate."

Another *Crossfire* panelist, Bob Guccione, Jr., defended Michael as "emotionally retarded—a child in his own way."

If there was any chance Michael might be easily persuaded to return, it vanished when Los Angeles police obtained a warrant for a strip search. "Why are they trying to humiliate me?" he asked his lawyers. "There is no way I am going through that. No way."

Where is Michael? It was the one question on everybody's lips—not to mention in front-page headlines around the world. He was rumored to be hiding in a resort hotel in the French Alps, at Elizabeth Taylor's Gstaad chalet, even in Connecticut at the prestigious Silver Hill sanitarium, where Joan Kennedy, Truman Capote, and Liza Minnelli had all been treated.

Much of this was the handiwork of Anthony Pellicano, who spent thousands on Michael Jackson lookalike decoys who showed up at various locations around the world to confuse, confound, and generally mislead the press. One London tabloid went so far as to offer a £50,000 ($75,000) reward to anyone who could lead them to "Wacko Jacko."

On November 18 Jackson phoned Eddie Reynoza, a featured dancer in the *Thriller* video and a friend for three years. Reynoza, who claimed Michael had made sexual overtures to him back in the mid-1980s, taped the fourteen-minute conversation. According to Reynoza, a morose-sounding Michael said he was "never coming back. My lawyers are going to get me out of it. It's nothing but scandal. They want my money. . . . I can't come back and face that. I can't, I can't, I can't."

Reynoza, speaking from his own experience, had no doubts about Michael's guilt. "He's had little boys for nine years straight, twenty-four hours around the clock," he told *Vanity Fair*. "People in show business couldn't understand how long it took to get the talk going. The public is one hundred years behind on this."

With the world abuzz about his disappearance, Michael took over the entire fourth floor of the London's Charter Nightingale Clinic for the detoxification phase of his treatment. The cost: $50,000 a week. The nineteenth-century building was once the Florence Nightingale Hospital for Gentlewomen and was run by the legendary nurse. Now it more closely resembled a luxury hotel, with a massage parlor, Jacuzzi, two gyms, a game room, and a three-star restaurant. All bedrooms had color televisions and marble baths.

Michael's lawyers stated that his treatment would take from six to eight weeks. Curiously, the clinic's brochure claimed most patients were cured within three weeks and "some within a matter of days." The clinic treated phobias, sexual dysfunction, eating disorders, and stress as well as alcohol and drug dependency. All patients were expected to participate in "group counseling, psychosexual counseling, behavior therapy, and evaluation of lifestyle."

"All medical care is totally confidential," the brochure continued, "and, with such short periods away from work, colleagues may think the patient has just taken a holiday."

As soon as Michael arrived at the clinic, he was searched for drugs. Inside Jackson's yellow duffel bag nurses found and promptly confiscated thirteen bottles of pills. Jackson responded by locking himself in his room and turning the volume on his radio up all the way. Then, evading the bodyguard assigned to him, Michael sneaked out and began wandering the halls, asking other patients how to get out of the building.

Caught by clinic staffers before he could escape, Michael was put on a Valium IV as part of the process to wean him off the painkillers (the official British diagnosis of Jackson's problem was "analgesia abuse"). The clinic's star therapist, Beechy Colclough, seemed an unlikely savior. A high school dropout, failed rock drummer, and former alcoholic and drug addict, Colclough got so drunk at his best friend's funeral that he fell into the grave and landed on the coffin. By 1980 Colclough was living on the streets, swigging Old Spice aftershave and digging through garbage cans for food. He landed in psychiatric wards four times and sought help in 1983 only after waking up in the gutter to find a dog urinating on his face. Just one year later he was counseling others on how to overcome their addictions.

At group therapy sessions led by Colclough, Michael spoke about his father's cruelty, his lost childhood, the pain of being falsely accused. Others in the group did what they were there to do—lend unquestioning support. If that wasn't enough, Michael could peek out the window and see dozens of fans keeping vigil, even though no one was certain he was really there. Several had unfurled a ten-foot-high banner across the street. It read: MICHAEL JACKSON IS 100% INNOCENT.

Such encouragement aside, Michael grew increasingly wary of the press's growing presence and asked that his treatment be continued back at the London mansion of Elton John's manager, John Reid. This time, doctors, nurses, and the patient himself donned disguises and left the clinic one by one to avoid arousing suspicion. London oddsmakers, meanwhile, were approached by gamblers wanting to bet on whether Jackson would commit suicide by the end of the year. "I was hoping," said one, "to get odds of fifty to one." "We have a stream of requests like this," one top bookmaker confessed. "People also want to bet on him being convicted of child abuse. But opening a book on Mr. Jackson's suicide would be in totally bad taste."

During a week-long break from regular treatment, Michael was smuggled out of London and driven south to Manor Farm, the Tudor estate of British banking tycoon Jack Dellal. The seventy-year-old millionaire, a family friend of Beechy Colclough, lent him the house so that Michael could continue his therapy in a more bucolic setting. Protected by six armed bodyguards, he never left the house. Instead he spent nearly all his time doing simple household chores as part of his therapy. His favorite task: vacuuming, which, according to the Portuguese caretaker, he did for hours at a stretch.

Back in California, Fields, Weitzman, Bonnie Eskenazi, and the rest of Michael's high-priced legal team were busy pressing their motion for a six-year delay. They were totally unprepared for the next blow. The day before the crucial hearing to delay, five former Jackson bodyguards filed suit in Los Angeles, claiming they had been fired the previous February because they knew too much about Michael's activities with young boys.

Morris Wiliams, Leroy Thomas, Donald Starks, Fred Hammond, and Aaron White had worked both at Hayvenhurst and at Neverland. Their suit described how they had helped smuggle Michael's special friends past his parents and the night he'd ordered Leroy Thomas to destroy the snapshot of a nude boy. The suit claimed that Michael had forgotten which bodyguard had been given this special assignment and determined the only way to handle the matter was to fire all five.

Also named as defendants in the lawsuit were Pellicano and Michael's housekeeper, Norma Staikos, who had actually handed the bodyguards their pink slips. The much despised "hatchet lady" of Neverland was now considered a key figure in the criminal investigation. Trouble was, she too had vanished.

Acting on an anonymous tip that Staikos was leaving the country, police held an Athens-bound British Airways jet at Los Angeles Airport and searched the plane. It was too late; she had left the country and joined her husband in Athens, where they had accumulated enough money to purchase their own shopping center.

With both Michael and Norma Staikos now out of the country, L.A. district attorney Gil Garcetti and Santa Barbara DA Tom Sneddon both doubted seriously if Michael would ever come back. "It looks," one detective said, "like we've got another Roman Polanski on our hands." (Film director Polanski fled to France in the early 1970s rather than face charges of having had sex with a thirteen-year-old girl. He never returned.)

Customs and immigration officials as well as agents of Interpol were asked to stop both Jackson and Staikos if they turned up at an airport. But since they were wanted only for questioning and not charged with any crimes, no warrants were issued for their arrest.

Meanwhile police raided the offices of Michael's dermatologist, Arnold Klein, and his plastic surgeon, Steven Hoefflin. They left with boxloads of medical records, but according to one investigator, Jackson's were missing.

At a Washington, D.C., AIDS clinic being named in her honor, Elizabeth Taylor implored the public to leave Michael alone while he was seeking help for his addiction to painkillers. "I saw for myself that Michael was in desperate need of specialized medical attention," she said, adding that she "made calls to arrange the very best treatment, and he is getting that treatment now in Europe."

As for Jackson's whereabouts: "Out of concern for his privacy, my regard for him, and my concern for his health, I will continue to be silent. I love him like a son," Taylor added. "I support him with all my heart." Her loyalty was admirable. If a warrant for his arrest were issued and she refused to disclose his whereabouts, however, some feared Taylor could run into her own problems with the law.

It was all a strain on her relationship with Fortensky. Reportedly, when he asked her to stop dashing to Michael's defense a bitter argument ensued. While Taylor stayed in Washington to accept her award, a seething Fortensky flew back to Los Angeles.

Even as network news programs were carrying coverage of Taylor's emotional appeal to protect Michael's privacy, the team of Fields and Weitzman was blundering its way through another televised court appearance. At the all-important hearing to delay the civil case until 2000—the year the criminal statute of limitations would run out—Fields let slip the erroneous information that a grand jury had been convened in Santa Barbara for the purpose of indicting Jackson.

"There's a grand jury sitting already in Santa Barbara County," Fields told Judge David Rothman. "You have a DA sitting up in Santa Barbara County about to indict, and if they do, we are going to have a criminal trial very soon. . . ."

Judge Rothman denied the defense's request for delay and set a March 21, 1994, trial date. Once they were outside, Weitzman scrambled frantically to undo the damage from Bert Fields's oddly casual remark that an indictment was imminent. He told reporters that Fields had "misspoken himself." Weeks later a Santa Barbara grand jury would, in fact, begin hearing witnesses—but, it would turn out, too late for Fields.

Famed New York divorce lawyer Raoul Felder was having a better time of it on Geraldo Rivera's syndicated talk show, where he "defended" Michael in a mock trial. Jackson, the audience's clear favorite, was unanimously acquitted. "Thank you for your sterling defense of Michael," Weitzman wrote Felder. "Now I know where to look if I need criminal defense co-counsel in any matters on the East Coast."

In stark contrast with Bert Fields, John Branca was back to working wonders for Michael. During his three years in exile Branca had bided his time, seldom speaking to Michael. But in the summer of 1993, just before the scandal broke, he had lunch with Sandy Gallin at L.A.'s chic restaurant Le Dome. Over coffee, Branca told Gallin that if Michael agreed to renegotiate the Sony deal, he could land him an even higher royalty rate than he was already getting. The bottom line–conscious Michael bit, inviting Branca back onto his legal team in an unspecified capacity. From that point on, Michael would refer to Branca's return as "the Second Coming."

On November 22, 1993, *People* magazine hit the stands with a cover story titled "Michael Jackson Cracks Up—Sex, Drugs and the Fall of the World's Biggest Star." Two days later, Michael took time out from his group therapy sessions to sign the biggest music publishing deal in history: a guaranteed $150 million, five-year deal with EMI to administer the ATV Music Publishing Catalog. On signing, Michael received $70 million.

Michael, for all his problems, was apparently a hands-on participant in the delicate negotiations. And Branca, who had so brilliantly engineered the sale, was well on his way back to preeminence among Michael's most trusted advisers.

Actually, apart from the child molestation charges and Michael's alleged narcotics addiction, the MJJ empire was flourishing—booming, in fact. Since the scandal broke, a few scattered radio stations had declined to play his records. But the overwhelming majority *increased* the number of times they aired Michael's songs.

Sales of Michael's records also soared. On the same day it announced that *Dangerous* had sold twenty million worldwide, Sony made a bold move by releasing *The Dangerous Tapes.* The home video documentary began with Michael being pursued by frenzied crowds to the theme music from *The Omen.*

Michael was holding up better than some members of his own family. Kicking off her concert tour in Cincinnati, Janet, wearing a fringed, midriff-baring outfit, stopped the show and asked the crowd to say "a silent prayer for my brother Michael." As the audience cheered, Janet broke down crying.

Janet may have been surprised by the reaction. Michael's old friends had been anything but vocal. Diana Ross, Liza Minnelli, Jackie Onassis, David Geffen, and hundreds more who once clamored to be photographed beside him now remained stonily silent. One who did come to his defense, more or less, was Paul McCartney. "Linda and I are parents," he told the Argentine newspaper *Clarin*, "and it's clear to us that Michael isn't that kind of person."

McCartney was still peeved that Michael had allowed Beatles songs to be used in advertisements. Nor was he convinced that Michael was really out of the country because he needed to be treated for drug addiction. "It's all very L.A.—I mean, Judy Garland, Elizabeth Taylor—these are people who became stars at a very young age. We, the Beatles, we were ordinary guys. When fame arrived, we went a bit crazy, but even so we had our feet on the ground; we had roots; we knew about life. Michael, instead . . . ah, well."

21

He'd rather cut his own wrist than harm a child.

—Elizabeth Taylor

Katherine Jackson was angry. Angry that her son was being accused of molesting a child. Angry that Michael never called her. Angry that he had replaced her with Elizabeth Taylor. Angry that the *Jackson Family Honors* was in jeopardy. Angry that Michael's advisers seemed to be committing one blunder after another.

In a twenty-four-hour television blitz, Katherine and Jermaine appeared on CNN and *Hard Copy* to speak out in Michael's defense. Joe, who was asking to be paid $150,000 to speak on his son's behalf, declined to appear with them. "He's never done anything like this, and he never will do anything like this," Katherine insisted, "because he's *not* a child molester. Being a mother, I have to let people know he didn't do this terrible thing."

They admitted for the first time that they had no idea where Michael was. "Michael's handlers don't want us to get to him," Jermaine complained.

Katherine slammed her son's accusers—particularly the bodyguards—as people who were "coming forth just to get paid. . . . I'm not going to sit by and watch them crucify him. The bodyguards know they're telling lies."

On *Hard Copy* she staunchly defended Michael's heterosexuality. "Michael's appearance makes a lot of people think he's gay. But you can tell when a person is gay; sometimes you look at a person's face and you say, 'Oh, my God, that guy is gay.' Michael is not gay."

Katherine admitted that she was surprised when she heard that Michael was addicted to painkillers but insisted that he was "too strong" to try to take his own life.

On CNN she issued a direct appeal to Michael. "You have to come home," she said, "to defend yourself." "He's an American citizen, and he *will* be coming home," Jermaine added. "He's ready to kick some butt." As for his counsel: "The lawyers make so many mistakes," Katherine said, "I wonder if it's intentional or not."

Katherine may have bitterly resented Elizabeth Taylor's interference. But it was Taylor who, with the help of her own lawyer, Neil Papiano, would manage to orchestrate a changing of the guard around Michael. Fields's November 23 courthouse comments were sufficient for Taylor, Bray, and the increasingly powerful John Branca to engineer a coup. By mid-December Fields and Pellicano would be out of the picture, replaced by Johnnie Cochran. "Cochran," Papiano had told Taylor in no uncertain terms, "is the man for the job."

Fields remained silent about his departure from the case, but not Pellicano. "You know families," he said of the criticism leveled at him by Katherine and Jermaine. "You can't keep families quiet." Pellicano admitted he would have done only one thing differently: "I'd be more forceful," he said. "Sometimes being a gentleman works, and sometimes it doesn't."

On December 7, 1993, La Toya Jackson was heading for Israel when she read about the sentencing of a former Rhode Island priest who had confessed to molesting hundreds of children in the 1950s and 1960s. The news reports of that story, she later said, would force her to make one of the most difficult decisions of her life.

Shortly after arriving in Tel Aviv, she called a midnight press conference at her hotel. "Michael is my brother, and I love him very much," she told reporters, "but I cannot and I will not be a silent collaborator in his crimes against young children. If I remain silent, then that means I feel the guilt and humiliation that these children are feeling, and I think it is very wrong.

"Forget about the superstar, forget about the icon," she said. "If he was any other thirty-five-year-old man who was sleeping with little boys, you wouldn't like this guy."

La Toya went on to say that she had seen evidence that suggested the parents of several boys had been paid off—the checks her angry mother had shown her years earlier. "I don't know if these children were apparently bought through the parents by Michael or not, but I have seen these checks . . . the sums are very, very large amounts.

"But I think it's sad," she continued, "because I am a victim myself, and I know what it feels like. These kids are going to be scarred for the rest of their life, and I don't want to see any more innocent small children being affected this way. I love Michael very dearly," she added, her voice trembling, "but I feel even more sorry for these children because they don't have a life anymore."

Why was she delivering such a stinging indictment of her brother? "I love Michael very dearly," she repeated. "I hope he gets help."

Outside Hayvenhurst, other Jackson family members held a rare impromptu news conference of their own to refute La Toya's explosive charges. "La Toya's lying, and I'll tell her to her face she's lying," said Katherine, who added that her daughter was "selling her own brother down the river. La Toya's been brainwashed by her moneygrubbing mongrel of a husband."

"Jack is doing this whole thing to make money off our family," big brother Jackie concurred. "He is a hustler, and he knows how to do it well." Jermaine insisted that there was "no validity to what she [La Toya] is saying. It is absolutely not true. My brother is not a child molester. This has got to stop!"

The Jackson family, claiming that it had launched its own investigation into the charges against Michael, continued its counterattack. After reports surfaced that a second boy had told police he was molested by Michael, the family rallied to his defense on Black Entertainment Television. La Toya's rebuttal: "Michael supports the entire Jackson family financially. They have to support him."

While Feldman stepped up the pressure on Michael to give a court-mandated deposition on January 18, 1994, Jackson's legal team negotiated the conditions for his return with prosecutors. After weeks of haggling, L.A. district attorney Gil Garcetti and Santa Barbara DA Tom Sneddon promised that Michael would not be met with an arrest warrant or a sealed indictment on his return. Still, Michael balked. It was not until U.S. officials contacted Scotland Yard, setting the wheels in motion for his arrest in London, that he agreed to return.

Meanwhile, British papers were reporting that Beechy Colclough, psychiatrist Brian Wells, and Michael's physician David Forecast had concluded that Michael was a virgin and "totally asexual." The team was reportedly prepared to testify that Michael could not have molested anyone, adult or child.

The therapists reportedly determined that Michael was "not capable of such activities. He is totally asexual. There is absolutely no sexual aspect to his personality, his character, or his behavior. If *Basic Instinct* came on the TV, he would just walk out of the room. His sexy stage act and raunchy videos are just a performance and have no sexual effect whatsoever on him."

Ever since he took the job as head of Michael's legal team, Johnnie Cochran had been urging him to come home. "For months *Hard Copy* and the tabloids had been beating up Michael," Cochran said. "I wanted to bring him back here, at the center of what was happening. Michael always has and always will be the most effective advocate for the fact of his innocence."

But it took La Toya's explosive statements to spur Michael to action. He ordered his lawyers to reach a settlement with Randall in exchange for Joey's silence. Although they had gathered testimony from numerous sources, the prosecutors had made the calculated decision to base their criminal case on the civil case. Under California law a child could not be forced to testify in a molestation case. And without Joey's testimony, Michael had been told, there was a good chance the criminal case would collapse completely.

Michael also had no intention of dipping into his coffers to pay for the settlement. He instructed his lawyers to find some ingenious way to take care of the bill. "I don't care how," he said, "just do it."

La Toya's comments also prompted Michael's decision to return home. Two days after her Tel Aviv press conference, Michael was smuggled out of the Charter Nightingale Clinic at six A.M. inside one of the clinic's "luxury ambulances" with blacked-out windows. At ten A.M. he took off from Heathrow on a 727 owned by the sultan of Brunei, the richest man in the world and a diehard Jackson fan. Keeping Michael company, as they had done even before the scandal broke: the Cascio brothers.

After a refueling stop in Boston, the plane landed in Billings, Montana, late that afternoon. Michael refused to get off the plane to go through customs. "I don't know if our deal is good here. They'll arrest me if I get off," he told Bill Bray. "I know they will. Don't let them take me." Instead a customs officer boarded the plane and checked Michael's passport. As he left, the customs officer asked the pilot, "Is that *the* Michael Jackson?"

That evening Michael's plane landed at Santa Barbara Airport. Trailed by the Cascio brothers, Michael, wearing a red hat, red silk shirt, black pants, and surgical mask, dashed to a waiting van and sped off to Neverland. An airport maintenance man flashed the peace sign (or was it V for victory?). Michael waved back.

As scores of news organizations gathered outside Neverland's Tudor-style gatehouse, a steady line of vans, cars, and limousines streamed through. When he arrived to welcome Michael home, one of his advisers looked at the Cascio brothers in astonishment. "Get those boys *out* of here," he said, "right away!" Michael told the adviser to mind his own business if he wanted to keep his job.

After all of Michael's cloak-and-dagger escapades, weary journalists were not convinced that he was really back. Michael, the most sought after figure in the world, would be back in the United States three days before the media actually felt confident enough to report rumors of his return.

His neighbors harbored no such doubts. For months they heard the din of crews laying track for Michael's new full-size railroad during the daylight hours. But after dusk there was only silence. On Saturday night, December 11—just twenty-four hours after his return—the sky over Neverland was aglow with lights from Michael's amusement park. And ranchers recognized the familiar sound of Michael's carousel playing "Like a Virgin."

At an L.A. Raiders game on Sunday, December 12, Larry Feldman just happened to bump into Michael's new lawyer, Johnnie Cochran. For the first time Cochran confirmed that Michael was indeed back in the country.

Feldman was skeptical about Michael's alleged drug problem. "It's very suspicious," he said, "that Mr. Jackson arrives and is now cured . . . exactly when the district attorney and the defense make a deal on his body search." Still, he agreed his homecoming was a wise move. "Up until now," said Feldman, "Michael has been very poorly advised."

As even more witnesses stepped forward to tell their stories about Michael, he looked to his few adult friends for support. Diana, Liza, Jackie, Brooke, Katharine Hepburn, Jane Fonda, David Geffen—all continued giving Michael the silent treatment.

Most conspicuously silent of all was Oprah Winfrey, whose live interview with Michael had made television history. A longtime champion of children's rights and herself a victim of sexual abuse as a child, Winfrey must have agonized over the no-win position in which she had inadvertently put herself. She did not want to prejudge a man idolized by the black community, but neither did she appreciate being used to further his image as the champion of children around the world. Her best approach at the time—her only approach—was to say nothing and wait.

One of the few who spoke out against Michael was Roseanne Arnold. Another self-described victim of sexual abuse as a child, Arnold attacked Jackson in a *Vanity Fair* cover story. Stating that she wanted to go on the record with her opinion, she said of Jackson: "He is the perfect picture of a child molester. He had the perfect circumstances. Everything. But you know what? People don't know anything, so these stupid fucking assholes go, 'Well, we let our kids sleep with him and share his bed, 'cause he took 'em to Toys "R" Us. He's a nice, nice boy.' He's thirty-five fucking years old, and I think he got all this facial surgery done to obscure his age. . . . He don't really look like a thirty-five-year-old man, so maybe he really *is* Peter Pan. Yeah: 'He's Peter Pan, so we can let our little boys sleep with him!' But there are a lot of people —most people, according to those awful polls—who don't believe the kid accusing him. Nobody believes any kid. . . ."

Michael did, however, find an unexpected ally in Nation of Islam leader Louis Farrakhan. Making his first public appearance in New York in years, the man who once denounced Michael's "sissified ways" now defended him. "This brother is not charged with a crime," Farrakhan told a rally. "The powers that be can't stand to see Michael Jackson politically aware and using his money for the advancement of his people. . . . White men are afraid of a powerful black billionaire awakening politically."

The Jackson camp's attempts at lining up support from more mainstream black leaders were less successful. Jesse Jackson had already been criticized for pressuring the *L.A. Times* and other publications not to pursue the story too vigorously. And when approached to make a statement on Michael's behalf, Martin Luther King's widow, Coretta Scott King, declined.

Michael had fought frantically to keep from being strip searched and photographed. But as police monitored Dr. Arnold Klein's frequent visits to Neverland, they became more and more concerned that Michael was altering the marks on his body—marks that, if they matched Joey's description, would prove that he had an intimate knowledge of Michael's body.

Authorities in both Los Angeles and Santa Barbara County finally issued an ultimatum. "Michael shall be advised," read the Santa Barbara warrant, "that he has no right to refuse the examination and photographs, and any refusal to comply with this warrant would be admissible at trial and would be an indication of his consciousness of guilt." Johnnie Cochran and Howard Weitzman told a sobbing Michael that he no longer had a choice.

On the morning of December 20, 1993, two police detectives accompanied by a department doctor, videocameraman, and still photographer arrived at Neverland. Michael threw a tantrum, but calmed down enough to answer questions. After more than an hour of police questioning, Jackson was asked to disrobe.

Michael pleaded one final time. "Please, do I have to go through with this?" he begged. The detectives patiently reminded Michael that they had agreed to his demands that no women be present and that his own doctor be on hand to witness the examination.

With that, the detectives looked the other way as Jackson undressed. When they turned around, they saw Michael, wearing two robes over a pair of swimming trunks, standing in the center of the room. He was staring at a portrait of Elizabeth Taylor.

Reluctantly Michael shed one robe, then another—all the while fixing his gaze on the portrait of Taylor. Finally, at the detectives' insistence, he pulled down his swimming trunks.

It had been speculated that police would be looking for a tattoo, specifically a tatoo of Winnie the Pooh. In truth they wanted to verify Joey Randall's description of Michael as being "half black and half white"—totally white above his beltline and dark brown below—as well as his description of the large black rings around Michael's thighs and buttocks, and the pink-white vitiligo blotches around his genitals. When he first saw Michael naked, Joey had pointed at the brown and pink-white blotches and laughed, "You look like a cow! You look just like a cow!"

The detectives were astonished at what they saw. According to sources close to the investigation, the markings on Michael's body matched Joey's description. (Interviewed months later, Jackson claimed that the markings didn't match Joey's description.)

Michael kept staring at the portrait of Elizabeth Taylor as the cameraman and the photographer circled him slowly, making a painstaking visual record of every millimeter of his torso, groin, and legs.

After five minutes Michael cried, "Make them stop!" They grudgingly agreed, but he still had to be examined by the police doctor, who spent another fifteen minutes scribbling down detailed notes about the distinguishing characteristics of Michael's buttocks and genitalia. The Santa Barbara DA had initially wanted the physician to bring a ruler to measure the size of Jackson's genitals and the dimensions of the skin discolorations as described by Randall, but Cochran successfully fought that request.

When it was all over, Michael pulled on his clothes and broke down in tears. "Don't ever, *ever,*" he sobbed to Bray, "let this happen to me again!"

On December 22 Michael broke his silence on the case with an emotional televised appeal written over a two-day period by him and his top advisers. The four-minute telecast, carried live worldwide on CNN and rebroadcast on all the network evening news programs, had all the markings of a presidential address—with some cosmetic differences. Strikingly effeminate even by his own standards, Michael wore a red shirt, red lipstick, and Bambi-like false eyelashes. Long strands of black hair hung down on either side of his face. The dateline "Live from Neverland Valley" was carried at the bottom of the screen.

Proclaiming his innocence, Jackson called for a "speedy end to this horrifying, horrifying experience." He railed against the "many disgusting statements" made about him by the "incredible, terrible mass media.... I ask you all to wait to hear the truth before you label or condemn me. Don't treat me like a criminal, because I am innocent."

Jackson also graphically described the "dehumanizing and humiliating" body search by police: "They served a search warrant on me which allowed them to view and photograph my body, including my penis, my buttocks, my lower torso, thighs, and any other areas that they wanted.

"It was the most humiliating ordeal of my life . . . a nightmare, a horrifying nightmare," Michael went on. "But if this is what I have to endure to prove my innocence, so be it." In declaring his love for "children of all ages and races," Michael then quoted scripture. "If I am guilty of anything," he said, "it is of believing what God said about children: 'Suffer little children to come unto me and forbid them not, for such is the Kingdom of Heaven.' In no way do I think that I am God, but I do try to be God-like in my heart."

He then signed off with his usual "I love you very much, and may God bless you all. I love you. . . ."

Weitzman, not surprisingly, praised the speech. "It's great to have a client," he said, "who participates with his lawyers and shows the world he's innocent of these charges."

Larry Feldman, on the other hand, pointed out that he couldn't put his thirteen-year-old client on camera. "I'm very sad," Feldman said, "that they just won't stop trying to manipulate the press and manipulate the jury."

It was indeed an emotional performance—ANGUISH was the *New York Post*'s one-word headline—but unconvincing to several leading lie detection experts who monitored Michael's statement. Charles R. McQuiston, who coinvented the Psychological Stress Evaluater used by law enforcement agencies in thirty-six states, declared it "one of the most damning tapes I've ever seen. The stress in Jackson's voice shows that he's lying."

Atlanta voice stress expert Dr. Martin Markowitz agreed. "My analysis shows that in his mind and his heart, Michael knows he has abused one or more children. . . . When he says 'I don't say I'm God, but I try to be God-like in my heart,' the stress nearly goes off the chart. That was too much even for Michael to stomach."

Even as Michael delivered his passionate appeal for sympathy from the American public, his lawyers were negotiating the terms of a settlement with Feldman—the settlement Michael himself had instructed them to work out in November.

The media was in a wild feeding frenzy, but Michael seemed determined not to let it interfere with his fun. On December 30 he flew to Las Vegas to spend the weekend with Michael Milken and Mirage Casino owner Steve Wynn. Michael and his advisers considered Las Vegas friendly territory; he was a familiar figure at the casino arcades, where he could often be found playing video games with young boys.

As he went on the Nile amusement ride at the Luxor Hotel, however,

Michael was clearly unprepared for the public reaction. A few supporters yelled words of encouragement, and several children asked for his autograph. But there were also cutting remarks from adults in the crowd and even shouts of "Pervert!" On New Year's Eve patrons booed and hissed when he walked through the casino of the MGM Grand.

Shaken, the next day Michael wore his Arab woman disguise—a hooded black chador with a veil and white running shoes—when he and Milken visited the MGM Grand theme park. After an hour he returned to his room; the weird outfit was attracting too much attention.

That evening Michael caught Barbra Streisand's much ballyhooed concert at the MGM Grand. He expected the crowd (which included a great many show business people) to react positively, and he was not disappointed. When Barbra introduced him, the audience burst into wild applause. After the show he met with a friend who just happened to be in town—his trusted dermatologist, Dr. Arnold Klein.

A week later Michael appeared at the nationally televised NAACP Image Awards, ostensibly to hand Debbie Allen her award as best choreographer. He was wearing another one of his braided Sgt. Pepper jackets, and in a lengthy, impassioned, and self-serving speech, he again spoke of his stolen childhood, his love of children, and his innocence.

"Not only am I presumed to be innocent," he told the black-tie crowd, "but I *am* innocent." That statement brought the audience, which included many of Hollywood's biggest stars, to its feet. "I am not fighting this battle alone," Michael went on. "Together we will see this thing through. The truth will be my salvation!"

Feldman's response was predictable. "Michael Jackson," he said, "just ought to cut out these staged media events and stop trying to influence potential jurors."

Feldman's repeated references to juries and jurors continued to vex Cochran. Four court-appointed psychiatrists unanimously agreed that Joey Randall would be scarred even further psychologically if he testified in open court. But Feldman kept pressing ahead with his plan to depose Michael on January 18—an appointment Michael had no intention of keeping.

Feldman upped the ante. As long as Michael seemed determined to try his case in the court of public opinion even while settlement talks were under way, he felt he could not remain silent. On January 10, 1994—the day before Joey Randall's fourteenth birthday—his lawyer asked the court for a detailed accounting of Michael's assets (which, had it been granted, would almost surely have found its way into the hands of reporters).

At the same time Feldman filed a four-page statement with the court in which Joey Randall described a few of the more shocking details of his alleged molestation at the hands of Michael. "It was psychological pressure," Feldman said of Michael's tactics. "Michael Jackson starts off slowly, gains the confidence of and involves the whole family, not just the child, into this relationship."

Again the world was buzzing about Michael's alleged pedophilia. His characteristically defiant response was to throw a party for two hundred underprivileged children at Neverland on January 16, Martin Luther King, Jr., Day. Katherine begged him not to go ahead with the annual event, but Michael ignored her.

KCAL-TV and Black Entertainment Television were called in to cover Michael cavorting with the kids, leading them Pied Piper–like on rides, driving bumper cars, trying out his new steam train. One by one the inner-city children were then paraded in front of the television cameras to praise their host. "Michael," said one little girl, "is too nice to do those things. He's totally innocent. He loves kids."

Two days later the devastating Northridge earthquake struck Southern California, killing more than fifty people and resulting in billions of dollars in damage. Hayvenhurst was badly shaken. Particularly hard hit was the Trophy Room, where Michael's platinum records and awards were dashed on the floor. Neverland sustained minor damage. But at the Hollywood Wax Museum, the quake knocked the head off the Michael Jackson statue.

At this stage, with a criminal investigation (and a possible jail sentence) hanging in the balance and Feldman pressing the civil case, the pressure on Jackson was greater than ever. Branca, Cochran, Weitzman, and Bray must have had the same thought: Michael must not be compelled to testify in court.

Feldman had rejected their first offer of $900,000 out of hand, reminding Cochran that back in July—before the scandal broke—a tentative settlement of $20 million was already being discussed. Adam Randall was not about to let Joey accept less now. A panel of three retired judges was brought in to preside over the negotiations.

From the very beginning Michael had no intention of digging into his own deep pocket to pay up. As far back as November of 1993, he had ordered his lawyers to approach his insurance company, Transamerica, and demand it pay not only any settlement costs, but also his legal fees. Such costs, he claimed, were covered under his personal liability policy. Since MJJ Productions was an important client, Transamerica agreed to have its lawyers explore the possibilities.

The first week in January Transamerica executives began to get nervous when rumors flew about a proposed settlement. They faxed Michael's lawyers, asking if they were indeed nearing a settlement in the case and stating they would need to know the details before they made a decision.

Michael's team wanted a commitment before the staggering dollar figures were revealed, however. On January 13, 1994, Johnnie Cochran fired off an angry letter to Transamerica, threatening to sue the company if it refused to cover Michael's costs. "I believe it is imperative that the matter be resolved immediately," wrote Cochran, pointing to the fact that his client had already incurred substantial financial losses.

"Transamerica has thus fallen woefully short of its obligation to cooperate in the defense of this matter," Cochran wrote. "In the event that this matter is settled without any participation by Transamerica, please be advised that Mr. Jackson will pursue all civil remedies available to him against Transamerica for a host of claims, including failure to pay defense costs, failure to contribute toward settlement costs . . . and/or punitive damages for bad faith."

Transamerica officials may have admired Michael's lawyers for their audacity, but they had no intention of knuckling under. That same day, claims analyst Russ Wardrip fired off a letter to Howard Weitzman, informing him that Michael's policy covered him only in the event he was injured in an accident. "Acts of sexual activity," Wardrip stated, "do not constitute an accident."

The letter went on to point out that "Transamerica declines coverage for any damages flowing from the allegations of sexual conduct in the complaint. Further, acts of sexual activity, especially those committed against a minor, are inherently intentional, wrongful, and harmful. Coverage for such acts is precluded by California Insurance Code Section 533. On that basis, as well, coverage is denied under the Transamerica policy for the allegations in the Randall lawsuit."

Twenty-four hours later a meeting was hastily arranged at Feldman's Santa Monica office before the three retired judges. In addition to Feldman, Transamerica attorney Lane Ashley attended the meeting, as did three Jackson attorneys—Cochran, Weitzman, and Allan Goldman. As Randall's lawyer, Feldman was committed to seeing that there was hard cash behind any settlement offer. The Transamerica lawyer reported back in a memo: "At the outset (and as is typical) counsel for Jackson 'beat up' on Transamerica for its denial of coverage."

Incredibly, the Jackson team's customary hardball tactics worked. Transamerica, without acknowledging any legal obligation to do so, agreed to pay a certain amount. Even more incredibly, the Jackson team turned it down. "An offer was made on behalf of Transamerica on a onetime only basis to resolve the claim," the memo stated. "This offer was rejected by the insured." Evidently, Michael wanted his insurance company to cover the whole cost and nothing less.

Within a week a final settlement was reached: $26 million—$1 million in cash to Adam Randall, the remainder to be paid into a trust for Joey at the rate of $5 million a year over five years. The trust would be administered by a retired judge. Transamerica was still considering whether to help defray the cost to Jackson.

On January 24, 1994, prosecutors cleared Adam Randall of extortion, stating that there were "no grounds whatsoever" for believing an extortion ever occurred. The next day lawyers for both sides held a joint press conference outside the Santa Monica courthouse (which had been heavily damaged in the Northridge quake) to announce a settlement.

"Michael Jackson maintains his innocence," Feldman said, "and he withdraws previous allegations of extortion. The civil suit will be dismissed to allow the parties to get on with their lives . . . to allow the parties to close this chapter of their lives with dignity." As for Joey: "The boy has shown enormous amounts of courage," Feldman said. "He is very happy with the resolution of this matter."

"Michael Jackson is an innocent man," Cochran told reporters. "The time has come for Michael Jackson to get on with his life."

It would have been impossible to make it a formal part of the settlement agreement, but many believed there was a tacit understanding that Joey Randall would not testify against Jackson in the criminal investigations. Nevertheless, prosecutors in both Los Angeles and Santa Barbara vowed to pursue the criminal investigations. "The district attorney's office," DA Garcetti said, "is taking Mr. Feldman at his word that the alleged victim will be allowed to testify and that there has been no agreement in the civil matter that will affect cooperation in the criminal investigation."

Still, there was no doubt that by cutting off the supply of evidence generated by the civil case, lawyers for both sides knew the criminal investigation had been dealt a severe blow.

That evening President Bill Clinton gave his State of the Union address. Later the ABC news program *Nightline* was devoted not to the state of the Union, but to the *really* important story of the day: the settlement in the Michael Jackson case. One of the panelists, New York attorney Raoul Felder (the same lawyer who'd won an "acquittal" for Michael during the mock *Geraldo* trial), was "disgusted" by the settlement. "It sends a terrible message," he said. "That statue on the courthouse should hang its head in shame that this could happen. If you're rich, you can buy justice—pure and simple."

A broadly grinning Feldman (who stood to collect as much as $10 million in contingency fees) also appeared on *Nightline*. After blasting prosecutors for "doing nothing" during the previous six months, he insisted that no deal had been struck to silence Joey Randall as a witness.

"If people believe that Michael Jackson paid millions of dollars," Felder retorted, "and he didn't get a promise that the boy wouldn't testify, then they also believe in the tooth fairy."

Among the many lingering questions about the case was the role of the Justice Department. FBI agents had reportedly compared Jackson to their own secret profile of a career pedophile and found that he matched virtually all the profile's characteristics—*excessive interest in children; refers to children as "pure," "innocent," etc.; age and gender preference; identifies with children more than adults; limited peer relationships;* etc. A particularly chilling passage in the FBI profile: "The homes of some pedophiles have been described as shrines to children or miniature amusement parks."

Why, then, hadn't federal authorities sought charges against him? According to Joey Randall, Michael had molested him in Las Vegas and in Monaco—meaning that Michael, if the charges were true, had taken his young victim across state lines and international borders for the purpose of committing a crime. Because of the high-profile nature of the case, the U.S. attorney in Los Angeles raised the issue with Attorney General Janet Reno. After conferring with the White House, it was agreed that—in the wake of the L.A. riots—the matter was best left in the hands of local law enforcement. "Nobody in the Clinton administration," said one official, "wants to be the one who put Michael Jackson in the slammer—including Bill and Hillary."

As always, Elizabeth Taylor could be counted on to put her particular spin on the settlement. "Thank God this case is being dismissed," she said in a press release. "As one of Michael's closest friends, who is convinced of his innocence, I agonized over the daily avalanche of lies, innuendos, and slurs, none of which Michael deserved. Michael's love of children is one of the purest things I have ever seen; it shines like an extra sun. . . . In spite of the media's distorted lens, I was repeatedly touched by the faith that so many of Michael's friends and fans had in his complete innocence."

Another old friend seemed to share the more widespread impression that the settlement was a tacit admission of guilt. If he had been the one accused, Elton John told Barbara Walters during a pre-Oscar television special, he would have fought it down to "the last penny."

22

I was sent forth for the world, for the children. But have mercy, for I've been bleeding a long time now.

On February 4, 1994, Norma Staikos reentered the United States through New York. She was stopped at the airport and served a summons to appear before the Santa Barbara grand jury looking into child molestation charges against her boss. If she thought the heat was off because of the settlement ("The Check Is in the Mail," cracked *Newsweek*), Staikos was mistaken. She was questioned by police.

The day Staikos was intercepted, Los Angeles County district attorney Gil Garcetti announced his support of new legislation that would compel a victim to testify if he or she sued the accused molester. "We think this law might erase the negative perception that if you're rich, you can get away with it." Garcetti went on to say, "Yes, it would apply to the Michael Jackson case, and yes, we are being told that the alleged victim is ready, willing, and able to step forward."

But suddenly Feldman, who for months had painstakingly gathered evidence and subpoenaed witnesses to prove that Michael had a history of molesting children, had a client whose interests had drastically changed.

"Victims ought to be able to control their own destiny," Feldman said. "I don't think anyone who has been the subject of a sexual assault should be forced to testify if they don't want to. What are you going to do, start locking up victims of sexual abuse? Lock this boy up?"

Feldman's attitude toward those who had helped him build his case against Michael had also shifted with the settlement. Charles "Ted" Mathews, the lawyer for the five fired bodyguards still pursuing their suit against Michael, had shared information with Feldman. Now Mathews claimed Feldman was no longer cooperating with him. Journalists Feldman had used to build his case were getting much the same treatment. "I was willing to talk to you before," he told one, "but why should I talk to you *now?*"

Charli Michaels came forward to tell her eyewitness account of Michael's grabbing another special friend's crotch because, as she put it, "the settlement sickened me enough." Tatiana, the dancer from Jackson's *The Way You Make Me Feel* video, had been carted out by the Jackson family only weeks earlier to hint at a romantic relationship on national television. She now admitted it was all a ruse. "Quite frankly," she said, "when I read he'd paid the boy millions, it turned my stomach."

Two private investigators who had worked for Feldman were so outraged that they, too, went public. San Francisco–based Sandra Sutherland and Jack Palladino, who had also worked previously on the Patty Hearst and Menendez cases, encountered a "significant number" of credible witnesses—boys and young men who said they had been molested by Michael.

"I've talked to two grown men crying on the phone, talking about their experiences with Michael as minors," Sutherland said. "Some are in prisons and mental hospitals abroad because of what happened to them." Sutherland went on to say that while a number claimed to have been victimized several times, there were also a few who had been picked up on tour or on the L.A. streets for "one-night stands." All were showered with money and gifts.

"There are still victims whose parents don't want to get involved," Sutherland said. "I was horrified by the lengths people will go to to protect their interests, even when it's contrary to human decency and justice." Sutherland and Palladino stressed that they believed Joey Randall's story largely because of the "specific erotic details—details a child wouldn't know unless he lived in a porno store."

José Gomez, thirty-three, reacted to the settlement by spraying orange paint over Jackson's star on Hollywood Boulevard. "I hate child molesters," he told police before pleading no contest to one count of vandalism.

Jermaine Jackson somehow managed to convince NBC to go ahead with its *Jackson Family Honors* telecast. In the hours before the show's February 19 taping at the Las Vegas MGM Grand, there was chaos as organizers scrambled to fill the auditorium. Tickets that were priced originally at $1,000 were now being scalped for $50. Not leaving anything to chance, several dozen fresh-scrubbed teenagers were pulled in off the street and handed placards by concert organizers that looked homemade. The signs read WE LOVE MICHAEL and were decorated with hearts.

The big question: Was La Toya going to show up and disrupt the Jackson family lovefest? Although Katherine and the others maintained that La Toya was welcome to join them on stage, the prodigal daughter was categorically excluded from participating. What's more, security had been alerted to bar her if she tried to crash the event.

At the last minute La Toya, who had taken a suite at a nearby hotel, called Katherine and begged to be a part of the show. According to La Toya, her mother said she could come only if she signed a gag order. La Toya refused, and Katherine hung up.

Backstage there was panic. The entire family was ninety minutes late. Then, when it looked as though Michael might not show up, a heated argument erupted among Jermaine, Joe, and the NBC executives who had paid $3.5 million in broadcast fees on the understanding that Michael would be part of the festivities.

Michael, wishing to avoid contact with his family as much as possible, refused a suite at the MGM Grand and stayed at the Mirage. Janet, sharing his sentiments, occupied a suite at the Luxor. Michael arrived a half hour before the show was to begin and refused to go on. Sitting in the front row were Katherine, dressed in white, and Joe, looking like a Mafia don in a black suit, black shirt, and red bow tie.

Katherine was summoned backstage to coax Michael into going through with the evening as planned. Michael told her he could not bear to face all those strangers, but most of all he couldn't bear to face Joe. As usual, Katherine prevailed, and the show went on. The supposed family unity was at best strained, as evidenced by the fact that Janet opened the show with "All Right" and then stormed out, refusing to participate in a family sing-along finale.

There were endless taped family reminiscences, video clips,

speeches (Lou Gossett, Jr., pledged his "unconditional support to the Jackson family"), and performances by Celine Dion, Gladys Knight, and Smokey Robinson, among others.

Calling Michael "caring and spiritual," Robinson then introduced him as the "king of pop." Michael, wearing a new Prince Valiant hairstyle, the standard black military outfit, and a red armband, then basked in a five-minute-long standing ovation. The cameras panned the audience and the teenagers waving the WE LOVE MICHAEL signs they had been given. Michael just stood giggling, managing now and then to toss an "I love you!" back to the cheering throng. The camera then focused on a boy of about seven clapping in the audience.

"Thank you to the fans," Michael said. "Thank you for your prayers. Thank you for your loyalty. Thank you for your love and your friendship." He then presented Berry Gordy with a "Life Achievement Award" from the family. The two-foot-high award was a diamond-studded globe topped with white doves. Ringing the equator were children, running hand in hand. Gordy embraced Michael warmly. It was noted that at no time did Michael look directly at his own father, much less hug him.

Michael reappeared later, flanked by two hundred white-robed teenage choir members, to present Elizabeth Taylor with *her* Life Achievement Award. "During my recent trials and tribulations," said Michael, who was interrupted constantly by cheering, "Elizabeth stood by my side with unwavering strength and support. She is not swayed by public opinion because she knows in the end, truth *always* triumphs."

At this point someone in the audience hollered, "So why did you pay the kid money, Michael?" The remark was edited out of the videotape.

Taylor, about to undergo hip replacement surgery, was rolled to the edge of the stage in a wheelchair, then got up and hobbled to the podium. "I'm honored to be here with my beloved Michael," she said. "Michael's kindness, genuine, remarkable, compassion beyond bounds. Michael, we who know you acknowledge the suffering you have endured, because we have suffered with you. But we knew you would prevail through the darkest hour, and that you would emerge tired, bruised, but still magically whole."

Taylor was only getting started. "Enough of tabloid media!" she proclaimed. "Enough of tabloid television! Michael, we know your recent torture is not going to change your compassion and love for children. You are the brightest star in the universe. Don't let anything dim your leading light. Surely, Michael, you are the king of pop without a doubt!"

The crowd kept chanting, "Michael, sing!" And when he declined, their mood changed measurably. "Michael hasn't prepared," Taylor said. "He doesn't have any music." There were unexpected boos. "That's not nice," scolded Taylor. "Don't boo. That's an ugly sound."

Later Michael did join the rest of the clan in singing "If You Only Believe." But the eleven thousand people who had come to hear him perform were greatly disappointed.

The event was quickly dubbed the "Jackson Family Fiasco." In its aftermath, Smith-Hemion Productions sued Michael and nine other family members for failing to pay Gary Smith $2.2 million—including his $400,000 fee and payments due two hundred cast and crew members.

The suit also charged that the Jacksons, while advertising the show as a charity event, kept $300,000 in cash from a loan to finance the show, spent $39,000 on room service (including $250 bottles of Dom Pérignon), bought $30,000 worth of clothes for themselves, and spent $7,500 to have a fleet of limousines sit unused at the curbside for four days.

The Jacksons claimed the show, which cost $5.7 million to mount, grossed only $4.5 million. Despite the millions spent, only $100,000 was set aside for charities. "What's really frustrating is how arrogant the Jacksons are," Gary Smith complained. "Now they have the nerve to say, 'We won't pay you.' Where's the honor in that?"

None of this ongoing melodrama sat well with Disney, where the decision was made to drop the *Captain EO* attraction. Disney's official excuse was that *Captain EO* needed to be replaced because attendance had dropped off. Not true. Attendance was higher than ever.

Even after settling the Randall lawsuit, Michael remained deep in litigation. Concert promoter Marcel Avram had filed a $20 million suit against Michael for canceling the second leg of the *Dangerous* world tour. Citing a clause in his contract, Michael's lawyers claimed he did not have to return $3 million in advances because illness caused him to cancel. Avram's lawyers fired back that the "illness" was an addiction that Jackson had concealed from the promoters.

The Children's Peace Foundation, meanwhile, filed a $150 million class action suit claiming Michael did not deliver on his legal obligation to lend his name to a line of Children's Peace Foundation merchandise. Then there were the rappers who filed a breach of contract suit claiming Michael reneged on his agreement to let them use Beatles material in their rap music.

To complicate matters even further, Michelle Flowers of Modesto, California, filed a $1.6 million paternity suit against Michael in the spring of 1994, claiming he was the father of her ten-year-old son, James Allen Hall. If nothing else, Flowers said, it proved that Michael was interested in women. "I know Michael is straight," she said. "James is living proof he's straight."

Beyond the damage to his reputation, Michael discovered that his dangerous fascination with young boys had cost him dearly. Between the settlement (including legal fees and case-related costs) and the gifts lavished on his special friends and their parents, Michael had spent over $40 million. Factor in the cost of canceling the *Dangerous* tour, as well as the lost future endorsements, and that price tag easily topped $100 million.

Michael would score two early (if modest) court victories in 1994, however. Former Jackson family friends Reynaud Jones and Robert Smith lost their copyright infringement suit claiming Michael had ripped off "Thriller," "The Girl Is Mine," and "We Are the World" from tapes they handed Joe Jackson years earlier.

Then, on February 14, Jackson flew into Denver and gave an impromptu a cappella rendition of *Billie Jean* to show how he went about writing songs—and to prove that he did not steal *Dangerous* from Crystal Cartier. In addition to copyrighting her song *Dangerous* a year earlier than Michael, Cartier testified that she had given a demo containing the song to Jackson's road manager in Denver in 1988.

It appeared to courtroom observers that Cartier stood an excellent chance of winning the case until Michael made his surprise appearance. Grinning broadly, Michael snapped his fingers and swayed in the witness box—just as he had done to such great effect years earlier when he was sued for allegedly stealing "The Girl Is Mine."

"He giggled while he was being sworn in!" Cartier recalled. "It was a joke. He kept smiling at the jury.... Michael did everything but moonwalk." Cartier had worn a tight leather dress and jacket to court, ostensibly to show that she, too, was in show business. Instead the judge deemed her attire inappropriate and ordered her out of the court.

"If I was supposed to dress like a conservative woman," Cartier said, "then the judge should have also demanded that Michael Jackson wash his face, remove his eye makeup, lashes, and lipstick, so he would look like a conservative man instead of a flaming drag queen." Cartier was even more disturbed when the judge brought his son to court to meet the defendant.

After Michael's dazzling performance, the spellbound jury ruled in his favor. Cassette tapes of Jackson's performance were later available from the court for $15 each.

Given Michael's demonstrated willingness to testify in court—not to mention spend millions in legal fees to defend copyright infringement charges—there were those who wondered why he would not do at least as much to clear his name. Had he decided to fight the child molestation charges in court, the odds would have been in his favor. Starstruck juries were, in fact, a major concern of prosecutors in Los Angeles and Santa Barbara. "The celebrityhood of this will affect every aspect of the investigation and prosecution," former Los Angeles district attorney Ira Reiner observed. "It usually helps the defendant. Juries are star-struck, like people generally, and like to be friends of celebrities. It's not impossible, but it's extremely difficult to convict celebrities of crimes."

That meant the molestation case against Michael had to be airtight if it was to result in conviction. Over the next four months more than a dozen witnesses would parade before the Santa Barbara grand jury. Marlon Brando, described as a "father confessor" to Michael, was called to testify, as was his son Miko. Norma Staikos, publicist Bob Jones, Dr. Arnold Klein, Bill Bray—not to mention the housekeepers, maids, cooks, bodyguards, and secretaries who had been privy to Michael's secret worlds at Hayvenhurst and Neverland—all testified.

In addition to the shocking testimony of Blanca Francia, Charli Michaels, Orietta Murdoch, Janet Jackson's ex-husband, James DeBarge, the bodyguards, and others, there was also the occasional, tantalizing new lead. Michael's chauffeur, Gary Hearne, reportedly told the grand jury that he was instructed to pick up a suitcase at the Century City condo an hour before the police raid. Anthony Pellicano and his wife were both called to testify about another mysterious suitcase that she had been asked to hold for him.

Several of Michael's "special friends" appeared before the grand jury. So did their parents. There was the oft repeated rumor that two more boys—spurred on, perhaps, by the promise of riches—would come forward any day with the story of how they were molested by Michael.

The search would also continue for one particular boy rumored to have been picked up by Michael while he was touring in Europe. Police investigators referred to him as "the German kid," and his story was supposed to have made Joey Randall's pale by comparison. By the summer of 1994 it remained unclear whether the German kid would ever go public with his story.

Many who stepped forward to tell what they knew did so despite the fear of reprisals. "There are some central witnesses," Feldman had said, "who are scared to death to testify."

Sometimes fear was enough. Bodyguard Charli Michaels said she hadn't come forward prior to the announcement of the settlement because "I was scared to death." Michael's executive assistant, Orietta Murdoch, claimed that Pellicano told her that if she ever told anyone what she had seen, she would be "labeled an extortionist. If I'd said anything [prior to the Randall suit], no one would have believed me. I'd have been labeled what everyone is being labeled—a disgruntled ex-employee."

There is no proof that either Jackson or anyone in his circle had made threats against potential witnesses. Still, threats were reported. "I was told you don't go up against Michael Jackson," said Leroy Thomas, one of the five bodyguards suing Michael. Another was told "blood will flow" if she said anything. There was reason to believe it was no empty threat. After going public, one of the bodyguards was almost run down by a white Cadillac; another of the bodyguards who now worked as a car salesman escaped injury when shots were fired through his showroom window.

Michael's former personal maid, Blanca Francia, was run off the road by a mysterious car. One evening Eddie Reynoza, the dancer who claimed Michael once touched him in an inappropriate way, emerged from a restaurant to find a dead cat on the roof of his car. Attached to it was a note that read "Stay away from Michael if you know what's good for you. Here's your cat." Reynoza went into hiding the next day.

The most frightening incident occurred in early January, when Joey Randall and the family housekeeper were crossing the road not far from Randall's home. Without warning a car came out of nowhere and nearly ran them down. They were still shaking when the same car screeched to a halt and then came at them in reverse. At the last moment the housekeeper managed to pull Joey out of the car's path. From that point until the settlement was finalized, Joey did not leave the house without armed bodyguards.

Michael remained silent throughout the weeks and months of grand jury testimony—until Katherine was subpoenaed by Gil Garcetti. "For the purpose of headline grabbing," Michael complained, "the L.A. District Attorney's Office continues to persecute me, and this has now expanded to include the harassment of my beloved mother." Katherine's lawyer, Richard Steingard, added, "Trying to pit a mother against her son crosses the boundaries of decency."

At about the same time that he lodged his protest on behalf of his "beloved" mother, Michael made the first multimillion-dollar payment into Joey Randall's trust fund as per the settlement.

By April of 1994 the Santa Barbara prosecutor, reluctant to proceed without Joey Randall's testimony, put its case on the back burner. Johnnie Cochran and Howard Weitzman, meanwhile, demanded that the DA hand over the nude photographs and videotape taken of Jackson at Neverland before they fell into the wrong hands. It was rumored that certain publications were offering $3 million for the pictures. Since the Los Angeles case was still proceeding apace, the lawyers' request was denied. The nude photos were to stay locked in a safe at the Santa Barbara Court House.

Michael left the legal wrangling behind and went to New York, where he planned to work on his delayed greatest hits album. Donald Trump put him up at one of his properties, the Plaza Hotel, and warned that "if anyone wants to mess with Michael, they have to come through me first."

On the rare occasions when he was spotted around town, Michael was often in the company of the Cascio brothers. At the Metropolitan Museum of Art, officials opened up the spectacular Temple of Dendur to Michael and his two friends for a rare nighttime tour.

In mid-April photographer Richard Oliveira was standing outside the Plaza Hotel at four forty-five in the afternoon when, through the zoom lens of his camera, he spotted something unusual across the street. There, in the grass next to the gilt-covered statue of General Sherman, was Michael Jackson. He was on his knees, bouncing to the rhythm of a street musician playing the steel drums.

Oliveira was snapping away when Michael's bodyguards spotted him. "They *attacked* me," the photographer recalled. "These huge guys grabbed me by the neck and were jerking me around like a little doll. They smashed my camera and took my film. They were animals."

It was then that Michael sprinted over. "At first I thought he was running over to tell his bodyguards to take it easy, but he just wanted to make sure they got the film," Oliveira said. "I said to him, 'Aren't you going to do anything?' But he just looked at me with those dead, expressionless eyes." At the urging of Central Park carriage drivers who witnessed the attack, Oliveira filed yet another lawsuit against Michael.

A few days later thousands of youngsters cheered Michael as he showed up at the second annual Children's Choice Awards to accept top honors. When one hundred thousand schoolchildren were asked to name any person in the world, male or female, as their "ideal role model," three out of four picked Michael Jackson.

Michael's life took another surreal turn in early 1994 when his friendship with Lisa Marie Presley began to intensify. This oddest of couples had been close since 1988, when he comforted her during an early separation from her husband, rocker Danny Keough. It was then, when Lisa Marie informed Michael she thought she would soon be giving birth to a boy, that he reportedly offered to serve as a surrogate father to her unborn child. After the birth of their child—a girl—Presley and Keough briefly reconciled.

In the early months of 1994 Lisa Marie, who was three when her father first brought her to meet the Jackson Five in Las Vegas, returned Michael's kindness by going out with him while he battled the child sex abuse charges swirling all around him. Their high-profile Las Vegas date on the eve of the ill-fated *Jackson Family Reunion* was intended to resurrect Jackson's image after he agreed to pay $26 million to settle the Joey Randall case.

The couple continued their relationship in New York, where Lisa was a frequent visitor to the Trump Tower duplex loaned Michael by his friend Donald Trump. That spring Lisa Marie, a devout member of the Church of Scientology, was serious enough about Michael to discuss the situation with her fellow Scientologists. While they approved, Lisa Marie's mother, Priscilla, was rumored to be less than enthusiastic about the idea. For his part, Michael was telling Donald and Marla Trump that he was in love with Lisa Marie. Clearly, it did not matter to her that Michael demanded to be called the "king of pop" because he so bitterly resented Elvis's undisputed status as the "king of rock and roll."

In May 1994, after signing a prenuptial agreement that would keep their fortunes separate, Michael, thirty-five, and twenty-six-year-old Lisa Marie flew to the Dominican Republic. At first the couple wanted to be married aboard a Sony-owned Falcon 900 jet—one of several aircraft at Michael's immediate disposal—as it circled the island, but they were informed that in order for the marriage to be legal, it had to be performed on Dominican soil.

At 9:30 on the morning of May 26, Michael, Lisa Marie, and their entourage drove to the home of Civil Judge Hugo Francisco Alvarez Perez in the tiny village of La Vega. They arrived in a rented white Toyota minibus with tinted windows. A blue van carrying lawyers and bodyguards followed. Michael and Lisa Marie then presented their passports to the judge for identification, and Alvarez led them to the living room where, according to Dominican law, he was required to conduct the entire ceremony in Spanish (one of Michael's bilingual attorneys served as interpreter).

The groom wore a black shirt, black pants, a slicked-back ponytail, a cowboy belt, a string tie, a broad-brimmed black Spanish hat, and red lipstick. The bride was wearing a skin-tight, strapless beige dress. Alvarez later claimed Michael spent most of the fifteen-minute-long somber ceremony staring at the floor. But when asked if he would take Lisa Marie as his wife, Michael softly replied, *"Sí."* They exchanged heavy gold bands, but Lisa Marie had to pull Michael toward her before he would kiss her on the mouth.

Michael said nothing to his bride, but as soon as the vows were exchanged, he complimented the judge on his tie, which was decorated with Flintstones cartoon characters. "I just *love* Fred," Michael gushed. The newlyweds then sped off for nearby Casa de Campo, the sprawling resort complex owned by designer Oscar de la Renta, fifty miles outside Santo Domingo. There they stayed in separate villas five miles apart.

Not surprisingly, reports of Michael's marriage to Elvis's only daughter met with disbelief. Although Lisa Marie was separated from her twenty-eight-year-old husband, rocker Danny Keough, it was not immediately clear whether they were in fact divorced. Yet a Dominican divorce could have been obtained within a few days, and in total secrecy. To further complicate matters, Danny's brother Thomas Keough and Thomas's wife, Eve Darling, who held Lisa Marie's twenty-month-old son, Benjamin, during the ceremony, had acted as witnesses. (Lisa Marie's daughter Danielle, five, was not present.)

Finally, on August 1, 1994, two months after the Dominican ceremony, Lisa Marie issued a stunning announcement through Michael's press office. She conceded that the marriage had indeed taken place, and that henceforth she was to be called Lisa Marie Presley Jackson. "I am very much in love with Michael," she said, "and will dedicate my life to being his wife. I understand and support him. We both look forward to raising a family and living a happy, healthy life together. We hope our friends and fans will understand and respect our privacy."

Priscilla Presley, who raised their daughter after her 1973 divorce from Elvis (Lisa Marie was nine when he died four years later), hastily issued a statement of her own. "Please assure everyone," Michael's new mother-in-law said, "I am very supportive of Lisa Marie and everything she does." Privately, however, Priscilla appeared to be anything but pleased with the newest addition to the Presley clan.

It was not the first time Elvis's heir had given her mother cause for concern. After Lisa Marie dropped out of high school, the two fought bitterly over Lisa Marie's drug-taking and rebellious behavior. Once she made the decision to settle down and raise her two children, the sullen-faced Lisa Marie became—like Elvis and Michael—one of the country's most hotly pursued recluses.

It was clear what Michael stood to gain from marrying Lisa Marie. Reeling from allegations that he had sexually abused young boys and still facing possible criminal charges, Michael would obviously benefit from being perceived as a devoted husband and stepfather. Equally important, reports of Michael's marriage to Elvis's daughter were generating mountains of publicity—just as Michael put the finishing touches on *History: His Story*, the new "greatest hits" album. By August 1994, Lisa Marie was spending every available moment with Michael in his New York recording studio, offering him moral support. Michael needed all the help he could get. The success or failure of the album—his first effort since the Randall settlement—would determine once and for all if his career had been irreparably harmed by the scandal.

It was less obvious why Lisa Marie would choose to marry Michael—although it was suggested that she had sought his advice on ways to jump-start her own stalled career as an actress and singer. Indeed, they plan to sing a duet as part of a tribute to Lisa-Marie's father in October. Frank Dileo, who so often heard Michael bitterly complain about the attention paid Elvis, speculated that Michael would produce a solo album for his new wife.

Certainly, given the recent settlement of the Joey Randall child molestation case and the ongoing criminal investigation, Lisa Marie's decision to have Michael raise Elvis's grandchildren may have seemed questionable to some. It remained to be seen whether or not they would ever have children of their own, though there was widespread doubt even within Jackson's camp that the couple—who never displayed affection and seldom even touched in public—had anything resembling a physical relationship. "It's a business deal—pure and simple," observed a former insider. "Michael was a virgin before he married Lisa Marie, and I'm convinced he is *still* a virgin."

At least the new Mrs. Presley-Jackson would not have to worry about her new husband's having designs on the $150 million estate she stands to gain complete control of in 1998; Michael's fortune was more than twice the size of hers. In terms of copyrights alone, they controlled much of the era's musical legacy—most notably the works of the Beatles, Elvis, and of course Jackson himself. (One of Michael's business associates pointed out that Michael, who owned a few Elvis tunes, had long had his eye on acquiring the rights to all of Presley's work.) Moreover, they constituted one of show business's most powerful couples, with a combined worth of nearly half a *billion* dollars.

For most, the very idea of the King of Pop marrying the King's daughter was nothing short of mind-boggling. "That whirring sound you hear," quipped talk-show host David Letterman about the reported marriage, "is the sound of a dead rock legend spinning in his grave." Amidst persistent rumors that the marriage was a hoax, the *Tonight Show*'s Jay Leno was equally skeptical. Commenting on the newlyweds' highly publicized trip to Budapest, where Michael taped a promotion video in which he was portrayed delivering Eastern Europe from communist oppression, Leno told viewers that the couple stopped off in Austria. There, Leno continued, "Lisa Marie bought Michael a beautiful, beautiful wedding gift—the Vienna Boys Choir."

Monologues aside, not long after Michael and his bride returned from Europe, there were reports that he had offered Lisa Marie's ex-husband Danny Keough $1 million to adopt Danielle and Benjamin. Keough allegedly rejected the offer, prompting speculation that he might contest Lisa Marie for custody. There were also persistent rumors that Lisa Marie was two months pregnant with Michael's child at the time of their marriage.

A lawsuit filed by David Schwartz in August 1994 did nothing to bolster Michael's qualifications for parenthood. Joey's stepfather claimed that, in "sexually assaulting" his stepson, Michael had "devastated" the Schwartz family. At about the same time, it was revealed that, in answering the suit filed by five former bodyguards who claimed he routinely had boys smuggled into his room at Hayvenhurst, Michael took the Fifth—seventeen times.

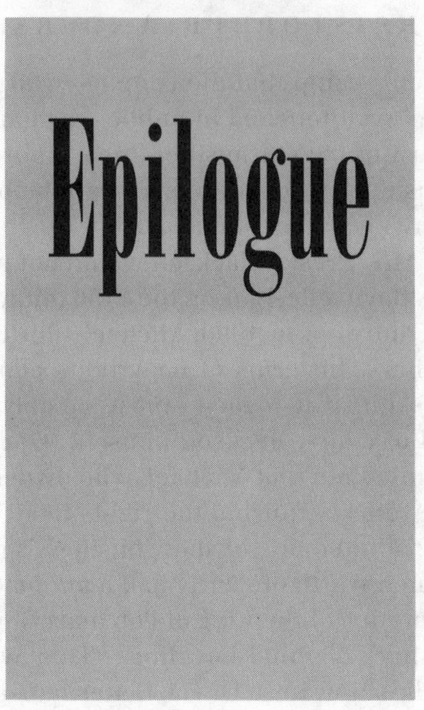

Epilogue

Like his life and career, the scandal that threatened Michael Jackson had all the properties of a supernova. After the blazing flare-up, the world was still waiting for the cosmic dust to clear. It was indeed the show business scandal of the century, and that was only fitting. Michael Jackson is, after all, generally conceded to be the greatest entertainer of our time.

It took *Thriller* to make him indisputably the world's top performer, yet it seemed as if the Gloved One had been around forever. Michael and his brothers had already sold over one hundred million records and collected armloads of Grammys after the Jackson Five exploded on the entertainment scene in a blaze of sequins in 1969. Yet even then the rest of the family conceded—if sometimes grudgingly—that its staggering success was due entirely to the formidable talent and bottomless energy of brother Michael.

From working-class Gary, Indiana, to the gated privilege of Hayvenhurst and Neverland, the Jacksons embodied the Horatio Alger dreams of millions of African Americans. Yet other poor blacks had achieved wealth and fame; Michael, in a search for his own identity, took it all to another level. "By blurring his gender, age, and race," wrote *Newsweek*'s Jonathan Alter, "he universalized himself as no other star had ever quite done before." That was the key to his global appeal. However weird the whole package, in Michael we all recognized something of ourselves.

The rags-to-riches fairy tale notwithstanding, Michael's was the sort of dysfunctional family that keeps talk-show hosts in business. Between various extramarital affairs, Joe abused Michael physically and emotionally, forced his sons to hone their act in sleazy strip joints, and—after the Jackson Five was signed by Motown—drove them mercilessly to record and tour.

Katherine Jackson, elevated to veritable sainthood in her children's eyes, looked the other way and quoted from scripture. The only god worshiped in the Jackson household, it would become clear even to Michael, was cold cash.

Like Judy Garland and his friend Elizabeth Taylor, Michael would forfeit his childhood for stardom and pay the awful price. Unlike them, he would go on to spend his adulthood in pampered isolation, seeking only the company of children in a sad effort to relive—or, rather, *live*—his childhood. Michael spent more and more time sequestered with his special friends at Neverland, and his mystique grew exponentially. However many times he sought to proclaim himself the king of pop, he was, more accurately, the Howard Hughes of pop.

As the preeminent pop culture giant of the twentieth century, Michael could be only a tangle of mind-spinning contradictions. He is the crotch-grabbing orgiast who at thirty-five remained a virgin; the giggling man-child who has used cutthroat tactics to build a $350 million fortune; the preening narcissist who hates his face so much that he has been transformed through plastic surgery; the idolized black role model who has done everything possible to make himself white; the onetime Jehovah's Witness whose work reflects a fascination with Satan and the occult; the abstemious teetotaler addicted to painkillers; the self-proclaimed lover of children who paid millions to silence charges that he sexually exploited a young boy. His stunning marriage to the only child of another pop-culture god—a union widely dismissed as a publicity ploy—left Michael's public more disbelieving than ever.

It had been said repeatedly that Michael was not like other mortals, that he was more extraterrestrial than human, that he was not of this earth. In truth he is very much of this earth and all too human, embodying the problems and frailties of a generation.

Michael has anguished through addictions to painkillers and plastic surgery, anxiety attacks, nervous breakdowns, and gender confusion.

Most painful of all would be the public scrutiny and condemnation of his relationships with children. Michael would befriend little boys, then go on to sleep with them and, inevitably, be accused of molesting them. Faced with these devastating allegations, he once again did the unexpected and openly flaunted his affection for boys before an astonished press and public. Was it merely arrogance or—more likely—an anguished cry for help?

Michael, it would seem, has been less a casualty of fame than of family—as much a victim as any he may have abused. Driven first by his father and then by his own demons, he tried to overcome his own feelings of worthlessness by fashioning himself into the world's greatest living pop culture icon. It could only be expected that his fall from grace would have all the makings of an epic tragedy.

"People," Michael once said, "don't treat me like a person." True, in an effort to cling to its own youth, the public played a role in infantilizing Michael. We were happy as long as he played Peter Pan and never grew up.

And that may be the greatest tragedy of all.

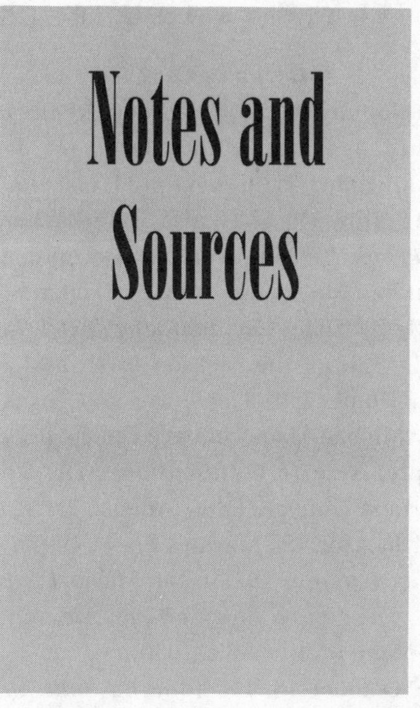

The following chapter notes are designed to give a general view of the sources drawn upon in preparing this book, but they are by no means all-inclusive. The author has respected the wishes of many interview subjects not to be named and, accordingly, has not listed them either here or elsewhere in the text.

Chapter 1

To re-create the raids on Neverland and Michael Jackson's Century City condominium, my researchers and I drew on interviews with Neverland guards and household staff members, police sources, and Michael's neighbors. Additional interviews included Don Ray, Vinnie Zuffante, Duane Bole, Rosemary McClure, Bill Dworin, Tony Brenna, Harry Benson, John Blossom, and Toi Saengswant. Accounts of the raids also appeared in numerous newspapers and magazines, including *The New York Times,* the *Los Angeles Times, The Washington Post, The Boston Globe,* the *San Francisco Chronicle,* the *Detroit Free Press,* the *Chicago Tribune,* the New York *Daily News,* the *New York Post, Time, People,* and *Newsweek.*

Notes and Sources

Chapters 2–4

Interviews included Johnny Jackson, Gordon Keith, Robert Smith, Beverly Washington, Reynaud Jones, Jack Gordon, Rosemary McClure.

Published sources included "The Jackson Five at Home" by Timothy Tyler, *Time,* June 14, 1971; "How Do You Raise Nine Rockers? Very Carefully" by Katherine Jackson, *People Extra,* November–December 1984; "Michael's Maturity at 13" by Lynn Van Matre, the *Chicago Tribune,* July 23, 1972; "No Star Trip for Teen Idol Michael Jackson" by Kathy Orloff, *Los Angeles Times,* September 1972; "Family Life of the Jackson Five" by Louie Robinson, *Ebony,* December 1974; "At Home with Jackie Jackson" by Robert A. DeLeon, *Jet,* February 13, 1975; "Michael Jackson: 'We Shacked Up with Diana . . . for a Year" by Marie Moore, New York *Amsterdam News,* October 22, 1977; "The Jackson Five" by Ernest Dunbar, *Look,* August 25, 1970; *The Jacksons—My Family* by Katherine Jackson (St. Martin's Press, 1990); *La Toya: Growing Up in the Jackson Family* (Dutton, 1991); *The Michael Jackson Story* by Nelson George (Dell, 1984); *The Untold Story—Berry, Me and Motown* by Raynoma Gordy Singleton (Contemporary Books, 1990).

Hollywood Palace, October 18, 1969; the *Ed Sullivan Show,* December 14, 1969; *Diana!,* April 18, 1971; *Goin' Back to Indiana,* September 19, 1971.

Chapters 5–8

For these chapters, the author drew on conversations with Terry George, Johnny Jackson, Lee Wohlfert, Wendy Leigh, Melinda Cooper, Steve Rubell, Truman Capote, Dick Scott, Hazel Southam, June Scott, Christopher Makos, Joy Wansley, Michael Gross, Patricia Lawford, Vinnie Zuffante.

Articles and books included "In Love with the Jackson Five" by Vince Aletti, *The Village Voice,* February 17, 1975; "Leaving Motown," *The New Yorker,* July 14, 1975; "Katherine Jackson: the Mother Who Made Michael a Superstar" by Elsie B. Washington, *Family Circle,* November 13, 1984; "The Jackson 5" by Richard Trubo, *Southland Sunday,* September 23, 1973; "Michael Jackson: the Innocent Idol" by Bob Weiner, the New York *Daily News,* April 10, 1977; "Michael Jackson: Sweet and Sexy, He's Pop's Greatest Thriller" by Mark Rowland, *Playgirl,* November 1984; " 'Wiz' Kid Michael Jackson Tries His Wings" by Ian Haremer, *US,* November 14, 1978; "Michael Jackson Digs the Wiz" by Edwin Miller, *Seventeen,* August 1978; "The Truth According to Michael Jackson" by Steve Manning, *Black Stars,* January 1978; "Blame It On the Boogie?" by Timothy White, *Crawdaddy,* December 1978; "An Exclusive Interview with the Jacksons" by J. Randy Taraborrelli, *Black Stars,* December 1978; "Michael Jackson: Hooked on the Spotlight" by Dennis Hunt, the *Los Angeles Times;* "The Jacksons: Famed Brothers Are No Longer Little Boys" by Charles L. Sanders,

Ebony, September 1979; "Michael Jackson and His World," *Black Stars,* April 1980; *Michael Jackson: The Magic and the Madness* by J. Randy Taraborrelli (Carol Publishing Group, 1991); *Moonwalk* by Michael Jackson (Doubleday, 1988); *Out of the Madness: the Strictly Unauthorized Biography of Janet Jackson* by Bart Andrews (HarperCollins, 1994); *On the Road with Michael* by Mark Bego (Grove Press, 1979).

The author also drew on more than 118 court documents, including copies showing the establishment of the Joh Vonnie Jackson Trust Corporation, Joh Vonnie Jackson's birth certificate listing Joe Jackson as her father, and Case No. 139795, *Michael Jackson et al.* v. *Motown Record Corporation of California et al.,* March 30, 1976.

CHAPTERS 9–12

Interviews included Norman Winter, John Branca, Katharine Hepburn, Jane Fonda, Bob Michaelson, Greg Phillinganes, Jack Gordon, Dick Clark, Allie Willis, Vinnie Zuffante, Charles T. Mathews, Margaret Lewis, Tina Weaver, May Pang, Arthur Collins, Angela Bowie, David McGough.

Thriller and the Victory tour generated thousands of newspaper and magazine articles worldwide. Only a few are listed here, including: "Is Michael Leaving the Jacksons?" by Robert E. Johnson, *Ebony,* October 1981; "Michael Jackson" by Andy Warhol and Bob Colacello, *Interview,* October 1982; "E.T. as Mr. Entertainment" by Vince Aletti, *The Village Voice,* December 14, 1982; "The Peter Pan of Pop" by Jim Miller, *Newsweek,* January 10, 1983; "Michael Jackson: Life in the Magical Kingdom" by Gerri Hirshey, *Rolling Stone,* February 17, 1983; "I'm the Mystery Billie Jean" by Leon Wagener, *Star,* April 24, 1983; "Diana Ross, the Concert, the Controversy, and Her Michael Jackson Connection" by Michael Small, *People,* August 8, 1983; "Thriller Chiller" by Carl Arrington, *People,* February 13, 1984; "Michael Jackson Inc.," *Newsweek,* February 27, 1984; "A Night of Michaelmania" by Dennis Hunt, the *Los Angeles Times,* March 1, 1984; "Why He's a Thriller," *Time,* March 19, 1984; "Michael Jackson: the World's Greatest Entertainer" by Robert E. Johnson, *Ebony,* May 1984; "Trouble in Paradise" by Michael Goldberg and Christopher Connelly, *Rolling Stone,* March 15, 1984; "Tour De Force," *People,* May 7, 1984; "The Jacksons' Summer Tour in Chaos as Businessmen Scramble for Power" by Michael Goldberg, *Rolling Stone,* June 7, 1984; "The Fabulous Show Begins," the *Boston Herald,* June 17, 1984; "Wheeling and Dealing as Jacksons Tour Approaches" by Michael Goldberg, *Rolling Stone,* June 21, 1984; "Countdown Begins for Jacksons' $50 Million Tour" by Leslie Bennetts, *The New York Times,* July 5, 1984; "Michael Stars in a Show of Flash, Passion" by Miles White, Jack Curry, and Jeff Levine, *USA Today,* July 9, 1984; "Bringing Back the Magic" by

Jay Cocks, *Time,* July 16, 1984; "The Tour, the Money, the Magic" by Jim Miller, *Newsweek,* July 16, 1984; "The Jackson Fireworks," *People,* July 23, 1984; "Michael Fumes: I'm NOT Gay," the *Los Angeles Times,* September 6, 1984; "Michael: On Stage and Off," *Life,* September 1984; "Victory on the Road" by Anthony DeCurtis, *Record,* October 1984; "Michael Jackson Stopped the Party Cold" by Jeannie Williams, *USA Today,* April 11, 1984; "My Michael—the New Messiah" by Steve Tinney, August 14, 1984; "Dissent Grows Among Jehovah's Witnesses" by Ari L. Goldman, *The New York Times,* August 29, 1984; "I Saw Michael and Sean Lennon in Bed Together" by Tina Weaver, *Today,* January 6, 1994.

Books included *The Industry* by Saul David (Times Books, 1981); *Trapped: Michael Jackson and the Crossover Dream* by Dave Marsh (Bantam Books, 1985); *We Are the World* by David Breskin (Perigee, 1985); *Jagger Unauthorized* by Christopher Andersen (Delacorte Press, 1993).

The author also referred to numerous court documents, depositions, sworn statements, and reports, including all those relating to: Gina Sprague's lawsuit against Katherine, Joe, Randy, and Janet Jackson (Case C383387); Katherine Jackson's two divorce actions (Case D076606); the divorce action *Hazel Gordy* v. *Jermaine Jackson* (Case D202224), and *Carlin Music Corporation* v. *Michael Jackson,* February 28, 1983.

CHAPTERS 13 AND 14

For these chapters, the author drew on conversations with Sandra Sutherland, Bob Michaelson, Norman Winter, Maureen Orth, Bebe Buell, Liz Derringer, Lawrence Straus, Jessica Malloy, Reynaud Jones, Rita Jenrette, Kimberly Walton, C. David Heymann, Erika Bell, June Scott, Bob Smith, and Vinnie Zuffante.

Articles include "All Star Record" by Joe Brown, *Washington Post,* March 8, 1985; "Let's Go to the Feelies" by Richard Corliss, *Time,* September 22, 1986; "The Pressure to Beat It" by Quincy Troupe, *Spin,* June 1987; "Michael Jackson: The Marketing of an Eccentric" by Bridget Byrne, *Los Angeles Times Magazine,* October 11, 1987; "Unlike Anyone, Even Himself," by Cutler Durkee and Todd Gold, *People,* September 14, 1987; "American Heavies Thank Their Stars" by Mitchell Fink, *Los Angeles Herald Examiner,* January 31, 1985; "Inside Those Secret Rooms" by Stuart White, *News of the World,* September 5, 1993; "Michael's First Epistle" by Michael Small, *People,* October 12, 1987; "The Badder They Come" by Jay Cocks, *Time,* September 14, 1987.

The author also consulted transcripts of the videotaped deposition of Blanca Francia in the case of *"Joey Randall"* v. *Michael Jackson and Does 1 Through 100* filed in the Superior Court of the State of California, County of Los Angeles (Case SC026226), and statements by bodyguards Morris Williams, LeRoy A.

Thomas, Donald Starks, Fred Hammond, and Aaron White in their lawsuit against Michael J. Jackson, MJJ Productions, Norma Staikos, Anthony Pellicano, et al. (Case BC093593).

La Toya Jackson's interview on *Geraldo*, February 3, 1994, was noted.

CHAPTERS 15 AND 16

Interviews included Norman Winter, Mark Quindoy, Faye Quindoy, Tony Brenna, Bob Michaelson, Charles T. Mathews, John Marion, Bobby Zarem, Lee Wohlfert, Maureen Orth, Crystal Cartier, Howard Manning, Jr., Diane Dimond, Karin Montoya.

Articles included "Michael Jackson, a Reluctant Spokesman" by Bruce Horovitz, the *Los Angeles Times*, September 15, 1989; "Michael to Wed His Backup Singer" by Beverly Williston, *Star*, May 9, 1989; "Estranged La Toya Fears Her Family" by Karen Thomas, *USA Today*, November 28, 1990; "So Long, Ryan: Gutsy AIDS Victim Dies at 18" by Jane Furse, the *New York Post*, April 9, 1990; "Peter Pan or Pervert?" by Andy Coulson, the London *Sun*, August 25, 1993; "Elite Lawyers Battle Over Michael Jackson" by Ellen Joan Pollock, *The Wall Street Journal*, December 27, 1993.

Among the legal documents consulted were the depositions of Jolie Levine and Blanca Francia in the case of *"Joey Randall"* v. *Michael Jackson* (Case SC026226).

CHAPTERS 17 AND 18

The author drew on conversations with Larry Feldman, Mark Quindoy, Ernie Rizzo, Sandra Sutherland, Crystal Cartier, Diane Dimond, Vinnie Zuffante, Swifty Lazar, Bill Dworin, Rosemary McClure, Jack Gordon, Harry Benson, Deborah Linden, Loretta Schwartz-Nobel, C. David Heymann. The debut of Michael's *Black or White* video and the release of the *Dangerous* album resulted in a veritable tidal wave of press coverage, as did the Oprah Winfrey interview. A few selected articles: "Thriller, Can Michael Jackson Beat It?" by Richard W. Stevenson, *The New York Times*, November 10, 1991; "Michael Aims to Foster Korean Boy: He's Obsessed with the Kid," the *Daily Mail*, April 1991; "New Video Opens the Jackson Blitz" by Jon Pareles, *The New York Times*, November 16, 1991; " 'Sorry' Michael Cleans Up His Raunchy Video" by Michele Greppi and Marianne Goldstein, the *New York Post*, November 16, 1991; "My Art Belongs to Daddy" by Stephen J. Dubner, *New York* magazine, November 29, 1993; "Michael Jackson: Crowned in Africa, Pop Music King Tells Real Story of Controversial Trip" by Robert E. Johnson, *Ebony*, May 1992; "Black or White Blues" by David Browne, *Entertainment Weekly*, November 29, 1991; "Michael Jackson's Latest in Shade of His Greatest" by Geraldine Fabrikant,

The New York Times, March 16, 1992; "Michael Jackson: The Making of the King of Pop" by Michael Goldberg, *Rolling Stone,* January 9, 1992; "The Jacksons: Not as Easy as ABC" by Tom Shales, *The Washington Post,* November 15, 1992; "Michael Picks the White One, Baby" by George Rush, *New York Post,* December 31, 1992; "Michael Jackson: He's Dangerous. He's Talking to Us" by Glenn Plaskin, New York *Daily News,* August 9, 1992; "Michael Jackson the Self-Promoter to Be More Open" by Matthew Gilbert, the *Boston Globe,* February 10, 1993; "Doctor Says Michael Jackson Has a Skin Disease" by Gina Kolata, *The New York Times,* February 13, 1993; "Peter Pan Speaks" by Richard Corliss, *Time,* February 22, 1993; "Beyond the Pale" by Ken Tucker, *Entertainment Weekly,* February 26, 1993; "Michael Jackson: Star's TV Confessions the Buzz of 90 Million" by Karen Thomas, *USA Today,* February 12, 1993; "Just What Does Michael Jackson's Story Add Up To?" by Ann Powers, *The New York Times,* February 21, 1993; "The Thriller Is Gone" by Diane Werts, *New York Newsday,* February 10, 1993; "Michael in Wonderland" by David Friend, *Life* magazine, June, 1993; "What Turns Ebony to Ivory" by Joel Garreau, *The Washington Post,* February 12, 1993; "I Watched Stars' Horror as Jackson Cuddled the Boy" by Piers Morgan, the London *Sun,* August 26, 1993; "Michael Jackson Exclusive" by Wayne Francis, the London *Sun,* October 4, 1993; "Streetwise Gumshoe to the Stars" by Shawn Hubler and James Bates, the *Los Angeles Times,* September 11, 1993; "Nightmare in Neverland" by Maureen Orth, *Vanity Fair,* January 1994.

Documents included: the official case activity log report of Los Angeles County Department of Children's Services, caseworker Ann T. Rosato, relating to "Joey Randall," as well as complaints, summonses, motions, and depositions pertaining to *"J. Randall"* v. *Michael Jackson* (Case SC026226). Also, the author obtained the *Articles of Incorporation for the Neverland Zoo Foundation for the Preservation and Breeding of Endangered and Other Species* (Document 1807564) filed with the office of California secretary of state March Fong on April 13, 1992. Material from Blanca Francia, Evangeline Aquilizan, Charli Michaels, Adrian McManus, and Gary Hearne was taken from their sworn depositions. Author also drew on comments made by Orietta Murdoch and investigative reporter Victor Gutierrez on CBS Television.

CHAPTERS 19–21

Interviews included Howard Manning, Jr., Charles T. Mathews, Lauren Weis, John Branca, La Toya Jackson, Richard Oliveira, Ernie Rizzo, Tom Sneddon, Tina Weaver, Harry Benson, Sandra Sutherland, Crystal Cartier, Diane Dimond, Bob Jones, Russell Turiak, Bill Dworin, Jessica Malloy, Susan Crimp, Wayne Darwen, Wendy Leigh, Jack Gordon, David McGough.

Notes and Sources

No scandal had ever been accorded more extensive press coverage than the Michael Jackson child sex-abuse story. Michael's surprise marriage to Lisa Marie Presley also triggered an avalanche of newspaper and magazine articles. Among the hundreds of published sources both here and abroad consulted by the author: "Liz Taylor Flies to Side of Close Pal Michael Jackson" by Marianne Goldstein, the *New York Post,* August 28, 1993; "Some Are Looking for Crime; Michael Jackson Sees a Plot" by Robert Reinhold, *The New York Times,* August 25, 1993; "Michael & the Innocents" by Megan Rosenfeld, *The Washington Post,* August 30, 1993; "The Jackson Dive" by Philip Norman, *The Sunday Times* of London, October 4, 1993; "McCartney Slams Michael" by William Neuman, the *New York Post,* November 29, 1993; "We Are the Weird" by Edwin Diamond, *New York* magazine, September 13, 1993; "Is This the End?" by Dana Kennedy, *Entertainment Weekly,* September 10, 1993; "Michael's World" by Cathleen McGuigan, *Newsweek,* September 6, 1993; "The Man in the Mire" by Ginia Bellafante, *Time,* December 6, 1993; "Hospital Brain Scan for Troubled Michael" by Richard Shears, the *Daily Mail,* September 1, 1993; "The Man Hoping to Save Michael Jackson," the London *Evening Standard,* November 15, 1993; "Secrets Michael's Private Eye Is Hiding from the World," by Kathleen Tracy, the *Globe,* December 21, 1993; "How I Helped Sneak Jacko into Britain" by Rob McGibbon, the *New York Post,* July 25, 1994; "Jackson Denies Molestation, Tells of Search" by Jim Newton and Carla Hall, the *Los Angeles Times,* December 23, 1993; "Lloyd's Faces $20 Million Claim Over Michael Jackson Tour" by Jon Ashworth, *The Times* of London, January 10, 1994; "The Price Is Right" by Richard Corliss, *Time,* February 7, 1994; "The Check Is in the Mail" by Jeff Giles with Stryker McGuire in Los Angeles, *Newsweek,* February 7, 1994; "Dodging the Bullet" by Bill Hewitt, *People,* February 7, 1994; "Jackson Can Never Say: 'I'm Innocent' " by Peter McDonald, *Evening Standard,* January 26, 1994; "Leave My Mom Alone," Reuters, March 17, 1994; "Vow? Wow!" by Karen S. Schneider, *People,* July 25, 1994.

The PBS *Frontline* documentary "Tabloid Truth: the Michael Jackson Scandal" of February 15, 1994, was also noted. The author obtained copies of the disputed $600,000 "payoff" document that triggered lawyer Bert Fields's suit against the *Globe,* and *Child Molesters: A Behavioral Analysis for Law Enforcement Officers Investigating Cases of Child Sexual Exploitation* by Kenneth V. Lanning, Supervisory Special Agent, Behavioral Science Unit, Federal Bureau of Investigation, FBI Academy, Quantico, Virginia.

Acknowledgments

So many people contributed in so many ways to the creation of *Michael Jackson: Unauthorized* that it is impossible to thank them all here. To those who preferred to remain anonymous, I express my deep gratitude for helping to make this book possible.

Once more I owe a special debt to my editor, Fred Hills, for his vision, skill, and passionate commitment to *Michael Jackson: Unauthorized.* My thanks as well to Burton Beals for his editorial contribution, and to Fred's assistant, Laureen Connelly Rowland.

For her wise counsel and friendship, I am grateful to my agent, Ellen Levine. My thanks as well to her talented associates—Diana Finch and Anne Dubuisson in New York and Lisa Eveleigh of A. P. Watt Ltd. in London—and to my British editor, Louise Haines.

For their unstinting support, my thanks to the entire Simon & Schuster family—especially Carolyn Reidy, Emily Remes, Victoria Meyer, Joann Di Gennaro, Leslie Ellen, Frank Metz, Eve Metz, Michele Martin, Marcella Berger, Marie Florio, and my friend Sandy Bodner, whom I have known longer than I am sure either of us care to remember.

My researchers, Wendi Rothman and Hazel Southam, were of incalculable help in unearthing fresh and often astonishing details about Michael Jackson's life. My thanks as well to Tony and Elena Brenna and to Tom Freeman for their generous assistance in helping me compile material for *Michael Jackson: Unauthorized.*

ACKNOWLEDGMENTS

My wife, Valerie, has again been a bottomless reservoir of encouragement, patience, and humor—as have our wonderful daughters, Kate and Kelly.

Hundreds of people cooperated in the writing of this book. While all my sources are not listed here, I am deeply grateful to every person who took the time to assist me. Additional thanks to: Jeanette Andersen, John Branca, Johnny Jackson, Norman Winter, Don Ray, Larry R. Feldman, Katharine Hepburn, Lauren Weis, La Toya Jackson, Bob Michaelson, Mark Quindoy, Jane Fonda, Elliot Mintz, Faye Quindoy, Jack Gordon, Ernie Rizzo, Terry George, Sandra Sutherland, Tina Weaver, Deborah Linden, Charles T. Mathews, Sandy Gallin, Greg Phillinganes, Gordon Keith, Reynaud Jones, Arthur Collins, Maureen Orth, David McGough, Robert Smith, Allie Willis, Crystal Cartier, Beverly Washington, Rosemary McClure, Harry Benson, Bebe Buell, Deborah Linden, Jessica Malloy, Howard Manning, Jr., Bob Jones, Wendy Leigh, Leroy Thomas, Lani Arst, Jack Palladino, Diane Dimond, Lawrence Straus, Bill Dworin, May Pang, Dick Clark, Steven Karten, Dick Scott, Vinnie Zuffante, Richard Oliveira, Bobby Zarem, Patricia Lawford Stewart, Daniel Stewart, Margaret Lewis, Liz Derringer, Edward Andersen, John Marion, Angela Bowie, Lee Wohlfert, Kimberly Walton; the late Truman Capote, Steve Rubell, and Swifty Lazar; Orietta Murdoch, John Wesley Cromer, Joy Wansley, David Switzer, C. David Heymann, Michael Gross, Erika Bell, Valerie Wimmer, Loretta Schwartz-Nobel, Dudley Freeman, Susan Crimp, Russell Turiak, Christopher Makos, Emily Schneider, Wayne Darwen, Kenneth V. Lanning, Bobby Zarem, Yvette Reyes, Ray Whelan, Linda Conte, Ron Galella; the Los Angeles Police Department and Office of the District Attorney; Office of the Santa Barbara District Attorney; the FBI; the National Center for Missing and Exploited Children; the Lincoln Center Library for the Performing Arts; the Margaret Herrick Library of the Academy of Motion Picture Arts and Sciences and Academy Foundation; the National Academy of Recording Arts and Sciences; the New York Public Library; the Beverly Hills Public Library; the Los Angeles Public Library; the Gary, Indiana, Public Library; the Hartford, Woodbury, Southbury, New Milford, Watertown, Middlebury, and Danbury, Connecticut, public libraries; the Silas Bronson Library; the Gunn Memorial Library; MTV, ASCAP, BMI, CBS; D.M.I., Wide World, the Associated Press, the Bettmann Archive, Globe, Movie Star News, the Gamma Liaison Network, Retna Ltd., the Image Works, Sygma, Graphictype.

Index

Index

Index

Index

Index

INDEX

Index

Index

PHOTO CREDITS

Christopher Andersen: 23, 45, 46
AP/Wide World Photos: 12, 18, 22, 24, 30, 31, 39, 51, 54, 55, 57, 60, 64
Albert Ferreira/DMI: 35
Ron Galella Ltd.: 20, 43
Gamma Ltd.: 50, 52, 58, 59
Globe Photos: 4, 5, 6, 10, 17, 19, 28, 62
Rosemary McClure: 21
David McGough/DMI: 9, 26, 29
Movie Star News: 1, 7, 14, 32
John Paschal/DMI: 15
Press Association/Topham: 34, 37, 53
Retna Ltd.: 36, 38, 47, 56, 61
Reuters/Bettmann: 27, 40, 41, 42, 48, 49, 65
Splash News: 63
UPI/Bettmann: 2, 3, 8, 11, 13, 16, 25
Walt Disney Company/Retna Ltd.: 33
Kevin Winter/DMI: 44